THE SCENIC ART

HENRY JAMES

THE SCENIC ART

Notes on Acting & the Drama:

1872–1901

EDITED, WITH AN INTRODUCTION

AND NOTES, BY

ALLAN WADE

A DRAMABOOK

HILL AND WANG, INC.

New York

1957

ACKNOWLEDGMENTS

The editor and the publishers wish to thank Charles Scribner's Sons for material from *The Life of Whitelaw Reid* by Royal Cortissoz, and the following publishers for their kind permission to use in this book certain writings by Henry James:

Columbia University Press for material from *Art and the Actor;* Houghton Mifflin Company for material from *A Roman Notebook;* and Charles Scribner's Sons for material from *Notes on Novelists,* from *The Letters of Henry James,* (Vol. I), and from *The Novels and Tales of Henry James* (New York Edition, Volume XIV).

This edition is published by special arrangement with the Trustees of Rutgers College in New Jersey.

Library of Congress Catalog Card Number 57-5841

MANUFACTURED IN THE UNITED STATES OF AMERICA

A.B.

ACKNOWLEDGMENTS

I desire to express my indebtedness to the late Mr. Henry James, of New York, for his kind permission to quote from unpublished letters and for his approval of this collection.

In compiling this book and in writing the notes I have made full use of Mr. LeRoy Phillips's Bibliography of the Writings of Henry James, *1906, and of the revised and enlarged edition of 1930, and acknowledge with much gratitude my debt to that invaluable work, which first revealed to the admirers of Henry James the existence of so much early and uncollected writing.*

I have also gladly availed myself of the Bibliographical Notes which Miss Edna Kenton contributed to the Henry James number of Hound and Horn, *April–June, 1934. To her untiring research is due the discovery of three of these dramatic criticisms not elsewhere recorded.*

To Mr. Leon Edel my debts are manifold: he discovered and at once notified to me the important unsigned essay on the London Theatres, 1880; he has read the proofs of this volume; and his extensive knowledge of Henry James's connection with the drama has been ungrudgingly placed at my disposal over a long period of time.

Allan Wade

Cornwall, England
1947

FOREWORD

The actor and the stage director, the men and women who practice the scenic art, live their creative lives through the spoken word within the make-believe of the theatre. They are not, on the whole, bookish people. They may read a great deal — and generally in dramatic literature. They often collect books. Less often, they write them. When they do, it is largely to chronicle their own lives, the anecdotes of their successes and failures, exhibiting themselves on the printed page even as their lives were spent exhibiting themselves in the glow of the footlights. There are exceptions, of course. They will, on occasions, display creative talent in the other arts. One thinks of Sir Johnston Forbes-Robertson (who once produced one of Henry James's plays) and his attachment to his palette and his canvases; of the late Harley Granville-Barker, who wrote plays, acted in them, renovated the British theatre at the turn of the century and in the end became a Shakespearian scholar; of Elizabeth Robins, who played so large a role in establishing Ibsen in England and in Henry James's own struggle to win a place on the stage of the 1890's, and who, in mid-career, slammed the stage door and became a successful novelist. One might multiply examples without, however, altering the general rule that the artists of the Book and of the Stage, by the very nature of their vocations, are destined to separate and independent courses. The stage is literature in action, on many levels and in many forms; and this very fact assigns to literature a passive role which the actor — his very name betrays it — embraces with difficulty.

The editor of this unusual volume has, in singular fashion, been able to bridge the gulf between the life of action, in the world of the stage, and the life of study and contemplation, in the world of books and bibliography. When Allan Wade was not at the theatre he was usually at the British Museum, haunting the circular reading room, hunting down the "facts," the "items," the stray clues which illuminate literary history much as a combination of disparate colors can light up a play. It was in the British Museum that the writer of this foreword first met him. He had sought him out to ask him some questions about Henry James's plays which it had fallen to his lot to edit. He found Allan Wade patiently copying out, in a meticulous hand, and with a refreshing disregard for the photostat (and later microfilm), the novelist's papers on the drama, relishing each phrase as he copied it, living through again the experience of the author himself, rescuing them from the old magazines and newspapers in which they had lain buried and unrecognized, some for more than half a century. Allan Wade explained that this was his peculiar whim born of a desire to have on his own shelves these papers, assembled so that they might be read and re-read and studied for their remarkable qualities — the accurately framed and richly imaged impressions of a sensitive spirit reacting, in the dimmed theatres of two continents, to the "traffic" of the stage. It was then and there that a suggestion was spontaneously made that perhaps Allan Wade would care to share his collection with kindred spirits by publishing it. The idea was readily accepted and thus The Scenic Art *came into being.*

Allan Wade, who had put students of William Butler Yeats in his debt by his careful bibliography of the poet's work, approached the Jamesian task in the same meticulous fashion. He had been an admirer of Henry James from his school days in England in the 1890's. He had been closely associated with Harley Granville-Barker during the great days of the Court Theatre, as actor, secretary, and playreader; he had been, in earlier days, a strolling player himself, and was later to be a translator of French plays; he had been business manager of several theatres and a founder of the Phoenix Society, directing more than twenty plays for that organization; he had been a joint manager of the Everyman Theatre, with Raymond Massey and George Carr, stepping out of managerial shoes now and again to assume a role on his own stage. He had achieved an honorable name in the annals of the Incorporated Stage Society and enjoyed the acquaintance or friendship of such diverse literary personalities as Yeats and Shaw, Conrad and George Moore. He had, shortly after Henry James's death, directed the novelist's long-forgotten light comedy, The Reprobate. *He had, moreover, read the novelist, with the care and affection that few — very few — of his critics have shown him.*

All this experience has gone into this book, so that it is far from being a mere collection of James's fugitive dramatic essays thrown casually together to make up a volume. The stage, for people who care, invites a very special kind of attention and evokes a very special kind of passion, whether from stage-struck young men and women, or long-experienced technicians and masters of stagecraft, or the persistent playgoer. Henry James possessed such a passion and no one reading his memoirs, A Small Boy and Others, *can fail to be charmed by the tenderness with which he evokes the theatres of old New York, when Chambers Street and Park Place were the precursors of Times Square, and Barnum's "Museum" offered to doughnut-munching small boys of that era all the excitement the cinema matinees of today offer to the generation of the ice cream cone and the "western."*

Reading these papers it is not difficult to discern the elements that went into the writing of Henry James's long novel of the stage, The Tragic Muse. *Even as Henry James's plays illuminate his novels, so his dramatic essays illuminate his "dramatic years" — the years in which he emerged from his novelist's study and sought with extraordinary energy to find a place for himself in the hurly-burly of the theatre. They constitute, in fact, an admirable introduction to his plays (most of them never published and shortly to see the light of day) and particularly when they come to us from the hands of a practical workingman of the theatre. Henry James, in his glowing pages, turns on the lights of old theatres, presents to our vision the painted faces of old comedians, and breathes life into plays long forgotten. And Allan Wade, on his side, fulfills his role of director and producer. He sets the scene; he furnishes the background; he identifies the actors; he even puts the programs into our hands, so that in turn, Henry James comes alive. Henry James captured for us a vanished phase of theatrical history that two world wars might have obliterated were there not such rich chroniclers as the novelist to preserve it for us, and faithful editors, such as Allan Wade, to cherish and illuminate the chronicles.*

Leon Edel

New York, 1948

CONTENTS

CONTENTS

INTRODUCTION

IN THIS VOLUME are assembled the notes and critical essays on plays and playwrights, actors and the art of acting, which Henry James contributed to various newspapers and periodicals in America and, on some few occasions, in England between 1872 and 1901. Covering so wide a span of time they will, of necessity, be found to represent his opinions at many different periods of his life. They show, also, the gradual development of his style, the first essay having been published before he had issued the earliest of his long novels, while the last was written immediately after he had completed *The Ambassadors*. Only six of these essays were ever reprinted by Henry James himself: the first, on the Parisian stage, in *Transatlantic Sketches*, 1875; the paper on the Comédie Française in *French Poets and Novelists*, 1878; "After the Play" in *Picture and Text*, 1893; the study of Ibsen in *Essays in London*, 1893; "Dumas the Younger" and the note on "John Gabriel Borkman" in *Notes on Novelists*, 1914. Most of these books have been out of print for many years; two of them were never issued in England.

The essay on Coquelin, first published in 1887 in the *Century Magazine*, was revised by Henry James as recently as 1915, the year before his death, for inclusion in a volume on "Art and the Actor" issued by the Dramatic Museum of Columbia University. This fact may perhaps be taken as an indication that, even if he would not himself have collected all these articles into a volume, he might, had the opportunity presented itself, have consented to a selection of them appearing, with due revision, as evidence of his enduring passion for the art of drama, and as one more tribute to his affectionate memory of "the interesting face of things as it mainly *used* to be."

I

Henry James has recorded, in the first volume of his autobiography, at how very early an age his playgoing adventures began; it seems to have been one of his father's amiable ideas that children could hardly begin that part of their necessary education too early. Almost as early, we may well be sure, was the process of criticism at work in the small spectator's mind. "It is an advantage," he wrote many years later, "when the sense of certain differences awakes early. I had that good fortune." And speaking, in his autobiography, of these early theatrical experiences, he notes that "it was a great thing to have a canon to judge by — it helped conscious criticism, which was to fit on wings (for use ever after) to the shoulders of appreciation. In the light of that advantage I could be *sure* my second Eliza [he is speaking of two different versions of *Uncle Tom's Cabin*] was less dramatic than my first, and that my first Cassy, that of the great and bloodcurdling Mrs. Bellamy of the lecture room, touched depths which made the lady of the National prosaic and placid."

Henry James remained a devoted playgoer almost to the end of his life; and in these early American days, as during the several visits he made in childhood and youth to Europe, it is evident that he was to miss no opportunity which was afforded him of seeing the best acting that the theatre then provided. The many references in the autobiographical volumes to plays seen, and the frequent mention of earlier plays and performances which he makes in these criticisms testify to his extraordinarily retentive memory of theatrical experience. It seems as though nothing that might have even a remote bearing for him on questions of form and expression was ever allowed to fade into obscurity. One might almost imagine that already he felt himself predestined to write for the theatre, so closely did his attention fix itself on the "scene." His earliest original writing submitted to an editor, as one gathers from a statement in *Notes of a Son and Brother*, was an appreciation of the acting of Miss Maggie Mitchell, a prominent American actress of the fifties and sixties seen in her performances at the Boston Athenaeum, though it is impossible to divine whether the proffered contribution was ever printed. From this time (about 1862) Henry James turned his attention to the writing of stories and the reviewing of books, and appears to have written nothing more about the theatre for ten years. The autumn of 1872, however, he spent in Paris, where, in company with James Russell Lowell, he became a very regular attendant at the Théâtre Français. The ineffaceable impression made on him by this experience is registered, the importance of it to him, seasoned playgoer as he already was, may be measured in his first essay on the Parisian stage. Here at last Henry James had found a standard which was to serve him consistently throughout the rest of his playgoing life. "The cultivated foreigner," he writes, "let him be as stuffed with hostile prejudices as you please . . . leaves the theatre an ardent Gallomaniac. This, he cries, is the civilized nation *par excellence*. Such art, such finish, such grace, such taste, such a marvellous exhibition of applied science are the mark of a chosen people." And he quotes with enthusiasm the overheard remark of one old playgoer to another, after a performance by Bressant and Madame Plessy: "Quelle connaissance de la scène . . . et de la vie!"

Some forty years later, one of my too few meetings with Henry James took place in London, in the stage-box of a theatre after the representation of a long one-act play by an Austrian dramatist, the action of which was laid during the French Revolution. Some-body asked James what he had thought of it, and in reply he demanded, in a tone of mild reproof, how he, with his early saturation in the French theatre, his early enthusiasm for the players of the Comédie Française, could be expected to attach any great importance to the doubtless commendable efforts he had just witnessed. This was a little chilling to the enthusiasm which the rest of us had felt justified in expressing — though per-haps we should have realized our temerity had we then been acquainted with his early criticisms. It is indeed possible that the reader of some of his essays, especially those which deal with American and, even more, with English theatre conditions in the seventies and eighties of the last century, may feel that the criti-cisms are sometimes harsh to the verge of unkindness, but James had now his standard, and his opinions therefore could not well be different. In *The Tragic Muse*, that novel in which so much of his feeling about the contemporary theatre is concentrated, he notes the effect on the theatre-struck young Embassy secretary, Peter Sherringham, of the Paris newspaper *feuilletons* "which he was committed to thinking important, but of which, when they were very good, he was rather ashamed. But," that young diplo-mat goes on to reflect, "if one was right in liking the actor's art one ought to have been interested in every candid criticism of it, which, given the peculiar conditions, would be legitimate in proportion as it should be minute. If the criticism that recognized frankly these conditions seemed an inferior or an offensive thing, then what was to be said for the art itself? What an implication, if the criticism was tolerable only so long as it was worthless — so long as it remained vague and timid."

Vague and timid Henry James's own criticisms certainly are not. If American theatre critics have today a reputation for being considerably more outspoken, more merciless than their English colleagues, they may claim with justice that their distinguished forerunner set them a brilliant example. How salutary might it not have been for the English stage if these criticisms had been, from the first, addressed to English readers! It should be remembered, however, that the majority of these papers were published in American periodicals only, and formed a part of that detailed report on French and English life and manners which, as a kind of unofficial literary ambassador, Henry James sent home from time to time for his compatriots' information.

II

These reports, taken together and in their chronological order, constitute a sort of intermittent diary of their author's playgoing adventures, and we are able to follow him from Paris (in 1872) back to America, where he criticises *The School for Scandal* at Boston in 1874 and reviews the conditions of the New York stage in 1874–75, noting the visit of Madame Ristori as well as those of several English performers. In the latter part of 1875 he returned to Europe and soon began to contribute to the *New York Tribune* a series of letters on French life and affairs. On his way to Paris, however, he stayed in London long enough to witness Irving's performance of Macbeth and to see Horace Wigan in the drama *All for Her*.

But he tired of French life after a twelvemonth (though not, certainly, of the French theatre) and transferred himself to London which now became his headquarters for a number of years, though in 1881 and 1882 he made two visits to the States in quick succession, on the second of which, occasioned by his father's death, he remained in America for a considerable time. When he left France, however, he summed up his impressions of the theatre there in the masterly essay on the Comédie Française, published in the *Galaxy* in April, 1877, to be followed in the same magazine the next month by a companion piece on the London theatres. It is illuminating to compare these impressions of the "peculiar conditions" affecting the French and English theatres respectively. After the regulated, formalized, traditional, classical art of the French, enshrined and protected in the National Théatre, he had to face the individualistic, wayward, often eccentric methods of the English actors of that day, in whom he could discover no evidence of training, no conscious aiming at a definite standard. Then, too, he had left the richness of the French classical repertory and a host of prolific and accomplished contemporary dramatists — Dumas *fils*, Augier, Pailleron, Sardou, and the rest — and was confronted with the poverty of the English dramatic output. Those, we must remember, were the days celebrated by Brander Matthews in his *Ballade of Adaptation*:

> *"The native drama's sick and dying,*
> *So say the cynic critic crew!*
> *The native dramatist is crying —*
> *Bring me the paste! Bring me the glue!*
> *Bring me the pen and scissors too!*
> *Bring me the works of E. Augier!*
> *Bring me the works of V. Sardou!*
> *I am the man to write a play!"*

Any successful French play was liable to be seized upon by one of the many busy play-factors of the epoch and hastily "adapted" (if the subject were not considered *too* scandalous) to suit the queasy taste of the British theatre patron. Henry James's onslaughts upon this questionable custom are severe, and his plea for the development of a native English drama, though it was to find no response for many years, must give his writings an honourable place in the roll of theatre criticism.

We can picture him, if we like, leaving his comfortable lodgings in Bolton Street, off Piccadilly, adventuring forth into that gas-lit

London which he was to describe just about this time, in an essay on Delacroix, as being "to the 'intelligent foreigner' in its superficial aspects a depressing and uncomfortable city," and in hansom cab or four-wheeler, accompanied sometimes by the venerable and venerated Fanny Kemble, exploring the dingy regions of theatreland.* This London was still almost the London of Dickens. No Shaftesbury Avenue nor Charing Cross Road had yet cut their way through the ill-reputed neighbourhood round Seven Dials, and theatres demolished long since and now almost forgotten were to be sought in Oxford street, in Holborn, and in the cluster of narrow streets at the eastern end of the Strand. The little Prince of Wales's, known before the Bancrofts refurbished it as the "Dust Hole," stood in its slum off Tottenham Court Road. No wonder Henry James laments "the repulsive character of many of the streets through which your aesthetic pilgrimage lies," contrasting this with "the very much more convenient form that playgoing assumes in Paris, where the various temples of the drama are scattered along the clean, bright Boulevard." The Adelphi Theatre, in the Strand, he found "musty and fog-haunted . . . a perpetual yellow mist, half dust, half dampness, seems to hover above the stalls, and to stretch itself across the stage, like a screen of dirty gauze." Yet for all this, strong in the persuasion that "the London theatres are highly characteristic of English civilization," and that "the plays testify indirectly if not directly to the national manners," his devotion to the theatre persists, and he faithfully reports his adventures for the information and entertainment of his fellow countrymen. There are few original plays

* Playgoing with Fanny Kemble evidently kept one on the higher altitudes. It was she, so Henry James informed an acquaintance in later years, who was so shocked at seeing Portia touch Bassanio during a performance of The Merchant of Venice. It was also she who turned to her "embarrassed companion," after witnessing a player (doubtless it was Adelaide Neilson) in her own old part of Julia in The Hunchback, "with a tragic, an unforgettable 'How could you bring me to see this thing?'"

to be found, and these are generally poor. True, there is Shake-speare, but it is Shakespeare as interpreted at the Lyceum, and this is one more disconcerting if enormously interesting element.

III

At this time—the late seventies and early eighties of the nine-teenth century—there was very great divergence of critical opinion concerning the acting of Henry Irving. Readers and play-goers of today, remembering only his later triumphs, his un-questioned leadership of his profession, his social eminence, and the pathetic circumstances of his death, are inclined to regard the old Lyceum days as the last high-water mark of a great tradition, and may possibly be surprised to realize how fiercely divided opinions were in those earlier days when Irving, still achieving his gradual conquest of his public, had nearly as many detractors as he had idolators. Henry James admired him only with con-siderable reservations, and in many ways did not admire him at all. But he gives his reasons fairly and squarely, and those who may be inclined to think his judgements severe should remember that Irving himself—as reported by Ellen Terry—made much the same adverse criticism of his own shortcomings of voice and movement. Henry James writes:

"In the opinion of many people, the basis, the prime condition, of acting is the art of finished and beautiful utterance—the art of speaking, of saying, of diction, as the French call it; and such persons find it impossible to initiate themselves into any theory of the business which leaves this out of account. Mr. Irving's theory eliminates it altogether, and there is perhaps a great deal to be said for his point of view."

And again:

"Mr. Irving is what is called a picturesque actor; that is, he de-pends for his effect upon the art with which he presents a certain

figure to the eye, rather than upon the manner in which he speaks
his part. He is a thoroughly serious actor, and evidently bestows an
immense deal of care and conscience upon his work; he meditates,
elaborates, and upon the line on which he moves, carries the part
to a high degree of finish. But it must be affirmed that this is a
line with which the especial art of the actor, the art of utterance,
of saying the thing, has almost nothing to do."

Here is a perfectly definite standpoint and it may perhaps be
said to mark the point of divergence between much of the modern
theatre's trend and the older way of doing things. The age of
"production" had begun, production not as understood to mean a
reasonable and considered *direction* of the actor's efforts to ex-
pound and illustrate the author's intentions, but as a method of
treating a play as something to be "decorated," "costumed,"
"lighted," and otherwise "presented" in a manner to reflect glory
on the producer, let the effect on the play itself be what it will.
This tendency was, of course, as yet in its early days, but the
clear-sighted Henry James observed the peril from afar. As early
as 1882 he wrote:

"The danger is common—the danger of smothering a piece in
its accessories; and the accident occurs at most of the London
theatres. The reason is doubtless that the art of putting a piece on
the stage, as it is called (*as if the only way to put a piece on the stage
were not to act it*), has lately made an advance in England which
is out of proportion to any improvement that has taken place in
the dramatic art proper."

The words which I have italicized seem to me one of those
pregnant utterances of which this book is full. That they have not
lost their significance in our own time is evident when one ob-
serves that the late Harley Granville-Barker in his broadcast

lecture on *The Perennial Shakespeare* had still—more than half a century later—to insist on the same point: "a play's interpretation lies in its acting and in nothing else that matters."

Had Henry James devoted more of his time to criticism of the theatre, it can hardly be doubted that the result might have been of very great importance. To the credit of English journalism it may be recorded that in 1883, about the time when one of his theatre criticisms first appeared in the English press, a proposal was made to him that he should become the official drama critic of an important London daily paper. To this he would not assent, perhaps feeling that as a "perpetual paying guest" in England, it would not be tactful to tell the English all he thought of their theatre. Yet how stimulating it might have been for them!

In all his criticism it is not merely the play and the acting that he has in mind, but also the social setting—the state of affairs, moral and intellectual, which makes it possible for that particular form of theatrical art, whatever it may be, to find acceptance. Compare his opinion that in France "even people of serious tastes look upon the theatre, not as one of the 'extras' but as one of the necessities of life," with what he has to say of audiences in New York (in 1875) and with his amusing description of the business of securing (in 1877) a ticket for a performance at a London theatre. And for a complete and delightful resumé of his whole theatrical "attitude," one has only to turn to that entertaining "imaginary conversation" *After the Play* (1889) where it is evident that the views of "Dorriforth" represent the views of Henry James. Those views are prophetic; and he comes, at one point, very near to prophesying something uncannily like the cinema. Consider this:

"I have no doubt that the scenic part of the art . . . is only in its infancy, and that we are destined to see wonders done that we now but faintly conceive. The possible extension of the mechanical arts is infinite. 'Built in,' forsooth! We shall see castles and cities and mountains and rivers built in. Everything points that way; especially the constitution of the contemporary multitude. It is huge and good-natured and common. It likes big, unmistakable, knock-down effects; it likes to get its money back in palpable, comfortable change. It's in a tremendous hurry, squeezed together, with a sort of generalized gape, and the last thing it expects of you is that you will spin things fine."

IV

After this summing-up Henry James wrote but little on the subject of actual theatre performances, only taking the occasion of the Lyceum production of *Cymbeline* in 1896 to pay a somewhat belated tribute to the art of Ellen Terry, to an appreciation of which it is evident he had arrived but slowly. He is still very guarded in his praise of Irving, and when he comes to write of the revival of *Richard III.* seems to reach—how many years in advance of the theatre!—the conclusion to which so many people have at last come, namely that in the staging of a Shakespeare play "the more it is painted and dressed, the more it is lighted and furnished and solidified, the less it corresponds or coincides, the less it squares with our imaginative habits."

One regrets again, after reading his notes on contemporary plays of the nineties in the essay called *The Blight of the Drama*, that he found so few occasions to develop his views of English drama when, with the advent of Henry Arthur Jones and Pinero, it showed some sign of original life, especially since it appears that, by this time, he would have been more ready to do so. But we have, in compensation, the three considered studies of those masters of drama—Dumas *fils*, Ibsen, Rostand—each of which, in its wide range of reflection, gives us the utmost reward for our trouble in following him as he pursues his way, carefully and steadily, to the heart of the matter. In the nineties Ibsen was, for the English theatre-goer, as much a cause of disputation as Irving's acting had been ten years earlier. Feeling ran high, the older critics expended much sound and fury, and the younger generation, rushing equally to extremes, proclaimed the supremacy of the "new movement" in an ecstasy of somewhat uncritical enthusiasm. Today, when the battle cries have long since died away, we can observe how exactly Henry James was able to assess the value, for the contemporary stage, of Ibsen and his influence. Nor did he fail to note, with amusement, the fact that the emotion provoked in England by Ibsen's work was "conspicuously and exclusively moral, one of those cries of outraged purity which have so often and so pathetically resounded through the Anglo-Saxon world." Today it is unlikely that many critics would be found to dissent from the opinions expressed by Henry James at the moment when Ibsen was not only a novelty but regarded by many as a danger. The English theatre has, as he foresaw it would, absorbed the immense influence of Ibsen's technical skill, while refusing, except for occasional brief revivals, to make much use of the plays themselves. An earlier instance of the English and American theatres' dislike of any approach to didacticism on the stage Henry James has noted in his essay on Dumas *fils*, pointing out that — *La Dame aux Camélias* apart — very few of the plays in his "rich argumentative series" made any mark in the Anglo-Saxon theatre. "The real difference, I take it, is that whereas we like to be good the French like to be better. We like to be moral, they like to moralize." But he notes also that Dumas was "the kind of artistic influence that is as inevitable as a medical specific; you may decline it from a black bottle today — you will take it from a green bottle tomorrow. The energy that went forth blooming as Dumas has come back grizzled as Ibsen, and would under the latter form, I am sure, very freely acknowledge its debt."

Very interesting it is, finally, to read his long analysis of the art of Edmond Rostand, whose plays might seem to be not at all the kind to appeal to Henry James. There is no mistaking the pleasure he took in them. It is only towards the end of his essay that he expresses the doubt which assailed him — the doubt as to whether Rostand would be able to "keep it up" — and asks what will happen then. Setting aside the question of a prophetic insight — for in the event it would appear that Rostand *was* only able to "keep it up" for one more play — there is food for reflection in the comparison that Henry James draws with the work of another French dramatist of no very lasting renown. Hervieu's talent, he suggests, at least brings him out "where life itself comes out," and so his source of inspiration will never of itself run dry. This constant demand for "the line of life" has persisted through all these criticisms from the earliest ("Quelle connaissance de la scène — et de la vie!"). For authors and actors alike fidelity to life is the supreme — though by no means the only — virtue.

In a letter of August, 1901, to the Editor of the *Cornhill Magazine* Henry James wrote: "I'm afraid my article will show you afresh how little *journalistic* talent I have — though perhaps some other . . . I've had to entitle (it) Edmond Rostand pure and simple — I found I couldn't talk of the rest of the matter in any coherent way in the space; and he is a distinct subject in himself." It is evident from the last paragraph of his essay that he had contemplated fuller consideration of the more realistic French dramatists of the period; that he never carried out this intention must add one more to the long list of our regrets for projects which, the right opportunity lacking, were doomed to remain intentions only, never to achieve that fullness of expression he would certainly have given them in the written page.

V

A French man of letters — a poet, a novelist, a critic of literature — will, as often as not, include a volume or two of dramatic
criticism in the list of his collected works. He will have regarded
the theatre as an important feature of normal civilized life. In
the English-speaking countries it is more usual to leave criticism
of theatrical matters to experts, men whose lifelong task it sometimes is, whose work, often valuable and profound, is then left
to moulder in the pages of the newspaper or periodical where it
was first printed. This is possibly one more symptom of that mild
contempt in which the theatre is still held among us. But from
time to time an English-speaking man of letters will devote a few
months or a few years to the study of the contemporary theatre,
and his work, reprinted, remains for our delight, instruction, or
amusement even though many of the plays he reviews have been
long since forgotten. Thus we have Bernard Shaw's *Our Theatres
in the Nineties*, Arthur Symons's *Plays, Acting and Music* (in its
first edition), and Max Beerbohm's *Around Theatres*, books in
which the playwright, the poet, the essayist have elaborated their
theories of the drama's function in the course of their "notices"
of a season's productions, good, bad, or indifferent. In *The Scenic
Art* I would like to suggest that we may now have another addition to the small shelf which contains these classics of theatre
criticism. Less systematic than any of those mentioned, because
they are spread over a lengthier period of time and seem to have
been written, as occasion or impulse prompted, in response to no
definite demand, these essays nevertheless, taken all together,
present a body of dramatic theory which still has much significance for us. It is by no means certain that we shall always agree
with Henry James's opinions — indeed it is probable that many
people will sometimes disagree violently — but even in disagree-

ment we shall, I think, be ready to admit the value of a critic who devoted his attention to the theatre with so passionate a seriousness, and who never ceased to urge the importance of a *standard*, without which he saw very well that the English-speaking theatre would be doomed to remain in that state of mediocrity in which he found it.*

Allan Wade

Menton, France

* In the course of his reviewing Henry James had occasion, between 1866 and 1877, to discuss the publication of some half-dozen plays and dramatic poems — by Swinburne, Bayard Taylor, W. W. Story, Tennyson and Browning; he writes of these only as poetry, as literature, and does not (except quite briefly in Tennyson's case) envisage their appearance in the theatre, for which indeed they were, most of them, but ill-fitted. It has not been thought apposite to include these book reviews in a volume of essays in which James writes exclusively of acted drama, and almost invariably of performances which he had himself seen.

THE SCENIC ART

THE PARISIAN STAGE

---------- **1 8 7 2** ----------

I T IS impossible to spend many weeks in Paris without observing that the theatre plays a very important part in French civilization; and it is impossible to go much to the theatre without finding it a copious source of instruction as to French ideas, manners, and philosophy. I supposed that I had a certain acquaintance with these complex phenomena, but during the last couple of months I have occupied a great many orchestra chairs, and in the merciless glare of the footlights I have read a great many of my old convictions with a new distinctness. I have had at the same time one of the greatest attainable pleasures; for, surely, among the pleasures that one deliberately seeks and pays for, none beguiles the heavy human consciousness so totally as a first-rate evening at the Théâtre Français or the Gymnase. It was the poet Gray, I believe, who said that his idea of heaven was to lie all day on a sofa and read novels. He, poor man, spoke while *Clarissa Harlowe* was still the fashion, and a novel was synonymous with an eternity. A much better heaven, I think, would be to sit all night in a fauteuil (if they were only a little better stuffed) listening to Delaunay, watching Got, or falling in love with Mademoiselle Desclée. An acted play is a novel intensified; it realizes what the novel suggests, and, by paying a liberal tribute to the senses, anticipates your possible complaint that your entertainment is of the meagre sort styled "intellectual." The stage throws into relief the best gifts of the French mind, and the Théâtre Français is not only the most amiable but the most characteristic

3

of French institutions. I often think of the inevitable first sensations there of the "cultivated foreigner," let him be as stuffed with
hostile prejudice as you please. He leaves the theatre an ardent
Gallomaniac. This, he cries, is the civilized nation, *par excellence*.
Such art, such finish, such grace, such taste, such a marvellous
exhibition of applied science, are the mark of a chosen people, and
these delightful talents imply the existence of every virtue. His
enthusiasm may be short and make few converts; but certainly
during his stay in Paris, whatever may be his mind in the intervals, he never listens to the traditional *toc — toc — toc* which
sounds up the curtain in the Rue Richelieu, without murmuring,
as he squares himself in his chair and grasps his lorgnette, that,
after all, the French are prodigiously great!

I shall never forget a certain evening in the early summer when,
after a busy, dusty, weary day in the streets, staring at charred
ruins and finding in all things a vague aftertaste of gunpowder,
I repaired to the Théâtre Français to listen to Molière's *Mariage
Forcé* and Alfred de Musset's *Il ne Faut Jurer de Rien*. The entertainment seemed to my travel-tired brain what a perfumed bath is
to one's weary limbs, and I sat in a sort of languid ecstasy of contemplation and wonder — wonder that the tender flower of poetry
and art should bloom again so bravely over blood-stained pave-
ments and fresh-made graves. Molière is played at the Théâtre
Français as he deserves to be — one can hardly say more — with the
most ungrudging breadth, exuberance and *entrain*, and yet with a
kind of academic harmony and solemnity. Molière, if he ever drops
a kindly glance on MM. Got and Coquelin, must be the happiest of
the immortals. To be read two hundred years after your death is
something; but to be acted is better, at least when your name does
not happen to be Shakespeare and your interpreter the great
American (or, indeed, the great British) tragedian. Such powerful,
natural, wholesome comedy as that of the creator of Sganarelle
certainly never was conceived, and the actors I have just named
give it its utmost force. I have often wondered that, in the keen

and lucid atmosphere which Molière casts about him, some of the effusions of his modern successors should live for an hour. Alfred de Musset, however, need fear no neighborhood, and his *Il ne Faut Jurer*, after Molière's tremendous farce, was like fine sherry after strong ale. Got plays in it a small part, which he makes a great one, and Delaunay, the silver-tongued, the ever-young, and that plain robust person and admirable artist, Madame Nathalie, and that divinely ingenuous ingénue, Mademoiselle Reichemberg. It would be a poor compliment to the performance to say that it might have been mistaken for real life. If real life were a tithe as charming it would be a merry world. De Musset's plays, which, in general, were not written for the stage, are of so ethereal a quality that they lose more than they gain by the interpretation, refined and sympathetic as it is, which they receive at the Théâtre Français. The most artistic acting is coarser than the poet's intention.

The play in question, however, is an exception and keeps its silvery tone even in the glare of the foot-lights. The second act, at the rising of the curtain, represents a drawing-room in the country; a stout, eccentric baronne sits with her tapestry, making distracted small talk while she counts her points with a deliciously rustic abbé; on the other side, her daughter, in white muslin and blue ribbons, is primly taking her dancing lesson from a venerable choreographic pedagogue in a wig and tights. The exquisite art with which, for the following ten minutes, the tone of random accidental conversation is preserved, while the baronne loses her glasses and miscounts her stitches, and the daughter recommences her step for the thirtieth time, must simply, as the saying is, be seen to be appreciated. The acting is full of charming detail — detail of a kind we not only do not find, but do not even look for, on the English stage. The way in which, in a subsequent scene, the young girl, listening at evening in the park to the passionate whisperings of the hero, drops her arms half awkwardly along her sides in fascinated self-surrender, is a touch quite foreign to

English invention. Unhappily for us as actors, we are not a gesticulating people. Mademoiselle Reichemberg's movement here is an intonation in gesture as eloquent as if she had spoken it. The incomparable Got has but a dozen short speeches to make, but he distils them with magical neatness. He sits down to piquet with the baronne. "You risk nothing, M. l'Abbé?" she soon demands. The concentrated timorous prudence of the abbé's "Oh! non!" is a master-stroke; it depicts a lifetime. Where Delaunay plays, how-ever, it is hard not to call him the first. To say that he *satisfies* may at first seem small praise; but it may content us when we remem-ber what a very loose fit in the poet's vision is the usual *jeune premier* of the sentimental drama. He has at best a vast deal of fustian to utter, and he has a perilous balance to preserve between the degree of romantic expression expected in a gentleman whose trade is love-making and the degree tolerated in a gentleman who wears a better or worse made black coat and carries the hat of the period. Delaunay is fifty years old, and his person and physi-ognomy are meagre; but his taste is so unerring, his touch so light and true, his careless grace so free and so elegant, that in his hands the *jeune premier* becomes a creation as fresh and natural as the unfolding rose. He has a voice of extraordinary sweetness and flexibility, and a delivery which makes the commonest phrases musical; and when as Valentin, as Perdican, or as Fortunio, he embarks on one of de Musset's melodious *tirades*, and his ut-terance melts and swells in trembling cadence and ringing empha-sis, there is really little to choose between the performance, as a mere vocal exhibition, and an aria by a first-rate tenor.

An actor equally noted for his elegance, now attested by forty years of triumphs, is Bressant, whose name, with old Parisians, is a synonym for *la distinction*. "Distingué comme Bressant" is an accepted formula of praise. A few years ago comedians were denied Christian burial; such are the revenges of history. Bressant's gentility is certainly a remarkable piece of art, but he always seems to me too conscious that an immense supply of the commodity is expected from him. Nevertheless, the Théâtre Français offers nothing more effective and suggestive than certain little comedies (the *Post Scriptum*, for instance, by Émile Augier), in which he receives the *réplique* from that venerable *grande coquette*, Madame Plessy, the direct successor, in certain parts, of Mademoiselle Mars. I find these illustrious veterans, on such occasions, more interesting even than they aspire to be, and the really picturesque figures are not the Comte nor the Marquise, but the grim and battered old comedians, with a life's length of foot-lights making strange shadows on their impenetrable masks. As a really august exhibition of experience, I recommend a tête-à-tête between these artists. The orchestra of the Théâtre Français is haunted by a number of old gentlemen, classic play-goers, who look as if they took snuff from boxes adorned with portraits of the fashionable beauty of 1820. I caught an echo of my impressions from one of them the other evening, when, as the curtain fell on Bressant and Plessy, he murmured ecstatically to his neighbour, "Quelle connaissance de la scène . . . et de la vie!"

The audience at the Parisian theatres is indeed often as interesting to me as the play. It is, of course, composed of heterogeneous elements. There are a great many ladies with red wigs in the boxes, and a great many bald young gentlemen staring at them from the orchestra. But *les honnêtes gens* of every class are largely represented, and it is clear that even people of serious tastes look upon the theatre, not as one of the "extras," but as one of the necessities of life; a periodical necessity hardly less frequent and urgent than their evening paper and their *demi-tasse*. I am always struck with the number of elderly men, decorated, grizzled, and grave, for whom the stage has kept its mysteries. You may see them at the Palais Royal, listening complacently to the carnival of lewdness nightly enacted there, and at the Variétés, levelling their glasses paternally at the lightly clad heroines of Offenbach. The truth is, that in the theatre the French mind *se reconnaît*, according to its own idiom, more vividly than elsewhere. Its supreme faculty,

7

the art of form, of arrangement and presentation, is pre-eminently effective on the stage, and I suppose many a good citizen has before this consoled himself for his country's woes by reflecting that if the Germans *have* a Gravelotte in their records, they have not a *Rabagas*, and if they possess a Bismarck and a Moltke, they have neither a Dumas nor a Schneider. A good French play is an admirable work of art, of which it behoves patrons of the contemporary English drama, at any rate, to speak with respect. It serves its purpose to perfection, and French dramatists, as far as I can see, have no more secrets to learn. The first half-dozen a foreign spectator listens to seem to him among the choicest productions of the human mind, and it is only little by little that he becomes conscious of the extraordinary meagreness of their material. The substance of the plays I have lately seen seems to me, when I think them over, something really amazing, and it is what I had chiefly in mind in speaking just now of the stage as an index of social character. Prime material was evidently long ago exhausted, and the best that can be done now is to rearrange old situations with a kind of desperate ingenuity. The field looks terribly narrow, but it is still cleverly worked. "An old theme, — but with a difference," the workman claims; and he makes the most of his difference — for laughter, if he is an *amuseur* pure and simple; for tears, if he is a moralist.

Do not for a moment imagine that moralists are wanting. Alexandre Dumas is one — he is a dozen, indeed, in his single self. M. Pailleron (whose *Hélène* is the last novelty at the Théâtre Français) is another; and I am not sure that, since *Rabagas*, M. Sardou is not a third. The great dogma of M. Dumas is, that if your wife is persistently unfaithful to you, you must kill her. He leaves you, I suppose, the choice of weapons; but that the thing must somehow be done, he has written a famous pamphlet, now reaching its fortieth edition, to prove. M. Pailleron holds, on the other hand, that if it was before your marriage, and before she had ever heard of you, and with her cousin, when she was a child and knew no better, you must — after terrific vituperation, indeed, and imminent suicide on the lady's part — press her relentingly to your bosom. M. Pailleron enforces this moral in capitally turned verse, and with Delaunay's magical aid; but as I sat through his piece the other evening, I racked my brain to discover what heinous offence Delicacy has ever committed that she should have to do such cruel penance. I am afraid that she has worse things in store for her, for the event of the winter (if a *coup d'état* does not carry off the honours) is to be the new play of Dumas, *La Femme de Claude*. Whatever becomes of the state, I shall go early to see the play, for it is to have the services of the first actress in the world. I have not the smallest hesitation in so qualifying Mademoiselle Desclée. She has just been sustaining by her sole strength the weight of a ponderous drama called *La Gueule du Loup*, in which her acting seemed to me a revelation of the capacity of the art. I have never seen nature grasped so in its essence, and rendered with a more amazing mastery of the fine shades of expression. Just as the light drama in France is a tissue of fantastic indecencies, the serious drama is an agglomeration of horrors. I had supped so full of these that, before seeing the *Gueule du Loup*, I had quite made up my mind to regard as an offence against civilization every new piece, whether light or serious, of which the main idea should not be *pleasing*. To do anything so pleasant as to please is the last thing that M. Dumas and his school think of. But Mademoiselle Desclée renders the chief situation of M. Laya's drama — that of a woman who has fancied herself not as other women are, coming to her senses at the bottom of a moral abyss, and measuring the length of her fall — with a verity so penetrating that I could not but ask myself whether, to become a wholesome and grateful spectacle, even the ugliest possibilities of life need anything more than rigorous exactness of presentation. Mademoiselle Desclée, at any rate, was for half an hour the most powerful of moralists. M. Laya, her author, on the other hand, is an atrocious one. His trivial dénouement, treading on the heels of the sombre episode I have mentioned, is an insult to the spectator's sympathies. Even Mademoiselle Desclée's acting fails to give it dignity. Here, as everywhere, an inexpressible want of moral intelligence is the striking point. Novel and drama alike betray an incredibly superficial perception of the moral side of life. It is not only that adultery is their only theme, but that the treatment of it is so singularly vicious and arid. It has been used now for so many years as a mere pigment, a source of dramatic color, a *ficelle*, as they say, that it has ceased to have any apparent moral bearings. It is turned inside out by hungering poetasters in search of a new "effect" as freely as an old glove by some thrifty dame intent on placing a prudent stitch. I might cite some striking examples, if I had space; some are too detestable. I do not know that I have found anything more suggestive than the revival, at the Gymnase, of that too familiar drama of the younger (the then very youthful) Dumas, the *Dame aux Camélias*. Mademoiselle Pierson plays the heroine — Mademoiselle Pierson, the history of whose *embonpoint* is one of the topics of the day. She was formerly almost corpulent — fatally so for that beauty which even her rivals admitted to be greater than her talent. She devoted herself bravely to a diet of raw meat and other delicacies recommended by Banting, and she has recently emerged from the ordeal as superbly spare as a racing filly. This result, I believe, "draws" powerfully, though it seemed to me, I confess, that even raw meat had not made Mademoiselle Pierson an actress. I went to the play because I had read in the weekly feuilleton of that very sound and sensible critic, M. Francisque Sarcey, that even in its old age it bore itself like a masterpiece, and produced an immense effect. If I could speak with the authority of Dr. Johnson, I should be tempted to qualify it with that vigorous brevity which he sometimes used so well. In the entr'actes I took refuge in the street to laugh at my ease over its colossal flimsiness. But I should be sorry to linger on the sombre side of the question, and my intention, indeed, was to make a note of none but pleasant impressions. I have, after all, received so many of these in Paris play-houses that my strictures seem gracelessly cynical. I bear the actors, at least, no grudge; they are better than the authors. Molière and de Musset, moreover, have not yet lost favour, and Corneille's *Cid* was recently revived with splendour and success. Here is a store of imperishable examples. What I shall think of regretfully when I have parted with the opportunity is, not the *tragédies bourgeoises* of MM. Dumas, Feuillet, and Pailleron, but the inimitable Got, strutting about as the podestà in the *Caprices de Marianne*, and twitching his magisterial train from the nerveless grasp of that delicious idiot, his valet; and Delaunay murmuring his love-notes in the ear of the blond Cécile; and Coquelin as Mascarille, looking like an old Venetian print, and playing as if the author of the *Étourdi* were in the coulisse, prompting him; and M. Mounet-Sully (the ardent young debutant of the *Cid*) shouting with the most picturesque fury possible the famous sortie, —

"Paraissez Navarrins, Maures et Castillans!"

To an ingenuous American the Théâtre Français may yet offer an aesthetic education.

Paris, December, 1872

"*The Parisian Stage*" first appeared, unsigned and as "From an occasional correspondent," in the Nation, *January 9, 1873*, and was reprinted as the eighth paper in Transatlantic Sketches, *1875*. It was, however, one of the four papers omitted from the Tauchnitz edition of the book, which was issued under the title Foreign Parts in *1883*. This paper, and the majority of those described in this volume as unsigned, was identified by LeRoy Phillips in his Bibliography of the Writings of Henry James (Boston, *1906*; revised and enlarged edition: New York, *1930*).

The essay was the outcome of Henry James's residence in Paris during the autumn of *1872*. He had arrived in Europe in May of that year, at the age of *29*, with an agreement to contribute travel sketches to the Nation. After visiting England, Switzerland, Northern Italy, and Bavaria, he settled down in the French capital, working in the mornings, visiting the Louvre in company with Emerson, and seeing much of James Russell Lowell, who at that time was living in a quiet hotel on the left bank of the Seine. Together they explored the city; "we both had the habit of long walks," James wrote in his essay on Lowell, "and he knew his Paris as he knew all his subjects." At night they assiduously frequented the Français or visited some other theatre, and it is evident that here was laid the foundation of that experience which permitted James to declare to his brother William a few years later: "I know the Théâtre Français by heart."

"THE SCHOOL FOR SCANDAL"
AT BOSTON

———— 1 8 7 4 ————

TO OFFER a few reflections on current theatrical matters in a
department devoted to the fine arts may seem to indicate a
rather startling measure of audacity, and we confess that if under
this title we proposed to take a general view of the field, we should
be open to the charge of making, as the French idiom says, an
arrow of any wood. The drama at large in America, just now, is
certainly neither artistic nor fine; but this is a reason for caring
with some tenderness for what it may be in particular cases. And
indeed we are by no means sure that its usual vulgarity is not in
itself a signal occasion for criticism. If tawdry plays, and acting to
match, were things that began and ended with themselves, we
could certainly very well afford to let them alone; for one of the
least comfortable signs of the times, to our sense, is the extension, the resonance, as it were, given by voluminous criticism to
poor performances. But a thousand theatres full of people con-
templating every night in the year spectacles artistically, at least,
more or less pernicious, suggest a number of accessory ideas. The
pertinence of these reflections depends very much of course upon
one's measure of the strict importance to people in general of the
artistic quality of their diversions. When a play is barbarous both
in form and in rendering, and ignoble in sentiment, there is little
doubt but that it can do no one any good. Often, however, one is
struck with the high—the oppressively high—moral tone of
dramas replete with aesthetic depravity; and we are thinking just

now of pieces in which sentiment is maintained at a reasonable level, but machinery, using the term broadly, comes out with especial strength. Does it really much matter, one sometimes wonders, whether such machinery is made to produce vulgar effects or charming ones? Is there any very tangible relation between the working consciousness and the play-going consciousness of people in general? American audiences are not demonstrative, and it has often seemed to us that, for good or for evil, impressions at the theatre are not penetrating. People go thither to be amused, and tacitly assume that amusement is one thing and workaday life another, and that the world exhibited in plays is a purely fictive and artificial world, with a logic quite distinct from that of the dusky world of umbrellas and street-cars, into which they hustle back when the play is over. If plays are artificial, so, in a minor degree, are pictures and novels; part of the machinery of that pleasure which is indeed in some degree tributary, as rest and relief, to the business of life, but not harmoniously interfused with it and animated by the same energies. We are inclined to think, in spite of the evidence, that this view of the case is exaggerated, and that it does seriously matter whether even uncultivated minds are entertained in good taste or in bad. Our point would be simply that it matters rather less than many of the people interested in the moral mission of art are inclined to admit. We are by no means sure that art is very intimately connected with a moral mission; and a picture that one dislikes, or a novel that one cannot read, or a play that one cannot sit out, is therefore to our sense a less melancholy phenomenon than to that of more rigid philosophers. We see no reason to believe that the mass of mankind will ever be more "artistic" than is strikingly convenient, and suspect that acute pleasure and pain, on this line, will remain the privilege of an initiated minority. A great many poor plays and pictures and novels will continue to be produced, in order that a few good ones may be floated to the front; and the few good ones, after all, will have but a limited influence. A brilliant work of art will always seem artificial — a fact, it seems to us, not on the whole to be deplored.

It is because our plays are trivial and our acting crude, and because, even if of necessity they awaken no echoes in the daylight world, they usurp for the evening the place of better things, and because, lastly, any marked exception to a vulgar fashion is agreeable, that the discriminating play-goer should make a note of the excellent performance of *The School for Scandal* given during the past month at the Boston Museum. *The School for Scandal* leads off the rather dreary list of the so-called old English comedies, but it stands a head and shoulders higher than its companions. Like most of the better pieces in the English repertory, it is more than a trifle threadbare, and has seen, in its day, no small amount of service. One should speak of it with respect, for, with all its faults, it has played a very useful part. It has often kept a worse play from being acted, and, odd as the fact may appear, it has been almost solely charged, for upwards of a century, with representing intellectual brilliancy on the English stage. There is Shakespeare, of course, but Shakespeare stands apart, and it never occurs to the critic to call him brilliant. We commend him in less familiar phrase. There are the old English comedies just mentioned, which, from Mrs. Inchbald down to *London Assurance*, are universally acknowledged to be very knowing affairs, and to contain a vast amount of talent, and of the superior sparkle and movement which is independent of the gasman and the machinery. But for real intellectual effort, the literary atmosphere and the tone of society, there has long been nothing like the *School for Scandal*. It has been played in every English-speaking quarter of the globe, and has helped English wit and taste to make a figure where they would otherwise, perhaps, have failed to excite observation. It has therefore, by this time, a certain venerable air; it is an historical relic, an ethnological monument. One might have fancied that it had earned its rest and passed into the province of the archaeologists, but we find it summoned once more to the front and bearing the brunt of the battle. It was revived a year ago in London under circumstances which gave it a new lease of life. These circumstances, it must be confessed, were for the most part chairs and tables, melancholy tokens that, for a sceptical age, even the *School for Scandal* cannot maintain itself on its intellectual merits alone. The spectacle in London was brilliant and the furniture very clever, being made up for the most part of genuine antiques of the Teazle period, in which the strongest opera-glass was challenged to detect a flaw. But if the chairs and tables in London were very natural, the actors were rather stiff, and the thing, on the whole, is better done at the Boston Museum. It is perhaps because here the acting is commendably natural, that the comedy, in spite of the traditional glamour that surrounds it, seemed to us so strangely lifeless and ghostly. For so lively an affair, the performance was almost funereal. The play must have been in its day prodigiously clever, and we are not at all surprised that with its first representation it should have taken its ticket for an apparently endless journey through the ages. We are far from saying too that its cleverness has altogether evaporated. When, on Lady Teazle's saying that her friends at Lady Sneerwell's are "people of fortune and remarkably tenacious of reputation," Sir Peter replies that, egad! they are tenacious of reputation with a vengeance, for they don't choose anybody shall have a character but themselves, one smiles as frankly as ever at the honest retort. When Mrs. Candour pretends to defend her near relation by marriage, Miss Sallow, by saying that great allowances should be made for her, and that a woman labours under many disadvantages who tries to pass for a girl of six and thirty, we are still struck not perhaps with the delicacy, but at least with the alertness, of the humour. But on the whole, to compare the *School for Scandal* with the part it has played seemed to us the other evening to tell a rather dismal tale of the poverty of the English stage. Here was the great comedy, the comedy *par excellence*, and yet, in sentiment, what a singularly

meagre affair it seemed! Its ideas, in so far as it has any, are coarse
and prosaic, and its moral atmosphere uncomfortably thin. The
main idea is that gossips and backbiters are brought to confusion,
that hypocrisy is a nasty vice, and that a fine young fellow who
lives freely and sociably and has a kindly word for great and small
is likely to turn out better, in the long run, than his elder brother,
who is an economist and a "man of sentiment." The types are
coarsely depicted and the morality is all vulgar morality. The
play is of course positively none the worse for this latter fact; it is
only less imaginative. It has hardly a ray of fancy, of the graceful
or the ideal, and even its merit — its smartness and smoothness and
rapidity — has something hard and metallic. Sir Peter Teazle
rather forfeits our commiseration by his cross-grained temper,
and his wife our charity by her cynicism. An ever very flighty
young wife, who tells her husband that she wishes he was dead,
goes rather too far to recover lost ground within the five acts. Sir
Oliver Surface is the regular old *oncle de comédie*, Joseph is a mere
walking gentleman who stands for hypocrisy and is labeled in
very large letters, and Charles, who is better, is rather a low fellow, even if he would not sell his uncle's portrait. He is made at
the Museum, indeed, a much lower fellow than he need be. The
gentleman who should deliver himself in the leering, hiccoughing
manner adopted by Mr. Barron, as he makes his exit after having
overturned Lady Teazle's screen, would have no allowable claim
to the hand of the exemplary — the too exemplary — Maria. Mr.
Barron's acting at this point is the one distinctly bad thing in the
play, and it is the more regrettable as the scene can ill afford to be
made coarse. Sheridan's sense of the delicate, we think, was not a
very fine one, but it told him that the situation should not be
treated as broadly comical. The speech he has put into Charles
Surface's mouth is therefore one that may be uttered with a sort of
ceremonious irony, much more effective than the uproarious
laughter and the incoherent shouts with which Mr. Barron goes
reeling away. The distinctively amusing scenes in the *School for*

17

Scandal are those in which Lady Sneerwell's guests assemble to pull their acquaintance to pieces. They are brilliantly clever, but they perhaps best illustrate our charge of coarseness and harshness. Crabtree and Mrs. Candour are absolutely brutal, and the whole circle settles down to its work with the ferocity of vultures and wolves. To measure the difference between small art and great, one should compare the talk of Sheridan's scandal-mongers with that scene in Molière's *Misanthrope* in which the circle at Célimène's house hit off the portraits of their absent friends. In the one case one feels almost ashamed to be listening; in the other it is good society still, even though it be good society in a heartless mood.

And yet there are numerous good reasons why the *School for Scandal* should have had a great popularity. The very fact that its wit is such as all the world can understand, at the same time that it has point enough to make the spectator, who seizes it as it flies, think himself a rather clever fellow; the fact, too, that it hits the average sense of fair play, and does not attempt too fine a discrimination of character; its robustness and smoothness of structure, and its extreme felicity and finish of style, — these things sufficiently account for its continued vitality. On its recent revival in London the play was remodeled in accordance with modern notions of symmetry, and to this version the Museum has apparently conformed. It is a very good one, and the only liberty it takes with the text is to transpose certain scenes and run others together. We have a great deal of tolerance for all audacities based on a desire to resolve an act into a single picture. Visible change of scene is rapidly becoming a barbarism, and we strongly suspect that this circumstance will end by giving a deathblow to Shakespeare as an *acting* dramatist. The Museum has blown its trumpet rather too loudly over its upholstery and costumes on this occasion. Things at the Museum are not exactly shabby, but a manager, nowadays, has no right to boast of his scenery who fails to close in his rooms with a ceiling and spare us the horrible little fringed curtains, like the valances of old-fashioned bedsteads, which hang down from the roof. This is rudimentary. It is to be observed also that the ladies walk through the play without a change of toilet; but on the other hand, Mr. Le Moyne wears a most beautiful embroidered coat, and Miss Clarke, indeed, looks so handsome from the first, that one feels sure she could not change her dress for the better. The play, as a whole, is acted with extreme finish and skill; the first act, in especial, is really artistic. The two scenes at Lady Sneerwell's have been compressed into one, and the manner in which they are rendered at the Museum touches the maximum of so-called genteel comedy on the American stage. Every one here is good, and Miss Clarke, and Mr. Le Moyne as Crabtree, prove themselves artists. Mrs. Vincent's Mrs. Candour is extremely amusing; the actress has a capital sense of humour. The fine lady is rather missed; but morality gains, perhaps, by so pernicious a personage not having even that claim to our esteem. Miss Clarke has rarely done better than in Lady Teazle; we prefer her comic manner to her sentimental. The two disputatious scenes with Sir Peter are charming, and the serious side of the character is very discreetly lighted. Lady Teazle has a serious side, and she seems to us the only figure in the play who is anything of a creation. Both in her folly and in her penitence she has a certain natural air, which loses nothing in Miss Clarke's hands. We have seen Mr. Warren do better than in Sir Peter; but it is not weakly good-natured to remember, apropos of Mr. Warren, that even Homer sometimes nods.

A noticeable feature in the performance at the Museum is the minuet danced at the end of the first act. It is thrust in by the shoulders, but if we suppose Lady Sneerwell to be giving a party, it may pass for picturesqueness' sake. It is very prettily done, and it justifies itself by reminding us of a statelier age than ours. People were coarse, in a thousand ways, a hundred years ago, and if you wish to know the books Lady Teazle read, you may turn and see what Lydia Languish, in the sister comedy of *The Rivals*, hides under her sofa-cushion when her aunt comes up-stairs. But it is nevertheless obvious that the men and women who found a pleasure in dancing a minuet had a certain gravity and dignity which has passed out of the habits of the heroes and heroines of the "German." A straw may show how the wind blows, and a minuet may testify to a civilization. We watched the dance the other evening with an almost foolish pleasure; by way of a change, it was *not* realistic! The play-goer in search of realism will have gone to see *Belle Lamar*, by Mr. Boucicault, at the Boston Theatre, and have discovered into what swamps of vulgarity that *ignis fatuus*, in its duskier moods, may lead him.

"*The School for Scandal at Boston*" appeared, unsigned, under the heading "*The Drama*," in the Atlantic Monthly, *December, 1874*.

Henry James had returned to America in September, 1874, and spent three months at Cambridge; he had, therefore, good opportunity for seeing the Boston production of The School for Scandal, which took place in October. But the same cannot be said in respect to the Bancrofts' production of the play in London, to which the article evidently refers. This ran from April 4 until August 7, 1874, after which date there was a holiday break until September 19, the run continuing to November 6. Henry James was certainly in Italy, as his letters and the dated essays in Transatlantic Sketches show, until the middle of June, and on June 23 he writes home from Baden Baden. At the end of July he was still in Baden Baden, and August was spent in visits to Holland and Belgium. He had sailed for America before the play's run was resumed.

It cannot at present be shown definitely that James did visit London during July — the only month for which his movements are unknown. This uncertainty has raised a doubt as to whether the essay was indeed written by him, since he would certainly not claim to have seen a performance which in fact he had not seen.

Mr. LeRoy Phillips says that the essay is twice ascribed to Henry James Jr. (under title and in the list of authors) in an Index to the Atlantic Monthly, *Volumes I-XXXVIII (1857–1876)*, published in 1877; he adds that, according to a penciled note on the title page of the copy in the Boston Athenaeum Library, the index was compiled by Horace E. Scudder, who edited the magazine from 1890 to 1898. This evidence, and certain other indications — the mention of strong opera glasses and of the actors being less important than the furniture, which is paralleled in the essay on The London Theatres of 1877 — the Jamesian use of such phrases as par excellence, oncle de comedié, "as French idiom says," and the comparison of the "scandal" scenes with Molière's Misanthrope — have inclined me to think that the essay may be taken as genuine Henry James. But the uncertainty exists, and so eminent an authority as Miss Edna Kenton has expressed a doubt, based chiefly on the evidence cited above as well as stylistic grounds, and on the fact that another essay, long attributed to Henry James and published in the May Atlantic of the same year — a study of the work of J. Foxcroft Cole — has been established by Miss Kenton and myself definitely to be from another's hand. Until further evidence comes to light the individual reader must be left to form his own judgment.

NOTES ON THE THEATRES:
NEW YORK

—————————— 1875 ——————————

IF ONE held the belief that there is any very intimate relation
between the stage, as it stands in this country, and the general
cause of American civilization, it would be more than our privilege, it would be our duty, as vigilant observers, to keep an attentive eye upon the theatres. For in New York, at least, these
establishments have rarely been more active than during the past
few weeks, and the moment would be highly opportune for drawing from the national diversions a critic's moral as to the national
state of mind. In fact, however, we suspect that moralizing too
rigidly here is a waste of ingenuity, inasmuch as the diversions
in question are not especially national. New York possesses
half-a-dozen theatres of the so-called first class, in addition to
a host of play-houses of the baser sort, whose performances are
dramatic only by that extension of the term under which the
romances in the Sunday papers may be spoken of as literary. These
theatres are all, for the time, working at high pressure. Each
has brought forward its *pièce de résistance*. The trumpets are
blown and the public is convoked. The public assembles in varying
numbers—on the whole, it seems to us, in very goodly ones. The
public evidently likes playgoing, and is willing to pay for it—
to pay a good deal, and to pay often. But except at the Fifth
Avenue Theatre, it does not go with the expectation of seeing the
mirror held up to nature as it knows nature—of seeing a reflection of its actual, local, immediate physiognomy. The mirror, as

the theatres show it, has the image already stamped upon it — an Irish image, a French image, an English image. The French and English images indeed are multiplied, and an Italian image, we perceive, looms above the horizon. The images may be true to an original or not; the public doesn't care. It has gone to look and listen, to laugh and cry — not to think. This is so true that we fancy it must have resented even the very slight intellectual effort necessary for finding *Women of the Day* at the Fifth Avenue as preposterous an attempt to portray as it was a dreary attempt to entertain. Nevertheless, if the theatre with us *is* a superficial institution, it shares the peculiarity with other social phenomena, and the observer may commit as great a fault in taking it too easily as in taking it too hard.

Our drama seems fated, when it repairs to foreign parts for its types, to seek them first of all in the land of brogue and "bulls." A cynic might say that it is our privilege to see Irish types enough in the sacred glow of our domestic hearths, and that it is therefore rather cruel to condemn us to find them so inveterately in that consoling glamour of the footlights. But it is true that an Irish drama is always agreeably exciting; whether on account of an inherent property in the material, or because it is generally written by Mr. Boucicault, we are unable to say. *The Shaugraun* will, we suppose, have been the theatrical event of the season; and if a play was to run for four or five months there might have been a much worse one for the purpose than this. There is no particular writing in it, but there is an infinite amount of acting, of scene-shifting, and of liveliness generally; and all this goes on to the tune of the finest feelings possible. Love, devotion, self-sacrifice, humble but heroic bravery, and brimming Irish *bonhomie* and irony, are the chords that are touched, and all for five liberal acts, with a great deal of very clever landscape painting in the background, and with Mr. Boucicault, Mr. Montagu, Mr. Becket and Miss Dyas in the foreground. For Mr. Boucicault, both as author and actor, it is a great triumph — especially as actor. His skill and shrewdness in knocking together effective situations and spinning lively dialogue are certainly commendable; but his acting is simply exquisite. One is hard cleverness, polished and flexible with use; the other is very like genius. The character of the Shaugraun is very happily fancied, but the best of the entertainment is to see the fancy that produced it still nightly playing with it. One hears it said sometimes that an actor acts with "authority;" certainly there is rarely a higher degree of authority than this. Mr. Boucicault smiles too much, we think; he rather overdoes the softness, the amiability, the innocence of his hero; but these exaggerations perhaps only deepen the charm of his rendering; for it was his happy thought to devise a figure which should absolutely, consummately, and irresistibly please. It has pleased mightily.

The Two Orphans at the Union Square Theatre, a piece which has been running a race with the *Shaugraun* in popularity, is an American rendering of an elaborate French *drame* of the old "boulevard" school. The original play ran all last winter in Paris, and fairly rejuvenated the rather defunct type to which it belonged. It is prodigiously clever, and we doubt whether for the time and the money one spends it would be possible to give one fuller measure, pressed down and running over, of surprises, sensations, and bewilderments. What is offered at the Union Square is the mere gaunt, angular skeleton of the original. The whole thing, both as to adaptation and rendering, is very brutally done. It hangs together as it can. There is no really delicate acting in the piece, with the exception, in a sense, of Miss Kate Claxton's representation of the blind maiden. She goes through the part with the pretty dismalness required, and with the enunciation of a young lady reciting a "piece" at a boarding-school. But *The Two Orphans* is worth seeing simply for the sake of sitting in one's place and feeling the quality of a couple of good old-fashioned *coups de théâtre* as your French playwright who really knows his business manages them. The first is when one of the Orphans, hearing in her garret the voice of the other, who is wandering in the street, sightless and helpless, and singing a song addressed, through the mercy of chance, to her sister's ear, and being about to fly to her rescue, is arrested on her threshold by a *lettre de cachet*. The other is the cry of that sadly unwholesome cripple, Pierre (badly played, we should say, if the part were not in its nature an impossible one), when, after being trampled upon through the whole play, he turns upon his hulking, blackguard brother: "As you say yourself, we come of a race that kills!" These are very telling strokes, but if you wait for them at the Union Square you pay for them well. You are kept in patience, it is true, by some very pretty scenery.

The Fifth Avenue Theatre, we believe, makes a specialty of "American comedy," eschews for the time at least Parisian orphans, and heroic bog-trotters, and gives us our fellow-citizens in their habits as they live. Some one ought to be held morally accountable for such an unqualifiable mass of vulgarity as *Women of the Day*. It is a pity to talk about this thing, even explicitly to pass it by; but we believe it is one of a series, and under these circumstances one strikes out instinctively in self-defence. It was ghastly, monstrous, a positive nightmare. It ran for several weeks, and one wonders whether the public was an active or a merely passive accomplice. Did it like it, or did it simply endure it? The public at large is very ignorant and very good-natured, and anything is possible.

One is bound to regret, in the presence of such a phenomenon as *Women of the Day*, that the wholesome old fashion of hissing has in the English theatre fallen into disuse. It was of course liable to abuse; but what is one to say, on the other hand, of the spectator's patience? It would seem at least that, short of the privilege of absolute hissing (which ceases to be brutal only when it is directed at the play, and not at the performers), the disappointed, the deceived spectator ought to hold in his hand some instrument of respectful but uncompromising disapproval.

We made this reflection as we watched the celebrated Mrs. Rousby, who had been interpreting historic blank-verse for a month at the Lyceum. It is hard to speak rigidly of so handsome a woman, but Mrs. Rousby's histrionic powers are about equivalent to those of some pretty trained animal — a pet lamb, say, or a white rabbit, or a snowy-breasted dove. Her acting is absolutely flat and weak — uninspired, untrained, unfinished. It was singular to see so extremely pretty a person take so little the critical chill off the atmosphere. Mrs. Rousby is distinctly incompetent. She has been followed at the same theatre by another English artist, a real artist this time — Mr. Toole. Mr. Toole has solved the problem of making low comedy charming. It must be admitted that in one of his parts — the "Artful Dodger" — the lowness is more apparent than the charm.

A more important dramatic enterprise than any we have mentioned has been the revival at Booth's Theatre, as a great spectacle, of *Henry V.* We can spare but a word to it. The play could be presented only as a kind of animated panorama, for it offers but the slenderest opportunities for acting. These all fall to the lot of Mr. George Rignold, a young English actor, who, as the victor of Agincourt, has made a very charming impression. He plays the part in the most natural fashion, looks it and wears it to perfection, and declaims its swelling harangues with admirable vigour and taste. He is worth looking at and listening to. The scenic splendours of the play have received many compliments, though, as such things go, they seem to us to have a number of weak spots. But even if they had fewer, they would still, to our sense, be founded on a fallacy. Illusion, as such an enterprise proposes to produce it, is absolutely beyond the compass of the stage. The compromise with verisimilitude is not materially slighter than in the simple days before "revivals" had come into fashion. To assent to this you have only to look at the grotesqueness of the hobby-horses on the field of Agincourt and at the uncovered rear of King

Harry's troops, when they have occasion to retire under range of your opera-glass. We approve by all means of scenic splendours, but we would draw the line at invading armies. Mr. Rignold, as we say, however, really produces a very grateful illusion.

"Notes on the Theatres" appeared, unsigned, under the rubric "Fine Arts," in the Nation, *March 11, 1875.*

MADAME RISTORI

WITH due recognition of the fact that Madame Ristori has entered into the final twilight, as we may call it, of her brilliant career, her appearance is yet incomparably the most important theatrical occurrence of the winter. Nothing that we can at present produce from our own resources is worthy of even a minute share of the consideration which people of taste feel prompted to offer this great foreign artist. One would rather this were not so; but so unfortunately it is. Madame Ristori's return to America is marked by circumstances not especially conciliatory. She is making, professionally, the circuit of the civilized world, and her *impedimenta*, of all kinds, have been selected with an eye to light weight. She reappears, too, after having bidden us farewell with some solemnity—an act in which there is always a certain awkwardness. But Madame Ristori, as an actress, is before all things stately, and her stateliness surmounts the disadvantage of a superlatively shabby *mise en scène*, a meagre company, and a somewhat surprised welcome. She apparently —probably very wisely— confines herself to a limited round of characters, and she offers us only one part in which she has not hitherto appeared. Fortunately, the parts left in her repertory are the strongest ones, and those which have done most to make her famous. She is indissolubly associated with the picturesque stage-figures of Medea and Mary Stuart, and though the strong colouring of these representations has suffered somewhat from the chill of years, they keep their place, in all essentials, among the most accomplished pieces of acting of our time. There are, indeed, things in each of them which it is safe to say the stage has never seen surpassed. Those who remember Madame Ristori twenty years ago may be conscious that here and there the execution drags a little; but young spectators should be assured that in witnessing the last act of *Mary Stuart*, or certain of the great points in *Medea*, they are looking at a supreme exhibition of the grand style of acting. No one whom we have seen, or are likely to see in this country, can interpret tragedy in the superbly large way of Madame Ristori—can distribute effects into such powerful masses. The abundance of her natural gifts makes the usual clever actress seem a woefully slender personage, and the extreme refinement of her art renders our most knowing devices, of native growth, unspeakably crude and puerile. Madame Ristori has the fortune to come of the great artistic race—the race in whom the feeling of the picturesque is a common instinct, and the gift of personal expression so ample that, even when quite uncultivated, it begins where our laborious attempts in the same line terminate. Coming thus of a pre-eminently expressive and demonstrative race, and watched by a peculiarly undemonstrative and impassive[1] public—a public among whom gesture, inflection of voice, and play of feature are comparatively unknown—it is natural that Madame Ristori should seem very often to exaggerate, to grimace, to tear a passion to tatters. It is very possible, too, that playing so much in foreign countries, to audiences ignorant of her language—audiences for whom the meaning is to be driven home *vi et armis*—has had the effect of imparting to the whole method of the actress a coarseness against which the constant presence of a really critical public would have been a protest. Unfortunately, the most artistic race in the world is not able to pay largely for its pleasure, and Italian actors and singers are almost of necessity wanderers and exiles. This fact, if one reflects upon it, gives a rather melancholy background to

---

[1] *Editor's emendation; the* Nation *printed the word "impressive." Henry James frequently did not see proofs before publication.*

one's admiration at the Lyceum just now. Of course, Madame Ristori, making the "farewell tour of the world," acquires fame on an immense scale and, on a somewhat commensurate scale, it is to be hoped, that grosser profit for which it smooths the way. But surely, looking at the thing the least bit from the ideal point of view, there is an essential dreariness in this great artist's expending her powers so exclusively upon populations for whom half of them are of necessity wasted. Between herself and her audience there is a gulf—a gulf which she certainly bravely does her best to overleap, and which is kept open by no ill-will on the spectators' part, but by the inexorable difference of race, of language, of national temperament. She is judged altogether from the outside—from a distance; and as she sweeps to and fro through all the variations of her art, she seems hardly more than a sort of magnificent curiosity. The "nature" that she represents is not the nature of the house.

But Madame Ristori's great merit—a merit that abundantly covers her defects, such as they are—is one that is perhaps especially appreciable here. She has *style*. The quality is so rare upon the English-speaking stage—especially, it is painful to observe, among the actresses—that one should make the most of any suggestion of it. It is the result in Madame Ristori of a combination of fine elements—her admirable stage presence, her incomparable language, and the peculiarly *masterly* way—the firmness, the certainty, the assurance—with which she deals with her part. Her Mary Stuart is full of style; the whole manner in which the part is "composed" to the eye is one of the great things of the stage. The intellectual conception, we think, is not particularly elevated; it is the natural woman simply—the woman of temper, the woman who talks loud, who struggles, hates, revenges, who is quite untouched by what Matthew Arnold calls "sweet reasonableness." But the part is superbly worn, and the last act is rendered as no one but Madame Ristori could render it. The expression of dignity here reaches a great height. No one but Madame Ristori could manage the farewell to her weeping servants, could gather the group about her, and handle it, as one may say, with that picturesque majesty. It is realism, especially in the closing moments, of a downright pattern; but it is realism harmonized by a great artistic instinct. Madame Ristori's Elizabeth is, in a manner, her *cheval de bataille*, but we have never liked the part. There are wonderfully skilful things in it, and it is an extraordinary piece of elaboration; but it is a thing made, as we say, for uncritical publics, painted with a big brush to be seen at a distance. It is better liked, probably, in New York than in Paris; it will be better liked in San Francisco than in New York, and it will make a *furor* in Australia. The objections to Madame Ristori's Medea are obvious; the lady is too much of a termagant—no wonder poor Jason would not go back to her. But the part is a dense tissue of superb action, and there are strokes in it—of tone, of attitude, of gesture, of facial play—any single one of which would make the fortune of a slighter artist. In *Lucrezia Borgia*, which Madame Ristori plays now for the first time in America, she has not found, to our sense, a very happy opportunity. The part is a hideous one, and it has the drawback that its climax, in its pursuit of the terrible, very distinctly grazes the ludicrous. We have heard it said that the way she plays it is a proof of enfeebled vigour. It seems to us, on the contrary, that she renders it with an energy quite adequate to its demands for vehemence, but that her acting is rather wanting in *finesse*. In the long scene with the Duke, in which there is a fine chance in the way of high comedy, she has some masterly touches, but the whole thing strikes us as too high pitched, and, here and there, as rather roughly executed. We should say, too, that the last words of the play, when Lucrezia has been stabbed by her son—"Gennaro, I am thy mother!"—would, as constituting its tragic consummation, be much more effective if delivered standing—discharged at him with passionate reproach. But these are details. In a general way one goes to see Madame Ristori with a serene certainty of observing a dramatic temperament of unsurpassable power, seconded by a language which gives to speech a lovely dignity, independent of its meaning.

"Madame Ristori" appeared, unsigned, under the rubric "Fine Arts," in the Nation, *March 18, 1875.*

MR. GEORGE RIGNOLD

———————— 1 8 7 5 ————————

W E SPOKE some weeks since in these columns of the successful and, in some respects, brilliant revival of *Henry V.* at the Booth's Theatre, and of the merits of Mr. George Rignold in the only part in the play which admitted of much acting. The management having found that Shakespeare could be made to pay, and having Mr. Rignold still in hand, have lately been offering *Macbeth* — by no means with the same splendour as the other play, but with some pretensions to care and completeness. Is it to be accounted an additional resource that they have also had the services of Miss Clara Morris? From an at all exacting point of view, we think not. It is one thing to make a great hit with Shakespeare in a case where much spectacle will carry off little acting, and another thing to succeed where, whether the spectacle be much or little, the acting must not in decency fall below a certain level. Mr. Rignold had immense good fortune with the part of Henry V., which seemed to give him a chance to do all he could, and to ask of him nothing he could not. With Macbeth he stands on different ground, and he stands much less firmly. He has great good-will, and good looks and good taste, such as prevent him from ever being disagreeable; he is what is called "sympathetic;" one rather likes him, even in his weaker moments, and one has a sort of sense of friendly relief in witnessing his stronger ones. But the part is too large for him, and he does not in the least fill it out; he occupies at best, now here, now there, an outlying corner of it. He desires to be natural and real — a most laudable ambition; but

33

there is reality and reality. When you have Shakespeare's speeches to utter, your reality must be a sort of imaginative compromise; you must wind your whole conception up to a certain exalted pitch, and there, at that impressive altitude, you may keep among the levels. Mr. Rignold is best when he has a chance for movement and violence, as in the scene with Banquo's ghost at the banquet. In passages of pure declamation he is ineffective; he gave such speeches as the "Duncan is in his grave," etc., quite without richness or resonance. He is an actor who probably can do certain parts so very well that it is a pity to see him doing certain others but half well. It is to be supposed that there are some things that Miss Clara Morris can also do well; but the utterance of the tremendous speeches of Lady Macbeth is not one of them; to speak frankly (this is a case for it), the disparity between the actress and the part was simply ludicrous. Miss Morris's meagre voice, her vulgar intonation, her trivial conception of her opportunities, are all fatal disqualifications. Every speech seemed to us distinctly missed, and the actress's facial play and the introduced business of her own invention struck us as an insufficient compensation. This is not harsh criticism. Miss Morris, it seems to us, has a large reserve of good fortune to draw upon in finding it so easy to display her incompetence on an eminent stage. The truth is, no artist need expect to play parts demanding style and elevation in this familiar juxtaposition and alternation with the "realistic" drama of the period. Realism is a very good thing, but it is like baking a pudding in a porcelain dish; your pudding may be excellent but your dish gets cracked. An actor who attempts to play Shakespeare must establish for himself a certain Shakespearean tradition; he must make sacrifices. We are afraid that as things are going, most actors find it easier to sacrifice Shakespeare than to sacrifice to him.

"Mr. George Rignold" appeared, in the Nation, *May 27, 1875. Henry unsigned, under the heading ".Notes," James had transferred himself from*

Cambridge to New York in December, 1874, and remained there, in East Twenty-fifth Street, well into the Spring. His busiest journalistic period had now begun, and reviews by him appear in almost every issue of the Nation, as well as occasional papers on art and the drama. In the late autumn of 1875 he sailed once more for Europe, intending to settle permanently in Paris.

MR. HENRY IRVING'S
MACBETH

———————— 1 8 7 5 ————————

MR. HENRY IRVING'S Macbeth, which, on the actor's first appearance in the part in London some six weeks ago, produced not a little disappointment in the general public, seems to have been accepted as an interesting if not a triumphant attempt, and is exhibited to audiences numerous if not overflowing, and deferential if not enthusiastic. Considering the actor's reputation, indeed, the very undemonstrative attitude of the spectators at the Lyceum is most noticeable. Mr. Irving's acting is, to my mind, not of a kind to provoke enthusiasm, and I can best describe it by saying that it strikes me as the acting of a very superior amateur. If Mr. Irving were somewhat younger, and if there existed in England any such school of dramatic training as the Conservatoire of Paris, any such exemplary stage as the Théâtre Français, a discriminating critic might say of him: "Here is an aspirant with the instincts of an artist, and who, with proper instruction, may become an actor." But, thanks to the absence of a school and of any formidable competition, success has come easily to Mr. Irving, and he has remained, as the first tragic actor in England, decidedly incomplete and amateurish. His personal gifts — face, figure, voice, enunciation — are rather meagre; his strong points are intellectual. He is ingenious, intelligent, and fanciful; imaginative he can hardly be called, for he signally fails to give their great imaginative value to many of the superb speeches he has to utter. In declamation he is decidedly flat; his voice is without charm, and his utterance without subtlety. But he has thought out his part, after a fashion of his own, very carefully, and the interest of his rendering of it lies in seeing a spare, refined man, of an un-histrionic—of a rather sedentary—aspect, and with a thick, un-modulated voice, but with a decided sense of the picturesque, grappling in a deliberate and conscientious manner with a series of great tragic points. This hardly gives an impression of strength, of authority, and it is not for force and natural magic that Mr. Irving's acting is remarkable. He has been much criticized for his conception of his part—for making Macbeth so spiritless a plotter before his crime, and so arrant a coward afterward. But in the text, as he seeks to emphasize it, there is fair warrant for the line he follows. Mr. Irving has great skill in the representation of terror, and it is quite open to him to have thrown into relief this side of his part. His best moment is his rendering of the scene with the bloody daggers—though it must be confessed that this stupendous scene always does much toward acting itself. Mr. Irving, however, is here altogether admirable, and his representa-tion of a nature trembling and quaking to its innermost spiritual recesses really excites the imagination. Only a trifle less powerful is his scene with Banquo's ghost at the feast, and the movement with which, exhausted with vain bravado, he muffles his head in his mantle and collapses beside the throne. Mr. Irving has several points in common with Edwin Booth, and belongs to the same general type of actor; but I may say that if, to my thinking, Ed-win Booth comes nearer being a man of genius, I find Mr. Irving more comfortable to see. Of Miss Bateman, who does Lady Mac-beth, the less said the better. She has good-will and a certain superficial discretion; but a piece of acting and declaiming of equal pretensions, more charmless in an artistic way, it has not been my fortune to behold.

November 6th, 1875

"*Mr. Henry Irving's Macbeth*" ap-peared, unsigned, and preceded by the *words* "*a correspondent writes us from London, under date of November 6,*" *in the* Nation, *November 25, 1875. On his way to France Henry James spent something like a fortnight in London and hastened to send the Nation his first impression of Henry Irving, who by this time was firmly established as the star actor at the Lyceum Theatre, though not yet under his own management. As James's later criticisms show, the unfavourable impression of Irving's acting which he received at this time was never entirely obliterated.*

PARIS REVISITED

IN PARIS the first symptoms of the winter are to be looked for at the theatres. Most of them are bringing out at this time the pieces which they expect to carry them through the next six months—or through as many of them as may be. The Français, as yet, has given only promises; but its promises cast the performances of the others in the shade. The Théâtre Français has in rehearsal a piece by the younger Dumas, and this constitutes, from the Parisian point of view, a very great event. A *coup d'état* by Marshal MacMahon, an invasion of France by Prussia—it would take something of that sort to equal it. M. Dumas is a great favorite with the *Figaro* newspaper, and the *Figaro's* compliments—which is saying a great deal—are almost as ingenious as its abuse. Either in good humour or in bad it is, to my sense, a most detestable sheet; but it certainly understands in perfection the art of advertising a man. It has kindled a crackling fire under the *Étrangère*, and it will keep the pot boiling until the play is produced. The greater part of the *Figaro*, the other day, was taken up with an article of many columns about the reading of the play to the actors. Of course the papers could say very little that was definite, for the subject was not to be deflowered. But everything that talking without telling could do the *Figaro* achieved; it even gave the names of the characters—a piece of information which, for Dumas's regular admirers, leaves infinite pasture for the imagination. The French have a particular word for this sort of literary service; they call it to *soigner* an artist or his work—to

39

take care of them. *L'Étrangère* is being very well taken care of.
Victorien Sardou has hitherto been supposed, I believe, to enjoy
the supreme good fortune in the way of having his plays talked
about, and even quarrelled about, beforehand. But I believe
Sardou has been accused of pulling the wires himself, and this
Alexandre Dumas neither needs nor would condescend to do.
Sardou, however, has just produced very quietly at the Gymnase a
long serio-comic drama which is pronounced good, but not good
for Sardou. There would some day be something interesting to say
about this supremely skillful contriver and arranger—a man who,
as one may phrase it, has more of the light and less of the heat
of cleverness than anyone else; and if *Ferréol* is still being played
when the day comes round, it will serve as a text.

A month ago the shop windows in New York were filled with
portraits of Ernesto Rossi, the Italian tragedian, who was coming
over to tread in the deep foot-prints of Salvini—or as he hoped,
I suppose, to make new ones of his own. You will have perceived
by this time that he has not arrived, though you may but imperfectly appreciate his motives for breaking his engagement. He is
having a quite extraordinary success in Paris, and he remembers
the adage about a bird in the hand. On his way to embark for
America he stopped a night in Paris to play, and the next morning
he found himself famous. I am very sure that his great part, Kean,
would not have encountered in America the prosperity it enjoys
here, where it has been played steadily for the last two weeks—
a great triumph for a drama in a foreign tongue. Kean is the late
Edmund Kean, the English tragedian, as portrayed by the late
Alexandre Dumas. The part was created by Frédéric Lemaître,
and was one of his most extraordinary achievements. I listened to
Rossi the other night in company with an old gentleman of a
retrospective turn, who would let nothing pass without assuring
me that "Frédéric" did it fifty times better. But in spite of my
neighbour I enjoyed Rossi—in spite of my neighbour and in spite
of *Kean*. The play is the most fantastic farrago of high-spirited

nonsense that even the impudent imagination of Alexandre Dumas could offer as a picture of "insular" manners. The first three quarters of the piece are mortally dull (in the Italian version) and Rossi is remarkable, but not exciting. But toward the end of the fourth act poor Edmund Kean is represented as refusing to act his part because he is in a passion of jealousy of George IV. who is making love to his mistress. He rages up and down his dressing-room, and declines to go on, though manager and prompter and dresser are all on their knees to him. At last George IV. comes in, and joins in the suppliant chorus, but Kean laughs in his face, and still keeps the house waiting. At last he is reminded that the performance is for the benefit of a crippled clown, who was his comrade in the days when he made his living by turning somersaults at fairs, and at this hint he collapses, wraps himself in the mantle of Hamlet, and plunges into his part. In the next scene we see him on the stage consorting with Ophelia, and feverishly watching George IV. in the house. This scene is brief and rapid, but it is admirably played, and it decides in a moment the actor's success. Kean, consumed with jealousy, sees George IV. enter the box of the woman he loves, and from this moment he is less in his part, and more and more certain to fling it aside and betray himself. At last he does so in a magnificently grotesque explosion of wrath at the Prince and sarcastic abuse of himself—tumbler, clown, vile histrion, Punchinello! He rushes to the footlights and pours out a volley of delirious bravado. "Punchinello?—so be it!" he cries, and he shoulders his princely sword, like Punch's stick, and executes a sort of furious mocking dance. It is horribly and yet most effectively fantastic, and it makes nearly all the tumult in the theatre that the real scene might have made. Rossi will doubtless do this quite as well in America, if he ever gets there; but will it be as highly relished? I doubt it. The Paris theatre-going public seizes an artist's intention with extraordinary alertness.

November 22nd, 1875

"Paris Revisited" appeared as the first of a series of letters from France in the New York Tribune, December 11, 1875; only that part of the letter which deals with the theatre is here reprinted.

Henry James had reached Paris at the end of 1875, and established himself in rooms whose windows, as he says, "looked into the Rue de Luxembourg—since then meagerly renamed Rue Cambon." Here, in December, began work on The American, and he mentions that he "had come back (to Paris), after earlier visitations, but a few weeks before." Besides his novel he continued to write regularly for the Nation and he began, almost immediately, his "Correspondence" in the New York Tribune.

The story of Henry James's contributions to the Tribune has been told in some detail in The Life of Whitelaw Reid by Royal Cortissoz (1922). Reid was anxious to strengthen his foreign correspondence department, and it seems that James was not unwilling to address his work to a larger audience than the readers of the Nation. The suggestion came first from John Hay who wrote to Reid on July 24, 1875: "Henry James, Jr., wants to write for The Tribune, letters from Paris, where he is going to live for some time to come. He considers The Tribune the only paper where business could be combined with literary ambition. I hope you will engage him . . . He will start in the autumn some time . . ."

So the engagement was made, and James contributed a series of twenty letters, usually, though not invariably, at fortnightly intervals, between December, 1875, and August, 1876. The earlier letters deal with politics, general news, literature, art, and the drama; among the later are some

travel sketches in the French provinces, which he reprinted in Portraits of Places, 1883.

At first all went well. Reid thought his readers enjoyed the letters and presumably James liked writing them. Presently, however, a letter to his father dated April 11 discloses that the effort to find "popular" material for his letter is becoming irksome. "The American papers over here are accablants, and the vulgarity and repulsiveness of the Tribune, whenever I see it, strikes me so violently that I feel tempted to stop my letter. But I shall not, though of late there has been a painful dearth of topics to write about. But soon comes the Salon . . ." And a few days later, on April 23, he is protesting to his editor, from 29 Rue de Luxembourg, against the use of subheadings, which were, he said, "in every way disagreeable to me."

Finally Reid wrote suggesting that the letters might with advantage be shorter, more varied, and above all more topical. To this James replied: "I have just received your letter of August 10th. I quite appreciate what you say about the character of my letters, and about their not being the right sort of thing for a newspaper. . . . They would, as you say, be more in place in a magazine. But I am afraid I can't assent to your proposal that I should try and write otherwise. I know the sort of letter you mean—it is doubtless the proper sort of thing for The Tribune to have. But I can't produce it . . . If my letters have been 'too good' I am honestly afraid that they are the poorest I can do, especially for the money! I had better, therefore, suspend them altogether . . ."

And so the episode came to a seemly and dignified end. It was destined, however, to bear fruit many years after, when James, writing his poignant story The Next Time (1895), recalled his own failure to achieve the "popular" journalistic tone and dramatised this in the situation of an author who is perpetually trying to write for the great public but can only turn out a series of masterpieces appreciated by "the happy few."

THAT the theatre plays in Paris a larger part in people's lives than it does anywhere else is by this time a fact too well established to need especial comment. It is one of the first facts that comes under the observation of the resident foreigner, who very soon perceives that the theatre is an essential part of French civilization, in regard to which it keeps up a lively process of action and reaction. It is not a mere amusement, as it is in other countries; it is an interest, an institution, connected through a dozen open doors with literature, art, and society. There are, of course, plenty of people who assure you that the French stage of to-day is nothing but a name; that its great days are over, and that to know the perfection of acting one should have been born seventy years ago. Born, unfortunately, more recently, I have seen neither Talma, nor Mlle. Mars, nor Mlle. Georges, nor Madame Dorval, nor Rachel, nor Frédéric Lemaître, and in such a case, though it is disagreeable to have to assent to invidious reflections, it is difficult to gainsay them. But even without this questionable privilege of depressing comparison, I must add that I find it easy to imagine the French stage being better than it is. I remember vaguely Rose Chéri, and distinctly Mlle. Desclée. The best acting in Paris is extremely good, at the present time, but the second best is not so much better than it is elsewhere, as it is sometimes assumed to be. I take it that the sign of a highly flourishing state of dramatic art is excellence in secondary positions—finish in out of the way places. That is what Mr. Ruskin praises in the art of the

44

greatest architecture, and the analogy may be carried into the labours of the actor. Is it true, then, that the golden days of the French stage are over? I shall not pretend to say, but I think that a critic of greater courage might find some support for an affirmative answer. He might, indeed, while he was about it, go on to argue that the happy time of the acted drama has passed away the world over. He might, if he were philosophically inclined, remark that the dramatic art requires, both in performers and spectators, a certain simplicity, a *naïveté*, an abeyance of the critical spirit, which are rapidly passing out of human life. To produce very good acting there should be a class of performers and a public in whom subtlety has not attained its maximum. If evidence in favour of this assertion were needed, I should venture to point to two striking cases of essentially modern acting which I have lately witnessed as samples of the harm that can be done by the absence of what I have called *naïveté*. One is the Macbeth of Mr. Henry Irving, which I lately saw in London; the other is the Macbeth of Signor Ernesto Rossi, which I saw the other night here. I do not know how Garrick or Charles Kemble or Edmund Kean played the part, or how Talma would have played it if he had been allowed; but as I watched the English and the Italian tragedian I murmured within myself, "Oh, for one touch of Kemble or of Talma!" one touch of good faith, of the ideal, the simple. But Irving and Rossi are very clever actors, and these remarks have perhaps an air of aberration. So far as such matters in Paris are concerned, it may be enough to allude, in confirmation of a gloomy view of the future of the stage, to the inordinate prosperity, of late years, of opera bouffe. This phenomenon, I should say, could only have been possible in a community which had ceased to take the theatre with that degree of seriousness which is necessary for its perfect good health.

A person fond of the stage and indifferent to opera bouffe has not just now a very comfortable time of it. At least a third of the theatres are given over to the strains of Offenbach, of Lecocq, and of Hervé, and the photographs of the actresses who impart to these melodies the requisite complement of grimace and gesture, simper at you from every second shop window. My present complaint of the *Cruche Cassée* and the *Créole* is not that they are vulgar or trivial or indecent, but simply that they are unhistrionic. They give up the stage to something which not only is not acting, but is a positive denial of acting. To act is to produce an illusion; to interpret Offenbach is to snap your fingers and thrust out your tongue at illusion — to try and make it appear that a young woman in the audience, too frolicsome, really, to be suffered to go at large, has scrambled upon the stage and is using the footlights in the interest of her sentimental relations with a plurality of individuals in the house. The favourite actress in opera bouffe at the present hour is Mme. Judic, an extremely pretty woman. An inventory of Mme. Judic's artistic stock in trade would be really a very curious document. After Mme. Judic in popular favour comes Céline Chaumont, who is not nearly so pretty, but infinitely cleverer. Mme. Chaumont is indeed so clever, and has such genuine dramatic gifts, that it is very dismal to see what opera bouffe is making of her.

The winter season is in full operation at the theatres, but I hardly know upon what novelties to confer the honour of an especial mention. I have already spoken of Rossi, to whom I just now alluded. He pursues his triumphant career, and having exhausted the popularity of *Kean*, has added *Macbeth* to his Shakespearean performances. His acting in this part, as in every other, is at once very fine and very coarse. I should say he was poorest in the best places and best in the comparatively unimportant ones. In this he resembles Mr. Henry Irving, who is so meagre in the essential and so redundant in the (relatively) superfluous. Rossi is a superb stage figure, and every now and then he has a cry, a movement, a look, which goes straight to the mark; but, as a whole, I thought his Macbeth a decidedly bungling affair. It was ludicrously Italian — I am sorry to associate so disrespectful an adverb with so glorious an adjective. It is true, however, that in most cases of an alternation of good taste and bad, the genius of modern Italy decides for the bad. The scene of Duncan's murder is disfigured by the most absurd ventriloquial effects on the part of the shuddering Thane, who makes an elaborate attempt to give his wife an idea of the way the voices of the sleeping grooms sounded. Fancy the distracted chieftain reeling out red-handed from his crime and beginning to give "imitations." The scene with Banquo's ghost was disappointing, and the address to the spectre singularly weak. It is a good indication of Rossi's calibre that he depends for his final effect here upon a very puerile piece of ingenuity. The scene has been vulgarly acted and vulgarly declaimed; Signor Rossi has been reserving himself. And for what? As Macbeth leaves the apartment with his wife, after the departure of the guests, he stumbles upon his long mantle, trips, falls, and rolls over with his heels in the air. His mind is so full of supernatural horrors that he thinks the ghost of Banquo is still playing him tricks, and he lies crouching and quaking, to see what is coming next. It is a handsome somersault, certainly, but I do not think it can be called acting Shakespeare. The actress who plays Lady Macbeth with Signor Rossi has obtained a great success—a success which owes nothing to felicity of costume. I spoke just now of "good faith," and of Italian bad taste; Mme. Pareti-Glech puts these two things together and produces a striking result. The Italians, after all, if you make them a certain allowance, have an instinctive sense of the picturesque which is beyond our culture. Grant that Lady Macbeth's influence over her husband was a purely physical one, and this obscure southern artist is superb. You should see the gesture with which, in her call upon nature to "unsex" herself, she utters the great "Hold, hold!"—or those with which, to raise Macbeth to his senses before the visitors who have been knocking at the gate are admitted, she shakes him about and chokes him by his coat-collar.

The most successful play of the winter, up to this time, has been

the *Ferréol* of Victorien Sardou, and it is an agreeable fact that
it is also the best. It is consummately clever, in M. Sardou's usual
way, and it is acted at the Gymnase in a manner to throw its
cleverness into extraordinary relief. It literally palpitates with
interest, as the phrase is, and from the first word and to the last
the spectator is under the charm. The charm with M. Sardou is not
of a very high quality; he makes a play very much as he would
make a pudding; he has his well-tested recipe and his little stores
of sugar and spice, from which he extracts with an unimpassioned
hand exactly the proper quantity of each. The pudding is capital,
but I can think of no writer of equal talent who puts so little of
himself into his writing. Search M. Sardou's plays through and
you will not find a trace of a personal conviction, of a moral emotion, of an intellectual temperament, of anything that makes the
"atmosphere" of a work. They seem to have been produced in a
sort of mental vacuum. But they are not played in a vacuum by any
means, and *Ferréol* bids fair to run for a good part of the rest of the
winter. It has made the reputation, and, theatrically, the fortune of
an admirably young actor named Worms. I don't know when I
have seen a piece of acting that has given me such unmitigated
satisfaction as M. Worms's representation of the distracted hero of
this piece. He has seen a man murdered as he himself was leaving
clandestinely at two o'clock in the morning the house of the
woman he loves, and his lips are sealed by the fact of his position.
His best friend is arrested on suspicion and condemned by the
strongest circumstantial evidence, and yet he cannot make a
declaration which involves publication of the circumstance that
his point of view, as a witness, was the garden wall of Mme. de
Bois-Martel. This lady (who had imprudently permitted his visit)
is in equal distress, and the unhappy couple are buffeted to and fro
between the sense of their duty and of their dangers. I need not say
how the problem is solved, for sooner or later, I suppose, *Ferréol*
will be "adapted." But in losing M. Worms it will lose half its
power. This young actor has a gift of quiet realism, of mingled

vehemence and discretion, of impassioned self-control, which places him at a jump beside Delaunay, the classic *jeune premier* of the Théâtre Français, whom, however, he resembles only in the perfection of his art. The Français has promptly marked him for her own. Under her fostering care he can ripen and develop at his ease.

Actors are just now indeed rather too much at their ease at this establishment, which has produced this winter but a single new piece — a little one-act comedy by M. Pailleron. When the Théâtre Français can do nothing else, as a critic said the other day, she can drape herself in her majesty — she can draw from her immense historical repertory. The drapery is most voluminous and becoming, but the terms of the Théâtre Français's magnificent contract with the State are that she shall increase her inheritance and think of the future as well as the past. M. Pailleron's comedy, *Petite Pluie* by name, has had a moderate success, which it owes wholly to the incomparable skill of Mme. Plessy. There is a double interest in watching Mme. Plessy, as with the present winter she is to close her long and brilliant career. She has probably never done anything more purely brilliant than the part she plays in the piece I have just mentioned. The comedy treats of a young woman who has eloped from a villa on the French Riviera, near the Italian frontier, with a secretary of legation, and who arrives with her lover in her ball-dress at a wayside inn, to which the guilty couple have been driven by a sudden storm and by a fracture of the shafts of their carriage. Here they are overtaken by the friend from whose domicile, while paying her a visit and dancing at her ball, the fair fugitive has fled — a clever woman of the world, who disapproves altogether of elopements, takes a skeptical view of love, and recommends Mme. de Thiais to return to her husband, shabby fellow as he is. While the secretary of legation is out under the shed, pottering over his broken shaft with the drowsy innkeeper, the two ladies have it out together. The elder one riddles her friend's illusions with her wit, gives her a wholesome fright, and with a courtesy to the naughty attaché takes her off under her arm. This scene is acted by Mme. Plessy with a spirit and style and grace — what the French call an authority — which are certainly the last word of high comedy. Mme. Plessy is not (to my thinking) a woman of genius; she is not even a sympathetic actress; there is something always rather hard and metallic in her style. But she is so consummate, so accomplished, so perfect a mistress of the subtlest resources of her art, that to follow her through the light and shade of a long speech is not merely an amusement, but a real intellectual profit. When I think of all the experience, the observation, the reflection, the contact with life and art which are summed up in such a mellow maturity of skill, I am struck with a kind of veneration.

Of the other theatres there is nothing very important to narrate. The *revue* prevails at several of them, notably at the Variétés, which is supposed to be its stronghold — that dreary, flimsy burlesque of the events of the year, which is the pretext for so many bad jokes and undressed *figurantes*. The Palais Royal is, as always, exhaustingly exhilarating, with *Le Panache*, a long farce in which the element of quiet comedy is thought to be more marked than usual. This speaks well for the farces of the past.

Lastly, the Vaudeville with *Les Scandales d'hier*, and a company augmented by Pierre Berton from the Français, and Mlle. Pierson from the Gymnase — mysterious fugitives both — has been expending some very good acting on a very indifferent play.

January 7th, 1876

"*The Parisian Stage*" *appeared in the* New York Tribune, *January 29, 1876, being the fifth letter of the series.*

NOTES FROM PARIS

——————————— 1 8 7 6 ———————————

1

I WENT too far just now in saying that nothing but politics is
talked about; every one finds a word for *Les Danicheff*, and I
suppose that I should therefore find a word for them too. *Les
Danicheff* is a drama of mysterious origin which has just been
brought out with extraordinary success at the Odéon Theatre, and
is attracting all Paris to that remote and unfriended establishment.
Its origin is as mysterious as anything can be with which M. Alexandre Dumas is associated — for the play has been largely re-
touched and manipulated by him. It is the work of a Russian
author who calls himself on the bills, fictitiously, M. Pierre
Neosky, but who is otherwise unknown. The story goes that he
brought his drama a year ago to the author of the *Demi-Monde* to
ask his opinion of it, and that Dumas replied that the subject was
magnificent, but the treatment in a high degree clumsy. Then, by
way of pointing out errors, he sat down with his docile petitioner
and fairly made the play over. Its success is in great measure owing to the more famous author's remarkable scenic science which
forms a distinct and easily recognizable ingredient. The smartness
is all Dumas's — the epigrams, the *tirades*, the aphorisms, by this
time rather drearily familiar, about the fathomless depravity of the
female sex. But the theme of the piece is so picturesque and effective that it carries Dumas's faults hardly less easily than his merits.

It has the charm of being strange and novel, and not dealing with the everlasting seventh commandment as interpreted on the boulevards. In spite of this, however, the story is easier to tell in French than in English. A Russian countess of autocratic temper picks out a wife for her only son, the ardent and gallant young Vladimir. He declines his mother's offer, and intimates that he is in love with a young girl, by birth a serf, whom she has educated and admitted into her drawing-room. Scandalized and horrified, she attempts to reason away his passion, but he is deaf to arguments and threats, and insists upon marrying the modest and amiable Anna. The countess obtains of him that he will at least absent himself for a year from home, to test the permanency of his affection — that he will repair to Moscow, frequent the society of his equals, and do his best to fall in love. He departs, and as soon as his back is turned she summons Anna and marries her, willy-nilly, out of hand, to the coachman. The coachman, a certain Osip, in his black velvet Knickerbockers and his red silk caftan, is the real hero of the piece. The scene of the marriage is very effective, and makes a striking picture — all the serfs convoked and ranged solemnly round, the long-bearded pope, the picturesque moujik, with a soul above his station, the high-handed old countess in the middle, flanked by her parrot, her lap-dog, and her two grotesque and servile old lady companions, and the poor young girl, vainly entreating and sobbing, in the pitying silence, and twisting herself at the feet of her mistress. Her resistance and her prayers are vain, and, secretly in love as she is with Vladimir, she is shuffled into the arms of Osip. The coachman is an old-time comrade of the heir of the house, who, when they were boys together, had treated him almost as an equal, and toward whom he has always preserved a devoted loyalty. Vladimir, on hearing of Anna's marriage, comes back from Moscow like a whirlwind, long before his year is out, and his savage irruption, whip in hand, into the cottage of the humble couple produces a great effect. This is so well rendered by the young actor who plays the part that the audience breaks out into long applause before he has spoken a word. Then follows a scene between the two young men which it required some delicacy to handle. The upshot of it is that Osip, instead of deserving his young master's opprobrium for what he has done, has earned his gratitude. He has contented himself with being Anna's husband but in name — he has piously abstained from the exercise of marital rights — he has accepted the young girl (whom of course he secretly adores), only as a sacred deposit. The marriage shall be broken and he will hand her over to Vladimir. I need not relate the conclusion of the piece, for after this exalted flight the most felicitous conclusion must be more or less of an anti-climax. The obvious objection to the story is that Osip is too ethereal a fellow for a Russian coachman; but the authors have made him plausible, the part is singularly well played, and for myself I do not object to fanciful creation. What I enjoyed in *Les Danicheff*, in spite of the very sensible presence of Dumas, is a certain imaginative good faith and *naïveté* which offers a grateful change from the familiar gyrations of that terribly tough and lean old performer, *l'esprit Parisien*.

I have it on my conscience, while touching on these matters, to say another word about Ernesto Rossi, of whom I have spoken hitherto with a certain meagreness of praise. He has lately appeared as Romeo, and though he has attracted less attention in the part than in some others, it is the one in which he has given me most pleasure. He has scandalously mutilated the play, but there is a certain compensation in the fact that what he has left of it sounds wonderfully well in Italian. One never sees Shakespeare played without being reminded at some new point of his greatness; the other night what struck me was the success with which, for the occasion, he had Italianized his fancy. The things that trouble us nowadays in *Romeo and Juliet* — the redundancy of protestation, the importunate conceits, the embarrassing frankness — all these fall into their place in the rolling Italian diction, and what one seems to see is not a translation, but a restitution. It is singular that Rossi should play best the part that he looks least, for a stout middle-aged man one would say that Romeo was rather a snare. But it is with Romeo very much as with Juliet; by the time an actor has acquired the assurance necessary for playing the part, he has lost his youth and his slimness. Robust and mature as he is Rossi does it as a consummate artist; it is impossible to imagine anything more picturesquely tender, more intensely ardent. As I have said, he has done very much what he chose with the play, but it is not to be denied that in one or two cases he has almost made his modifications pardonable. He makes Juliet come to her senses in the tomb and discover her inanimate lover before Romeo has utterly expired. Besides enabling the hapless couple to perish in each other's arms, this gives Rossi an opportunity for a great stroke of dumb show — the sort of thing in which he decidedly excels. He has staggered away from the tomb while the poison, which he has just drunk, is working, and stands with his back to it as Juliet noiselessly revives and emerges. He returns to it, finds it empty, looks about him, and sees Juliet standing a short distance off, and looking in the dim vault like a spectre. He has been bending over the empty tomb, and his eyes fall upon her as he slowly rises. His movement of solemn terror as he slowly throws up his arms and continues to rise and rise, until, with his whole being dilated, he stands staring and appalled, on tiptoe, is, although it is grotesque in description, very well worth seeing. Rossi's speeches are often weak, but when he attempts an acutely studied piece of pantomime, he never misses it. This superiority of his pantomime to his delivery seems to me to fix him, in spite of his great talent, in the second line of actors.

January 18th, 1876

Ernesto Rossi, whose acting was discussed in a previous essay, "Paris Revisited," and in this extract from the sixth letter, which appeared under the heading, "Parisian Life," in the New York Tribune, February 5, *1876, was a novelty to the Parisians but not to Henry James. James had already seen him in Rome three years earlier, and had written briefly about him in the chapter "From a Roman Notebook" in* Transatlantic Sketches *under a date in April, 1873. In quoting his words I give the text as he revised it for* Italian Hours *in 1909:*

"Last evening in H's box at the Apollo to hear Ernesto Rossi in "Othello." He shares supremacy with Salvini in Italian tragedy. Beautiful great theatre with boxes you can walk about in; brilliant audience . . . Rossi is both very bad and very fine; bad where anything like taste and discretion is required, but "all there," and much more than there, in violent passion. The last act reduced too much, however, to mere exhibitional sensibility. The interesting thing to me was to observe the Italian conception of the part — to see how crude it was, how little it expressed the hero's moral side, his depth, his dignity — anything more than his being a creature terrible in mere tantrums. The great point was his seizing Iago's head and whacking it half-a-dozen times on the floor, and then flinging him twenty yards away. It was wonderfully done, but in the doing of it and in the evident relish for it in the house there was I scarce knew what force of easy and thereby rather cheap expression."

2

In the midst of her political turmoil Paris had had time to drop a sigh over the grave of Frédéric Lemaître, who died at a very advanced age a fortnight ago. The newspapers have been full of tributes to his memory, and his death following so close upon that of that other grotesquely aged veteran, Déjazet, has been a piece of good luck for the anecdote-mongers. I incline to think, from what I have heard and read of him, that he was one of the greatest of actors, but that he needed a great license, a great margin, to show his powers. The present generation had seen him — for poverty had repeatedly driven him back to the stage after the chill of age had settled upon him — but it did not know him. It is only our elders — those who remember Victor Hugo's *Marion Delorme* and *Ruy Blas* and Alexandre Dumas's *Antony* as new pieces, that know him. He was formed by the passionate romantic drama that began its career in 1830. He was the actor for the time; he inspired Victor Hugo, and Victor Hugo inspired him in turn. He never succeeded at the Français — he was too fantastic and audacious — he played tragedy with a sense of humour. For an actor he grew old very young. He reminds one of what we hear of Garrick, in having had equal triumph in tragedy and comedy. The theatre of our own

day, with its relish for small, realistic effects, produces no more
actors of these heroic proportions. The nearest approach to them
is perhaps to be found in Got at the Théâtre Français, who has an
element of high fantasy, as those who have seen him in the curious
revival of the mediaeval farce of *Maître Pathelin* must remember.
But Got is on the whole really a philosophic actor, and Frédéric
Lemaître was an imaginative one. The ideal actor nowadays — an
actor formed by Sardou and Dumas *fils* and Feuillet — is Worms of
the Gymnase, who renders prose, not verse, and whose minute and
exquisite strokes are like a masterly etching. But Frédéric
Lemaître, as we see him in his *legende*, is like a huge fantastic
shadow, a moving silhouette, projected duskily against the wall
from a glowing fire. The fire is the "romantic" movement of 1830.

February 11th, 1876

*An extract from the eighth letter, which appeared under the heading, "Paris in
Election Time," in the* New York Tribune, *March 4, 1876.*

3

If it is true that the country is going to the bad, and that the
celebrated "era of revolutions" is again to open, people are beguiling the interval in such fashion as they may. A convenient
sedative to suspense is found to be an evening at the Théâtre
Français, where they are now playing Alexandre Dumas's long-
expected drama *L'Étrangère*. Besides your evening, in this case,
you can get plenty to talk about afterward. The production of this
piece has been the event of the winter. Besides its intrinsic importance, there were several accessory reasons for its attracting
attention. It is the first play (if I am not mistaken) that Dumas
has produced since his election to the Academy, as well as the
first that he has presented to the Théâtre Français. The curiosity
of the public, moveover, had been very skillfully stimulated, and
the last rehearsal of the play had all the honours of a first representation. *L'Étrangère*, after all, has been but a moderate success —
though, certainly, many a poor playwright would be enchanted

that "moderation" should deal out his laurels and his percentage in this particular fashion. The great theatre is crowded, and for the least little orchestra chairs you have to apply a week in advance. Nevertheless the play is pronounced indifferent by some people, and shockingly bad by others. No one, as far as I have observed, has had the originality to call it good. I happened to hear it discussed, a few days since, among several gentlemen who are more or less of the same guild as its author, and it was as pretty a cutting-up as one could desire to see. The general verdict was that Alexandre Dumas has so much wind in his sails (from former successes) that he will float safely across his present shallows, but that his decline (since decline it is) will be cumulative; that another piece as bad as *L'Étrangère* will have much worse luck, and that the more gentle the public has been for the author hitherto, the more pitiless it will be when he begins to sink. Has he already begun to sink? I confess that *L'Étrangère* strikes me as a rather desperate piece of floundering in the dramatic sea. It is a long story, and I cannot pretend to relate it in detail. Suffice it that the "Foreigner" who gives its title to the piece, and who is played by that very interesting actress, Mme. Sarah Bernhardt, is a daughter of our own democracy, Mrs. Clarkson by name. She explains, in the second act, by a mortal harrangue — the longest, by the watch, I have ever listened to — that she is the daughter of a mulatto slave-girl and a Carolinian planter. As she exprésses it herself, "My mother was pretty: he remarked her; I was born of the remark." Mrs. Clarkson, however, has next to nothing to do with the action of the play, and she is the least successful figure that the author has ever drawn. Why she should be an American, why she should have negro blood, why she should be the implacable demon that she is represented, why she should deliver the melodramatic and interminable *tirade* I have mentioned, why she should come in, why she should go out, why, in short, she should exist — all this is the perfection of mystery. She is like the heroine of an old-fashioned drama of the Boulevard du Crime who has strayed unwittingly into a literary work, in which she is out of time with all her companions. She is, on Dumas's part, an incredible error of taste. It must be confessed, however, that her entrance into the play has a masterly effectiveness. The whole first act indeed is an excellent start, though the goal is never really reached. As one of the characters says, we are *en pleine décomposition sociale*. The Duchess de Sept-Monts is giving a charity ball, and the circle of her particular intimates is collected about her in one of her apartments. The lady in question has been sold by her father, a retired tradesman of immense fortune, to a penniless and exhausted little rake, who, driven to bay by his creditors, has been delighted to raise money on his ducal title by the simple expedient of matrimony. Her father and her husband are present, and the conversation alights upon Mrs. Clarkson, the mysterious American, her beauty, her diamonds, her sinister reputation, her innumerable conquests, and her total absence of female friends. No respectable woman has ever entered her house or has ever received her. It so happens that the Duchess's father, her husband and her lover are all entangled in Mrs. Clarkson's toils, and these facts more or less explicitly transpire. The baleful beauty is moreover even now on the premises; she has been seen in the garden among the visitors present by right of having purchased their ticket — seen on the arm of the Duchess's lover (a lover who is as yet, I hasten to add, sincerely platonic). Abruptly the Duchess is approached by a servant with a card, which she reads in deep agitation. She writes a few words on another card and gives it to the footman; he goes off with it, and then she reads aloud to the company the contents of the first missive. Mrs. Clarkson requests permission to be admitted to the salon in which the Duchess sits apart with her intimates, there to receive from the Duchess's own hands a cup of tea. In compensation, she offers to pay for her cup of tea the sum of 25,000 francs, which the Duchess will make over to the charity for which the ball has been given. At the revelation of this audacity the little circle is aghast, and demands with a single voice what the Duchess has answered. The Duchess has answered that Mrs. Clarkson may be admitted if one of the gentlemen actually about the hostess will go out, offer his arm and conduct her into the ducal presence. There is a particular silence— half a dozen gentlemen are present, but not one of them moves. Finally the shaky, unclean little Duke himself (admirably played by Coquelin) stands forth and declares that he will play the gallant part. The announcement makes a great sensation, for it is his presumed mistress that he proposes to introduce to his wife. He departs and shortly afterward returns, bearing Mrs. Clarkson on his arm, in all the effectiveness of the strange physiognomy and the fantastic toilet of yellow and black which Mme. Sarah Bernhardt has conferred upon her. "A cup!" shouts the outraged Duchess, sticking to her bargain and nothing but her bargain. I must not relate what follows. The real heroine of the play is Mlle. Croizette, who played the Duchess with a great deal of skill and with all that strangely meretricious charm for which she is renowned. She has one really magnificent scene—a scene in which the ill-used (but on her own side by no means unpeccant) heroine, the cup of whose disgust at her husband's turpitude is full, pours it all forth in rage and scorn upon his ignoble head. This is nature caught in the act—Mlle. Croizette's cries and gestures, the passionate reality of her imprecations, electrify the house. The author makes his duchess say things which have never before been said on the stage, but the artistic good faith of the actress carries them off.

I should mention that there is also a Mr. Clarkson in the play— a gentleman engaged in gold-washing in Utah, while his wife drinks tea at five thousand dollars the spoonful in Paris. Half the merit of this figure is with Febvre, who represents it, and who, in particular, has dressed his Yankee with great felicity—quite in the occidental taste, and yet without the least exaggeration. On the whole, as I have said, *L'Étrangère* has been a disappointment, and it is unquestionably a very unsatisfactory piece of work for so clever a man as Dumas. It hangs very loosely together, and the story is both extremely improbable and profoundly disagreeable. Disagreeable above all, for there is not a person in the play who is not, in one way or another, misbehaving grossly. Every one is in the wrong, and the author most of all. And then his drama is saturated with that aroma of bad company and loose living which is the distinctive sign of M. Dumas's muse. This lady is afflicted with a congenital want of perception of certain rudimentary differences between the possible, for decent people, and the impossible. She has also on this occasion abused her characteristic privilege of indulging in pretentious *tirades* of the would-be philosophic order — explaining that love is physics and marriage is chemistry, etc.

February 28th, 1876

An extract from the ninth letter, which appeared under the heading, "Parisian Affairs," in the New York Tribune, *March 25, 1876.*

4

The adventurous American in Paris at the present moment is deriving much entertainment from going to see the highly successful melodrama of the *Chevaliers de la Patrie*, at the Théâtre Historique. I say "adventurous" because the theatre in question is very far off, and, though of splendid aspect and proportion, much frequented by that class of amateurs who find the suspense of the entr'actes intolerable without the beguilement of an orange. The drama in question treats bravely of the American civil war, and the "chevaliers" from whom it takes its name are Abraham Lincoln and Stonewall Jackson. It is in no less than eight acts, but I sat to the end, for it is a most exhilarating affair. The author, one M. Delpit, is, I believe, by birth a Louisianian. He evidently "knows better," but he knows that his audience does not, and he gives them their money's worth of local colour. In the first act the greater part of the *dramatis personae* are assembled on a steamboat on the Potomac, and they all come to the side of the vessel and narrate their histories to the audience. Meanwhile the steamboat is racing with a craft of an opposition line, and the captain has formally announced that his boat must win the race or blow up. One or other of the boilers must burst—they can only hope it will be the other. The passengers exclaim in chorus, "All right!" and await further developments. At last the rival steamboat comes along-side, and, after a moment of painful suspense, explodes. "It's the other!" cry the passengers, and continue their promenade on the deck. The sequel is worthy of this beginning, but I cannot begin to unweave its tangled web. Abraham Lincoln is ever administering justice in one of the saloons of the White House, like a primitive chieftain under the spreading oak. The White House, indeed, appears to open out in the rear into the forest primeval. The scene is of course in a high degree farcical, but the actor who represents Mr. Lincoln has succeeded in making up his head into a very tolerable likeness of the original. Then we are transported to the Southern army, in which two gallant young Frenchmen have come to seek commissions, and introduced to Stonewall Jackson and the famous cavalry chieftain, Stuart. This, of course, furnishes the opportunity for a very dramatic contrast— Jackson sitting reading the Bible on one side of the stage, Stuart draining his glass on the other, and the Southern army displayed in the background. Stuart proposes to give a "fête" in the evening, but Jackson piously protests. Stuart, however, insists, Jackson goes off in sorrow, if not in anger, and the fête—consisting of a dozen negro minstrels and as many ballet girls—is promptly put forward. It is interrupted, however, by the return of Jackson on a litter, fresh from the field of battle, and mortally wounded. During the fête a battle has been raging, at which Stuart's attendance appears to have been deemed superfluous. Jackson, in his death agony, struts and stamps about the stage, and requests the two French officers to repair straightway to Washington and kidnap Mr. Lincoln. This they proceed to do in the next act; but Wilkes Booth—whose name has been altered by the censorship—

comes very near being beforehand with them. They are all baffled, however, by the sublimity of Mr. Lincoln's conversation, and
the curtain falls upon the reunion of the French officers and their
sweethearts in one of the parlours of the White House, where the
President fraternally blesses them.

March 10th, 1876

*An extract from the tenth letter, which appeared under the heading, "Parisian
Topics," in the* New York Tribune, *April 1, 1876.*

5

In comparison with Michelet's early struggles to climb the
ladder of knowledge, it may seem that such a career as that of
Madame Plessy, who has just bidden farewell to the stage at the
Théâtre Français, offers but a trivial interest, but certainly nothing that is thoroughly well done has been easily done, and I
am sure that the extraordinary perfection of Madame Plessy's art
was the fruit of a great deal of labour. Her last appearance the
other night was a very brilliant solemnity. She acted portions of
three or four of her most successful parts, and in conclusion, with
the whole company of the Comédie Française gathered about her,
she declaimed some very good verses by M. Sully-Prudhomme.
She is a really irreparable loss to the stage, which in spite of her
advanced age she might for some time have continued to adorn.
Her age was not seriously perceptible; she is 57 years old and had
belonged to the Théâtre Français from her fifteenth year. In 1845
she seceded, without ceremony, and repaired to Russia, where she
enjoyed fame and fortune for some ten years. In 1855 she returned
to the Comédie Française, quite *en princesse*, making her own terms
and paying none of the fines and penalties to which she had been
legally condemned. Since then, from year to year, her talent has
been growing richer and more perfect, and it has now a blooming
maturity which might long bid defiance to time. The especially
regrettable point is that her place will probably never be filled,

for she was the last depositary of certain traditions which can never, in the nature of things, be renewed. She was the perfect great lady of high comedy, as high comedy was possible before the invention of slang. She represented certain instincts and practices which have passed out of manners. The other night, as she finished her verses, she took Mesdemoiselles Sarah Bernhardt and Croizette by the hands, and, with admirable grace, presented them to the public as her substitutes. It is more than likely that she had measured the irony of her gesture; for from the moment it takes two actresses to make up a Madame Plessy, the cause is obviously lost. Clever as these young ladies are they will not fill the void. Their art is small art; Madame Plessy's was great art.

May 27th, 1876

An extract from the sixteenth letter, which appeared under the heading, "Parisian Topics," in the New York Tribune, *June 17, 1876.*

6

If the success of M. Parodi's *Rome Vaincue* at the Théâtre Français may be taken as a pledge of the prosperity of the season of 1876–77, the present winter will, in theatrical matters, be brilliant. If we may be allowed to make the distinction, however, it is the success of M. Parodi's tragedy that has been brilliant rather than the tragedy itself. The latter is a highly respectable production, but it certainly would not have been much talked of if Mlle. Sarah Bernhardt had not given it the aid of her extraordinary talent. The play is pompous and tedious, and it is already the fashion among fastidious spectators to arrive only towards ten o'clock, in time for the last two acts, in which Mlle. Bernhardt comes out, as the phrase is, "very strong." The presumption, beforehand, was certainly against the success of M. Parodi's drama. A tragedy in five acts, in verse, on a fine old Roman subject, would hardly have been said to fall in with the taste of the period. Add to this that the author is a foreigner—an Italian—who has been liv-

ing but two or three years in Paris, where he has exercised the
modest function of teacher of his native tongue. His play, given the
almost intolerable restrictions of its form and the fact that its
author was not to the manner born, is a very honourable performance. There is too much talk and too little action, but there is
a great deal of dramatic feeling, some very fine *tirades*, and some
very happy lines. The author's style has often a masculine ring,
and his mastery of the formidable art of French verse is proof of a
truly impressive combination of ambition and industry. There is
every reason to expect that he will go on to greater things. The
story of the play is the crime of a vestal virgin who has lapsed
from chastity, and who, Hannibal being at the gates of Rome, is
denounced by the oracles as the cause of the city's peril. This can
only be averted by her submitting to the orthodox punishment—
burial alive. At the supreme moment she is rescued from her horrible fate by her grandmother, a blind octogenarian, who stabs her
to the heart. Mlle. Sarah Bernhardt plays not, as might be expected, the guilty vestal, but the heroic ancestress. The manner
in which she renders the part is one more proof of her extraordinary intelligence and versatility; it is in the highest degree
picturesque. She muffles her youth and beauty in long veils and
grey tresses, until she looks like a perfect Mater Dolorosa—a
Madonna of a *pietà*. How it is that, to simulate blindness, she contrives for half an hour at a time to show only the whites of her
eyes, is her own affair; the effect is highly relished by the audience. Her narration of the accident by which she lost her eyesight
provokes immense applause by its terrible tranquility—applause
which is equally bestowed upon the movement and exclamation
by which, when in the presence of the consul and the decemvirs,
who are quite *au courant*, and who are assembled to judge the
crime, her granddaughter whispers her dreadful secret—"Ma
mère, j'ai failli"—she instantly bids the young girl speak lower
lest she be overheard. I may add that *Rome Vaincue* has had the
good fortune to be "endorsed" in the highest terms by the critic

whose weekly manifesto, in the *Temps*, makes and unmakes the success of plays — M. F. Sarcey.

November 16th, 1876

An unsigned essay which appeared under the heading "Notes" and as written by "a correspondent from Paris," in the Nation, *November 16, 1876.*

7

Having mentioned a few weeks ago that the winter season of the Théâtre Français promised to be "lively," as it would be called in commercial circles, I may add that events have since then done something to justify my prevision. MM. Erckmann-Chatrian's *L'Ami Fritz* has lately been brought out under circumstances of peculiar vivacity. The *Figaro*, with characteristic impudence and acerbity, began a campaign against the piece a month before the first representation, and did its best to prepare a 'manifestation' and prevent a hearing. By publishing a certain number of garbled and manipulated extracts it undertook to show that the authors of the *Conscrit de 1813* 'insulted' the French army; that they were anti-patriotic, and that patriotism must hiss them off the stage. It is, of course, not safe to embrace any cause with one's eyes shut; but if this were ever reasonable, it would be in taking blindly on any occasion the directly opposite ground to the *Figaro*. Such ground was taken by the friends of MM. Erckmann-Chatrian, and, as the event has proved, by the public at large. The newspapers discussed the 'patriotism' of these charming story-tellers, the publishers brought out new editions of the incriminated work, and M. Perrin, the very clever director of the Comédie Française, flattered himself that *L'Ami Fritz* was being splendidly advertised. The play was brought forward on the 2nd of December, before an immense audience, but the performance was something of an anticlimax. Every one, as it turned out, went to see the 'manifestation,' but no one went to make it. The evening passed off most smoothly, the play was very pretty, and the only incident was M. Got's fling at the *Figaro*, when, according to the custom of the theatre, he came before the curtain to announce the names of the authors: "The play which we have had the *honour* of performing," said M. Got, in the very largest letters and emphasizing the words by a long stop, "is by MM. Erckmann-Chatrian," etc. The only consolation of the *Figaro* has been to publish a long article on M. Got's impudence. The whole affair has been, according to the French adage, a good deal of noise about an *omelette au lard*. The little novel of *L'Ami Fritz*, published many years since, was a real masterpiece — a savoury idyll, a succulent pastoral. It was a Dutch picture of the daily life of an honest bachelor in an Alsatian town, who spends his hours in washing down heavy dinners and suppers with draughts of Rhennish wine, until at last, at the instigation of a good old Jewish rabbi who has a passion for match-making, he falls in love with a blonde young woman, marries her, and is converted from lonely gluttony to the functions of a good citizen and a paterfamilias. Upon this very slender basis the authors have built a play which, it must be confessed, is signally wanting in dramatic interest. The story was a very pretty cabinet picture, in which especially the soft fumes curling up from the hero's excellent dinner were rendered in the most natural manner. But it is hard to make a drama out of good smells. The authors have helped themselves along by introducing one of the questions of the hour, which seems rather pushed in by the shoulder. There has been of late a good deal of talk in France about the decrease of the population and its being the duty of good citizens to try and check it. The old rabbi, admirably played by Got, is made the apostle of propagation, and whenever the play drags a little he delivers a little rhapsody upon the beauty of a numerous progeny. The piece owes everything to the actors and to the delightful picturesqueness of the *mise-en-scène*. As regards this latter feature, there is in particular a certain Sunday dinner, in the first act, of which the lavish realism makes the reader's mouth water. Got, as I have said, plays the rabbi, as he plays everything, with incomparable richness and depth of humour; Febvre, whose usual line is the injured husband or the dangerous lover of fashionable life, renders the rustic epicure in perfection; and Mlle. Reichemberg has only to be herself and to climb into a cherry-tree above the garden-wall to be the most charming of Suzels. The exertions of these artists and the curiosity of the public—curiosity especially to see the table linen and crockery of the first act—will ensure *L'Ami Fritz* a certain amount of success; but I suspect that before very long the piece will succumb to the excessive tranquility of its interest.

January 4th, 1877

An unsigned essay which appeared under the title, "MM. Erckmann-Chatrian's 'Ami Fritz'," in the Nation, *January 4, 1877.*

———————————— 1 8 7 6 ————————————

M. FRANCISQUE SARCEY, the dramatic critic of the Paris *Temps*, and the gentleman who, of the whole journalistic fraternity, holds the fortune of a play in the hollow of his hand, has been publishing during the last year a series of biographical notices of the chief actors and actresses of the first theatre in the world. *Comédiens et Comédiennes: la Comédie Française*—such is the title of this publication, which appears in monthly numbers of the *Librairie des Bibliophiles*, and is ornamented on each occasion with a very prettily etched portrait, by M. Gaucherel, of the artist to whom the number is devoted. By lovers of the stage in general and of the Théâtre Français in particular the series will be found most interesting; and I welcome the pretext for saying a few words about an institution which—if such language be not hyperbolical—I passionately admire. I must add that the portrait is incomplete, though for the present occasion it is more than sufficient. The list of M. Sarcey's biographies is not yet filled up; three or four, those of Madame Favart and of MM. Febvre and Delaunay, are still wanting. Nine numbers, however, have appeared—the first being entitled *La Maison de Molière*, and devoted to a general account of the great theatre; and the others treating of its principal *sociétaires* and *pensionnaires* in the following order:

Regnier,
Got,
Sophie Croizette,

THE THÉÂTRE FRANÇAIS

Sarah Bernhardt,
Coquelin,
Madeleine Brohan,
Bressant,
Madame Plessy.

(This order, by the way, is purely accidental; it is not that of age or of merit.) It is always entertaining to encounter M. Francisque Sarcey, and the reader who, during a Paris winter, has been in the habit, of a Sunday evening, of unfolding his *Temps* immediately after unfolding his napkin, and glancing down first of all to see what this sturdy *feuilletoniste* has found to his hand — such a reader will find him in great force in the pages before us. It is true that, though I myself confess to being such a reader, there are moments when I grow rather weary of M. Sarcey, who has in an eminent degree both the virtues and the defects which attach to the great French characteristic — the habit of taking terribly *au sérieux* anything that you may set about doing. Of this habit of abounding in one's own sense, of expatiating, elaborating, reiterating, refining, as if for the hour the fate of mankind were bound up with one's particular topic, M. Sarcey is a capital and at times an almost comical representative. He talks about the theatre once a week as if — honestly, between himself and his reader — the theatre were the only thing in this frivolous world that is worth seriously talking about. He has a religious respect for his theme and he holds that if a thing is to be done at all it must be done in detail as well as in the gross.

It is to this serious way of taking the matter, to his thoroughly businesslike and professional attitude, to his unwearying attention to detail, that the critic of the *Temps* owes his enviable influence and the weight of his words. Add to this that he is sternly incorruptible. He has his admirations, but they are honest and discriminating; and whom he loveth he very often chasteneth. He is not ashamed to commend Mlle X., who has only had a curtsy to make, if her curtsy has been the ideal curtsy of the situation; and he is not afraid to overhaul Mr. A., who has delivered the *tirade* of the play, if Mr. A. has failed to hit the mark. Of course his judgement is good; when I have had occasion to measure it I have usually found it excellent. He has the scenic sense — the theatrical eye. He knows at a glance what will do, and what will not do. He is shrewd and sagacious and almost tiresomely in earnest, and this is his principal brilliancy. He is homely, familiar and colloquial; he leans his elbows on his desk and does up his weekly budget into a parcel the reverse of compact. You can fancy him a grocer retailing tapioca and hominy — full weight for the price; his style seems a sort of integument of brown paper. But the fact remains that if M. Sarcey praises a play the play has a run; and that if M. Sarcey says it will not do it does not do at all. If M. Sarcey devotes an encouraging line and a half to a young actress, mademoiselle is immediately *lancée;* she has a career. If he be-stows a quiet "bravo" on an obscure comedian, the gentleman may forthwith renew his engagement. When you make and unmake fortunes at this rate, what matters it whether you have a little ele-gance the more or the less? Elegance is for M. Paul de St. Victor, who does the theatres in the *Moniteur*, and who, though he writes a style only a trifle less pictorial than that of Théophile Gautier him-self, has never, to the best of my belief, brought clouds or sunshine to any playhouse. I may add, to finish with M. Sarcey, that he contributes a daily political article — generally devoted to watch-ing and showing up the "game" of the clerical party — to Edmond About's journal, the *XIXième Siècle;* that he gives a weekly *conférence* on current literature; that he "confers" also on those excellent Sunday morning performances now so common in the French theatres, during which examples of the classic repertory are presented, accompanied by a light lecture upon the history and character of the play. As the commentator on these occasions M. Sarcey is in great demand, and he officiates sometimes in small provincial towns. Lastly, frequent playgoers in Paris observe that the very slenderest novelty is sufficient to insure at a theatre the (very considerable) physical presence of the conscientious critic of the *Temps*. If he were remarkable for nothing else he would be remarkable for the fortitude with which he exposes himself to the pestiferous climate of the Parisian temples of the drama.

For these agreeable "notices" M. Sarcey appears to have mended his pen and to have given a fillip to his fancy. They are gracefully and often lightly turned; occasionally, even, the author grazes the epigrammatic. They deal, as is proper, with the artistic and not with the private physiognomy of the ladies and gentlemen whom they commemorate; and though they occasionally allude to what the French call "intimate" matters, they contain no satisfaction for the lovers of scandal. The Théâtre Français, in the face it presents to the world, is an austere and venerable establishment, and a frivolous tone about its affairs would be almost as much out of keeping as if applied to the Académie herself. M. Sarcey touches upon the organization of the theatre, and gives some account of the different phases through which it has passed during these latter years. Its chief functionary is a general administrator, or director, appointed by the State, which enjoys this right in virtue of the considerable subsidy which it pays to the house; a subsidy amounting, if I am not mistaken (M. Sarcey does not mention the sum) to 250,000 francs. The director, however, is not an absolute but a constitutional ruler; for he shares his powers with the society itself, which has always had a large deliberative voice.

Whence, it may be asked, does the society derive its light and its inspiration? From the past, from precedent, from tradition— from the great unwritten body of laws which no one has in his keeping but many have in their memory, and all in their respect. The principles on which the Théâtre Français rests are a good deal like the Common Law of England—a vaguely and inconveniently registered mass of regulations which time and occasion have welded together and from which the recurring occasion can usually manage to extract the rightful precedent. Napoleon I. who had a finger in every pie in his dominion, found time during his brief and disastrous occupation of Moscow to send down a decree re-modelling and regulating the constitution of the theatre. This document has long been a dead letter, and the society abides by its older traditions. The *traditions* of the Comédie Française—that is the sovereign word, and that is the charm of the place—the charm that one never ceases to feel, however often one may sit beneath the classic, dusky dome. One feels this charm with peculiar intensity as a foreigner newly arrived. The Théâtre Français has had the good fortune to be able to allow its traditions to accumulate. They have been preserved, transmitted, respected, cherished, until at last they form the very atmosphere, the vital air, of the establishment. A stranger feels their superior influence the first time he sees the great curtain go up; he feels that he is in a theatre that is not as other theatres are. It is not only better, it is different. It has a peculiar perfection—something consecrated, historical, academic. This impression is delicious, and he watches the performance in a sort of tranquil ecstasy.

Never has he seen anything so smooth and harmonious, so artistic and completed. He has heard all his life of attention to detail, and now, for the first time, he sees something that deserves that name. He sees dramatic effort refined to a point with which the English stage is unacquainted. He sees that there are no limits to possible "finish," and that so trivial an act as taking a letter from a servant or placing one's hat on a chair may be made a suggestive and interesting incident. He sees these things and a great many more besides; but at first he does not analyse them, he gives himself up to sympathetic contemplation. He is in an ideal and exemplary world—a world that has managed to attain all the felicities that the world we live in misses. The people do the things that we should like to do; they are gifted as we should like to be; they have mastered the accomplishments that we have had to give up. The women are not all beautiful—decidedly not, indeed—but they are graceful, agreeable, sympathetic, ladylike;

they have the best manners possible and they are perfectly well dressed. They have charming musical voices and they speak with irreproachable purity and sweetness; they walk with the most elegant grace and when they sit it is a pleasure to see their attitudes. They go out and come in, they pass across the stage, they talk, and laugh, and cry, they deliver long *tirades* or remain statuesquely mute; they are tender or tragic, they are comic or conventional; and through it all you never observe an awkwardness, a roughness, an accident, a crude spot, a false note.

As for the men, they are not handsome either; it must be confessed, indeed, that at the present hour manly beauty is but scantily represented at the Théâtre Français. Bressant, I believe, used to be thought handsome; but Bressant has retired, and among the gentlemen of the troupe I can think of no one but M. Mounet-Sully who may be positively commended for his fine person. But M. Mounet-Sully is, from the scenic point of view, an Adonis of the first magnitude. To be handsome, however, is for an actor one of the last necessities; and these gentlemen are mostly handsome enough. They look perfectly what they are intended to look, and in cases where it is proposed that they shall seem handsome, they usually succeed. They are as well mannered and as well dressed as their fairer comrades and their voices are no less agreeable and effective. They represent gentlemen and they produce the illusion. In this endeavor they deserve even greater credit than the actresses, for in modern comedy, of which the repertory of the Théâtre Français is largely composed, they have nothing in the way of costume to help to carry it off. Half-a-dozen ugly men, in the periodic coat and trousers and stove-pipe hat, with blue chins and false moustaches, strutting before the foot-lights, and pretending to be interesting, romantic, pathetic, heroic, certainly play a perilous game. At every turn they suggest prosaic things and the usual liability to awkwardness is meantime increased a thousand fold. But the comedians of the Théâtre Français are never awkward, and where it is necessary they solve triumphantly the problem of being at once realistic to the eye and romantic to the imagination.

I am speaking always of one's first impression of them. There are spots on the sun, and you discover after a while that there are little irregularities at the Théâtre Français. But the acting is so incomparably better than any that you have seen that criticism for a long time is content to lie dormant. I shall never forget how at first I was under the charm. I liked the very incommodities of the place; I am not sure that I did not find a certain mystic salubrity in the pestilent air. The Théâtre Français, it is known, gives you a good deal for your money. The performance, which rarely ends before midnight, and sometimes transgresses it, frequently begins by seven o'clock. The first hour or two is occupied by secondary performers; but not for the world at this time would I have missed the first rising of the curtain. No dinner could be too hastily swallowed to enable me to see, for instance, Madame Nathalie in Octave Feuillet's charming little comedy of *Le Village*. Madame Nathalie was a plain, stout old woman, who did the mothers and aunts and elderly wives; I use the past tense because she retired from the stage a year ago, leaving a most conspicuous vacancy. She was an admirable actress and a perfect mistress of laughter and tears. In *Le Village* she played an old provincial bourgeoise whose husband takes it into his head, one winter night, to start on the tour of Europe with a roving bachelor friend, who has dropped down on him at supper-time, after the lapse of years, and has gossiped him into momentary discontent with his fireside existence. My pleasure was in Madame Nathalie's figure when she came in dressed to go out to vespers across the *place*. The two foolish old cronies are over their wine, talking of the beauty of the women on the Ionian coast; you hear the church-bell in the distance. It was the quiet felicity of the old lady's dress that used to charm me; the Comédie Française was in every fold of it. She wore a large black silk mantilla, of a peculiar cut, which looked as if she had just taken it tenderly out of some old wardrobe where it lay folded in lavender, and a large dark bonnet, adorned with handsome black silk loops and bows. Her big pale face had a softly frightened look, and in her hand she carried her neatly kept breviary. The extreme suggestiveness, and yet the taste and temperance of this costume, seemed to me inimitable; the bonnet alone, with its handsome, decent, virtuous bows, was worth coming to see. It expressed all the rest, and you saw the excellent pious woman go pick her steps churchward among the puddles, while Jeanette, the cook, in a high white cap, marched before her in sabots with a lantern.

Such matters are trifles, but they are representative trifles, and they are not the only ones that I remember. It used to please me, when I had squeezed into my stall — the stalls at the Français are extremely uncomfortable — to remember of how great a history the large, dim *salle* around me could boast; how many great things had happened there; how the air was thick with associations. Even if I had never seen Rachel, it was something of a consolation to think that those very footlights had illumined her finest moments and that the echoes of her mighty voice were sleeping in that dingy dome. From this to musing upon the "traditions" of the place, of which I spoke just now, was of course but a step. How were they kept? by whom, and where? Who trims the undying lamp and guards the accumulated treasure? I never found out — by sitting in the stalls; and very soon I ceased to care to know. One may be very fond of the stage and yet care little for the green-room; just as one may be very fond of pictures and books and yet be no frequenter of studios and authors' dens. They might pass on the torch as they would behind the scenes; so long as during my time they did not let it drop I made up my mind to be satisfied. And that one could depend upon their not letting it drop became a part of the customary comfort of Parisian life. It became certain that the "traditions" were not mere catchwords, but a most beneficent reality.

Going to the other Parisian theatres helps you to believe in them. Unless you are a voracious theatre-goer you give the others up; you find they do not "pay;" the Français does for you all that they do and so much more besides. There are two possible exceptions — the Gymnase and the Palais Royal. The Gymnase, since the death of Mademoiselle Desclée, has been under a heavy cloud; but occasionally, when a month's sunshine rests upon it, there is a savour of excellence in the performance. But you feel that you are still within the realm of accident; the delightful security of the Rue de Richelieu is wanting. The young lover is liable to be common and the beautifully dressed heroine to have an unpleasant voice. The Palais Royal has always been in its way very perfect; but its way admits of great imperfection. The actresses are classically bad, though usually pretty, and the actors are much addicted to taking liberties. In broad comedy, nevertheless, two or three of the latter are not to be surpassed, and (counting out the women) there is usually something masterly in a Palais Royal performance. In its own line it has what is called style, and it therefore walks, at a distance, in the footsteps of the Français. The Odéon has never seemed to me in any degree a rival of the Théâtre Français, though it is a smaller copy of that establishment. It receives a subsidy from the State, and is obliged by its contract to play the classic repertory one night in the week. It is on these nights, listening to Molière or Marivaux, that you may best measure the superiority of the greater theatre. I have seen actors at the Odéon, in the classic repertory, imperfect in their texts; a monstrously insupposable case at the Comédie Française. The function of the Odéon is to operate as a *pépinière* or nursery for its elder — to try young talents, shape them, make them flexible and then hand them over to the upper house. The more especial nursery of the Français, however, is the Conservatoire Dramatique, an institution dependent upon the State, through the Ministry of the Fine Arts, whose budget is charged with the remuneration of its professors. Pupils graduating from the Conservatoire with a prize have *ipso facto* the right to *débuter* at the

Théâtre Français, which retains them or lets them go, according to its discretion. Most of the first subjects of the Français have done their two years' work at the Conservatoire, and M. Sarcey holds that an actor who has not had that fundamental training which is only to be acquired there never obtains a complete mastery of his resources. Nevertheless some of the best actors of the day have owed nothing to the Conservatoire — Bressant, for instance, and Aimée Desclée, the latter of whom, indeed, never arrived at the Français. (Molière and Balzac were not of the Academy, and so Mlle. Desclée, the first actress after Rachel, died without acquiring the privilege which M. Sarcey says is the day-dream of all young theatrical women — that of printing on their visiting-cards, after their name, *de la Comédie Française.*)

The Théâtre Français has, moreover, the right to do as Molière did — to claim its property wherever it finds it. It may stretch out its long arm and break the engagement of a promising actor at any of the other theatres; of course after a certain amount of notice given. So, last winter, it notified to the Gymnase its design of appropriating Worms, the admirable *jeune premier*, who, returning from a long sojourn in Russia and taking the town by surprise, had begun to retrieve the shrunken fortunes of that establishment.

On the whole, it may be said that the great talents find their way, sooner or later, to the Théâtre Français. This is of course not a rule that works unvaryingly, for there are a great many influences to interfere with it. Interest as well as merit — especially in the case of the actresses — weighs in the scale; and the ire that may exist in celestial minds has been known to manifest itself in the councils of the Comédie. Moreover, a brilliant actress may prefer to reign supreme at one of the smaller theatres; at the Français, inevitably, she shares her dominion. The honor is less, but the comfort is greater.

Nevertheless, at the Français, in a general way, there is in each case a tolerably obvious artistic reason for membership; and if

you see a clever actor remain outside for years, you may be pretty
sure that, though private reasons count, there are artistic reasons
as well. The first half dozen times I saw Mademoiselle Fargueil,
who for years ruled the roost, as the vulgar saying is, at the
Vaudeville, I wondered that so consummate and accomplished an
actress should not have a place on the first French stage. But I
presently grew wiser, and perceived that, clever as Mademoiselle
Fargueil is, she is not for the Rue de Richelieu, but for the Boulevards; her peculiar, intensely Parisian intonation would sound
out of place in the Maison de Molière. (Of course if Mademoiselle Fargueil has ever received overtures from the Français, my
sagacity is at fault—I am looking through a millstone. But I
suspect she has not.) Frédéric Lemaître, who died last winter,
and who was a very great actor, had been tried at the Français
and found wanting—for those particular conditions. But it may
probably be said that if Frédéric was wanting, the theatre was too,
in this case. Frédéric's great force was his extravagance, his fan-
tasticality; and the stage of the Rue de Richelieu was a trifle too
academic. I have even wondered whether Desclée, if she had lived,
would have trod that stage by right, and whether it would have
seemed her proper element. The negative is not impossible. It is
very possible that in that classic atmosphere her great charm—
her intensely modern quality, her super-subtle realism—would
have appeared an anomaly. I can imagine even that her strange,
touching, nervous voice would not have seemed the voice of the
house. At the Français you must know how to acquit yourself of a
tirade; that has always been the touchstone of capacity. It would
probably have proved Desclée's stumbling-block, though she
could utter speeches of six words as no one else surely has ever
done. It is true that Mademoiselle Croizette, and in a certain sense
Mademoiselle Sarah Bernhardt, are rather weak at their *tirades;*
but then old theatre-goers will tell you that these young ladies,
in spite of a hundred attractions, have no business at the Français.

In the course of time the susceptible foreigner passes from that superstitious state of attention which I just now sketched to that greater enlightenment which enables him to understand such a judgement as this of the old theatre-goers. It is borne in upon him that, as the good Homer sometimes nods, the Théâtre Français sometimes lapses from its high standard. He makes various reflections. He thinks that Mademoiselle Favart rants. He thinks M. Mounet-Sully, in spite of his delicious voice, insupportable. He thinks that M. Parodi's five-act tragedy, *Rome Vaincue*, presented in the early part of the present winter, was better done certainly than it would have been done upon any English stage, but by no means so much better done as might have been expected. (Here, if I had space, I would open a long parenthesis, in which I should aspire to demonstrate that the incontestable superiority of average French acting to English is by no means so strongly marked in tragedy as in comedy—is indeed sometimes not strongly marked at all. The reason of this is in a great measure, I think, that we have had Shakespeare to exercise ourselves upon, and that an inferior dramatic instinct exercised upon Shakespeare may become more flexible than a superior one exercised upon Corneille and Racine. When it comes to ranting—ranting even in a modified and comparatively reasonable sense—we do, I suspect, quite as well as the French, if not rather better.) Mr. G. H. Lewes, in his entertaining little book upon *Actors and the Art of Acting*, mentions M. Talbot, of the Français, as a surprisingly incompetent performer. My memory assents to his judgement at the same time that it proposes an amendment. This actor's special line is the buffeted, bemuddled, besotted old fathers, uncles and guardians of classic comedy, and he plays them with his face much more than with his tongue. Nature has endowed him with a visage so admirably adapted, once for all, to his rôle, that he has only to sit in a chair, with his hands folded on his stomach, to look like a monument of bewildered senility. After that it does not matter what he says or how he says it.

The Comédie Française sometimes does weaker things than in

keeping M. Talbot. Last autumn, [1876] for instance, it was really depressing to see Mademoiselle Dudley brought all the way from Brussels (and with not a little flourish either) to "create" the guilty vestal in *Rome Vaincue*. As far as the interests of art are concerned, Mademoiselle Dudley had much better have remained in the Flemish capital, of whose language she is apparently a perfect mistress. It is hard, too, to forgive M. Perrin (M. Perrin is the present director of the Théâtre Français) for bringing out *L'Ami Fritz* of MM. Erckmann-Chatrian. The two gentlemen who write under this name have a double claim to kindness. In the first place, they have produced some delightful little novels; every one knows and admires *Le Conscrit de 1813*; every one admires, indeed, the charming tale on which the play in question is founded. In the second place, they were, before the production of their piece, the objects of a scurrilous attack by the *Figaro* newspaper, which held the authors up to reprobation for having "insulted the army," and did its best to lay the train for a hostile manifestation on the first night. (It may be added that the good sense of the public out-balanced the impudence of the newspaper, and the play was simply advertised into success.) But neither the novels nor the persecutions of MM. Erckmann-Chatrian avail to render *L'Ami Fritz*, in its would-be dramatic form, worthy of the first French stage. It is played as well as possible, and upholstered even better; but it is, according to the vulgar phrase, too "thin" for the locality. Up-holstery has never played such a part at the Théâtre Français as during the reign of M. Perrin, who came into power, if I mistake not, after the late war. He proved very early that he was a radical, and he has introduced a hundred novelties. His administration, however, has been brilliant, and in his hands the Théâtre Français has made money. This it had rarely done before, and this, in the conservative view, is quite beneath its dignity. To this conservative view I should humbly incline. An institution so closely pro-tected by a rich and powerful State ought to be able to cultivate art for art.

The first of M. Sarcey's biographies, to which I have been too
long in coming, is devoted to Regnier, a veteran actor, who left
the stage four or five years since, and who now fills the office of
oracle to his younger comrades. It is the indispensable thing, says
M. Sarcey, for a young aspirant to be able to say that he has had
lessons of M. Regnier, or that M. Regnier had advised him, or that
he has talked such and such a point over with M. Regnier. (His
comrades always speak of him as M. Regnier—never as simple
Regnier.) I have had the fortune to see him but once; it was the
first time I ever went to the Théâtre Français. He played Don
Annibal in Émile Augier's romantic comedy of *L'Aventurière*, and
I have not forgotten the exquisite humour of the performance. The
part is that of a sort of seventeenth century Captain Costigan, only
the Miss Fotheringay in the case is the gentleman's sister and not
his daughter. This lady is moreover an ambitious and designing
person, who leads her threadbare braggart of a brother quite by
the nose. She has entrapped a worthy gentleman of Padua, of mature years, and he is on the eve of making her his wife, when his
son, a clever young soldier, beguiles Don Annibal into supping
with him, and makes him drink so deep that the prating adventurer
at last lets the cat out of the bag and confides to his companion that
the fair Clorinde is not the virtuous gentlewoman she appears, but
a poor strolling actress who has had a lover at every stage of her
journey. The scene was played by Bressant and Regnier, and it has
always remained in my mind as one of the most perfect things I
have seen on the stage. The gradual action of the wine upon Don
Annibal, the delicacy with which his deepening tipsiness was indicated, its intellectual rather than physical manifestation, and, in
the midst of it, the fantastic conceit which made him think that
he was winding his fellow drinker round his fingers—all this was
exquisitely rendered. Drunkenness on the stage is usually both
dreary and disgusting; and I can remember besides this but two
really interesting pictures of intoxication (excepting always, indeed, the immortal tipsiness of Cassio in *Othello*, which a clever

actor can always make touching.) One is the beautiful befuddle-
ment of Rip Van Winkle, as Mr. Joseph Jefferson renders it, and
the other (a memory of the Théâtre Français) the scene in the
Duc Job, in which Got succumbs to mild inebriation, and dozes in
his chair just boosily enough for the young girl who loves him to
make it out.

It is to this admirable Edmond[1] Got that M. Sarcey's second
notice is devoted. Got is at the present hour unquestionably the
first actor at the Théâtre Français, and I have personally no hesitation in accepting him as the first of living actors. His younger
comrade, Coquelin, has, I think, as much talent and as much art; as
the older man Got has the longer and fuller record and may therefore be spoken of as the master. If I were obliged to rank the half-
dozen *premiers sujets* of the last few years at the Théâtre Français
in their absolute order of talent (thank Heaven, I am not so
obliged!) I think I should make up some such little list as this:
Got, Coquelin, Madame Plessy, Sarah Bernhardt, Mademoiselle
Favart, Delaunay. I confess that I have no sooner written it than I
feel as if I ought to amend it, and wonder whether it is not a great
folly to put Delaunay after Mademoiselle Favart. But this is idle.

As for Got, he is a singularly interesting actor. I have often
wondered whether the best definition of him would not be to say
that he is really a *philosophic* actor. He is an immense humourist
and his comicality is sometimes colossal; but his most striking
quality is the one on which M. Sarcey dwells — his sobriety and
profundity, his underlying element of manliness and melancholy,
the impression he gives you of having a general conception of
human life and of seeing the relativity, as one may say, of the
characters he represents. Of all the comic actors I have seen he is
the least trivial — at the same time that for richness of detail his
comic manner is unsurpassed. His repertory is very large and
various, but it may be divided into two equal halves — the parts
that belong to reality and the parts that belong to fantasy. There

[1] *By a slip of memory Henry James wrote Émile instead of Edmond.*

is of course a great deal of fantasy in his realistic parts and a great
deal of reality in his fantastic ones, but the general division is just;
and at times, indeed, the two faces of his talent seem to have little
in common. The *Duc Job*, to which I just now alluded, is one of the
things he does most perfectly. The part, which is that of a young
man, is a serious and tender one. It is amazing that the actor who
plays it should also be able to carry off triumphantly the frantic
buffoonery of Maître Pathelin, or should represent the Sganarelle
of the *Médecin Malgré Lui* with such an unctuous breadth of
humor. The two characters, perhaps, which have given me the
liveliest idea of Got's power and fertility are the Maître Pathelin
and the M. Poirier who figures in the title to the comedy which
Émile Augier and Jules Sandeau wrote together. M. Poirier, the
retired shopkeeper who marries his daughter to a marquis and
makes acquaintance with the incommodities incidental to such a
piece of luck, is perhaps the actor's most elaborate creation; it is
difficult to see how the portrayal of a type and an individual can
have a larger sweep and a more minute completeness. The *bon-
homme* Poirier, in Got's hands, is really great; and half-a-dozen
of the actor's modern parts that I could mention are hardly less
brilliant. But when I think of him I instinctively think first of some
rôle in which he wears the cap and gown of a period as regards
which humorous invention may fairly take the bit in its teeth.
This is what Got lets it do in Maître Pathelin, and he leads the
spectator's exhilarated fancy a dance to which the latter's aching
sides on the morrow sufficiently testify.

The piece is a *réchauffé* of a mediaeval farce which has the credit
of being the first play not a "mystery" or a miracle-piece in
the records of the French drama. The plot is extremely bald and
primitive. It sets forth how a cunning lawyer undertook to purchase a dozen ells of cloth for nothing. In the first scene we see
him in the market-place, bargaining and haggling with the draper,
and then marching off with the roll of cloth, with the understanding that the shopman shall call at his house in the course of an hour

for the money. In the next act we have Maître Pathelin at his fireside with his wife, to whom he relates his trick and its projected
sequel, and who greets them with Homeric laughter. He gets into
bed, and the innocent draper arrives. Then follows a scene of
which the liveliest description must be ineffective. Pathelin pretends to be out of his head, to be overtaken by a mysterious
malady which has made him delirious, not to know the draper
from Adam, never to have heard of the dozen ells of cloth and
to be altogether an impossible person to collect a debt from. To
carry out this character he indulges in a series of indescribable
antics, out-Bedlams Bedlam, frolics over the room dressed out in
the bed-clothes and chanting the wildest gibberish, bewilders the
poor draper to within an inch of his own sanity and finally puts
him utterly to rout. The spectacle could only be portentously flat
or heroically successful, and in Got's hands this latter was its
fortune. His Sganerelle, in the *Médecin Malgré Lui*, and half-a-
dozen of his characters from Molière besides — such a part, too,
as his Tibia, in Alfred de Musset's charming bit of romanticism,
the *Caprices de Marianne* — have a certain generic resemblance
with his treatment of the figure I have sketched. In all these things
the comicality is of the exuberant and tremendous order, and yet
in spite of its richness and flexibility it suggests little connection
with high animal spirits. It seems a matter of invention, of reflection and irony. You cannot imagine Got representing a fool
pure and simple — or at least a passive and unsuspecting fool.
There must always be an element of shrewdness and even of contempt; he must always be the man who knows and judges — or at
least who pretends. It is a compliment, I take it, to an actor, to say
that he prompts you to wonder about his private personality; and
an observant spectator of M. Got is at liberty to guess that he is
both obstinate and proud.

In Coquelin there is perhaps greater spontaneity, and there is a
not inferior mastery of his art. He is a wonderfully brilliant,
elastic actor. He is but thirty-five years old, and yet his record

is most glorious. He too has his "actual" and his classical repertory, and here also it is hard to choose. As the young *valet de comédie* in Molière and Regnard and Marivaux he is incomparable. I shall never forget the really infernal brilliancy of his Mascarille in *L'Étourdi*. His volubility, his rapidity, his impudence and gaiety, his ringing, penetrating voice and the shrill trumpet-note of his laughter, make him the ideal of the classic serving-man of the classic young lover — half rascal and half good fellow. Coquelin has lately had two or three immense successes in the comedies of the day. His Duc de Sept-Monts, in the famous *Étrangère* of Alexandre Dumas, last winter, was the capital creation of the piece; and in the revival, this winter, of Augier's *Paul Forestier*, his Adolphe de Beaubourg, the young man about town, consciously tainted with *commonness*, and trying to shake off the incubus, seemed while one watched it and listened to it the last word of delicately humorous art. Of Coquelin's eminence in the old come-dies M. Sarcey speaks with a certain pictorial force: "No one is better cut out to represent those bold and magnificent rascals of the old repertory, with their boisterous gaiety, their brilliant fancy and their superb extravagance, who give to their buffoonery *je ne sais quoi d'épique*. In these parts one may say of Coquelin that he is incomparable. I prefer him to Got in such cases, and even to Regnier, his master. I never saw Monrose, and cannot speak of him. But good judges have assured me that there was much that was factitious in the manner of this eminent comedian, and that his vivacity was a trifle mechanical. There is nothing whatever of this in Coquelin's manner. The eye, the nose, and the voice — the voice above all — are his most powerful means of action. He launches his *tirades* all in one breath, with full lungs, without troubling himself too much over the shading of details, in large masses, and he possesses himself only the more strongly of the public, which has a great sense of *ensemble*. The words that must be detached, the words that must decisively 'tell,' glitter in this delivery with the sonorous ring of a brand-new louis d'or. Crispin,

Scapin, Figaro, Mascarille have never found a more valiant and joyous interpreter."

I should say that this was enough about the men at the Théâtre Français, if I did not remember that I have not spoken of Delaunay. But Delaunay has plenty of people to speak for him; he has, in especial, the more eloquent half of humanity — the ladies. I suppose that of all the actors of the Comédie Française he is the most universally appreciated and admired; he is the popular favorite. And he has certainly earned this distinction, for there was never a more amiable and sympathetic genius. He plays the young lovers of the past and the present, and he acquits himself of his difficult and delicate task with extraordinary grace and propriety. The danger I spoke of a while since — the danger, for the actor of a romantic and sentimental part, of being compromised by the coat and trousers, the hat and umbrella of the current year — are reduced by Delaunay to their minimum. He reconciles in a marvellous fashion the love-sick gallant of the ideal world with the "gentlemanly man" of to-day; and his passion is as far removed from rant as his propriety is from stiffness. He has been accused of late years of falling into a mannerism, and I think there is some truth in the charge. But the fault in Delaunay's situation is certainly venial. How can a man of fifty, to whom, as regards face and figure, Nature has been stingy, play an amorous swain of twenty without taking refuge in a mannerism? His mannerism is a legitimate device for diverting the spectator's attention from certain incongruities. Delaunay's juvenility, his ardour, his passion, his good taste and sense of fitness, have always an irresistible charm. As he has grown older he has increased his repertory by parts of greater weight and sobriety — he has played the husbands as well as the lovers. One of his most recent and brilliant "creations" of this kind is his Marquis de Presles in *Le Gendre de M. Poirier* — a piece of acting superb for its lightness and *désinvolture*. It cannot be better praised than by saying it was worthy of Got's inimitable rendering of the part opposed to it. But I think

I shall remember Delaunay best in the picturesque and romantic comedies — as the Duc de Richelieu in *Mademoiselle de Belle-Isle;* as the joyous, gallant, exuberant young hero, his plumes and love knots fluttering in the breath of his gushing improvisation, of Corneille's *Menteur;* or, most of all, as the melodious swains of those charmingly poetic, faintly, naturally Shakespearean little comedies of Alfred de Musset.

To speak of Delaunay ought to bring us properly to Mademoiselle Favart, who for so many years invariably represented the object of his tender invocations. Mademoiselle Favart at the present time rather lacks what the French call "actuality." She has recently made an attempt to recover something of that large measure of it which she once possessed; but I doubt whether it has been completely successful. M. Sarcey has not yet put forth his notice of her; and when he does so it will be interesting to see how he treats her. She is not one of his high admirations. She is a great talent that has passed into eclipse. I call her a great talent, although I remember the words in which M. Sarcey somewhere speaks of her: "Mademoiselle Favart, who, to happy natural gifts, *soutenus par un travail acharné,* owed a distinguished place," etc. Her talent is great, but the impression that she gives of a *travail acharné* and of an insatiable ambition is perhaps even greater. For many years she reigned supreme, and I believe she is accused of not having always reigned generously. However that may be, there came a day when Mesdemoiselles Croizette and Sarah Bernhardt passed to the front and the elder actress receded, if not into the background, at least into what painters call the middle distance. The private history of these events has, I believe, been rich in heart-burnings; but it is only with the public history that we are concerned. Mademoiselle Favart has always seemed to me a powerful rather than an interesting actress; there is usually something mechanical and overdone in her manner. In some of her parts there is a kind of audible creaking of the machinery. If Delaunay is open to the reproach of having let a mannerism get the better of him, this accusation is much more fatally true of Mademoiselle Favart. On the other hand, she knows her trade as no one does — no one, at least, save Madame Plessy. When she is bad she is extremely bad, and sometimes she is uninterruptedly bad for a whole evening. In the revival of Scribe's clever comedy of *Une Chaîne,* this winter (which, by the way, though the cast included both Got and Coquelin, was the nearest approach to mediocrity I have ever seen at the Théâtre Français,) Mademoiselle Favart was, to my sense, startlingly bad. The part had originally been played by Madame Plessy; and I remember how M. Sarcey in his *feuilleton* treated its actual representative. "Mademoiselle Favart does Louise. Who does not recall the exquisite delicacy and temperance with which Madame Plessy rendered that difficult scene in the second act?" etc. And nothing more. When, however, Mademoiselle Favart is at her best, she is remarkably strong. She rises to great occasions. I doubt whether such parts as the desperate heroine of the *Supplice d'une Femme,* or as Julie in Octave Feuillet's lugubrious drama of that name, could be more effectively played than she plays them. She can carry a great weight without flinching; she has what the French call "authority;" and in declamation she sometimes unrolls her fine voice, as it were, in long harmonious waves and cadences the sustained power of which her younger rivals must often envy her.

I am drawing to the close of these rather desultory observations without having spoken of the four ladies commemorated by M. Sarcey in the publication which lies before me; and I do not know that I can justify my tardiness otherwise than by saying that writing and reading about artists of so extreme a personal brilliancy is poor work, and that the best the critic can do is to wish his reader may see them, from a quiet *fauteuil,* as speedily and as often as possible. Of Madeleine Brohan, indeed, there is little to say. She is a delightful person to listen to, and she is still delightful to look at, in spite of that redundancy of contour which time has

contributed to her charms. But she has never been ambitious and
her talent has had no particularly original quality. It is a long time
since she created an important part; but in the old repertory her
rich, dense voice, her charming smile, her mellow, tranquil gaiety,
always give extreme pleasure. To hear her sit and *talk*, simply,
and laugh and play with her fan, along with Madame Plessy, in
Molière's *Critique de l'École des Femmes*, is an entertainment to be
remembered. For Madame Plessy I should have to mend my pen
and begin a new chapter; and for Mademoiselle Sarah Bernhardt
no less a ceremony would suffice. I saw Madame Plessy for the
first time in Émile Augier's *Aventurière*, when, as I mentioned, I
first saw Regnier. This is considered by many persons her best
part, and she certainly carries it off with a high hand; but I like
her better in characters which afford more scope to her talents for
comedy. These characters are very numerous, for her activity and
versatility have been extraordinary. Her comedy of course is
"high;" it is of the highest conceivable kind, and she has often
been accused of being too mincing and too artificial. I should
never make this charge, for, to me, Madame Plessy's *minauderies*,
her grand airs and her arch-refinements, have never been anything but the odorous swayings and queenly tossings of some
splendid garden flower. Never had an actress grander manners.
When Madame Plessy represents a duchess you have no allowances to make. Her limitations are on the side of the pathetic.
If she is brilliant, she is cold; and I cannot imagine her touching
the source of tears. But she is in the highest degree accomplished;
she gives an impression of intelligence and intellect which is produced by none of her companions — excepting always the extremely exceptional Sarah Bernhardt. Madame Plessy's intellect
has sometimes misled her — as, for instance, when it whispered to
her, a few years since, that she could play Agrippine in Racine's
Britannicus, on that tragedy being presented for the *débuts* of
Mounet-Sully. I was verdant enough to think her Agrippine very

fine. But M. Sarcey reminds his readers of what he said of it the Monday after the first performance. "I will not say"—he quotes himself—"that Madame Plessy is indifferent. With her intelligence, her natural gifts, her great situation, her immense authority over the public, one cannot be indifferent in anything. She is therefore not indifferently bad. She is bad to a point that cannot be expressed and that would be distressing for dramatic art if it were not that in this great shipwreck there rise to the surface a few floating fragments of the finest qualities that nature has ever bestowed upon an artist."

Madame Plessy retired from the stage six months ago and it may be said that the void produced by this event is irreparable. There is not only no prospect, but there is no hope of filling it up. The present conditions of artistic production are directly hostile to the formation of actresses as consummate and as complete as Madame Plessy. One may not expect to see her like, any more than one may expect to see a new manufacture of old lace and old brocade. She carried off with her something that the younger generation of actresses will consistently lack—a certain largeness of style and robustness of art. (These qualities are in a modified degree those of Mademoiselle Favart.) But if the younger actresses have the success of Mesdemoiselles Croizette and Sarah Bernhardt, will they greatly care whether they are not "robust"? These young ladies are children of a later and eminently contemporary type, according to which an actress undertakes not to interest but to fascinate. They are charming—"awfully" charming; strange, eccentric, imaginative. It would be needless to speak specifically of Mademoiselle Croizette; for although she has very great attractions I think she may (by the cold impartiality of science) be classified as a secondary, a less inspired, and (to use the great word of the day) a more "brutal" Sarah Bernhardt. (Mademoiselle Croizette's "brutality" is her great card.) As for Mademoiselle Sarah Bernhardt, she is simply, at present, in Paris, one of the great figures of the day. It would be hard to imagine a more brilliant embodiment of feminine success; she deserves a chapter for herself.

December, 1876

"The Theatre Francais" appeared in The Galaxy, *April, 1877, and was reprinted in* French Poets and Novelists, 1878, *where it formed the twelfth and last paper.*

Late in life Henry James professed to think lightly of this essay. When Brander Matthews asked his permission to include it in The Oxford Book of American Essays *(1914) he replied in an unpublished letter of April 29, 1914;* "I don't remember the paper on the Théâtre Français as any great affair (I haven't looked at it for years and I haven't now a volume containing it near me;) so that I should frankly have preferred to be represented in the Oxford Book of American Verse [*sic*] by some better thing. But if the sketch on the T.F. is absolutely the one you prefer I resign myself and authorize you to make use of it. Only I very earnestly beg you to affix to it the year of its original appearance, which must have been, I think, 1878. It *dates*—and has no great sense save as dating."

And on February 2, 1915 he writes: "I have your letter of the 21st as I also received with thanks the Oxford Book of American Essays, as to which I hope you won't think me ungracious if I say I wish my contribution might have made rather a more characteristic and consequent figure there."

The last sentence of the essay: "As for Mademoiselle Sarah Bernhardt . . . she deserves a chapter for herself" suggests the hope that Henry James may have written and published such a "chapter," but hitherto research has nowhere discovered one. In the autumn of 1877, *however, when he again visited France, he included the following short passage in an essay, "Paris Revisited," in* The Galaxy, *January, 1878, which he renamed "Occasional Paris" when reprinting it in* Portraits of Places, 1883:

"There are two things that the returning observer is likely to do with as little delay as possible. One is to dine at some *cabaret* of which he retains a friendly memory; another is to betake himself to the Théâtre Français. It is early in the season; there are no new pieces; but I have taken great pleasure in seeing some of the old ones. I lost no time in going to see Mademoiselle Sarah Bernhardt in *Andromaque*. *Andromaque* is not a novelty, but Mademoiselle Sarah Bernhardt has a perennial freshness. The play has been revived, to enable her to represent not the great part, the injured and passionate Hermione, but that of the doleful, funereal widow of Hector. This part is a poor one; it is narrow and monotonous, and offers few brilliant opportunities. But the actress knows how to make opportunities, and she has here a very sufficient one for crossing her thin white arms over her nebulous black robes, and sighing forth in silver accents her dolorous rhymes. Her rendering of the part is one more proof of her singular intelligence—of the fineness of her artistic nature. As there is not a great deal to be done with it in the way of declamation, she has made the most of its plastic side. She understands the art of motion and attitude as no one else does, and her extraordinary personal grace never fails her. Her Andromaque has postures of the most poetic picturesqueness — something that suggests the broken stem and drooping head of a flower that has been rudely plucked. She bends over her classic confidant like the figure of Bereavement on a bas-relief, and she has a marvellous manner of lifting and throwing back her delicate arms, locking them together, and passing them behind her hanging head."

THE LONDON THEATRES

A PERSON taking up his residence in a foreign city is apt, I think, to become something of a play-goer. In the first place he is usually more or less isolated, and in the absence of complex social ties the theatres help him to pass his evenings. But more than this, they offer him a good deal of interesting evidence upon the manners and customs of the people among whom he has come to dwell. They testify to the civilization around him, and throw a great deal of light upon the ways of thinking, feeling, and behaving of the community. If this exotic spectator to whom I allude is a person of a really attentive observation, he may extract such evidence in very large quantities. It is furnished not by the stage alone, but by the *theatre* in a larger sense of the word: by the audience, the attendants, the arrangements, the very process of getting to the playhouse. The English stage of to-day, of which I more particularly speak, certainly holds the mirror as little as possible up to nature—to any nature, at least, usually recognized in the British islands. Nine-tenths of the plays performed upon it are French originals, subjected to the mysterious process of "adaptation"; marred as French pieces and certainly not mended as English; transplanted from the Gallic soil into a chill and neutral region where they bloom hardly longer than a handful of cut flowers stuck into moist sand. They cease to have any representative value as regards French manners, and they acquire none as regards English; they belong to an order of things which has not even the merit of being "conventional," but in which barbarism, chaos, and crudity hold undisputed sway. The English drama of the last century deserved the praise, in default of any higher, of being "conventional"; for there was at least a certain method in its madness; it had its own ideal, its own foolish logic and consistency. But he would be wise who should be able to indicate the ideal, artistic and intellectual, of the English drama of to-day. It is violently and hopelessly irresponsible. When one says "English drama" one uses the term for convenience' sake; one means simply the plays that are acted at the London theatres and transferred thence to the American. They are neither English nor a drama; they have not that minimum of ponderable identity at which appreciation finds a starting-point. As the metaphysicians say, they are simply not cognizable. And yet in spite of all this, the writer of these lines has ventured to believe that the London theatres are highly characteristic of English civilization. The plays testify indirectly if not directly to the national manners, and the whole system on which play-going is conducted completes the impression which the pieces make upon the observer. One can imagine, indeed, nothing more characteristic than such a fact as that a theatre-going people is hopelessly destitute of a drama.

I ventured a month ago to record in these pages a few reminiscences of the Comédie Française; and I have a sort of feeling that my readers may, in the light of my present undertaking, feel prompted to accuse me of a certain levity. There is a want of delicacy, they may say, in speaking of the first theatre in the world one day and of the London stage the next. You must choose, and if you talk about one, you forfeit the right to talk about the other. But I think there is something to be done in the way of talking about both, and at all events there are few things it is not fair to talk about if one does so with a serious desire to understand. Removing lately from Paris to the British metropolis, I received a great many impressions — a sort of unbroken chain, in which the reflections passing through my fancy as I tried the different orchestra-stalls were the concluding link. The impressions of which I speak were impressions of outside things—the things with which in a great city one comes first into contact. I supposed that I had gathered them once for all in earlier years; but I found that the edge of one's observation, unlike that of other trenchant instruments, grows again if one leaves it alone. Remain a long time in any country, and you come to accept the manners and customs of that country as the standard of civilization—the normal type. Other manners and customs, even if they spring from the same soil from which you yourself have sprung, acquire by contrast an unreasonable, a violent, but often a picturesque relief. To what one may call a continentalized vision the aspect of English life seems strange and entertaining; while an Anglicized perception finds, beyond the narrow channel, even greater matter for wonderment.

The writer of these lines brought with him, at the outset of a dusky London winter, a continentalized, and perhaps more particularly a Parisianized, fancy. It was wonderful how many things that I should have supposed familiar and commonplace seemed strikingly salient and typical, and how I found, if not sermons in stones and good in everything, at least examples in porter-pots and reflections in coal-scuttles. In writing the other day of the Théâtre Français, I spoke of M. Francisque Sarcey, the esteemed dramatic critic; of the serious and deliberate way in which he goes to work—of the distance from which he makes his approaches. During the first weeks I was in London, especially when I had been to the play the night before, I kept saying to myself that M. Francisque Sarcey ought to come over and "do" the English theatres. There are of course excellent reasons why he should not. In the first place, it is safe to assume that he comprehends not a word of English; and in the second, it is obligatory to believe that he would, in the vulgar phrase, not be able to "stand" it. He would probably pronounce the English stage hopelessly and unmitigably bad and beneath criticism, and hasten back to Delaunay and Sarah Bernhardt. But if we could suppose him to fight it out, and give the case a hearing, what a solid dissertation we should have upon it afterward at the bottom of the *Temps* newspaper! How he would go into the causes of the badness, and trace its connections with English civilization! How earnestly he would expatiate and how minutely he would explain; how fervently he would point the moral and entreat his fellow countrymen not to be as the English are lest they should lapse into histrionic barbarism!

I felt, to myself, during these days, in a small way, very much like a Francisque Sarcey; I don't mean as to the gloominess of my conclusions, but as to the diffusiveness of my method. A spectator with his senses attuned to all those easy Parisian harmonies feels himself, in London, to be in a place in which the drama cannot, in the nature of things, have a vigorous life. Before he has put his feet into a theatre he is willing to bet his little all that the stage will turn out to be weak. If he is challenged for the reasons of this precipitate scepticism, he will perhaps be at a loss to give them; he will only say, "Oh, I don't know, *cela se sent.* Everything I see is a reason. I don't look out of the window, I don't ring the bell for some coals, I don't go into an eating-house to dine, without seeing a reason." And then he will begin to talk about the duskiness and oppressiveness of London; about the ugliness of everything that one sees; about beauty and grace being never attempted, or attempted here and there only to be woefully missed; about the visible, palpable Protestantism; about the want of expression in people's faces; about the plainness and dreariness of everything that is public and the inaccessibility of everything that is private; about the lower orders being too miserable to know the theatre, and the upper classes too "respectable" to understand it.

And here, if the audacious person we are conceiving is very far gone, he will probably begin to talk about English "hypocrisy" and prudery, and to say that these are the great reason of the feebleness of the stage. When he approaches the question of English "hypocrisy" you may know that he is hopelessly Galli-cized, or Romanized, or Germanized, or something of that sort;

and indeed his state of mind at this point strikes me myself with a certain awe. I don't venture to follow him, and I discreetly give up the attempt. But up to this point I can see what he may have meant, in the midst of his flippancy, and I remember how to my own imagination at first everything seemed to hang together, and theatres to be what they were because somehow the streets, and shops, and hotels, and eating-houses were what they were. I remember something I said to myself after once witnessing a little drama of real life at a restaurant. The restaurant in question is in Piccadilly, and I am trying to think under which of the categories of our Gallicized observer it would come. The remarkable façade, covered with gilded mosaics and lamps, is certainly a concession to the idea of beauty; though whether it is a successful one is another question. Within it has, besides various other resources, one of those peculiar refectories which are known in England as grill-rooms, and which possess the picturesque feature of a colossal gridiron, astride of a corresponding fire, on which your chops and steaks are toasted before your eyes. A grill-room is a bad place to dine, but it is a convenient place to lunch. It always contains a number of tables, which accommodate not less than half-a-dozen persons; small tables of the proper dimensions for a *tête-à-tête* being, for inscrutable reasons, wholly absent from English eating-houses.

The grill-room in question is decorated in that style of which the animus is to be agreeable to Mr. William Morris, though I suspect that in the present application of his charming principles he would find a good deal of base alloy. At any rate, the apartment contains a number of large medallions in blue pottery, pieced together, representing the heathen gods and goddesses, whose names are inscribed in crooked letters in an unexpected part of the picture. This is quite the thing that one would expect to find in one of those cloisters or pleasances, or "pleached gardens," in which Mr. Morris's Gothic heroines drag their embroidered petticoats up and down, as slow-pacedly as their poet sings. Only, in these pretty, dilettantish cloisters there would probably be no large tickets suspended alongside of the pictorial pottery, inscribed with the monstrous words, *Tripe! Suppers!* This is one of those queer eruptions of plainness and homeliness which one encounters at every turn in the midst of the massive luxury and general expensiveness of England — like the big, staring announcement, *Beds*, in the coffee-house windows, or *Well-aired Beds* painted on the side walls of taverns; or like a list of labels which I noticed the other day on a series of japanned boxes in a pastry-cook's shop. They seemed to me so characteristic that I made a note of them.

The reason of my being in the pastry-cook's shop was my having contracted in Paris the harmless habit of resorting to one of these establishments at the luncheon hour, for the purpose of consuming a little *gateau*. Resuming this innocent practice on English soil, I found it attended with serious difficulties — the chief of which was that there were no *gateaux* to consume. An appreciative memory of those brightly mirrored little shops on the Paris boulevards, in which tender little tarts, in bewildering variety, are dispensed to you by a neat-waisted *patissière*, cast a dusky shadow over the big buns and "digestive biscuits" which adorn the counter of an English bakery. But it takes a good while to eat a bun, and while you stand there solemnly disintegrating your own, you may look about you in search of the characteristic. In Paris the pastry-cooks' shops are, as the French say, coquettish — as coquettish as the elegant simplicity of plate glass, discreet gilding, polished brass, and a demonstrative *dame de comptoir* can make them. In London they are not coquettish — witness the grim nomenclature alluded to above; it was distributed over a series of green tin cases, ranged behind the counters: Tops and bottoms — royal digestives — arrow-root — oat-cake — rice biscuit — ratafias.

I took my seat in the grill-room at a table at which three gentlemen were sitting: two of them sleek British merchants, of a familiar and highly respectable type, the other a merchant too presumably, but neither sleek nor British. He was evidently an American. He was a good-looking fellow and a man of business, but I inferred from the tentative, experimental, and even mistrustful manner with which he addressed himself to the operation of lunching, and observed the idiosyncrasies of the grill-room, that he found himself for the first time in England. His experiment, however, if experiment it was, was highly successful; he made a copious lunch and departed. He had not had time to reach the door when I perceived one of the British merchants of whom I just now spoke beginning to knock the table violently with his knife-handle, and to clamour, "Waiter, waiter! Manager, manager!" The manager and the waiter hastened to respond, while I endeavoured to guess the motive of his agitation, without connecting it with our late companion. As I then saw him pointing eagerly to the latter, however, who was just getting out of the door, I was seized with a mortifying apprehension that my innocent compatriot was a dissembler and a pickpocket, and that the English gentleman, next whom he had been sitting, had missed his watch or his purse. "He has taken one of these—one of these!" said the British merchant. "I saw him put it into his pocket." And he held up a bill of fare of the establishment, a printed card, bearing on its back a coloured lithograph of the emblazoned façade that I have mentioned. I was reassured; the poor American had pocketed this light document with the innocent design of illustrating his day's adventures to a sympathetic wife awaiting his return in some musty London lodging. But the manager and the waiter seemed to think the case grave, and their informant continued to impress upon them that he had caught the retiring visitor in the very act. They were at a loss to decide upon a course of action; they thought the case was bad, but they questioned whether it was bad enough to warrant them in pursuing the criminal. While this weighty point was being discussed the criminal escaped, little suspecting, I imagine, the perturbation he had caused. But the British merchant continued to argue, speaking in the name of outraged morality. "You know he oughtn't to have done that—it was very wrong in him to do it. That mustn't be done, you know, and you know I ought to tell you—it was my duty to tell you—I couldn't *but* tell you. He oughtn't to have done it, you know. I thought I *must* tell you." It is not easy to point out definitely the connection between this little episode, for the triviality of which I apologize, and the present condition of the English stage; but—it may have been whimsical—I thought I perceived a connection. These people are too highly moral to be histrionic, I said; they have too stern a sense of duty.

The first step in the rather arduous enterprise of going to the theatre in London is, I think, another reminder that the arts of the stage are not really in the temperament and the manners of the people. The first step is to go to an agency in an expensive street out of Piccadilly, and there purchase a stall for the sum of eleven shillings. You receive your ticket from the hands of a smooth, sleek, bottle-nosed clerk, who seems for all the world as if he had stepped straight out of a volume of Dickens or of Thackeray. There is almost always an old lady taking seats for the play, with a heavy carriage in waiting at the door; the number of old ladies whom one has to squeeze past in the stalls is in fact very striking. "Is it good?" asks the old lady of the gentleman I have described, with a very sweet voice and a perfectly expressionless face. (She means the play, not the seat.) "It is thought very good, my lady," says the clerk, as if he were uttering a "response" in church; and my lady being served, I approach with my humbler petition. The dearness of places at the London theatres is sufficient indication that play-going is not a popular amusement; three dollars is a high price to pay for the privilege of witnessing any London performance that I have seen. (One goes into the stalls of the Théâtre Français for eight francs.) In the house itself everything seems to contribute to the impression which I have tried to indicate—the impression that the theatre in England is a social luxury and not an artistic necessity. The

white-cravatted young man who inducts you into your stall, and
having put you in possession of a programme, extracts from
you, masterly but effectually, a sixpence which, as a stranger,
you have wondered whether you might venture to give him,
and which has seemed a mockery of his grandeur—this excellent young man is somehow the keynote of the whole affair.
An English audience is as different as possible from a French,
though the difference is altogether by no means to its disadvantage. It is much more "genteel"; it is less Bohemian, less *blasé*,
more *naïf*, and more respectful—to say nothing of being made up
of handsomer people. It is well dressed, tranquil, motionless; it
suggests domestic virtue and comfortable homes; it looks as if it
had come to the play in its own carriage, after a dinner of beef
and pudding. The ladies are mild, fresh coloured English mothers;
they all wear caps; they are wrapped in knitted shawls. There are
many rosy young girls, with dull eyes and quiet cheeks—an
element wholly absent from Parisian audiences. The men are
handsome and honourable looking; they are in evening dress; they
come with the ladies—usually with several ladies—and remain
with them; they sit still in their places, and don't go herding out
between the acts with their hats askew. Altogether they are much
more the sort of people to spend a quiet evening with than the
clever, cynical, democratic multitude that surges nightly out of
the brilliant Boulevards into those temples of the drama in which
MM. Dumas, *fils*, and Sardou are the high priests. But you might
spend your evening with them better almost anywhere than at the
theatre.

As I said just now, they are much more *naïf* than Parisian
spectators—at least as regards being amused. They cry with
much less facility, but they laugh more freely and heartily. I
remember nothing in Paris that corresponds with the laugh of the
English gallery and pit—with its continuity and simplicity, its
deep-lunged jollity and its individual guffaws. But you feel that an
English audience is intellectually much less appreciative. A Paris

audience, as regards many of its factors, is cynical, sceptical, in-different; it is so intimately used to the theatre that it doesn't stand on ceremony; it yawns, and looks away and turns its back; it has seen too much, and it knows too much. But it has the critical and the artistic sense, when the occasion appeals to them; it can judge and discriminate. It has the sense of form and of manner; it heeds and cares how things are done, even when it cares little for the things themselves. Bohemians, artists, critics, connoisseurs — all Frenchmen come more or less under these heads, which give the tone to a body of Parisian spectators. They do not strike one as "nice people" in the same degree as a collection of English patrons of the drama — though doubtless they have their own virtues and attractions; but they form a natural, sympathetic public, while the English audience forms only a conventional, accidental one. It may be that the drama and other works of art are best appreciated by people who are not "nice"; it may be that a lively interest in such matters tends to undermine niceness; it may be that, as the world grows nicer, various forms of art will grow feebler. All this *may* be; I don't pretend to say it is; the idea strikes me *en passant*.

In speaking of what is actually going on at the London theatres I suppose the place of honour, beyond comparison, belongs to Mr. Henry Irving. This gentleman enjoys an esteem and consideration which, I believe, has been the lot of no English actor since Macready left the stage, and he may at the present moment claim the dignity of being a bone of contention in London society second only in magnitude to the rights of the Turks and the wrongs of the Bulgarians. I am told that London is divided, on the subject of his merits, into two fiercely hostile camps; that he has sown dissention in families, and made old friends cease to "speak." His appearance in a new part is a great event; and if one has the courage of one's opinion, at dinner tables and elsewhere, a con-versational godsend. Mr. Irving has "created," as the French say, but four Shakespearean parts; his Richard III. has just been given to the world. Before attempting Hamlet, which up to this moment has been his greatest success, he had attracted much attention as a picturesque actor of melodrama, which he rendered with a refinement of effect not common upon the English stage. Mr. Irving's critics may, I suppose, be divided into three categories: those who justify him in whatever he attempts, and consider him an artist of unprecedented brilliancy; those who hold that he did very well in melodrama, but that he flies too high when he attempts Shakespeare; and those who, in vulgar parlance, can see nothing in him at all.

I shrink from ranging myself in either of these divisions, and indeed I am not qualified to speak of Mr. Irving's acting in general. I have seen none of his melodramatic parts; I do not know him as a comedian—a capacity in which some people think him at his best; and in his Shakespearean repertory I have seen only his Macbeth and his Richard. But judging him on the evidence of these two parts, I fall hopelessly among the sceptics. Mr. Henry Irving is a very convenient illustration. To a stranger desiring to know how the London stage stands, I should say, "Go and see this gentleman; then tell me what you think of him." And I should expect the stranger to come back and say, "I see what you mean. The London stage has reached that pitch of mediocrity at which Mr. Henry Irving overtops his fellows — Mr. Henry Irving figuring as a great man—*c'est tout dire.*" I hold that there is an essential truth in the proverb that there is no smoke without fire. No reputations are altogether hollow, and no valuable prizes have been easily won. Of course Mr. Irving has a good deal of intelligence and cleverness; of course he has mastered a good many of the mysteries of his art. But I must nevertheless declare that for myself I have not mastered the mystery of his success. His defects seem to me in excess of his qualities and the lessons he has not learned more striking than the lessons he has learned.

That an actor so handicapped, as they say in London, by nature and culture should have enjoyed such prosperity is a striking proof of the absence of a standard, of the chaotic condition of taste. Mr. Irving's Macbeth, which I saw more than a year ago and view under the mitigations of time, was not pronounced one of his great successes; but it was acted, nevertheless, for many months, and it does not appear to have injured his reputation. Passing through London, and curious to make the acquaintance of the great English actor of the day, I went with alacrity to see it; but my alacrity was more than equalled by the vivacity of my disappointment. I sat through the performance in a sort of melancholy amazement. There are barren failures and there are interesting failures, and this performance seemed to me to deserve the less complimentary of these classifications. It inspired me, however, with no ill-will toward the artist, for it must be said of Mr. Irving that his aberrations are not of a vulgar quality, and that one likes him, somehow, in spite of them. But one's liking takes the form of making one wish that really he had selected some other profession than the histrionic. Nature has done very little to make an actor of him. His face is not dramatic; it is the face of a sedentary man, a clergyman, a lawyer, an author, an amiable gentleman—of anything other than a possible Hamlet or Othello. His figure is of the same cast, and his voice completes the want of illusion. His voice is apparently wholly unavailable for purposes of declamation. To say that he speaks badly is to go too far; to my sense he simply does not speak at all—in any way that, in an actor, can be called speaking. He does not pretend to declaim or dream of declaiming. Shakespeare's finest lines pass from his lips without his paying the scantiest tribute to their quality. Of what the French call *diction*—of the art of delivery—he has apparently not a suspicion. This forms three-fourths of an actor's obligations, and in Mr. Irving's acting these three-fourths are simply cancelled. What is left to him with the remaining fourth is to be "picturesque"; and this even his partisans admit he has made his specialty. This concession darkens Mr. Irving's prospects as a Shakespearean actor. You can play hop-scotch on one foot, but you cannot cut with one blade of a pair of scissors, and you cannot play Shakespeare by being simply picturesque. Above all, before all, for this purpose you must have the art of utterance; you must be able to give value to the divine Shakespearean line — to make it charm our ears as it charms our mind. It is of course by his picturesqueness that Mr. Irving has made his place; by small ingenuities of "business" and subtleties of action; by doing as a painter does who "goes in" for colour when he cannot depend upon his drawing. Mr. Irving's colour is sometimes pretty enough; his ingenuities and subtleties are often felicitous; but his picturesqueness, on the whole, strikes me as dry and awkward, and, at the best, where certain essentials are so strikingly absent, these secondary devices lose much of their power.

Mr. Fechter in Hamlet was preponderantly a "picturesque" actor; but he had a certain sacred spark, a heat, a lightness and suppleness, which Mr. Irving lacks; and though, with his incurable foreign accent, he could hardly be said to *declaim* Shakespeare in any worthy sense, yet on the whole he spoke his part with much more of the positively agreeable than can possibly belong to the utterance of Mr. Irving. His speech, with all its fantastic Gallicisms of sound, was less foreign and more comprehensible than that strange tissue of arbitrary pronunciations which floats in the thankless medium of Mr. Irving's harsh, monotonous voice. Richard III. is of all Shakespeare's parts the one that can perhaps best dispense with declamation, and in which the clever inventions of manner and movement in which Mr. Irving is proficient will carry the actor furthest. Accordingly, I doubt not, Mr. Irving is seen to peculiar advantage in this play; it is certainly a much better fit for him than Macbeth. He has had the good taste to discard the vulgar adaptation of Cibber, by which the stage has so long been haunted, and which, I believe, is played in America to the complete exclusion of the original drama. I believe that some of the tenderest Shakespeareans refuse to admit the authenticity of *Richard III.*; they declare that the play has, with all its energy, a sort of intellectual grossness, of which the author of *Hamlet* and *Othello* was incapable. This same intellectual grossness is certainly very striking; the scene of Richard's wooing of Lady Anne is a capital specimen of it. But here and there occur passages which, when one hears the play acted, have all the vast Shakespearean sense of effect.

> "— *To hear the piteous moans that Edward made*
> *When black-faced Clifford shook his sword at him.*"

It is hard to believe that Shakespeare did not write that. And when Richard, after putting an end to Clarence, comes into Edward IV.'s presence, with the courtiers ranged about, and announces hypocritically that Providence has seen fit to remove him, the situation is marked by one or two speeches which are dramatic as Shakespeare alone is dramatic. The immediate exclamation of the Queen —

> "*All-seeing heaven, what a world is this!*"

— followed by that of one of the gentlemen —

> "*Look I so pale, Lord Dorset, as the rest?*"

— such touches as these, with their inspired vividness, seem to belong to the brushwork of the master. Mr. Irving gives the note of his performance in his first speech — the famous soliloquy upon "the winter of our discontent." His delivery of these lines possesses little but hopeless staginess and mannerism. It seems indeed like staginess gone mad. The spectator rubs his eyes and asks himself whether he has not mistaken his theatre, and stumbled by accident upon some preposterous burlesque. It is fair to add that Mr. Irving is here at his worst, the scene offering him his most sustained and exacting piece of declamation. But the way he renders it is the way he renders the whole part — slowly, draggingly, diffusively, with innumerable pauses and lapses, and without a hint of the rapidity, the intensity and *entrain* which are needful for carrying off the improbabilities of so explicit and confidential a villain and so melodramatic a hero.

Just now, when a stranger in London asks where the best acting is to be seen, he receives one of two answers. He is told either at the Prince of Wales's theatre or at the Court. Some people think that the last perfection is to be found at the former of these establishments, others at the latter. I went first to the Prince of Wales's, of which I had a very pleasant memory from former years, and I was not disappointed. The acting is very pretty indeed, and this little theatre doubtless deserves the praise which is claimed for it, of being the best conducted English stage in the world. It is, of course, not the Comédie Française; but, equally of course, it is absurd talking or thinking of the Comédie Française in London. The company at the Prince of Wales's play with a finish, a sense of detail, what the French call *ensemble*, and a general good grace, which deserve explicit recognition. The theatre is extremely small, elegant, and expensive, the company is very carefully composed, and the scenery and stage furniture lavishly complete. It is a point of honour with the Prince of Wales's to have nothing that is not "real." In the piece now running at this establishment there is a representation of a boudoir very delicately appointed, the ceiling of which is formed by festoons of old lace suspended tent fashion or pavilion fashion. This lace, I am told, has been ascertained, whether by strong opera glasses or other modes of enquiry I know not, to be genuine, ancient, and costly. This is the very pedantry of perfection, and makes the scenery somewhat better than the actors. If the tendency is logically followed out, we shall soon be having Romeo drink real poison and Medea murder a fresh pair of babes every night.

The Prince of Wales's theatre, when it has once carefully mounted a play, "calculates," I believe, to keep it on the stage a year. The play of the present year is an adaptation of one of Victorien Sardou's cleverest comedies — *Nos Intimes* — upon which the title of *Peril* has been conferred. Of the piece itself there is nothing to be said; it is the usual hybrid drama of the contemporary English stage — a firm, neat French skeleton, around which the drapery of English conversation has been adjusted in awkward and inharmonious folds. The usual feat has been attempted — to extirpate "impropriety" and at the same time to save interest. In the extraordinary manipulation and readjustment of French immoralities which goes on in the interest of Anglo-Saxon virtue, I have never known this feat to succeed. Propriety may have been saved, in an awkward, floundering, in-spite-of-herself fashion, which seems to do to something in the mind a violence much greater than the violence it has been sought to avert; but interest has certainly been lost. The only immorality I know on the stage is the production of an ill-made play; and a play is certainly ill made when the pointedness of the framework strikes the spectator as a perpetual mockery upon the flatness of the "developments." M. Sardou's perfectly improper but thoroughly homogeneous comedy has been flattened and vulgarized in the usual way; the pivot of naughtiness on which the piece turns has been "whittled" down to the requisite tenuity; the wicked little Jack-in-the-Box has popped up his head only just in time to pull it back again. The interest, from being intense, has become light, and the play, from being a serious comedy, with a flavor of the tragic, has become an elaborate farce, salted with a few coarse grains of gravity. It is probable, however, that if *Peril* were more serious, it would be much less adequately played.

The Prince of Wales's company contains in the person of Miss Madge Robertson (or Mrs. Kendal, as I believe she is nowadays called) the most agreeable actress on the London stage. This lady is always pleasing, and often charming; but she is more effective in gentle gaiety than in melancholy or in passion. Another actor at the Prince of Wales's — Mr. Arthur Cecil — strikes me as an altogether superior comedian. He plays in *Peril* (though I believe he is a young man) the part of a selfish, cantankerous, querulous, jaundiced old East Indian officer, who has come down to a country house to stay, under protest, accompanied by his only son, a stripling in roundabouts, whom he is bringing up in ignorance of the world's wickedness, and who, finding himself in a mansion well supplied with those books which no gentleman's library should be without, loses no time in taking down Boccaccio's *Decameron*. Mr. Arthur Cecil represents this character to the life, with a completeness, an extreme comicality, and at the same time a sobriety and absence of violence which recalls the best French acting. Especially inimitable is the tone with which he tells his host, on his arrival, how he made up his mind to accept his invitation: "So at last I said to Percy, 'Well, Percy, my child, we'll go down and have done with it!' "

At the Court theatre, where they are playing, also apparently by the year, a "revived" drama of Mr. Tom Taylor — *New Men and Old Acres* — the acting, though very good indeed, struck me as less finished and, as a whole, less artistic. The company contains, however, two exceptionally good actors. One of them is Mr. Hare, who leads it, and who, although nature has endowed him with an almost fatally meagre stage presence, has a considerable claim to be called an artist. Mr. Hare's special line is the quiet natural, in high life, and I imagine he prides himself upon the propriety and good taste with which he acquits himself of those ordinary phrases and light modulations which the usual English actor finds it impossible to utter with any degree of verisimilitude. Mr. Hare's companion is Miss Ellen Terry, who is usually spoken of by the "refined" portion of the public as the most interesting actress in London. Miss Terry is picturesque; she looks like a preRaphaelitish drawing in a magazine — the portrait of the crop-haired heroine in the illustration to the serial novel. She is intelligent and vivacious, and she is indeed, in a certain measure, interesting. With great frankness and spontaneity, she is at the same time singularly delicate and lady-like, and it seems almost impertinent to criticize her harshly. But the

favour which Miss Terry enjoys strikes me, like that under which
Mr. Henry Irving has expanded, as a sort of measure of the
English critical sense in things theatrical. Miss Terry has all the
pleasing qualities I have enumerated, but she has, with them, the
defect that she is simply *not* an actress. One sees it sufficiently in
her face—the face of a clever young Englishwoman, with a hundred merits, but not of a dramatic artist. These things are indefinable; I can only give my impression.

Broadly comic acting, in England, is businesslike, and high
tragedy is businesslike; each of these extremes appears to constitute a trade—a *métier*, as the French say—which may be
properly and adequately learned. But the acting which covers the
middle ground, the acting of serious or sentimental comedy and
of scenes that may take place in modern drawing-rooms—the
acting that corresponds to the contemporary novel of manners—
seems by an inexorable necessity given over to amateurishness.
Most of the actors at the Prince of Wales's—the young lovers, the
walking and talking gentlemen, the house-keeper and young
ladies—struck me as essentially amateurish, and this is the impression produced by Miss Ellen Terry, as well as (in an even
higher degree) by her pretty and sweet-voiced sister, who plays
at the Haymarket. The art of these young ladies is awkward and
experimental; their very speech lacks smoothness and firmness.

I am not sorry to be relieved, by having reached the limits of
my space, from the necessity of expatiating upon one of the more
recent theatrical events in London—the presentation, at the St.
James's theatre, of an English version of *Les Danicheff*. This
extremely picturesque and effective play was the great Parisian
success of last winter, and during the London season the company
of the Odéon crossed the channel and presented it with an added
brilliancy. But what the piece has been reduced to in its present
form is a theme for the philosopher. Horribly translated and badly
played, it retains hardly a ray of its original effectiveness. There
can hardly have been a better example of the possible infelicities

of "adaptation." Nor have I the opportunity of alluding to what is going on at the other London theatres, though to all of them I have made a conscientious pilgrimage. But I conclude my very desultory remarks without an oppressive sense of the injustice of omission. In thinking over the plays I have listened to, my memory arrests itself with more kindness, perhaps, than elsewhere, at the great, gorgeous pantomime given at Drury Lane, which I went religiously to see in Christmas week. They manage this matter of the pantomime very well in England, and I have always thought Harlequin and Columbine the prettiest invention in the world. (This is an "adaptation" of an Italian original, but it is a case in which the process has been completely successful.) But the best of the entertainment at Drury Lane was seeing the line of rosy child faces in the boxes, all turned towards the stage in one round-eyed fascination. English children, however, and their round-eyed rosiness, would demand a chapter apart.

"The London Theatres" appeared in The Galaxy, *May, 1877. If, as it seems, Henry James had stayed in Paris for the premiere of "L'Ami Fritz" on December 2, 1876, he must have crossed the Channel very soon afterwards, and before the end of the year had taken "rooms" at 3, Bolton Street. Here is his own account, thirty years later, in his preface to the fourteenth volume of the New York Edition of his Novels and Tales:*

"This scene consisted of small chambers in a small street that opened, at a very near corner, into Piccadilly, and a view of the Green Park; I had dropped into them almost instantaneously, under the accepted heavy pressure of the autumnal London of 1876, and was to sit scribbling in them for nearly ten years. The big human rumble of Piccadilly (all human and equine then and long after) was close at hand; I liked to think that Thack-

eray's Curzon Street, in which Becky Sharp, or rather Mrs. Rawdon Crawley, had lived, was not much further off: I thought of it preponderantly, in my comings and goings, as Becky's and her creator's; just as I was to find fifty other London neighbourhoods speak to me almost only with the voice, the thousand voices, of Dickens.

"A 'great house', forming the southwest corner of Piccadilly and with its long and practically featureless side, continued by the high wall of its ample court, opposite my open-eyed windows, gloomed, in dusky brick, as the extent of my view, but with a vast convenient neutrality which I found, soon enough, protective and not inquisitive, so that whatever there was of my sedentary life and regular habits took a sort of local wealth of colour from the special greyish-brown tone of the surface always before me.

This surface hung there like the most voluminous of curtains — it masked the very stage of the great theatre of the town. To sit for certain hours at one's desk before it was somehow to occupy in the most suitable way in the world the proportionately ample interests of the mightiest of dramas. When I went out it was as if the curtain rose; so that, to repeat, I think of my tolerably copious artistry of that time as all the fruit of the inter-acts, with the curtain more or less quietly down and with the tuning of fiddles and only the vague rumble of shifted scenery playing round it and through it."

May not the abundant use of theatrical imagery in this passage have been occasioned by recollection of his intensive playgoing at this epoch?

Evidently during his first three months or so of London life he applied himself to a close study of what the English theatre had then to offer. He was, as yet, in his own words, "more or less isolated" and without "complex social ties," so that he would often dine alone and go to the theatre unaccompanied. The restaurant he amusingly describes was possibly the St. James's — familiarly "Jimmy's" — which occupied the site where the Piccadilly Hotel now stands; the ticket agency probably the famous Mitchell's in Bond Street.

His "tolerably copious artistry" of the year will have included The Europeans, *some short stories, a constant succession of reviews and art criticism for the* Nation, *a paper almost every month for* The Galaxy, *and some impressions of English life for* Lippincott's Magazine.

HENRY IRVING AS LOUIS XI.
OLIVIA AT THE COURT THEATRE

———— 1 8 7 8 ————

IT IS still something of an event in London when Mr. Henry Irving undertakes a new part; and I hope I shall not seem to speak brutally if I say that it is a good deal of an event when he undertakes it successfully. This happened several weeks ago, and the interval has proved the success. Mr. Irving appeared as *Louis XI.*, in an English "arrangement" of which I believe the perennial Mr. Boucicault has the credit, of Casimir Delavigne's rather dull and dreary drama of that name. It makes, as now performed at the Lyceum, quite what is called on the English stage (where alone the monstrosity is known) a "one-part play." But Mr. Irving plays his one part very well, and it is probably his most satisfactory creation. In this elaborate, picturesque representation of a grotesque old tyrant, at once passionate and cunning, familiar and ferocious, he has the good fortune that some of his defects positively come to his assistance. He is an incongruous Hamlet or Macbeth, but he is a very consistent Louis XI. The part was a favourite one with Charles Kean, who played it with more delicacy, and, at the same time (according to my recollection) with more *rondeur*, as the French say; but certainly, in the actual state of the English stage, there is no actor capable of doing the thing so cleverly and picturesquely as Mr. Henry Irving—in spite of his always saying "gaw" for *go*, "naw" for *no*, etc. Mr. Irving's eccentricities of utterance, however, are very numerous, and on this point the auditor must make a large concession at the outset.

Apropos of the actual state of the English stage, I may add that it has just been very oddly illustrated by the remarkable success, at the Court Theatre, of Mr. Wills's play of *Olivia*, a pathetic drama extracted — violently extracted — from the *Vicar of Wakefield*. The idea of making an effective play, adapted to the modern appetite, of Goldsmith's delicate and humorous masterpiece, whose charm is almost wholly the exquisite narrative style, could have originated only with a playwright desperately at a loss for a subject. Yet *Olivia*, with all Goldsmith's humor and delicacy left out, is a great success — a success rivalling that of the cleverly-played *Diplomacy*, at the Prince of Wales's, of which a report was some time since given in your columns. It seemed to me at the Court Theatre that the success could only be accounted for by an extraordinary apathy of taste on the part of the public, and a good-natured disposition in the well-fed British playgoer who sits in the stalls after dinner to accept a pretty collection of eighteenth-century chairs, and buffets, and pottery, with which *Olivia* is elaborately equipped, as a substitute for dramatic composition and finished acting. The play is tame, dull, and puerile, and the acting can hardly be condemned in a piece which offers such meagre opportunities. The only opportunities, in fact — and they are singularly few — are those of Miss Ellen Terry, as the heroine. Miss Ellen Terry, whom it is greatly the fashion to admire, has a great deal of charm and an interesting, pathetic, even beautiful countenance. But, whether it is the amateurishness of the piece or not, the representative of the Vicar's erring daughter seems amateurish. The goody-goody, namby-pamby element in *Olivia* is its most striking feature, and, combined with the extreme thinness of its interest, it really makes a thoughtful spectator revert longingly to those skilful productions of the French theatre in which, if the moral tone is loose, the dramatic texture is of the finest. It provokes him to declare that the highest morality, for a play, is that it be very well made. It would be interesting to hear the judgment of a first-rate French critic —

of M. Francisque Sarcey, for example—upon such a drama and such a performance as *Olivia*.

London, May 18th, 1878

"Henry Irving as Louis X.; Olivia at the Court Theatre" appeared, unsigned and without title, under the general rubric "Notes," preceded by the words "A correspondent writes to us from London, under date of May 18:" in the Nation, *June 13, 1878.*

M. ÉMILE AUGIER

M. ÉMILE AUGIER has just published his drama of *Les Fourchambault*, which is at present in the enjoyment of high success at the Théâtre Français, and forms, obviously, the most important contribution to the French stage — in other words, to the contemporary stage — during the present year. If to see a play from one of the best French hands acted as such things are acted at the Maison de Molière is one of the greatest possible pleasures, we may perhaps say that in the case of this pleasure being inaccessible by reason of remoteness, a fair substitute for the entertainment may be found in reading the published drama. *Les Fourchambault*, at any rate, reads extremely well, and forms a worthy supplement to that collective edition of the author's works which has been issued during the past year, in seven substantial volumes, by Calmann Lévy. In these seven volumes, by the way, M. Émile Augier makes a very honorable show; the modern theatre has few stronger pieces than *L'Aventurière* and *Le Mariage d'Olympe*, *Les Lionnes Pauvres* and *Maître Guerin*, just as it has nothing more charming than *Philiberte*. Alexandre Dumas the younger, alone, can contest the supremacy on their common line of the author of these masterly dramas. The two writers have many points of contact. The list of their works is of about equal length; both are members of the Academy; both are would-be moralists; both attempt the social, it may even be said the didactic, rather than the romantic or the simply entertaining, drama. In Paris there is scarcely any event so important as the appearance of a new play by one of these gentlemen, unless it be the production of a piece by the other. M. Émile Augier, on his social side, is preoccupied with the sanctity of the family, as they say in France; he "goes in," as they say in England, for the importance of the domestic affections. This is his most frequent thesis. He does not wage war quite so unremittingly as his brilliant rival upon misplaced gallantry and the encroachments of mercenary wiles; but the most earnest effort of his muse may be said to be to keep the family well together. In *Les Fourchambault*, thanks to a variety of causes, it is in terrible danger of falling apart; but cohesion is ultimately restored — the manner in which it is restored forming the subject of the play. In French plays these results are sometimes brought about very oddly. Here, for instance, the good example is set to the household of M. Fourchambault by a lady who has been M. Fourchambault's mistress and by her son, who is also that of M. Fourchambault. This is a curious example of the assumption, so frequent in French novels and plays, that to take a high attitude one must have done something very improper. Upon the didactic properties of these productions English readers are always certain to make their own reflections; they think it strange to see so much pleading of causes which, among themselves, are not in the way of being lost. They reflect, too, doubtless, upon some of their other properties — their finish and shapeliness, their neat, artistic, scientific form. Only, if on one side they feel no need of learning the lesson, on the other, too often, they seem unable to apply it.

"*M. Emile Augier*" appeared, unsigned, under the general rubric "*Notes*," in the Nation, *June 27, 1878*.

After his visit to Paris in the early autumn of 1877, Henry James went by way of Florence to Rome where he spent seven weeks. At the end of the year he was in Paris again on his way back to London, and complained from there in a letter to Miss Grace Norton that his acquaintances in Paris took up so much of his time that he couldn't even go to the Théâtre Français. His circle of friends in England was, by this time, expanding rapidly. He still visited the London theatres, doubtless seeing more plays than he wrote about; but the note on Augier shows how much he still regretted the Théâtre Français.

From London, on May 1, 1878, he

wrote to *William James* of his intention to begin playwriting. "*My inspection of the French theatre will fructify. I have thoroughly mastered Dumas, Augier and Sardou.*" In June and July of this year the Cornhill Magazine *published* Daisy Miller and James enjoyed one of the greatest successes of his earlier career. On September 15, writing from Scotland to his sister he said: "*Did I tell you I was now London correspondent of the* Nation?"

1 8 7 9

M R. MATTHEW ARNOLD, in his volume of *Mixed Essays*,
lately published, in speaking somewhere of some of the
less creditable features of English civilization, alludes to the
British theatre as "probably the most contemptible in Europe."
The judgement is a harsh one, but he would be a bold man who,
looking round him at the condition of the London stage at the
present moment, should attempt to gainsay it. I have lately made
a point of gathering such impressions on the subject as were
easily obtainable, and a brief record of them may not be without
interest. The first impression one receives in England on turning
one's attention at all in this direction, is that a very large number
of people are doing the same. The theatre just now is the fashion,
just as "art" is the fashion and just as literature is not. The
English stage has probably never been so bad as it is at present,
and at the same time there probably has never been so much care
about it. It sometimes seems to an observer of English customs
that this interest in histrionic matters almost reaches the proportions of a mania. It pervades society—it breaks down barriers. If
you go to an evening party, nothing is more probable than that
all of a sudden a young lady or a young gentleman will jump up
and strike an attitude and begin to recite a poem or a speech.
Every pretext for this sort of exhibition is ardently cultivated,
and the London world is apparently filled with stage-struck young
persons whose relatives are holding them back from a dramatic
career by the skirts of their garments. Plays and actors are per-

petually talked about, private theatricals are incessant, and members of the dramatic profession are "received" without restriction. They appear in society, and the people of society appear on the stage; it is as if the great gate which formerly divided the theatre from the world had been lifted off its hinges. There is, at any rate, such a passing to and fro as has never before been known; the stage has become amateurish and society has become professional. There are various explanations of this state of things, of which I am far from expressing disapproval; I mention it only because, superficially, it might seem that the theatre would have drawn strength from this large development of public favor. It is part of a great general change which has come over English manners — of the confusion of many things which forty years ago were kept very distinct. The world is being steadily democratized and vulgarized, and literature and art give their testimony to the fact. The fact is better for the world perhaps, but I question greatly whether it is better for art and literature; and therefore it is that I was careful to say just now that it is only *superficially* that one might expect to see the stage elevated by becoming what is called the fashion. They are in the truth of the matter very much more in France. In France, too, the democratizing, vulgarizing movement, the confusion of kinds, is sufficiently perceptible; but the stage has still, and will probably long have, the good fortune of not becoming the fashion. It is something at once more and less than the fashion, and something more respectable and permanent, and a part of the national life. It is a need, a constant habit, enjoying no fluctuations of credit. The French esteem the theatre too much to take rash liberties with it, and they have a wholesome dread, very natural in an artistic people, of abusing the source of their highest pleasure. Recitations, readings, private theatricals, public experiments by amateurs who have fallen in love with the footlights, are very much less common in France than in England, and of course still less common in the United States. Another fact that helps these diversions to flourish in England is the immense size of society, the prevalence of country life, the existence of an enormous class of people who have nothing in the world to do. The famous "leisure class," which is the envy and admiration of so many good Americans, has certainly invented a great many expedients for getting through the time; but there still remains for this interesting section of the human race a considerable danger of being bored, and it is to escape this danger that many of the victims of leisure take refuge in playing at histrionics.

In France (as I spoke just now of France) the actor's art, like the ancient arts and trades, is still something of a "mystery" — a thing of technical secrets, of special knowledge. This kind of feeling about it is inevitably much infringed when it becomes the fashion, in the sense that I have alluded to, and certainly the evidences of training — of a school, a discipline, a body of science — are on the English stage conspicuous by their absence. Of how little the public taste misses these things or perceives the need of them, the great and continued success of Mr. Henry Irving is a striking example. I shall not here pretend to judge Mr. Irving; but I may at least say that even his most ardent admirers would probably admit that he is an altogether irregular performer, and that an artistic education has had little to do with the results that he presents to the public. I do not mean by this, of course, that he has not had plenty of practice; I mean simply that he is an actor who, in default of any help rendered him, any control offered him by the public taste, by an ideal in the public mind, has had to get himself together and keep himself together as he could. He is at present the principal "actuality" of the London stage, and his prosperity has taken a fresh start with his having at the beginning of the winter established a theatre of his own and obtained the graceful assistance of Miss Ellen Terry. I say I shall not pretend to judge Mr. Irving, because I am aware that I must in the nature of the case probably do him injustice. His starting-point is so perfectly opposed to any that I find conceivable that it would be idle to attempt to appreciate him. In the opinion of many people the basis, the prime condition, of acting is the art of finished and beautiful utterance — the art of speaking, of saying, of diction, as the French call it; and such persons find it impossible to initiate themselves into any theory of the business which leaves this out of account. Mr. Irving's theory eliminates it altogether, and there is perhaps a great deal to be said for his point of view. I must, however, leave the task of elucidating it to other hands. He began the present season with a revival of *Hamlet* — a part, one would say, offering peculiar obstacles to treatment on this system of the unimportance of giving value to the text; and now, for some weeks past, he has been playing the *Lady of Lyons* with great success. To this success Miss Ellen Terry has very greatly contributed. She is greatly the fashion at present, and she belongs properly to a period which takes a strong interest in aesthetic furniture, archaeological attire, and blue china. Miss Ellen Terry is "aesthetic"; not only her garments but her features themselves bear the stamp of the new enthusiasm. She has a charm, a great deal of a certain amateurish, angular grace, a total want of what the French call *chic*, and a countenance very happily adapted to the expression of pathetic emotion. To this last effect her voice also contributes; it has a sort of monotonous husky thickness which is extremely touching, though it gravely interferes with the modulation of many of her speeches. Miss Terry, however, to my sense, is far from having the large manner, the style and finish, of a *comédienne*. She is the most pleasing and picturesque figure upon the English stage, but the other night, as I sat watching the *Lady of Lyons*, I said to myself that her charming aspect hardly availed to redeem the strange, dingy grotesqueness of that decidedly infelicitous drama.

The two best theatres in London are the Court and the Prince of Wales's, and the intelligent playgoer is supposed chiefly to concern himself with what takes place at these houses. It is certainly true that at either house you see the London stage at its best; they possess respectively the two most finished English

actors with whom I am acquainted. Mr. Arthur Cecil, at the Prince
of Wales's, has a ripeness and perfection of method which reminds
me of the high finish of the best French acting. He is an artist
in very much the same sense that Got and Coquelin are artists.
The same may be said of Mr. Hare at the Court, whose touch is
wonderfully light and unerring. Indeed, for a certain sort of
minute, almost painter-like elaboration of a part that really suits
him, Mr. Hare is very remarkable. But the merit of these two
actors, and those of some of their comrades at either theatre, only
serve to throw into relief the essential weakness of the whole
institution — the absolute poverty of its repertory. When Matthew
Arnold speaks of the "contemptible" character of the contemporary English theatre, he points of course not merely at the bad
acting which is so largely found there; he alludes also to its perfect
literary nudity. Why it is that in the English language of our day
there is not so much even as an unsuccessful attempt at a dramatic
literature — such as is so largely visible in Germany and Italy,
where "original" plays, even though they be bad ones, are produced by the hundred — this is quite a question by itself, and one
that it would take some space to glance at. But it is sufficiently
obvious that the poverty of the modern English theatre is complete, and it is equally obvious that the theatre is all one — that
the drama and the stage hold together. There can be no serious
school of acting unless there is a dramatic literature to feed it;
the two things act and react upon each other — they are a reciprocal
inspiration and encouragement. Anything less inspiring than the
borrowed wares, vulgarized and distorted in the borrowing, upon
which the English stage of to-day subsists, cannot well be imagined. Coarse adaptations of French comedies, with their literary
savor completely evaporated, and their form and proportions
quite sacrificed to the queer obeisances they are obliged to make
to that incongruous phantom of a morality which has not wit
enough to provide itself with an entertainment conceived in its
own image — this is the material on which the actor's spirit is

obliged to exert itself. The result is natural enough, and the plays and the acting are equally crude.

There can be no better proof of the poverty of the repertory than the expedients to which the Court and the Prince of Wales's have been reduced during the present winter. The Court has been playing a couple of threadbare French pieces of twenty and thirty years ago — a stiff translation of Scribe's *Bataille de Dames*, and a commonplace version of a commonplace drama entitled *Le Fils de Famille*. Scribe's piece is a clever light comedy — it is still sometimes played at the Théâtre Français; but it belongs at this time of day quite to the dramatic scrap-bag. There is something pitiful in seeing it dragged into the breach and made to figure for weeks as the stock entertainment at one of the two best English theatres. At the Prince of Wales's they have been playing all winter and are still playing Robertson's *Caste* — a piece of which, in common with the other productions of the same hand, it is only possible to say that it belongs quite to the primitive stage of dramatic literature. It is the infancy of art; it might have been written by a clever under-teacher for representation at a boarding-school. At the Criterion there is a comedy entitled *Truth*, by an American author, Mr. Bronson Howard. Even the desire to speak well of American productions is insufficient to enable me to say that Mr. Bronson Howard offers a partial contradiction to Matthew Arnold's dictum. *Truth* may be an "original" drama; I know nothing of its history; but it produces the effect of the faint ghost of any old conventional French vaudeville — the first comer — completely divested of intellectual garniture, reduced to its simplest expression, and diluted in British propriety.

London, May 24th, 1879

"*The London Theatres*" *appeared, signed XX., in the* Nation, *June 12, 1879.*

THE COMÉDIE FRANÇAISE
IN LONDON

——————————— 1 8 7 9 ———————————

THE Comédie Française gives to-night the last representation of its extraordinarily successful series, and I am reminded that I am on the point of losing my opportunity for carrying out an intention long deferred, and making a few remarks upon this very interesting episode of the visit to London of the children of Molière. The first remark to be made is that this visit has been a brilliant, a complete, an unclouded success. It is saying little for it to say that it is incomparably the most noteworthy event that has occurred for many a long year in the theatrical annals of London; these annals are not so rich as to impart any great force to such a compliment. But what I may say is that the episode will have been a memorable one in the annals of the house of Molière itself. Its members, individually, have refreshed their laurels and renewed their fame, and the beauty and power of the best French acting have affirmed themselves under circumstances which give an added value to the triumph. The appeal has been made to a foreign audience, an audience whose artistic perceptions are the reverse of lively, whose ear does not respond quickly to the magic French utterance, and whose mind does not easily find its way among the intricacies of French sentiment; and yet the triumph has been perfect, and the Comédie Française and the London public have been thoroughly pleased with each other. I am far from intimating that the Théâtre Français in its collective or ideal capacity has gained in prestige or in dignity by its visit to London and its successful exploitation of English curiosity. This is another question, and there are various things to be said about it. If London has been charmed by this delightful episode, Paris has by no means been affected in the same manner. Parisian irritation has been almost in direct proportion to English applause. It is hardly too much to say that Parisian opinion has been to a certain point scandalized. The conservative view of the case is easy to understand, and (inconsistent as the declaration may appear) it wholly commands my sympathy. In this view the Comédie Française has no right to detach itself from French soil; it is beneath its dignity to wander off to foreign lands like a troupe of common strollers, to fill its cash-box and make barbarians stare. If it leaves Paris it should betake itself to some other French city; it should speak only to French-speaking audiences; it should find a temporary home at Lyons, at Marseilles, at Bordeaux. Indeed, in the view of many fastidious spirits, the Comédie Française should not think too much about the cash-box at all. It should enjoy its copious subvention; it should live in comfort and credit; but it should never propose to itself to make money. It should never, as the French say, *courir les aventures.* Such vulgar ambitions are for other companies — they are not for the house of Molière, which belongs to the Gallic soil, to the climate, to the atmosphere, and has as little right to absent itself as the French Academy or the Chamber of Deputies would have to hold their sittings in neighbouring states. The pretext of this brilliant escapade on the part of an austere institution was the undertaking of certain repairs and embellishments in the great theatre of the Rue de Richelieu, where it must be confessed that some such labours had long been urgently needed. The house was to be put in order, the theatre was to be closed for six weeks. It was decided to spend these six weeks in London, and a rich pecuniary harvest was guaranteed beforehand. The Comédie assumed no risks, and no one connected with the enterprise can have been a loser — not even the tattered persons, of both sexes, whose share in it has been to thrust the play-book into the windows of the long train of carriages slowly advancing to the Gaiety Theatre. This is all very well; but if I were a consistent Parisian I should be no better pleased. I have spent as many evenings at the Gaiety Theatre as I have found possible, and I have always enjoyed my privilege; but, distinctly, the institution which I just spoke of as austere has lost to my eyes a part of that sanctity in which it was formerly clad. I have enjoyed it in London, but I am afraid that in case of paying it a visit in Paris I shall not enjoy it so much. I have seen it out of its element—I have seen it in the Strand! I have seen it vulgarized, reduced to the level of ordinary commercial ventures, departing from its traditions and compromising with its ideal. I don't know a more striking example of the spirit of the age, of the march of a civilization before which old scruples and reserves, old sentiments and sanctities are successively toppling over.

But of course if the Comédie Française was willing, we were only too delighted, and I must restrict myself to talking of our charming impressions. It is true that we have talked of them a great deal already—a certain section of the London world may be said for the last five weeks to have talked of nothing else. It had found a topic, and in a community addicted to dinner-giving a topic has precious uses. Indeed, there came a time when the Comédie Française threatened to take rank with the weather, or with Mrs. Langtry, as a subject available only for persons who had resigned themselves to the apparent sacrifice of originality. I almost feel tempted to say that the most entertaining part of the episode has been the performances, not of the Comédie, but of the audience. The Théâtre Français, as exhibited to London society, is one branch of the affair; London society, as exhibiting itself to the Théâtre Français, is another. The most amusing comedians have not always been before the footlights, and the drama has gone on in the world as well as on the stage. The whole thing, on the part of the public, has been very characteristic, very English—

the Parisian mind would probably say very provincial. I shall not attempt, however, to go into details on this point—it is enough to say that the hospitality of the London world has been extreme and complete. The Comédie Française has been "taken up," collectively and individually, with a warmth which must have taxed the preconceptions of the French imagination, and which does great honour to English courtesy. How the French imagination may have reconciled all this—especially in some of its phases— with the familiar traditions about English stiffness and coldness, English prudery and false delicacy, it profits not to enquire. It is enough that it must occasionally have been sorely puzzled, and have carried away a considerable store of tough problems, to be solved at leisure. One of these, for instance, will be connected, as we may surmise, with the extraordinary vogue of Mademoiselle Sarah Bernhardt, and will concern itself with enquiring into the sources of the tender interest excited by this lady. I speak of her "vogue" for want of a better word; it would require some ingenuity to give an idea of the intensity, the ecstasy, the insanity as some people would say, of curiosity and enthusiasm provoked by Mlle. Bernhardt. I spoke just now of topics, and what they were worth in the London system. This remarkable actress has filled this function with a completeness that leaves nothing to be desired; her success has been altogether the most striking and curious, although by no means, I think, the most gratifying, incident of the visit of the Comédie. It has not been the most gratifying, because it has been but in a very moderate degree an artistic success. It has been the success of a celebrity, pure and simple, and Mlle. Sarah Bernhardt is not, to my sense, a celebrity because she is an artist. She is a celebrity because, apparently, she desires with an intensity that has rarely been equalled to be one, and because for this end all means are alike to her. She may flatter herself that, as regards the London public, she has compassed her end with a completeness which makes of her a sort of fantastically impertinent *victrix* poised upon a perfect pyramid of ruins—the ruins of a hundred British prejudices and proprieties. Mlle. Sarah Bernhardt has remarkable gifts; her success is something quite apart as the woman herself is something quite apart; but her triumph has little to do with the proper lines of the Comédie Française. She is a child of her age—of her moment —and she has known how to profit by the idiosyncrasies of the time. The trade of a celebrity, pure and simple, had been invented, I think, before she came to London; if it had not been, it is certain she would have discovered it. She has in a supreme degree what the French call the *génie de la réclame*—the advertising genius; she may, indeed, be called the muse of the newspaper. Brilliantly as she had already exercised her genius, her visit to London has apparently been a revelation to her of the great extension it may obtain among the Anglo-Saxon peoples, and the *dénoûment* of this latest chapter in the history of the Comédie Française is that Mlle. Sarah Bernhardt has resigned her place as *sociétaire*. You will, of course, have heard long before this reaches you that she has formed projects, more or less definite, for visiting the United States. I strongly suspect that she will find a triumphant career in the Western world. She is too American not to succeed in America. The people who have brought to the highest development the arts and graces of publicity will recognize a kindred spirit in a figure so admirably adapted for conspicuity. Mlle. Bernhardt will be a loss to the Comédie Française, but she will not be a fatal one. Charming as are some of her gifts, peculiar and picturesque as is her whole artistic personality, it cannot in the least be said that she is a consummate actress, or even what the French call a real *comédienne*. She is far from belonging to the race of Rachel and Desclée, she has something sceptical and cynical which was wholly foreign to the manner of those concentrated and serious artists. There are, indeed, actresses now at the Théâtre Français who are very much more complete than Mlle. Sarah Bernhardt. Mlle. Favart knows her trade as her more youthful and more captivating successor will probably never pretend to do. But unfortunately Mlle. Favart lacks charms; she pleases no one but the people whose judgement is complicated by an appreciation of technicalities. It is to be added that Mlle. Sarah Bernhardt's repertory is a singularly narrow and disadvantageous one; in a single part, in Phèdre alone, has she a chance to give the measure of a great talent. The plaintive and pathetic passages of *Phèdre* she renders with admirable delicacy and grace; but in the violent scenes she forces her note beyond all reason, and becomes painfully shrill and modern. Her only other opportunity is in the last act of *Hernani*, which apparently has been her great success in London. In *Ruy Blas* her part is pale and savourless, and in *L'Étrangère* it is an almost grotesquely bad one. In *Zaïre* she has failed in London to make her mark; and in *Andromaque* she has little or nothing to do but to assume the attitude of a weeping willow, rustling and murmuring in melancholy zephyrs. This, it must be confessed, however, she does to perfection.

Her rival, Mademoiselle Croizette, has obtained a very much scantier share of the public favour, and this lady's failure to please the English public has been, I believe, for the administration of the Comédie Française, one of the surprises of the visit to London. This accident will have been less of a surprise to many spectators; yet I nevertheless think that Mlle. Croizette has not received her due. She has the misfortune of lacking a certain indispensable delicacy of interest, and it must be added that the amplitude of her person has reached a point at which, in the parts of young girls, illusion tends to vanish. But Mlle. Croizette is a very handsome woman and a very vigorous and definite actress, and it would have been in the interest of ideal justice that English applause should have been rather more equally divided between the most eminent of the younger ladies of the Comédie Française. As regards the elder ones, we have had the entertainment — and found it an excellent one — of seeing Madeleine Brohan and Mademoiselle Favart in the parts of mothers and aunts. The latter lady, in consenting to undertake the representation of maturity and maternity, has opened for herself a fresh and honourable career; and nothing can be more charming, more brilliant and picturesque, than Madeleine Brohan's creation of the old Marquise de Villemer, in George Sand's agreeable drama of that name. The striking thing in London, however, as it has long been in Paris, is the great superiority of the masculine side of the house. The great trio of Got, Delaunay, Coquelin, is unapproached, and from present appearances unapproachable, by any feminine combination. Each of these great actors has won himself large honours with the English public; each of them has done with a rich perfection that which he has had to do. If I were to put forward one of these artists rather than another as the source of my own highest pleasure, I think I should have little hesitation in naming the rich, the rare, the admirable and inimitable Coquelin. There was a time when I thought Got the first of living actors, and Got is certainly still a consummate, a superb comedian. But as Coquelin has advanced in life and in his art, he has attained a command of his powers and developed an intelligence of the whole dramatic mystery which place him, to my sense, almost alone. His variety, his versatility, the extent of his scale, are extraordinary; he is at once the most joyous and exuberant of pure comedians and the most powerful and touching of serious actors. He has a deeper intelligence than is often seen upon the stage; he strikes at once the note of high comicality and the note of passion, of deep seriousness; and he does both of these things with a certain touching, moving, exciting ardour. I said just now that Mlle. Sarah Bernhardt was supposed to be going to America. That is all very well; but what I really wish is that M. Coquelin would go.

London, July 12th, 1879

"The Comédie Française in London" appeared, signed xx., in the Nation, July 31, 1879.

At the end of the first week of this season Henry James wrote to Miss Grace Norton, dating his letter Sunday a.m., June 8: "I am to dine to-night at Sir Frederick Pollock's, to meet one or two of the (more genteel) members of the Comédie Française, who are here just now, playing with immense success and supplying the London world with that invaluable boon, a topic. I mean the whole Comédie is *here* en masse *for six weeks. I have been to see them two or three times and I find their artistic perfection gives one an immense lift out of British air."*

The essay is dated July 12, the day on which the season terminated, and in it James says: "*I have spent as many evenings at the Gaiety Theatre as I have found possible;*" they may have been many, as the répertoire brought over was extensive.

This appears to have been James's last contribution to the Nation for many years. In the issue of July 8, 1915, he contributed a note on "*The Founding of the* Nation" and after mentioning the "*adverse pressure*" his habit of contributing had learnt to know in '76, '77, and '78, in Paris and in London, he concludes that "*though I suppose I should have liked regularly to correspond from London, nothing came of that but three or four pious efforts which broke down under the appearance that people liked most to hear of what I could least, of what in fact nothing would have induced me to, write about. What I could write about they seemed, on the other hand, to view askance.*" Actually his regular journalism was now to cease for many years, though he continued to contribute, intermittently, to the monthly magazines.

THE LONDON THEATRES

THE AUTHOR of these remarks was on the point of pre-
fixing to them a different title from the one he has actually
made use of, when it occurred to him that the latter would give a
much better idea of his subject. "The London Theatres" stands
for something that may, more or less profitably, be talked about,
but "The English Stage" is a conception so purely intellectual, so
confined to the region of theory, or reminiscence, or desire, that
it eludes the most ingenious grasp. There are a great many theatres in London, enjoying various degrees of credit and prosperity;
but there is nothing cynical in saying that there is no such thing in
existence as an English stage. The stage is a collective organism,
composed of the harmonious vitality diffused through a number of
individual play-houses, which are nourished by a dramatic literature native to the country, and expressing its manners and feelings,
and which work together to an effective end. When it substantially
exists, it is usually summed up, typified to the world, in a theatre
more distinguished than the rest, in which the education of the
actor has reached its highest point, and in which it is the supreme
ambition of the dramatic authors of the country to see their productions represented. There is a stage in France, of which the
Comédie Française is the richest expression; and we are told that
there is a very honourable stage in Germany, where two or three
excellent theatres — literary theatres — maintain the standard of
finished and brilliant acting. It appears to be generally conceded
that there was formerly a stage in England. In the last century,

the English theatres went hand-in-hand with a literature which sprang substantially from the English mind itself, and which, though it has not proved of any value to posterity, ministered, for the time, to what we have called the vitality of the stage. At that time the actor's profession was looked upon as a hill of difficulty, not to be scaled at a bound, nor trodden by every comer. His art was not thought an easy one to master, and a long pro-bation, an apprenticeship of humility, was the portion of even the most promising aspirants. The two great "patented" houses, Drury Lane and Covent Garden, performed very much the same function that the Comédie Française has long been supposed to discharge (in spite of many lapses and errors) on the other side of the Channel. They protected the drama, and they had a high responsibility. They monopolized, in London, the right to play Shakespeare and the poetical repertory, and they formed the ob-jective point of actors and authors alike. They recruited them-selves from the training-school which the provincial theatres then supplied, and they rewarded merit, and consecrated reputations. All this is changed, as so many things are changed in literature and art. The conditions of production are immensely different from those of an age in which the demand for the things that make life agreeable had not become so immoderate as to create a stand-ing quarrel between the quality and the quantity of the supply. The art of writing a play has apparently become a lost one with the English race, who are content to let their entertainment be made for them by a people whose whole view of life is, however, ingenious, essentially different from their own. The comparatively simple and homogeneous character of the English stage has be-come a sort of musty tradition, and in its place we have several dozen small theatrical enterprises, some of which are very suc-cessful, and others not at all so, but all of which live entirely on what the French call "expedients," and compass their degree of success by methods decidedly incongruous.

It is of the actual, however, that we pretend to speak, and not of the possible or impossible. Talking simply of the actual, the first thing to say of it is that the theatre is nowadays decidedly the fashion in London. People go to it a great deal, and are willing to pay high prices for the privilege; they talk of it, they write about it, and, in a great many of them, the taste for it takes the form of a desire to pass from the passive to the active side of the footlights. The number of stage-struck persons who are to be met with in the London world is remarkable, and the number of prosperous actors who are but lately escaped amateurs is equally striking. The older actors regard the invasion of this class with melancholy disapproval, and declare that the profession is going to the dogs. By amateurs we mean young men "of the world" (for of the other sex, naturally, there is much less question) not of theatrical stock, who have gone upon the stage after being educated for something very different, and who have managed to achieve success without going through the old-fashioned processes. The old actors are probably right from their own point of view — the point of view from which a long course of histrionic gymnastics was thought indispensable, and from which the touchstone of accomplishment was the art of delivering the great Shakespearean speeches. That way of considering the matter has lost credit, and the clever people on the London stage to-day aim at a line of effect in which their being "amateurs" is almost a positive advantage. Small, realistic comedy is their chosen field, and the art of acting as little as possible has — doubtless with good results in some ways — taken the place of the art of acting as much. Of course, the older actors, with all their superfluous science, as they deem it, left on their hands, have no patience with the infatuation of a public which passes from the drawing-room to the theatre only to look at an attempt, at best very imperfect, to reproduce the accidents and limitations of the drawing-room.

All this tends to prove, however, that the theatre is what is called an actuality, and that if it labours under appreciable disadvantages, these are not the result of a want of patronage. There is no want of patronage to complain of when many hundreds of people are found every night prepared to pay the sum of ten shillings for a stall. The privilege of spending the evening in a stall at any theatre in London is dearly purchased at that cost; the disparity between the price paid for your entertainment and the quality of the entertainment provided is often almost ludicrous. It is in the power of an enterprising play-goer to endeavour to extract a portion of that large amount of pleasure which is represented (to our possibly too frugal sense) by two dollars and a half, from a spectacle not unworthy of a booth at a fair. Pleasure, however, is usually expensive in England, and the theatre conforms simply to the common law. Books are dear, pictures are dear, music is dear, travelling is dear. Play-going, in other ways besides, comes under the usual London disadvantages — the great distance to be traversed before reaching the theatre, the repulsive character of many of the streets through which your aesthetic pilgrimage lies, the necessity of dining earlier than usual and of dressing as if for a private entertainment. These things testify to the theatre's being the fashion among a certain class, and the last luxury of a few, rather than taking its place in the common habits of the people, as it does in France. The difference in favour of the French is indicated by the very much more convenient form that play-going assumes in Paris, where the various temples of the drama are scattered along the clean, bright Boulevard and are guarded by no restriction, tacit or other, as to the costume of their frequenters. In New York as well, in these respects, we are better off than the good people who embark for an evening of the play in London. The New York theatres are all more or less adjacent to the great thoroughfare of the town, and the ceremony of "dressing" does not, even feebly, impose itself. It must be admitted, however, that when once you are dressed and seated in London, your material comfort is greater than it is in Paris, greater, too, than it is in New York. The atmosphere, for inscrutable reasons, is a very much less poisonous compound than the suffocating medium through which the unexhausted Parisian is condemned to witness the masterpieces of Molière and Victor Hugo, of Sardou and the younger Dumas. You are much better seated, less crowded and jostled, than in Paris, and you are not bullied and irritated by the terrible tribe of *ouvreuses*. Your neighbours sit quietly and reasonably in their places, without trooping out between the acts, to the deep discomfort of your toes and knees. You have, in a word, the sense of passing your evening in better company than in Paris, and this, if it be not what you go to the theatre for, and if it be but a meagre compensation for a lame performance, may, nevertheless, be numbered among the encouragements to play-going. These encouragements, in all matters independent of the great matter—the acting itself—have multiplied greatly in London during the last few years, and have now reached a very high perfection. Everything has been done that can be done by beauty of scenery, completeness of furniture and costume, refinement of machinery, to put the auditor into good humour with what he is about to listen to. What will it matter what he listens to if he have real buhl cabinets, Persian carpets, and Venetian mirrors to look at? These tendencies have found a sumptuous home, within a small number of months, in three theatres which divide between them the honour of being the most important in London. To a stranger, inquiring which should be deemed the first of these houses, it would be difficult to give a very definite answer. "Oh, the Lyceum," it might be said, "because at the Lyceum they play Shakespeare." Yes; at the Lyceum they play Shakespeare; but the question is, *how* they play him. The greatest of poets is not, to our mind, interpreted at the Lyceum in a manner to assign a very high place to the scene of the attempt. At the St. James's, they play translations of MM. Bayard and Scribe, and original productions of Mr. Tom Taylor. At the Haymarket, they play Lord Lytton and M. Sardou. It is a nice question whether it is a nobler task to render Shakespeare inadequately, or to represent with sufficient skill rather pale adaptations of French *vaudevillistes*.

It is a question, however, that we are not called upon to solve; and we will content ourselves with saying that at the three theatres just mentioned a great many things are very cleverly done.

Upward of two years ago the Lyceum passed into the hands of Mr. Henry Irving, who is without doubt at present the most distinguished actor in England. He had been acting at the Lyceum for some years before, while the house was under the management of the late Mr. Bateman, and then of his widow, who has within a few months, with a great deal of courage and zeal, attempted to awaken the long dormant echoes of Sadler's Wells—a theatre which had its season of prosperity (many years ago), but which finally, in its out-of-the-way position, was left stranded by ebbing tides. Mrs. Bateman, to whom much of the credit of originally introducing Mr. Irving to the public belongs, succeeded in some degree, we believe, in turning the tide back to the little theatre to which the late Mr. Phelps's "revivals" at one period attracted the town. Mr. Irving for the last two years, then, has had his own way at the Lyceum, and a very successful way it has been. Hamlet and Shylock have constituted the stock of his enterprise, though he has also acted several of the parts in which he built up his reputation—Richelieu; Eugene Aram and Charles I., in Mr. W. G. Wills's plays; Louis XI., in a translation of Casimir Delavigne's rather dull drama, and Matthias in *The Bells*. During the whole of last winter, however, *The Merchant of Venice* held the stage, and this performance disputes with that of *Hamlet* the chief place in his list of successes as an actor. Among his triumphs as a manager, the former play, we believe, quite heads the list; it has every appearance of being an immense financial success, and startling stories are told of the great sums of money it brings in to the happy lessee of the theatre. It is arranged upon the stage with a great deal of ingenuity and splendour, and has a strong element of popularity in the person of Miss Ellen Terry, who is the most conspicuous actress now before the London public, as the picturesque Shylock of her Portia is the most eminent **actor**. Mr. Irving has been a topic in London any time these five years, and Miss Terry is at least as much of one. There is a difference, indeed, for about Mr. Irving people are divided, and about Miss Terry they are pretty well agreed. The opinion flourishes on the one side that Mr. Irving is a great and admirable artist, and on the other the impression prevails that his defects outnumber his qualities. He has at least the power of inspiring violent enthusiasms, and this faculty is almost always accompanied by a liability to excite protests. Those that it has been Mr. Irving's destiny to call forth have been very downright, and many of them are sufficiently intelligible. He is what is called a picturesque actor; that is, he depends for his effects upon the art with which he presents a certain figure to the eye, rather than upon the manner in which he speaks his part. He is a thoroughly serious actor, and evidently bestows an immense deal of care and conscience upon his work; he meditates, elaborates, and, upon the line on which he moves, carries the part to a very high degree of finish. But it must be affirmed that this is a line with which the especial art of the actor, the art of utterance, of saying the thing, has almost nothing to do. Mr. Irving's peculiarities and eccentricities of speech are so strange, so numerous, so personal to himself, his vices of pronunciation, of modulation, of elocution so highly developed, the tricks he plays with the divine mother-tongue so audacious and fantastic, that the spectator who desires to be in sympathy with him finds himself confronted with a bristling hedge of difficulties. He must scramble over the hedge, as best he can, in order to get at Mr. Irving at all; to get at him, that is, as an exponent of great poetic meanings. Behind this hedge, as we may say, the actor disports himself with a great deal of ingenuity, and passes through a succession of picturesque attitudes and costumes; but we look at him only through its thorny interstices. In so doing, we get glimpses of a large and various ability. He is always full of intention, and when the intention is a matter of by-play, it is brilliantly carried out. He is, of course, much better in the modern drama than in the Shakespearean; because, if it is a question of sacrificing the text, the less we are obliged to sacrifice the better. It is better to lose the verses of Mr. Wills than to fail to recognize those of the poet whom the French have sometimes spoken of as Mr. Williams. Mr. Irving's rendering of Shakespeare, however, is satisfactory in a varying degree. His Macbeth appeared to us wide of the mark, but his Hamlet is very much better. In *Macbeth*, as we remember his performance, he failed even to look the part satisfactorily — a rare mistake in an actor who has evidently a strong sense of what may be called the plastic side of the characters he represents. His Hamlet is a magnificent young prince: few actors can wear a cloak and a bunch of sable plumes with a greater grace than Mr. Irving; few of them can rest a well-shaped hand on the hilt of a sword in a manner more suggestive of the models of Vandyke. The great trouble with the Hamlet was that it was inordinately slow — and this, indeed, is the fault throughout of Mr. Irving, who places minutes between his words, and strange strides and balancings between his movements. Heat, rapidity, passion, magic — these qualities are the absent ones, and a good general description of him is to say that he is picturesque but diffuse. Of his Shylock during last winter, it was often said that it presents his faults in their mildest and his merits in their highest form. In this there is possibly a great deal of truth; his representation of the rapacious and rancorous Jew has many elements of interest. He looks the part to a charm, or rather we should say, to a repulsion, and he might be painted as he stands. His conception of it is a sentimental one, and he has endeavoured to give us a sympathetic, and, above all, a pathetic Shylock. How well he reconciles us to this aspect of the character we ourselves shall not undertake to say, for our attention was fixed primarily upon the superficial execution of the thing, and here, without going further, we found much to arrest and perplex it. The actor struck us as rigid and frigid, and above all as painfully behind the stroke of the clock. The deep-welling malignity, the grotesque horror, the red-hot excitement of the long-baffled, sore-hearted member of a despised trade, who has been all his life at a disadvantage, and who at last finds his hour and catches his opportunity — these elements had dropped out. Mr. Irving's Shylock is neither excited nor exciting, and many of the admirable speeches, on his lips, lack much of their incision; notably the outbreak of passion and prospective revenge after he finds that Antonio has become forfeit, and that his daughter has fled from him, carrying off her dowry. The great speech, with its grim refrain: "Let him look to his bond!" rising each time to an intenser pitch and culminating in a pregnant menace, this superb opportunity is missed; the actor, instead of being "hissing hot," as we have heard Edmund Kean described at the same moment, draws the scene out and blunts all its points. The best thing that Mr. Irving does is, to our taste, the Louis XI. of Casimir Delavigne, a part in which his defects to a certain degree stand him in stead of qualities. His peculiarities of voice and enunciation are not in contradiction to those of the mumbling old monarch and dotard whom he represents with so much effective detail. Two years ago he played Claude Melnotte for several months, sacrificing himself with the most commendable generosity to the artistic needs of Miss Ellen Terry, who was the Pauline of the season. We say sacrificing himself, for his inaptitude for the part was so distinct that he must have been aware of it. We may mention two other characters in which Mr. Irving composes a figure to the eye with brilliant taste and skill, — the Charles I. of Mr. Wills, and the Vanderdecken, of (if we mistake not) the same author. His Charles I. might have stepped down from the canvas of Vandyke, and his Vanderdecken is also superb. We say he looks these parts, but we do not add that he acts them, for, to the best of our recollection, there is nothing in them to act. The more there is to act, and the less there is simply to declaim, the better for Mr. Irving, who owes his great success in *The Bells* to the fact that the part of the distracted burgomaster is so largely pantomimic.

Miss Terry is at present his constant coadjutor, and Miss Terry is supposed to represent the maximum of feminine effort on the English stage. The feminine side, in all the London theatres, is regrettably weak, and Miss Terry is easily distinguished. It is difficult to speak of her fairly, for if a large part of the public are wrong about her, they are altogether wrong, and one hesitates to bring such sweeping charges. By many intelligent persons she is regarded as an actress of exquisite genius, and is supposed to impart an extraordinary interest to everything that she touches. This is not, in our opinion, the truth, and yet to gainsay the assertion too broadly is to fall into an extreme of injustice. The difficulty is that Miss Terry has charm—remarkable charm; and this beguiles people into thinking her an accomplished actress. There is a natural quality about her that is extremely pleasing—something wholesome and English and womanly which often touches easily where art, to touch, has to be finer than we often see it. The writer of these lines once heard her highly commended by one of the most distinguished members of the Comédie Française, who had not understood a word she spoke.

> *"Ah, Miss Terry, for instance; I liked her extremely."*
> *"And why did you like her?"*
> *"Mon Dieu, I found her very natural."*

This seemed to us an interesting impression, and a proof the more of the truism that we enjoy things in proportion to their rarity. To our own English vision Miss Terry has too much nature, and we should like a little more art. On the other side, when a French actress is eminent she is eminent by her finish, by what she has acquired, by the perfection of her art, and the critic I have just quoted, who had had this sort of merit before his eyes all his life, was refreshed by seeing what could be achieved in lieu of it by a sort of sympathetic spontaneity. Miss Terry has that excellent thing, a quality; she gives one the sense of something fine. Add to this that though she is not regularly beautiful, she has a face altogether in the taste of the period, a face that Burne-Jones might have drawn, and that she arranges herself (always in the taste of the period) wonderfully well for the stage. She makes an admirable picture, and it would be difficult to imagine a more striking embodiment of sumptuous sweetness than her Ophelia, her Portia, her Pauline, or her Olivia, in a version of Goldsmith's immortal novel prepared for the Court Theatre a couple of years ago by the indefatigable Mr. Wills. Her Ophelia, in particular, was lovely, and of a type altogether different from the young lady in white muslin, bristling with strange grasses, whom we are accustomed to see in the part. In Miss Terry's hands the bewildered daughter of Polonius became a somewhat angular maiden of the Gothic ages, with her hair cropped short, like a boy's, and a straight and clinging robe, wrought over with contemporary needlework. As for her acting, she has happy impulses; but this seems to us to be the limit of it. She has nothing of the style, nothing of what the French call the authority, of the genuine *comédienne*. Her perception lacks acuteness, and her execution is often rough; the expression of her face itself is frequently amateurish, and her voice has a curious husky monotony, which, though it often strikes a touching note in pathetic passages, yet on the whole interferes seriously with finish of elocution. This latter weakness is especially noticeable when Miss Terry plays Shakespeare. Her manner of dealing with the delightful speeches of Portia, with all their play of irony, of wit and temper, savours, to put it harshly, of the school-girlish. We have ventured to say that her comprehension of a character is sometimes weak, and we may illustrate it by a reference to her whole handling of this same rich opportunity. Miss Terry's mistress of Belmont giggles too much, plays too much with her fingers, is too free and familiar, too osculatory, in her relations with Bassanio. The mistress of Belmont was a great lady, as well as a tender and a clever woman;

but this side of the part quite eludes the actress, whose deportment is not such as we should expect in the splendid spinster who has princes for wooers. When Bassanio has chosen the casket which contains the key of her heart, she approaches him, and begins to pat and stroke him. This seems to us an appallingly false note. "Good heavens, she's touching him!" a person sitting next to us exclaimed — a person whose judgement in such matters is always unerring. But in truth there would be a great deal to say upon this whole question of demonstration of tenderness on the English stage, and an adequate treatment of it would carry us far. The amount of kissing and hugging that goes on in London in the interest of the drama is quite incalculable, and to spectators who find their ideal of taste more nearly fulfilled in the French theatre, it has the drollest, and often the most displeasing effect. Of such demonstrations French comedians are singularly sparing; it is apparently understood that French modesty may be ruffled by them. The English would be greatly — and naturally — surprised if one should undertake to suggest to them that they have a shallower sense of decency than the French, and yet they view with complacency, in the high glare of the footlights, a redundancy of physical endearment which the taste of their neighbours across the channel would never accept. It is wholly a matter of taste, and taste is not the great English quality. English spectators delight in broad effects, and English actors and authors are often restricted to them. It is a broad effect, it tells, or "fetches," as the phrase is, to make a lover and his mistress, or a husband and his wife, cling about each other's necks and return again to the charge, and when other expedients are wanting, this one always succeeds. It is when the embrace is strictly conjugal that it is especially serviceable. The public relish of it is then extreme, and is to be condemned only on aesthetic grounds. It speaks of the soundness and sincerity of the people, but it speaks also of their want of a certain delicacy. The French contention is that such moments, such situations should be merely hinted at — that they are too sacred, too touching to linger upon, and that, moreover, at bottom they are not dramatic. Mr. George Rignold, an actor who has had some success in America, has lately been playing in *Black-eyed Susan*, Douglas Jerrold's curiously antiquated drama, which tells so strange a tale of what the English stage had become fifty years ago; and this performance consists almost exclusively of the variety of situation in which the unfortunate William presses his devoted spouse to his bosom. It is admirable, but it is too admirable; and it is as great a mistake to give us so much of it as it would be to represent people saying their prayers. We have a vivid recollection of the tone in which a clever French lady narrated to us her impressions of a representation of Robertson's comedy of *Caste*, which she had seen at the Prince of Wales's Theatre. One of the principal incidents in this piece is the leave-taking of a young officer and his newly wedded wife, he being ordered away on foreign service. The pangs of parting, as the scene is played, are so protracted and insisted upon that our friend at last was scandalized; and when the young couple were indulging in their twentieth embrace—"*Mais, baissez donc le rideau!*" she found herself crying—"Put down the curtain! Such things are not done in public!"—while the company about her applauded so great a stroke of art, or rather, we ought to say, of nature,—a distinction too often lost sight of in England.

In speaking of the performances of Shakespeare at the Lyceum just now as "inadequate," we meant more particularly that no representation of Shakespeare can be regarded as at all adequate which is not excellent as a whole. Many of the poet's noblest and most exquisite speeches are given to secondary characters to utter, and we need hardly remind the reader how the actors who play secondary characters (putting, for the moment, those who play primary ones quite aside) are in the habit of speaking poetic lines. It is usually a misery to hear them, and there is something monstrous in seeing the most precious intellectual heritage of the human race so fearfully knocked about. Mr. Irving has evidently done his best in distributing the parts in *The Merchant of Venice*, and with what sorry results this best is attended! What an Antonio! what a Bassanio! what a Nerissa! what a Jessica! The scene between Lorenzo and Jessica on the terrace at Belmont, in which the young lovers, sitting hand in hand, breathe out, in rhythmic alternation, their homage to the southern night — this enchanting scene, as it is given at the Lyceum, should be listened to for curiosity's sake. But who, indeed, it may be asked, can rise to the level of such poetry? who can speak such things as they should be spoken? Not, assuredly, the untrained and undedicated performers of whom the great stock of actors and actresses presenting themselves to the English and American public is composed. Shakespeare cannot be acted by way of a change from Messrs. Byron and Burnand, Messrs. Robertson and Wills. He is a school and a specialty in himself, and he is not to be taken up off-hand by players who have been interpreting vulgarity the day before, and who are to return to vulgarity on the morrow.

Miss Marie Litton, an enterprising actress, has lately been conducting the small theatre attached to the Westminster Aquarium, and wooing success by revivals of "old comedies." Success, we believe, was at first rather coy; for about the Westminster Aquarium there hovers a sensibly bad odour. The impurities of its atmosphere, however, are chiefly perceptible after nightfall, and Miss Litton has conjured away ill-fortune by giving her performances during the more innocent hours, and renaming the little play-house the "Afternoon Theatre." It is a dusky and incommodious establishment, with that accidental, provincial look which is so fatal to the spectator's confidence in a would-be "home of the drama." But, such as it is, it has lately witnessed an attempt to bring out *As You Like It* in style, as they say at the restaurants. The style consists chiefly in Miss Litton's doing Rosalind, in Mr. Lionel Brough's doing Touchstone, and in Mr. Hermann Vezin's doing Jacques. Mr. Hermann Vezin, who is of American origin, is one of the best actors in London. He plays a remarkable variety of parts, and plays some of them extremely well. He is what is called in London an elocutionist—he speaks blank verse more artfully than most of his neighbours. His Jacques, however, appeared to us to lack colour and vivacity, humour and irony. The last occasion on which we had seen Mr. Lionel Brough was that of his playing in a fierce burlesque, at the Folly Theatre, in conjunction with Miss Lydia Thompson. As for Miss Litton herself, she has this qualification for the part of Rosalind, that as Rosalind, during most of the play, endeavours to pass herself off as a young man, so the actress's natural organism is remarkably man-like. Miss Litton is too bulky for Rosalind's nimble wit. But what an artistic education it supposes, a proper rendering of the part! What grace, what finish, what taste, what sentiment, what archness! In London there is no House of Shakespeare, as there is in Paris a House of Molière, and in his undomiciled condition, between the Lyceum and the "fishy" Aquarium, the poor great poet has strange bedfellows.

Among the three or four best theatres there has lately been a changing of hands. The company of the Prince of Wales's have lately established themselves at the Haymarket, which has been "done up," as they say in England, with great magnificence; and that of the Court has transferred itself to the St. James's, where, for a long time, no such promise of prosperity had reigned. The two forsaken theatres have meanwhile re-opened their doors in creditable conditions. The Prince of Wales's, indeed, has been the scene of an interesting performance, of which we shall presently speak. The Haymarket has gained by being taken by Mr. and Mrs. Bancroft, but we are not sure that this humorous couple have bettered themselves with the public by leaving the diminutive play-house to which they taught the public the road. The Prince of Wales's is a little theatre, and the pieces produced there dealt mainly in little things—presupposing a great many chairs and tables, carpets, curtains, and knickknacks, and an audience placed close to the stage. They might, for the most part, have been written by a cleverish visitor at a country-house, and acted in the drawing-room by his fellow-inmates. The comedies of the late Mr. Robertson were of this number, and these certainly are among the most diminutive experiments ever attempted in the drama. It is among the habits formed upon Mr. Robertson's pieces that the company of the Prince of Wales's have grown up, and it is possible that they may not have all the success they desire in accommodating themselves to a larger theatre. Upon this point, however, it is quite too early to pronounce; and meanwhile Mr. Bancroft has transformed the Haymarket — which was an anti-quated and uncomfortable house with honourable traditions, which had latterly declined — into the perfection of a place of entertainment. Brilliant, luxuriant, softly cushioned and perfectly aired, it is almost entertainment enough to sit there and admire the excellent device by which the old-fashioned and awkward proscenium has been suppressed and the stage set all around in an immense gilded frame, like that of some magnificent picture. Within this frame the stage, with everything that is upon it, glows with a radiance that seems the very atmosphere of comedy.

So much for the house, but for the rest, there is less to say. As soon as we come to speak of a theatre of which the specialty is the comedy of contemporary manners, our appreciation stumbles into the bottomless gulf of the poverty of the repertory. There can be no better proof of such poverty than the fact that the *genius loci* at the Prince of Wales's was always the just-mentioned Mr. Robertson. This gentleman's plays are infantile, and seem addressed to the comprehension of infants. Mr. and Mrs. Bancroft's actors and actresses could not go on playing them for year after year without falling into the small manner. It is not incumbent on us to say that this manner has been found wanting on being applied to larger things, for the simple reason that it has been rarely put to the test. To consecrate his new enterprise, Mr. Bancroft has brought forward the late Lord Lytton's hackneyed comedy of *Money*, and the acting of this inanimate composition cannot be said to make formidable demands. That it should have been brought forward at all at a moment when a brilliant stroke was needed, speaks volumes as to the degree in which an English manager may be unacquainted with the *embarras de choix*. In opening anew the best of English theatres, Mr. and Mrs. Bancroft were probably conscious of high responsibility; they had apparently decided that they ought to be local and national, and that it would be a false note to usher in their season with a drama extorted, after the usual fashion, from the French. They looked about them for an "original" English comedy, and it is certainly not their fault if they found nothing fresher nor weightier than this poor artificial *Money*, covered with the dust of a hundred prompters' boxes, and faded with the glare of a thousand footlights. An original English comedy is not to be had by whistling—no, nor apparently even by praying—for it. There are, however, members of the company at the new Haymarket who are fit for better things; fit, some of them, for the best things. The weak side, as on the London stage throughout, is that of the women. With the exception of Mrs. Bancroft, there is not an actress who calls for mention. Miss Marion Terry, who does the young ladies, is a pale reflection of her sister, and, although a graceful and sympathetic figure, has, as an actress, no appreciable identity whatever. It will be interesting to see what they will do at the Haymarket when they have to mount a piece with an important part for a young woman. What they will do apparently will be—not to mount it. Mrs. Kendal (Miss Madge Robertson), at the Prince of Wales's, used to play the important young women; but Mrs. Kendal has now passed over to the new St. James's, the management of which her husband divides with Mr. Hare. Mrs. Bancroft in the line of broad comedy is a delightful actress, with an admirable sense of the humorous, an abundance of animation and gaiety, and a great deal of art and finish. The only other actress in London who possesses these gifts (or some of them) in as high a degree is Mrs. John Wood, who is even more broadly comic than Mrs. Bancroft, and moves the springs of laughter with a powerful hand. She is brilliantly farcical, but she is also frankly and uncompromisingly vulgar, and Mrs. Bancroft has more discretion and more taste. The part most typical of Mrs. Bancroft's best ability is that of Polly Eccles, in *Caste*, of which she makes both a charming and an exhilarating creation. She also does her best with Lady Franklin, the widow with a turn for practical jokes, in *Money*, but the part has so little stuff that there is not much to be made of it. Mrs. Bancroft is limited to the field we have indicated, which is a very ample one; she has made two or three excursions into the region of serious effect, which have not been felicitous. Her Countess Zicka, in a version of Sardou's *Dora*, is an example in point.

Since we have begun to speak of the ladies, we will remain a little longer in their company — apologizing for our want of gallantry in again expressing our vivid sense of the fact that they do not shine on the London stage at the present hour. It takes more to make an accomplished actress than the usual English-woman who embraces the profession can easily lay her hands upon; a want of frankness, of brightness, of elegance, of art, is commonly, before the footlights, this lady's principal impediment. The situation may be measured by the fact that Miss Adelaide Neilson (whose principal laurels, we believe, were won in the United States) was one of its most brilliant ornaments. Miss Neilson was a remarkably pretty woman; but she added to this advantage, so far as we could perceive, none of the higher qualifications of an actress. We shall not soon forget a visit we paid over a year ago to the musty and fog-haunted Adelphi, where Miss Neilson was then representing the character of Julia in *The Hunchback*. The performance lingers in our mind as something ineffaceably lugubrious. Mr. Hermann Vezin did Master Walter, and Mr. Henry Neville, Sir Thomas Clifford. They are both clever actors; but either they were very much out of place, or they were playing without their usual spirit; for a sense of melancholy

poverty lay heavily upon the auditor's mind, which was not en-
livened by the manner in which Miss Lydia Foote, an actress
enjoying great credit, expressed the characteristics of the merry-
making Helen. We have passed some bad hours at the Adelphi—
an establishment which we remember in the "good old" days, as
they are called, of Mr. Benjamin Webster and Madame Celeste.
Mr. Benjamin Webster used to be very effective in *The Dead
Heart*, a drama of the French Revolution, pervaded by the clanking
of chains and the uproar of rescuing populace. As for Madame
Celeste, who that ever saw her in the *Green Bushes* can forget the
manner in which, as The Huntress of the Mississippi, she stalked
about the stage with a musket on her shoulder, her fine eyes
rolling, as the phrase is, all over the place, and her lower limbs,
much exposed, encased in remarkably neat Indian leggings? It is
not these memories that are painful, but several more recent ones.
We spoke of the Adelphi just now as a "fog-haunted" house, and
literally, from some mysterious reason, of winter nights the
murky atmosphere of the Strand is as thick within the theatre as
outside of it. It is a very palpable presence at most of the London
theatres; but at the Adelphi a perpetual yellow mist, half dust,
half dampness, seems to hover above the stalls, and to stretch
itself across the stage, like a screen of dirty gauze. Was it because
we beheld it through this unflattering medium that a certain
performance of *Nicholas Nickleby*, which Mr. Andrew Halliday
had done into a drama, recently appeared to us a terribly abortive
entertainment? We are unable to say; but we remember receiving
the impression that it was vain to attempt to galvanize the drama
into life by expensive upholstery, for a public whose taste could
resist the shock of such a performance. There was a vulgar ferocity, a shabby brutality about it which were quite indefinable;
and we felt that the taste of the community that could tolerate it
really offered no soil in which the theatre might revive. If that
was possible, better things were impossible. Mr. Hermann Vezin,
Mr. Henry Neville, Miss Lydia Foote, were again in the cast,

together with Mrs. Alfred Mellon, a praiseworthy actress, who many years ago was almost brilliant, and who now, in a costume worthy of a masquerade in Bedlam, gave visible form to the savage humours of Mrs. Squeers. In spite of the valuable aid of these performers, however, there is nothing comfortable in our recollection of *Nicholas Nickleby*, unless it be the acquirement of a conviction. We mean the conviction that it is a great mistake to attempt to transform Dickens's works into dramas. The extreme oddity of his figures, which constantly endangers them for the reader, is doubled when they are presented to the eye. Dramatic effect is not missed, but overdone, and we receive an impression of something intolerably salient and violent. Add to which the simple cutting up of a novel into episodes, tacked together anyhow, is always an abomination.

Mrs. Kendal (to return to the ladies whom we have left) is a thoroughly accomplished, business-like, lady-like actress, with a great deal of intelligence, a great deal of practice, and a great deal of charm. She is not, we should say, highly imaginative, but she has always the manner of reality, and her reality is always graceful. At the St. James's she carries the weight of the whole feminine side of the house — she reigns alone; and it is a proof of the great value which in London attaches to a competent actress, once she is secured, that Mrs. Kendal does all sorts of business. Yesterday she was a young girl, of the period of white muslin and blushes; to-day she plays Mrs. Sternhold, in a revival of Tom Taylor's *Still Waters*. The former Court and the former Prince of Wales's (that is, the St. James's and the Haymarket) keep very well abreast of each other, and their rivalry is altogether friendly; but as we cited the recent revival of *Money* at the second-named of these houses as an evidence of scanty resources, so we may say that it was rather pitiful to see Mr. Hare, when he came to open his new theatre, with nothing to set out as a birthday feast but an adaptation of a stale French vaudeville of twenty or thirty years ago, entitled *Le Fils de Famille*. This performance had not even the merit of novelty, for it had been played at the Court for many weeks before Mr. Hare left this house. *The Queen's Shilling*, however, as the English version of the play is called, offered Mr. Kendal some opportunities for very good acting. He and his wife, a few weeks after the opening of the St. James's, undertook the grave responsibility of making a success of the little drama which Mr. Tennyson has lately contributed to the stage. *The Falcon* is an attempt to convert into a poetic comedy one of the most familiar and most touching of the tales of Boccaccio, a tale which a dozen poets have reproduced in narrative verse. Mr. Tennyson's verse, in this last reproduction, aspires to be dramatic; but it works in awkward conditions. The story of the poor gentleman who, to give a breakfast to the proud lady whom he secretly adores, sends his falcon — a solitary treasure — to the pot, and then learns that the purpose of the lady's visit (she is a noble widow, of the neighbourhood) had been to ask for the gift of the bird for her little boy, who is lying ill and has taken a fancy to it — this simple and affecting tale is capital reading, but it is very indifferent acting. The *dénouement* consists exclusively in the poor man's saying "My falcon? why, madam, you have had it for your break-fast!" — and before an audience with an irreverent sense of the ridiculous such a *dénouement*, in a pathetic piece, might have pro-voked a dangerous titter. The English public, however, is not ironical, nor analytic; it takes things on the whole very simply. *The Falcon* therefore was for a few weeks a moderate success — the author having taken the precaution not to bid for loud applause by any great splendour of verse. Mr. and Mrs. Kendal, on the other hand, who recited the text with a great deal of care — the former indeed with a degree of ready art remarkable in an actor who has formed his manner upon current colloquialism, and has had the fear of the artificial constantly in his eyes — Mr. and Mrs. Kendal, in their Italian dresses of the fifteenth century, were splendidly picturesque figures. The arrangement of the stage also remains in our mind as a supremely successful thing of the kind —

the cool, inclosed light of a thick-walled cabin among Italian hills, with a glimpse of a glowing summer's day outside. So you stand and look, from a window with a deep embrasure, at the country about Siena.

We have spoken of Miss Ellen Terry, of Mrs. Bancroft, of Mrs. Kendal; but we have not spoken of the most interesting actress in London. It is agreeable to be able to say that she is an American; but as she is doubtless as well known in New York as in London, we ought perhaps to do no more than briefly allude to her. Miss Geneviève Ward's appearances in London take place at considerable intervals, and she has seemingly never made it her business to obtain a regular footing here. Indeed, to the best of our knowledge, she has not, until the present year, made what is called a hit. This fact is remarkable when Miss Ward's exceptional ability is considered. She acts with a finish, an intelligence, a style, an understanding of what she is about, which are as agreeable as they are rare. We know not whether she was born under an evil star, or whether there is an insufficient demand for her peculiar qualities to produce a reputation; at any rate, the actress strikes us as having hitherto been less appreciated than she deserves. It may be hoped that now she has made a hit she will obtain her deserts; it is only a pity that her success is not bound up with a more solid opportunity. *Forget-Me-Not*, the piece in which Miss Ward has lately appeared at the Prince of Wales's under the new management (she had already brought it out, shortly before the close of the summer season at the Lyceum), is the joint production of Messrs. Herman Merivale and Crawford Grove. The play is of very slender pattern, being almost totally destitute of action, and much overburdened with talk. The worst of it is that the talk is about nothing worth while—hovering perpetually round the question of whether a low French adventuress, whom the authors have not attempted to make anything but sordid, shall or shall not quarter herself upon certain young English ladies in Rome, with whom she is connected by mysterious ties. An English gentleman, befriending his young countrywomen, undertakes to dislodge the intruder, who resists with great energy, but is finally eliminated. Of these materials Miss Ward has made herself a part. It is a very bad one, but such as it is, she plays it with uncommon brilliancy. Her natural advantages are great, and, to our perception, she comes nearer than any other actress upon the London stage to being a mistress of her art.

At the Haymarket, among the men, Mr. Arthur Cecil is easily first — first, we mean, in the sense of being most of an artist. His art is the art of pure comedy, but it never loses sight of nature; it is always delicate and fine. Few English actors, we suspect, have ever achieved such a command of laughter with an equal lightness of touch. It is true that we remember Charles Mathews. There was more of Charles Mathews than of Arthur Cecil — he was much greater in quantity; but we doubt whether he was more exquisite in quality. Mr. Arthur Cecil is young; but it is his fate to represent elderly men — though when he occasionally does one of his own contemporaries (Sam Gerridge, for instance, in *Caste*) he loses nothing of his cunning. An actor whose situation is the same, who in the vitality of youth is often condemned to depict senility, is Mr. Hare, of the St. James's. He does many things admirably, his line, however, being less humorous than Arthur Cecil's. He is less genial and less comical, but his old men, whether natural or grotesque, are always minutely studied, and brought before us with elaborate art. He should be seen in a little piece called *A Quiet Rubber* (an adaptation of *Une Partie de Piquet*), in which his Lord Kildare, an impoverished and irascible Irish nobleman, whose high temper and good-breeding are constantly at odds, is a remarkable creation. Among the actors of the younger school, the votaries of that quiet realism which brings down on the heads of those who practise it the denomination of "amateurs," John Hare certainly divides with Arthur Cecil the first place. Among the latter's companions, at the Haymarket, Mr. Bancroft and Mr. Conway must be mentioned. Mr. Bancroft has always had a specialty — that of the well-dressed, drawling, empty-headed but presumably soft-hearted heavy dragoon, or man about town, of whom a specimen is usually found in the comedies of Mr. Robertson. Mr. Bancroft represents him with a humour that is not too broad, and in which the characteristics of the gentleman are not lost sight of. But he recently gave proof that he was capable of more serious work; and his Count Orloff, in the version of Victorien Sardou's *Dora*, played at the Prince of Wales's two years ago, was a vigorous and manly piece of acting. In *Diplomacy*, indeed, several of the performers we have mentioned, with two or three others, showed to exceptional advantage. Mrs. Kendal was not so good as the heroine as we have sometimes seen her; she was too mature for the part. We have also said that Mrs. Bancroft, as the Countess Zicka, showed a good deal of mis-directed energy. But Arthur Cecil, Mr. Kendal, and Mr. Clayton were all excellent, and the critical scene of the play, the scene of the three men, which on the first production of the piece in Paris did so much to secure its success, was rendered by the two latter gentlemen and by Mr. Bancroft in a manner which left little to be desired. We may say here, in parenthesis, that the part of the mother, in *Diplomacy*, the grotesque old widow of a South American general, was weakly filled. We mention the fact as a sign that on the London stage there is a plentiful lack of accomplished old women. There is no one that seems to us half so good as that wonderful Mrs. Vernon, who for so many years was the delightful old lady of comedy at Wallack's. Mr. Clayton, of whom we just spoke, deserves a paragraph to himself — though he has lately, if we are not mistaken, been playing in New York, and taking care himself of his credit. He is one of the best representatives of what may be called the man of the world in the contemporary drama. He has an agreeable combination of polish and robustness, and he cultivates ease without that tendency to underact which is the pitfall of the new generation. He made a great hit some five or six years ago in the *All for Her*, of Messrs. Herman Merivale

and Palgrave Simpson, a drama suggested by Charles Dickens's
Tale of Two Cities. We remember thinking his acting picturesque,
but the piece infelicitous. At the time we write, he is playing
Sir Horace Welby, the gentleman who fights a duel with Miss
Geneviève Ward in *Forget-Me-Not.* The part is a painfully weak
one, but Mr. Clayton acts it in a manner which shows that he is
capable of much more brilliant things. Mr. Conway, whose name
we set down above, is at present an ornament of the Haymarket,
where he plays the young lovers. We say an ornament advisedly;
for Mr. Conway's first claim to distinction is his remarkably good
looks, which may be admired, along with those of the other professional beauties, at half the photograph shops in London. Mr.
Conway follows the same line as that elegant young actor, the
late Mr. Montague, who was for several years, at Wallack's, the
admiration of New York. He acts with care and intention; but
the spectator can hardly rid himself of the feeling that the cut of
his garments bears an unduly large part in his success. He has been
playing Alfred Evelyn in the revival of *Money*, of which we have
already spoken, and he throws a great deal of effort and animation
into the part. But he is overweighted by it, flimsy as it is, and he
labours under the disadvantage of a harsh and inflexible voice.
We remember seeing Mr. Charles Coghlan play Alfred Evelyn,
upward of five years since, when the play was brought out at the
Prince of Wales's. He did it better, for Mr. Coghlan is a serious
and interesting actor. Mr. Coghlan is *par excellence* a votary of
quiet realism; the only criticism we shall make of him is that he
sometimes confounds the real with the quiet. He has lately been
playing in an English arrangement of an American piece — *The
Banker's Daughter. The Old Love and the New*, as it is renamed,
was brought out by the new management of the Court, with every
appearance of success. There is something so truthful, touching
and manly in Mr. Coghlan's acting that it is a satisfaction to see
him; but he should remember that good acting consists in doing,
not the real thing, but the thing which from the scenic point of

view *appears* the real thing—a very different affair. This would be
a guarantee against his turning his back too much to the audience
and delivering too many of his speeches into corners and cup-
boards. We cannot speak of *The Old Love and the New* without a
word of applause for a very clever actor, Mr. Anson, who plays
the part of a New York commercial traveller with remarkable
comic force. The wonder of it is that the actor is not, as we at
first supposed, an American. His rendering of the part is a real
study in linguistics. The intonation, the accent of his model, are
reproduced with a verity and a sobriety together which do great
honour to Mr. Anson's powers of observation. He has caught the
vulgar side of his dealer in "samples" so well that for the actor's
sake we could not wish the former less vulgar. We have reached
our limits, and we have left a great many things unsaid and a great
many names unnoted. We have pretended only to mention the
actors of the moment; we have no space even for immediate re-
trospect. We have omitted, for instance, to say anything of Mr.
Toole, who has at present a small theatre of his own, an establishment of frivolous traditions, known as the "Folly." Mr. Toole
is a rich and elaborate comedian, whom we remember seeing and
enjoying in all his parts when he visited the United States some
years ago; but in London, we must confess, he does not interest
us so much as he did in America. This is partly, we suspect,
because much of the quality that we enjoyed in him, the savour of
the soil, the cockney humour, was generic, as we may say, and
not individual. In London this quality is in the air; every one, in
certain classes, has a little of it; so that it becomes commonplace
and ceases to be picturesque. Moreover Mr. Toole sometimes
nods, and when he does, it is portentous. No less an adjective than
this will express the lugubrious quality of his unsuccessful attempt
to produce a great comic effect in Mr. Byron's dreary little drama
entitled *A Fool and His Money*. The source of laughter, for the
spectator of this misguided effort of actor and author alike, converts itself into a fountain of tears,—tears of humility for our

common liability to err. Though we have not said it hitherto, we must here say a good word for Mr. Charles Warner, who for unnumbered months distinguished himself as the Anglicized hero of the dramatization of Emile Zola's *Assommoir*, which Mr. Charles Reade did into English (under the name of *Drink*) for the Princess's. Mr. Warner's Coupeau is one of the best pieces of acting seen in London for many a day; it revealed, as the French say, the actor, who, though he had played much, had never played half so well. His Coupeau was an inspiration. We know not whether Mr. Edward Terry, who is the comic gentleman at the Gaiety, ever has inspirations, but it would be a happy one for him that should lead him to escape from the baleful circle of the punning farces and burlesques of Messrs. Byron and Burnand. He is one of the most amusing actors in London, and strikes us as having a comic vein that might be worked much more profitably than we see it worked in *Little Doctor Faust* and *Robbing Roy*. The same may be said of his comrade, Miss Nelly Farren, whom we ought to have included in our group of noticeable actresses. Many knowing critics in London will tell you that Miss Farren is a great actress, and that if she only had a chance her genius would kindle a blaze. This may be; but meanwhile the chance is wanting. We have seen Miss Farren in two or three parts in which she gave a glimpse of original comic power; but these bright moments were swallowed up in the inanities and vulgarities of the comic drama, as practised by the indefatigable punsters we have mentioned. Both she and Mr. Terry appear to be sacrificed to that infantile conception of dramatic entertainment which is the only contribution of the English imagination of the day to the literature of the theatre.

POSTSCRIPT. LONDON, NOVEMBER, 1880.

Since the foregoing pages were written, nothing has occurred to falsify the various judgements they contain. Very little, indeed, has occurred in any way — the months of August, September, and

October being usually a period of theatrical repose and sterility. At the present writing, however, most of the play-houses are open, and the winter season may be said to have begun. The writer may add that if he was warranted a few months since in deploring the destitution of the English stage, — its want of plays, of authors, of resources, — he is to-day even more justified by the facts. Mr. Irving, desiring to open his winter brilliantly at the Lyceum, can invent nothing better than a revival of that hackneyed and preposterous drama, *The Corsican Brothers* — a piece of which the principal feature is a gentleman of supernatural antecedents, in a blood-stained shirt, moving obliquely along a groove in the stage, under a shower of electric light. *The Corsican Brothers* is brilliantly mounted, with that perfection of detail, that science of the picturesque, which, in default of more pertinent triumphs, is the great achievement of the contemporary stage. It contains a little of everything except acting. Mr. Irving's proceedings in the first act of this drama, and especially the manner in which he delivers himself of the long explanatory narrative put into the mouth of the hero, are of a nature to cause a fiendish satisfaction on the part of such critics as may hitherto have ventured to judge him severely. An incident which points in exactly the same direction as this extremely successful, but none the less significant, enterprise at the Lyceum is the production (unattended in this case with great success) of *William and Susan* at the St. James's. *William and Susan* is an arrangement of *Black-eyed Susan*. Douglas Jerrold's first two acts have been rewritten and provided with scenery as trim and tidy as a Dutch picture — Mr. Wills being the author charged with the delicate task of pouring the old wine into new bottles. Mr. Wills has made a flat and monotonous little play, into which even the singularly charming and touching acting of Mrs. Kendal has failed to infuse the vital spark. Mrs. Kendal is natural and delightful; she has the art of representing goodness and yet redeeming it from insipidity. Mr. Kendal, who plays the high-toned and unfortunate tar, is a graceful and gentlemanly actor, but he is not another T. P. Cooke. He has not the breadth and body the part requires. The play, as it now stands, is of about the intellectual substance of a nursery-rhyme. The *mise en scène* is as usual delightful.

By far the most agreeable theatrical event that has lately taken place in London is the highly successful appearance of Madame Modjeska, who is so well known and generally appreciated in America. This charming and touching actress has hitherto appeared but in two parts; but in these parts she has given evidence of a remarkably delicate and cultivated talent. There are actresses in London whose proceedings upon the stage are absolute horse-play by the side of the quiet felicities of Madame Modjeska. A dismal translation of *La Dame aux Camélias* (in which the situation of the heroine is enveloped in the most bewildering and mystifying pruderies of allusion) permitted Madame Modjeska to achieve a success which was not assisted by any element of the real or the reasonable in the character represented. But she has lately been playing a business-like version of Schiller's *Mary Stuart*, and in this case has shown herself able to handle with brilliancy a part of greater solidity. She is a very exquisite and pathetic Queen of Scots. Madame Modjeska is the attraction of the hour; but it only points the moral of these desultory remarks that the principal ornament of the English stage just now should be a Polish actress performing in a German play.

"The London Theatres" appeared, unsigned, and with many illustrations, in Scribner's Monthly, *January, 1881.*

The discovery of this extensive essay was made by Leon Edel who identified it from a reference to "my theatrical article in January Scribner's" *in an unpublished letter of 1880. It may be noted that all the productions to which James refers in the main body of his article were made either late in 1879 or in the earlier part of 1880. It was therefore probably written at about the middle of 1880 and Mr. Edel suggests that publication was delayed to await the illustrations; this no doubt made it possible for Henry James to add his postscript, dated November.*

This essay is of much importance for students of the English theatre in the nineteenth century, surveying, as it does, a period which has been almost entirely neglected by reprinted criticism. With the paper that followed it two years later it helps to bridge the gap between Joseph Knight's Theatrical Notes *(1893), in which the chronicle stops short at the end of 1879, and A. B. Walkley's* Playhouse Impressions *(1892), which touches nothing earlier than 1889.*

LONDON PLAYS

I F ALL art is supposed to be one, and if its different manifes-
tations, to the truly penetrating eye, are supposed to minister
a mutual light, there should be no great violence of transition in
passing from the exhibitions to the theatres. The British stage
has indeed a considerable analogy to British painting, and the
reflections which present themselves at the Lyceum and the Haymarket are not very different from those which illuminate the
devious path of the visitor to Burlington House and the eccentric
temple in Bond Street [the Grosvenor Gallery]. Both at the
play-houses and at the exhibition he encounters a good deal of
Philistinism. On the other hand, both the art of the painter and
that of the actor are said to be improving, and if the training-
school for young actors, for which an appeal has just been made to
the English public by a group of more or less distinguished *dilett-
anti*, becomes a working institution, the dramatic profession may
spread its wings indeed. It is proposed to establish a dramatic
conservatory, modelled upon that of the Conservatoire in Paris,
at which the young ladies and gentlemen who aspire to brave the
footlights may acquire what may be roughly termed a little ease
of manner. The more ease the better; for English acting is for the
most part distinguished by a consummate want of study. There is
good material—though not so good, I think, as we sometimes
hear affirmed; but it remains undeveloped and ineffective,—it
doesn't see its way. It will take more, however, than even the
hottest histrionic forcing-house to make an English school of

actors which shall rival the French; it will take a transformation of English life, of the English temperament, of the English tongue. That a place of serious study for young persons proposing to adopt this very difficult profession is much to be desired, I shall, however, not pretend to deny. Such an institution would perhaps be even less valuable for what it might produce than for what it might prevent. There is an immense deal to prevent on the English stage. Would a training-school have, for instance, prevented Mr. Henry Irving, who has for some time past been offering us such a Romeo as we never dreamed of? A training-school, assiduously frequented by Mr. Irving in his youth, would not, perhaps, have suppressed him altogether, but it would have suppressed some of his extraordinary peculiarities. That these peculiarities should have blossomed and flowered at such a prodigious rate — a most rank and bristling vegetation — is the best possible proof of the absence of taste, of criticism, of knowledge, of a standard, on the part of the public. More extraordinary even than Mr. Irving's eccentricities is the fact that they have not interfered with his success. The part, of all the parts he has played, in which it might have been thought they would be most destructive is this exquisite part of the graceful and passionate Romeo; but, as it happens, the play has thriven mightily, and though people are sadly bewildered by what they see and hear in it, they appear to recommend the performance to their friends. It has the advantage of that splendid scenic presentation which Mr. Irving understands so well, and which converts the play from a splendid and delicate poem into a gorgeous and over-weighted spectacle. Mr. Irving does these things very handsomely; he is a most liberal and intelligent manager. It may, indeed, not be thought a proof of his intelligence that he himself should play the hero, or that he should entrust the girlish Juliet to the large, the long, the mature Miss Terry. Miss Terry has great charm; she is what the French call, in artistic parlance, a "nature"; she is almost always interesting, and she is often a delightful presence: but she is not Juliet; on the contrary! She is too voluminous, too deliberate, too prosaic, too English, too unversed in the utterance of poetry. How little Mr. Irving is Romeo it is not worth while even to attempt to declare; he must know it, of course, better than anyone else, and there is something really touching in so extreme a sacrifice of one's ideal. It remains to be ascertained why he should have wished to bring out the play. Mr. Irving is not a Romeo; Miss Terry is not a Juliet; and no one else, save Mrs. Stirling, is anything in particular. Was it for Mrs. Stirling, then, that this elaborate undertaking was set on foot? She plays the Nurse, and plays it very well—too well, almost, since it is pushed forward, out of its relations to the total. Mrs. Stirling, to-day a very old woman, is a rich and accomplished actress; she belongs to a more sincere generation; she knows her art, and it is from her rendering of the garrulous, humorous, immoral attendant of the gentle Juliet that the spectator receives his one impression of the appropriate and the adequate. It was probably for the spectacle that Mr. Irving took the play in hand, and the spectacle has richly rewarded him. It is the last word of stage-carpentering, and is full of beautiful effects of colour and costume. The stage is crowded with figures; there are at moments too many; the play moves slowly through a succession of glowing and deceptive pictures. The fault of all this splendour of detail is that, in the homely phrase, it puts the cart before the horse. The play is not acted, it is costumed; the immortal lovers of Verona become subordinate and ineffectual figures. I had never thought of *Romeo and Juliet* as a dull drama; but Mr. Irving has succeeded in making it so. It is obstructed, interrupted; its passionate rapidity is chopped up into little tableaus. In a word, it is slow,—mortally slow; for much of the dialogue is incomprehensibly spoken, and the rest ineffectively. To make this enchanting poem tame,—it was reserved for the present management of the Lyceum to accomplish that miracle. The danger, however, is common,—the danger of smothering a piece in its accessories; and the accident occurs at most of the London theatres. The reason is doubtless that the art of putting a piece on the stage, as it is called (as if the only way to put a piece on the stage were not to act it), has lately made an advance in England which is out of proportion to any improvement that has taken place in the dramatic art proper. Scenery and decorations have been brought to their highest perfection, while elocution and action, the interpretation of meanings, the representation of human feelings, have not been made the objects of serious study. There is plenty of talent in the London theatres, but it wants cultivation and direction. Of course, when Shakespeare is sacrificed to the machinist and the gas-man, the case is at the worst; the sacrifice of M. Sardou is a less tragic event. He is, however, mildly immolated every evening at the Haymarket, with Mrs. Bancroft and Madame Modjeska as high-priestesses of the altar. His ingenious comedy of *Odette* (which is by no means the triumph of his ingenuity) is represented at that theatre with every refinement of *mise en scène*. In its way it is as fine as the *Romeo and Juliet* of the Lyceum, — though of course it matters less that it should be so superfluously pictorial. It consists of a series of interiors, each of which is more elegant, as the play-bill would say, than the others. The acting is another affair, but the acting is very good. Madame Modjeska plays the erring but repentant wife (as the play-bill again would say); and if there were nothing else that was satisfactory in her performance it would be a satisfaction to see a "star" reduced to the level of an ordinary luminary, taking a regular place in a good stock company, and content to forego the use of staring capitals in the play-bill. But Madame Modjeska plays with a great deal of art; with grace, with force, with intelligence, with a certain personal distinction. The piece has been arranged for English life, but the heroine continues to be a Frenchwoman; a fact which eases off, for the actress charged with the part, the question of pronunciations. Madame Modjeska, moreover, has made progress with her English. There are few actresses more delightful than Mrs. Bancroft, when she appears in a part that exactly suits her, and such a part has been arranged for her in this somewhat heterogeneous *Odette*,—a brief, incidental part, of which, however, she has seized all the opportunities, opportunities for rich yet natural comedy. The comic power of Mrs. Bancroft is remarkable; it flows with abundance and freedom; you never hear the creaking of the pump. The whole piece is acted with an amount of care and finish which it would be ungracious not to acknowledge, and which certainly indicates a rise of the level of theatrical criticism. It is not the finish of the best French acting, but it is very well for a theatre operating in English conditions. If I were asked to specify the best piece of comedy in the play, I should say it was the manner in which a young actor, of high promise and of a peculiar and original talent, Mr. Charles Brookfield, representing the major-domo of a private gaming-house at Nice, acquits himself of the single scene of which his part consists. The man is a scoundrel, a charlatan, a Frenchman, a jackanapes, and various other things besides, and the art with which these elements are interfused and expressed is so remarkable as to convert Mr. Brookfield's purely episodic opportunity into a brilliant triumph. His acting is more than clever, it is imaginative; more than humorous, it is creative. The best thing in it—and the rarest thing—is the vividness with which he has perceived the figure which he wishes to represent. In short, it is a real portrait, and Mr. Brookfield, who has made a great hit, will be watched with interest in future. What I have said of *Romeo and Juliet* and of *Odette* is less true of *The Squire*, at the St. James's, by the distance that divides Mr. Pinero, the author of this successful but not original dramatic effort, not only from Shakespeare, but from Sardou. *Odette* is by no means the best Sardou; if the author of the most successful pieces of our time had produced nothing but this drama he would not be known to fame. But the play hangs neatly together, thanks simply to French scenic traditions—to the French habit of making things stick. *The Squire* doesn't stand very straight, but it is beautifully mounted and very carefully played. The author appears to have borrowed it from Mr. Thomas Hardy's novel of *Far from the Madding Crowd*,—though its origin was, I believe, very sharply contested when the piece was produced, and is at present involved in impenetrable mystery. The pictures are charming, Mrs. Kendal's acting is interesting, and the rest as good as there is occasion for. On the whole, like the exhibitions, the London theatres are improving.

"London Plays" formed the second part of an essay "London Pictures and London Plays," which appeared, un-signed, in the Atlantic Monthly, *August, 1882.*

The winter months of 1881 Henry James spent in Boston and New York, and in the Spring of 1882 he visited Washington. In February, 1882, his mother died suddenly, and for some time he was disinclined to work. But his father wished him to take up his life again in London and he returned to England in May. The plays he here chronicles had all been staged during his absence, and since he probably did not find in the current productions enough matter for an article wholly devoted to the theatre, he accordingly combined his observations on pictorial art and drama in a single essay.

TOMMASO SALVINI

i. *In Boston* (1883)

IT HAS often been said that the great actors who flourished in
the times preceding our own gave a more striking proof of
genius than their successors are called upon to give. They produced their famous effects without aids to illusion. They had no
help from scenery and costume; the background was nothing;
they alone were the scene. Garrick and Mrs. Siddons, wandering
over England, and interpreting Shakespeare as they went, represented the visions of Hamlet and the sorrows of Constance with
the assistance of a few yards of tinsel and a few dozen tallow
candles. The stage was dim and bare, but the great artists triumphed, so that the tradition of their influence over their auditors
has been sacredly preserved. For the most part, to-day we have
changed all that. There is to be seen in London at the present
moment a representation of one of Shakespeare's comedies which
is the last word of picture-making on the stage. It is a series of
exquisite pictorial compositions, in which nothing that can delight
the eye or touch the imagination has been omitted—nothing,
that is, save the art of the actor. This part of the business has not
been thought indispensable, and the performance is a great success, in spite of the fact that a fastidious spectator, here and there,
feels vaguely that he misses something. What he misses is what
Garrick and Mrs. Siddons had it in their power to give; what he

enjoys is a wealth of scenic resource of which they never dreamed. It is unreasonable to expect to have everything, and we must doubtless take our choice. I mention the case of the comedy in London, which fairly glows to the eye, like a picture by a great colourist, because, besides being a topic of the moment, it is probably the most perfect example the English stage has seen of the value of costume and carpentry. We have lately been having in Boston an illustration equally perfect of success achieved, in the old-fashioned manner, by personal art as distinguished from me-chanical. The famous Italian actor, Tommaso Salvini, giving us an opportunity to admire him in far too small a number of per-formances, has played to us under conditions very similar to those with which the actors of the last century had to struggle. There are differences, of course, — as in the Globe Theatre being an exceedingly comfortable house for the spectator, and in the stage being illuminated by gas rather than by tallow. Apart from this, it is difficult to imagine an actor surrounded with fewer of those advantages which I have called aids to illusion. Salvini's triumph — a very great triumph — is therefore, like that of Garrick and Mrs. Siddons, a proof of extraordinary power. He had no scenery, and he had no "support;" in this latter respect we feel sure that Garrick and Mrs. Siddons were very much better off. His fellow-actors were of a quality which it is a charity not to specify; un-mitigated dreariness was the stamp of the whole episode, save in so far as that episode was summed up in the personality of the hero. Signor Salvini naturally played in Italian, while his comrades answered him in a language which was foreign only in that it sometimes failed to be English. It was in this manner that *Mac-beth*, *Othello*, *King Lear*, were given. Signor Salvini uttered the translated text, and the rest of the company recited the original. This extraordinary system, which has been in operation in various parts of the country for many months past, has only to be described to be characterized; it has all the barbarism of an over-civilized age. It is grotesque, unpardonable, abominable. It is the condemnation of a public that tolerates it. If I were capable of saying anything unkind about the admirable Salvini, I should say it was also the condemnation of an actor who could lend himself to it. But of course he is well aware of his offence, and he is equally well aware that, unpardonable as it is, he induces us to pardon it. He has discovered that, rather than not have Salvini at all, the American public will take him as he offers himself, or as his impresario sees fit to offer him, — with a mixture of tongues, with a melancholy company, with pitiful scenery. The American public is either very superficial or very deep; in the presence of the large houses to which Salvini played, it was possible to be at once exhilarated and depressed. It was to the honour of the people of Boston that they should come in such numbers to see a great actor deliver himself in a language which conveyed no meaning to the great majority of them, — should come because they had the wit to perceive his greatness through the veil of his alien speech. It was not to their honour, on the other hand, that they should gaze without a murmur at the rest of the spectacle, and condone so profusely the aberrations of his playmates. Their attitude involved a contradiction, and it was difficult to get to the bottom of it. I frankly confess I have not done so yet! That people who have a taste for Salvini should not have a distaste — I mean an effective and operative distaste — for his accessories is a proof, as I just now hinted, either of density or of self-control. Were they culpably good-natured, or were they nobly magnanimous? Two things, at any rate, are certain. One is that the way in which the theatrical enterprise is conducted leaves much to be desired; the other is, there is that about Tommaso Salvini which excites the geniality, the tenderness, I may almost say the devotion, of the spectator. I am free to declare that, if he were to appear with a company of Hottentots, I should regret that a happier arrangement might not have been made, but I should go every night to see him.

This is as much as to say that Salvini is a charmer; he has the art of inspiring sympathy. Not the least of the drawbacks of the manner in which he appears is the consequent reduction of his repertory to five or six parts. To teach Italian cues to American actors is a work of time and difficulty; to learn American cues may be assumed to be, for an Italian, no more attractive a task. We see Salvini, therefore, in only half his range; we take the measure of only a part of him, though it possibly is the better part. The auditor who once has felt the deep interest of his acting desires ardently to know the whole artist. He is essentially a large, rich, abundant genius, capable of sounding a wide variety of notes. However, we are thankful for what is offered us, — thankful for *Macbeth*, thankful for *King Lear*, thankful for *La Morte Civile*, thankful above all for *Othello*. We scan the horizon in vain; no other artist to-day begins to be capable of giving us such an exhibition of tragic power. Othello headed the short list of his performances, and there is an artistic propriety in his playing Othello first. It is a sort of compendium of his accomplishments; he puts everything into it, and the part, as he plays it, has so full a volume that it may almost be said that it embraces all the others. There are touches in Salvini's Macbeth, touches in his Lear, very naturally, that are absent from his picture of the over-wrought Moor; but it carries him to his maximum, and what he puts into it above all is an inexhaustible energy. There are twenty things to be said about it, and half a dozen criticisms which it is impossible that we spectators of English speech should not make. But the depth, the nobleness, the consistency, the passion, the visible, audible beauty of it, are beyond praise. Nature has done great things for the actor; with the aid of a little red paint, the perfect Othello is there. But I assume too much in talking off-hand about the "perfect Othello," who is after all a very complex being, in spite of his simplicity. It may seem to many observers that Salvini's rendering of the part is too simple, too much on two or three notes, — frank tenderness, quick suspicion, passionate rage. Infinite are the variations of human opinion; I have heard this performance called ugly, repulsive, bestial. Waiving these considerations for a moment, what an immense impression—simply as an impression—the actor makes on the spectator who sees him for the first time as the turbaned and deep-voiced Moor! He gives us his measure as a man; he acquaints us with that luxury of perfect confidence in the physical resources of the actor which is not the most frequent satisfaction of the modern play-goer. His powerful, active, manly frame, his noble, serious, vividly expressive face, his splendid smile, his Italian eye, his superb, voluminous voice, his carriage, his tone, his ease, the assurance he instantly gives that he holds the whole part in his hands and can make of it exactly what he chooses,—all this descends upon the spectator's mind with a richness which immediately converts attention into faith, and expectation into sympathy. He is a magnificent creature, and you are already on his side. His generous temperament is contagious; you find yourself looking at him, not so much as an actor, but as a hero. As I have already said, it is a luxury to sit and watch a man to whom an expenditure of force is so easy. Salvini's perfect ease is a part of the spell he exercises. The straining, the creaking, the overdoing, the revelation of the inadequacy of the machinery, which we have been condemned to associate with so much of the interpretation of the dramatic gems of our literature,—there is no place for all this in Salvini's complete organization and consummate manner. We see him to-day perforce at the latter end of his career, after years of experience and practice have made him as supple as he is strong, and yet before his strength has begun to feel the chill of age. It is a very fine moment for a great artistic nature. The admirable thing in this nature of Salvini's is that his intelligence is equal to his material powers; so that if the exhibition is, as it were, personal, it is not simply physical. He has a great imagination; there is a noble intention in all he does. It is no more than natural, surely, that his imagination, his intentions, should be of the Italian stamp, and this is at the bottom of his failure to satisfy some of us spectators of English speech, — a failure that is most marked when he plays Shakespeare. Of course we have our own feelings about Shakespeare, our own manner of reading him. We read him in the light of our Anglo-Saxon temperament, and in doing so it is open to us to believe that we read him in the deepest way. Salvini reads him with an Italian imagination, and it is equally natural to us to believe that in doing so he misses a large part of him. It is indeed beyond contradiction that he does miss a large part of him, — does so as a necessary consequence of using a text which shuts the door on half the meaning. We adore the exorbitant original; we have sacred associations with all the finest passages. The loose, vague language of the Italian translation seems to us a perpetual sacrifice to the conventional: we find *ottima creatura*, for instance, a very colourless translation of "excellent wretch." But in the finest English rendering of Shakespeare that we can conceive, or are likely to enjoy, there would be gaps and elisions enough, and Salvini's noble execution preserves much more than it misses. Of course it simplifies, but any acting of Shakespeare is a simplification. To be played at all, he must be played, as it were, superficially.

Salvini's Othello is not more superficial than the law of self-preservation (on the actor's part) demands; there is, on the contrary, a tremendous depth of feeling in it, and the execution is brilliant — with the dusky brilliancy that is in the tone of the part — at every point. No more complete picture of passion can have been given to the stage in our day, — passion beginning in noble repose and spending itself in black insanity. Certain exquisite things are absent from it, — the gradations and transitions which Shakespeare has marked in a hundred places, the manly melancholy, the note of deep reflection, which is sounded as well as the note of passion. The pathos is perhaps a little crude; there is in all Shakespeare's sentiment a metaphysical side, which is hard to indicate and easy to miss. Salvini's rendering of the part is the portrait of an African by an Italian; a fact which should give the judicious spectator, in advance, the pitch of the performance. There is a class of persons to whom Italians and Africans have almost equally little to say, and such persons must have been sadly out of their account in going to see Salvini. I have done with strictures, and must only pay a hasty tribute to his splendour of execution. If those critics who dislike the Othello find it coarse (some people, apparently, are much surprised to discover that the representation of this tragedy is painful), there is at least not a weak spot in it from beginning to end. It has from the first the quality that thrills and excites, and this quality deepens with great strides to the magnificent climax. The last two acts constitute the finest piece of tragic acting that I know. I do not say it is the finest I can imagine, simply because a great English Othello would touch us more nearly still. But I have never seen a great English Othello, any more, unfortunately, than I have ever seen a great English Macbeth. It is impossible to give an idea of the way in which Salvini gathers force as he goes, or of the superior use he makes of this force in the critical scenes of the play. Some of his tones, movements, attitudes, are ineffaceable; they have passed into the stock of common reference. I mean his tiger-like pacing at the back of the room, when, having brought Desdemona out of her bed, and put the width of the apartment between them, he strides to and fro, with his eyes fixed on her and filled with the light of her approaching doom. Then the still more tiger-like spring with which, after turning, flooded and frenzied by the truth, from the lifeless body of his victim, he traverses the chamber to reach Iago, with the mad impulse of destruction gathered into a single blow. He has sighted him, with the intentness of fate, for a terrible moment, while he is still on one knee beside Desdemona; and the manner in which the spectator sees him — or rather feels him — rise to his avenging leap is a sensation that takes its place among the most poignant the actor's art has ever given us. After this frantic dash, the one thing Othello can *do*, to relieve himself (the one thing, that is, save the last of all), he falls into a chair on the left of the stage, and lies there for some moments, prostrate, panting, helpless, annihilated, convulsed with long, inarticulate moans. Nothing could be finer than all this; the despair, the passion, the bewildered tumult of it, reach the high-water mark of dramatic expression. My remarks may suggest that Salvini's rage is too gross, too much that of a wounded animal; but in reality it does not fall into that excess. It is the rage of an African, but of a nature that remains generous to the end; and in spite of the tiger-paces and tiger-springs, there is through it all, to my sense at least, the tremor of a moral element. In the Othello, remarkable in so many respects, of Salvini's distinguished countryman, Ernesto Rossi, there is (as I remember it) a kind of bestial fury, which does much to sicken the English reader of the play. Rossi gloats in his tenderness and bellows in his pain. Salvini, though the simplicity, credulity, and impulsiveness of his personage are constantly before him, takes a higher line altogether; the personage is intensely human.

The reader who has seen him in *La Morte Civile* will have no difficulty in believing this. The part of Corrado, in that play, is an elaborate representation of a character that is human almost to a fault. Before speaking of this extraordinary creation in detail, however, I must give proper honour to Salvini's Macbeth, the second part in which he appeared in Boston. This is a very rich and grave piece of acting; like the Othello it is interesting at every step. Salvini offers us a Macbeth whom we deeply pity, and whose delusions and crimes we understand, and almost forgive. Simple, demonstrative, easily tempted; pushed and bitten by the keener nature of his wife; dismayed, overwhelmed, assailed by visions, yet willing to plunge deeper into crime, and ready after all to fight and die like a soldier, if that will do any good, his picture of the character preserves a kind of gallantry in the midst of its darkness of colour.

This Macbeth is sombre enough, of course, but he is wonderfully frank and transparent; he gives us a strange sense of being honest through it all. Macbeth, like Othello, but unlike Lear, to my mind, is an eminently actable character; the part is packed with opportunities. Salvini finds the first of these in the physical make-up of the figure; presenting us with a fair-coloured, sturdy, rather heavy, and eminently Northern warrior, with long light hair, a tawny beard, and an eye that looks distractedly blue, as it stares at the witches, at the visionary dagger, at the spectre of Banquo. In the matter of dress I venture to remark that our actor is not always completely felicitous; something is occasionally wanting to the artistic effect of his costume; he is liable to wear garments that are a little dull, a little conventional. I cannot help regretting, too, that in four out of the five parts he played in Boston he should have happened to be so profusely bearded. His face is so mobile, so living, that it is a pity to lose so much of it. These, however, are small drawbacks, for, after all, his vigorous person is in itself a picture. His Macbeth deserves the great praise of being temperate and discreet; much of it is very quiet; it has a deal of variety; it is never incoherent, or merely violent, as we have known Macbeths to be; and there is not a touch of rant in it, from the first word to the last. It changes, from scene to scene; it is really, broadly rendered, the history of a human soul. I will not declare that with the scene of the murder of Duncan, which would be in its opportunities the great scene of the play if the scene at the banquet were not as great, I was absolutely satisfied. I thought that a certain completeness of horror was absent, that the thing was not as heart-shaking as it might have been. When the late Charles Kean—an actor to whom, on so many grounds, it is almost a cruelty to allude if one is speaking of Salvini— staggered out of the castle, with the daggers in his hands, blanched and almost dumb, already conscious, in the vision of his fixed eyes, of the far fruits of his deed, he brought with him a kind of hush of terror, which has lingered in my mind for many years as a great tragic effect. It is true that that was many years ago, and that if I were to have seen Charles Kean to-day I might

possibly be ashamed to mention him in this company. In the scene
in question, prodigious as it is, however acted, everything hangs
together; the lightest detail has much to do with the whole. We
are usually condemned to see it with a weak Lady Macbeth, and
we always feel—we felt the other night—that the effect would
be doubled if the Thane of Cawdor should have a coadjutor of his
own quality. Perhaps, therefore, it was the short-comings of the
actress alone that made us feel we had lost something; perhaps it
was the fact that the knocking at the gate was by no means what
it should be. That knocking is of great importance,—that knocking is almost everything; this is what I mean by saying that
everything in the scene hangs together. Signor Salvini should
have read De Quincey's essay before he arranged those three or
four vague, muffled, impersonal thumps, behind the back scene.
Those thumps would never have frightened Macbeth; there is
nothing heart-shaking in those thumps. They should have rung
out louder, have filled the whole silence of the night, have smitten
the ear like the voice of doom; for the more they break into the
scene, the more they add to the tension of the nerves of the
guilty couple, to say nothing of the agitation of the spectators.
This, however, is more than I meant to say. In the rest of the
play Salvini is admirable at a hundred points; admirable in
sincerity, in profundity, in imaginative power; and in the scene
of the banquet he is magnificent. The banquet was grotesque—
so grotesque as to bring out the full force of the analogy I have
suggested between our great Italian and his handful of lean
strollers and those celebrated players who flourished before the
introduction of modern improvements; but the actor rose to a
great height. He keeps this height to the end. The last part of
the play is the wonderful picture that we all know, of the blind
effort of a man who once was strong to resist his doom and contradict his stars, and Salvini rides the situation like a master. His
Macbeth is less brilliant, less prodigious than his Othello, and it is
not so peculiarly and exhaustively successful as his portrait, in

La Morte Civile, of the escaped convict who finds himself without social, almost without human, identity. But it comes third, I am inclined to think, in the list of his triumphs, and it does him, at any rate, the greatest honour.

I place Macbeth third on the list, in spite of the fact that the principal event in Signor Salvini's short visit to Boston was his appearance for the first time as King Lear. He achieved an immense success, and his rendering of the most arduous and formidable of Shakespearean parts was as powerful, as interesting, as might have been expected. It is a most elaborate composition, studied with extreme care, finished without injury to its breadth and massiveness, and abounding in impressive and characteristic features. It is both terrible and touching; it has remarkable beauty. But for all that, I do not put it before the Macbeth. I should make haste to add that I saw the representation of Lear but once, and that on a single occasion one can do but scant justice to a piece of acting so long, so rich, and, I may add, so fatiguing to the attention. One can do very little toward taking possession of it; one can only get a general impression. My own impression, on this occasion, was more than ever that *King Lear* is not a play to be acted, and that even talent so great as Salvini's, employed in making it real to us, gives us much of the pain that attends misdirected effort. *Lear* is a great and terrible poem, — the most sublime, possibly, of all dramatic poems; but it is not, to my conception, a play, in the sense in which a play is a production that gains from being presented to our senses. Our senses can only be afflicted and overwhelmed by the immeasurable complexities of *Lear*. If this conviction is present to us as we read the drama, how much more vivid does it become in the presence of an attempt to act it! Such an attempt leaves the vastness of the work almost untouched. At the risk of being accused of shameless blasphemy, I will go so far as to say that in representation the play is tremendously heavy. I say this with a perfect consciousness that the principal part gives extraordinary opportunities to a great actor.

Almost all great tragic actors have attempted it, and almost all have won honour from it, — as Salvini did, the other evening, when a theatre crowded from floor to dome recalled him again and again. The part, with all its grandeur, is monotonous; the changes are constantly rung on the same situation; and something very like a climax is reached early in the play. Regan, Goneril, Edgar, the Fool, are impossible in the flesh. Who has ever seen them attempted without thinking it an unwarrantable violence? When all this has been said, Salvini's Lear is, like everything he does, magnificent. We miss the text at times almost to distraction; for the text of *Lear* is one of the most precious possessions of our language, and the Italian version is a sadly pale reflection of it. Allowing for this, and for the way that the play resists the transmutation of the footlights, it has elements which will probably give it a foremost place henceforth in the great actor's repertory. The tenderness, the temper, the senility, the heart-broken misery, the lambent madness, the awful desolation of the king, — he touches all these things as a man of genius alone can touch them. He has great qualifications for the part, for he has reached the age at which an actor may lawfully approach it, and his extraordinary bodily and vocal powers give definite assurance of sustaining him. I have no space to dwell on particular points, but I may mention his delivery of the curse that the infuriated king launches on the head of Goneril, at the end of the first act, — "Hear Nature, hear! dear goddess, hear!" In this there was really a touch of the sublime, and the wild mixture of familiarity and solemnity that he throws into the "Ascolta — ascolta!" with which, in the Italian translation, the terrible invocation begins, was an invention quite in his grandest manner. The third and fourth acts are full of exquisite strokes; the manner, for instance, in which he replies to Gloster's inquiry, "Is't not the King?" is a wonderfully bold piece of business. He stares for a moment, — his wits have wandered so far, — while he takes in the meaning of the question; then, as the pang of recollection comes over him, he rushes to a neighbouring tree, tears off a great twig, grasps it as a sceptre, and, erecting himself for a moment in an attitude intended to be royal, launches his majestic answer: "Ay, every inch a king!" I do not say that this touch will commend itself to every taste. Many people will find it too ingenious, and feel that the noble simplicity of the words is swallowed up in the elaboration of the act. But it produces a great effect. All this part of the play is a wonderful representation of madness in old age, — the madness that is mixed with reason and memory, and only add a deeper depth to suffering. The final scene, the entrance with the dead Cordelia, is played by Salvini in a muffled key, — the tone of an old man whose fire and fury have spent themselves, and who has nothing left but weakness, tears, and death. The "Howl, howl, howl!" has not, on his lips, the classic resonance; but the pathos of the whole thing is unspeakable. Nothing can be more touching than the way in which, after he has ceased to doubt that Cordelia has ceased to live, he simply falls on his face on her body.

The unhappy hero of *La Morte Civile* is, however, the character which he has made most exclusively his own, and in which we watch him with the fewest mental reservations. Here is no sacrifice of greater admirations; here is none of the torment of seeing him play a Shakespeare that is yet not Shakespeare. It is Salvini pure and simple that we have; for of Giacometti there is, to begin with, as little as possible. Signor Giacometti's play has but a single part (to speak of), and it is Salvini who makes that part. The play is none of the best; it is meagre and monotonous; but it serves its purpose of giving the great actor a great opportunity. It deals with the unfortunate situation of an honest man, who, in spite of his honesty, has had the folly to kill his brother-in-law. The circumstances were of the most extenuating character, but he has been condemned (with a degree of rigour to which Italian justice resorts, we fear, only on the stage) to penal servitude for life. After fifteen years of imprisonment at Naples, he succeeds in escaping; and, having eluded pursuit, he feels a natural desire to see what has become of his wife and daughter. They are getting on perfectly without him; this fact, simply stated, is the great situation in Signor Giacometti's play. The child has been adopted by a benevolent physician, and by the mother's consent passes for the daughter of her benefactor. The mother, meanwhile, for whom there is no honour in her relationship to a murderer, lives under the same roof in the character of governess to the young girl, who is not in the secret of these transformations. When Corrado turns up, with a legitimate wish to claim his own, he finds that for these good people he has quite dropped out of life; they don't know what to do with him; he is civilly dead. How can he insist upon his paternity to his innocent child, when such paternity must bring her nothing but anguish and disgrace? How can he ask his wife to leave their daughter, in the tender care of whom she finds her one compensation for past shame and suffering, to go and live with him in hiding, and share at once the dangers and the infamy of his life? The situation is without an issue; it is the perfection of tragedy. At last poor Corrado, after a terrible struggle, determines to sacrifice himself to accomplished facts, and, since he is dead civilly, to die personally as well. He relieves his embarrassed relatives of his presence; he expires, abruptly and publicly, as people expire on the stage, after hearing his daughter, who is still not in the secret, but who obeys the pitying adjuration of his wife, address him for the first and last time as her father. Such is the subject of *La Morte Civile*, which is very effective in matter, though not very rich in form. It is interesting to compare Signor Giacometti's piece with the successful compositions of contemporary French dramatists, and to observe what the French would call the extreme *naïveté* of the Italian writer. It is not with the latter that we are dealing, however; for, after all, Signor Giacometti has provided Salvini with an occasion which an infinite infusion of French cleverness could not have improved. His Corrado is a most remarkable, most interesting, most moving creation. This is the great point, that it is really a creation; the conception, from the innermost germ, the construction, the revelation, of an individual. Corrado is a special nature. We live in an age of psychology; and it is not going too far to say that Signor Salvini's exhibition of this character has in it something of psychological research. Given a simple, well-meaning, generous, hot-blooded, uncultivated, and above all affectionate Sicilian; a man personally sympathetic, but charged with the perilous ingredients of his race and climate, — given such a nature as this, how will it have been affected by years of suffering, by the sting of disgrace, by the sense of injustice, by the reaction that comes with recovered freedom, by the bewilderment of a situation unexpected, unconceived, unendurable? Salvini undertakes to show us how, and his demonstration, in which every step is taken with the security of a master, is a triumph of art, of judgement, of taste. His acting is absolutely perfect: the ripeness, the sobriety, the truthfulness of it will remain in the minds of many people as a permanent standard. There is a piece of acting with which the American public has long been familiar which has something of this same psychological quality, as I have ventured to call it; but the material of Mr. Jefferson's admirable Rip Van Winkle is infinitely lighter and more limited. There is something extraordinarily affecting in the impression we get that Corrado was meant to be a good fellow; that he feels himself that he is a good fellow; that he eloped with his wife, it's true, but that, after that little adventure was over, he would so willingly have settled down to domestic felicity. He was not intended for false situations, for entanglements and agonies and insoluble problems; though he is all of one piece, as it were, he is not aggressive, and all that he asked was to be let alone and to let others alone. He is dazed and stupefied, although his southern blood spurts up occasionally into flame; he doubts of his own identity, and could easily believe that the whole story is a bad dream, and that these horrible things have not happened to himself. The description of the manner of his escape from prison, which he gives to his old friend Ferdinando and to the treacherous ecclesiastic, Don Giacchino, a long, uninterrupted narrative, which it takes some minutes to deliver, is the most perfect thing in the play. He begins it with difficulty, with mistrust, with diffidence; but as he goes on, his excitement, his confidence, a sense of doing it all over again, take possession of him, and he throws himself, as it were, with a momentary sense of freedom and success—it breaks out in a dozen touches of nature, of rapture, of familiarity—into the hands of his listeners, one of whom is only waiting to betray him. He not only describes his flight, he lives it over again; for five minutes he is off his guard, and his native good faith is uppermost. I have used the word which sums up the whole of this masterly performance. Corrado is a living figure.

In leaving *The Gladiator* to the last I have left myself no room to speak of it. This, however, I do not particularly regret, as there is little good to be said of the play, and there is less good to be said of Salvini's acting of the principal part than his performance of other characters would lead us to suppose. He can do nothing that is not powerful and interesting; but, all the same, I cannot help thinking his devotion to this feeble and ridiculous piece rather a mistake. The play is full of the incongruous, the impossible; if it had no other fault, it would be open to the objection that it is neither English nor Italian. With a text translated into one language for Salvini, and into another for his assistants, the polyglot system seems peculiarly vicious. *Le Gladiateur* of Alexandre Soumet, of the French Academy, was produced for the first time at the Théâtre Français, in 1841; but it had little success, and has, to the best of my belief, never been revived in France. It treats of a Roman empress, whose proceedings are incomprehensible; of a Christian young girl, a slave, of whom the empress is jealous, and whom she dedicates to a martyr's death; and of one of the heroes of the arena, who, when he is on the point of slaying the young girl,—a peculiar task for a gladiator,—discovers, from a scar on her arm, that she is his long-lost daughter. All this is terribly conventional and awkward, and even Salvini's vigorous acting fails to carry it off; there is a terrible want of illusion. The mounting of the play presents insuperable difficulties, and the scene in the arena makes a fearful draught upon the imagination without giving us anything in return. An Italian audience will rise to such occasions; it has good faith, a lively fancy, an abundant delight in a story, and a singular absence of perception of the ridiculous. But we poor Americans are made of sterner stuff, and there was something very dull in the house the night *The Gladiator* was played. What I mainly brought away was a recollection of Salvini's robust figure, invested in a very neat *maillot*, of the always magnificent tones of his voice, and of the admirable delivery of several speeches. It did not seem to me the gladiator killed his daughter so well as Salvini does some of his killing; but this young lady was a very difficult person to kill. It is a curious fact that Salvini's make-up in this piece gave him a striking resemblance to the late Edwin Forrest, who also used to represent a gladiator. It need scarcely be added that the resemblance was superficial.

Salvini's performances in Boston were lamentably few, and we take leave of him with the ardent hope that he will come back to us. We even go so far as to hope that he will, in that case, as on the occasion of his first visit to this country, bring with him an Italian company; though we are sadly afraid there is little ground for either of these hopes. We part from him, at any rate, in admiration and gratitude, and we wish him a continuance of triumphs and honours, with plenty of rest at last. Our American stage is in a state of inexpressible confusion; our American taste is sometimes rather wanting in light. It can do us nothing but good to have among us so noble and complete an artist. His example must be in some degree fruitful; his influence must be in some degree happy. And, fortunately, it is not to be said that we have not appreciated him.

In Boston "Tommaso Salvini" appeared in the Atlantic Monthly, *March, 1883.*

After spending some months of 1882 in London Henry James visited France in the autumn, commemorating his travels there in A Little Tour in France, 1884. *He spent a few weeks in Paris and on returning to London in December was called to America where his father now lay ill. He arrived, however, too late. Back in America, he remained there for the greater part of a year, and it was during his residence in Boston that Salvini played a season of two weeks at the Globe Theatre there; his repertory consisted of* Othello, Macbeth, The Outlaw (La Morte Civile), The Gladiator *and* King Lear, *played in that order; evidently Henry James saw all of these.*

II. *In London* (1884)

I HAVE, as an occasional playgoer, been waiting, to attempt to express my sense of what we owe him, till the great Italian actor who has been among us for the last three weeks should have added to the list of his parts, as his admirers have earnestly hoped, certain characters in which the English public had not already seen him, and which would give us still a larger impression of his repertory. He had not, I believe, on his former visits to England, played King Lear, but his American audiences, during his late long sojourn in the United States, have had the opportunity to admire his beautiful illustration of this most difficult of parts. Our allowance of opportunities completely new has therefore been small, the measure has now been definitely set, and it is safe to say there will have been deep disappointment. Signor Salvini will have played *Othello* repeatedly and *Il Gladiatore* often enough; but he will not have done, for the rest, what was expected of him. His former repertory was immense, and we shall in the course of some five weeks have been treated to a very limited revelation of it. We are thankful, devoutly thankful, for what we have had; but when I think what Salvini represents on the stage of to-day, how high he stands, and how much alone, and how little prospect there is—as one looks about—of his having a successor who can even distantly approach him, I cannot help regretting that a visit to England which probably will have been his last should not have been made splendid by the exhibition of the various sides of his genius. We have had variety, it is true, for nothing could be less like the *Gladiatore*, for instance, than the *Morte Civile;* but we have had hardly more than enough of it to whet our appetite. It must be added that the "splendour" for which I just expressed a wish has not been in any way a characteristic of the great actor's visit. He has had a company which, though capable of excellent efforts, has not given him the support which should be the proper honour of a talent like his, and which, when exposed to Shake-spearean tests, has seemed rather dingy and feeble; he has played in a theatre huge, cold, looking void even when it is tolerably full, and in every way disadvantageous for an actor whose exquisite finish is as remarkable as his force; and, lastly, he has encountered on the part of a large section of the London public a failure of appreciation, a stolidity in which assuredly there has been nothing brilliant.

His visit has been full of surprises, and I may as well say at once that one of the greatest is his having found encouragement to play *La Morte Civile* but once or twice. The perfection of his rendering of the hero of this lugubrious drama strikes the author of these lines as one of those artistic successes which leave the spectator nothing to say—leave him dumb and almost reverent, under the impression of absolute truth, of an execution that satisfies to luxury every demand of the imagination. It is puzzling, therefore, to see this incomparable representation of tragic feeling relegated to the limbo of things that "don't draw;" and a critic who expresses himself with the licence of an amateur may perhaps be allowed to add that he has lately observed few signs that have indicated more the comparative indifference of the London audience to the question of form, of execution, the manner in which an effect is produced. There are certain *rapprochements*, certain com-

parisons and contrasts, that might be made just now, which would
open up vistas in this direction; but they would lead us too far,
and I confess, moreover, that to my sense—perhaps I take things
too hard—the subject is rather portentous. Suffice it that *La Morte
Civile* is a heavy, melancholy piece, with very little richness of
texture—though in this respect it does not compare unfavourably,
surely, with the usual pabulum of the London playgoer—and that,
giving, with its faults, occasion for the most perfect representation
of moral suffering that our generation can have seen, it has been
promptly shelved as not being sufficiently amusing. To witness
La Morte Civile is a very serious affair, I admit; the manner in
which Salvini plays it is a constant challenge of the attention.
The ripeness and richness of his acting give every tone and gesture
their place in a conception extraordinarily complete; the whole
thing has a surface as firm and polished as the glaze of a precious
porcelain. The Othello is more brilliant, but it has not more truth,
and does not surpass the Corrado in the supreme merit of the
latter creation—the expression of life. The manner in which life
is produced in *La Morte Civile* is one of the most wonderful
triumphs I have seen in the actor's art; we seem to touch it, to
feel the depth of its throbs, the warmth of its breath, to live, ourselves, in the given situation, rather than to watch and follow, in a
greater or less degree of detachment. Like everything that Salvini
does, it is an expression of pure feeling, and no expression was
ever at once more real and more beautiful. The beauty that his
admirable artistic organization gives to everything he does is a
matter apart from the truth of his inspiration, apart from the
mastery that great experience has given him; but they add to his
genius that quality which converts the happy confidence of the
spectator into what I ventured just now to call a luxury. No other
word will express this sense of the degree to which nature has
been generous to the great Italian actor, and of such qualities of
voice and glance, such a magnificent apparatus of expression,
being in themselves a high entertainment. The facility, the im-

mediacy, with which he produces his great effects, has an extraordinary charm. Throughout *La Morte Civile* his splendid voice carries, as it were, the whole drama; without a note of violence, of effort, deep and intensely quiet from beginning to end, it reflects the finest shades of concentrated emotion, and goes to the depths of the listener's mind. The facility of execution is as delightful as the conception is simple and sincere. The long speech in which Corrado relates to Don Fernando and the malicious priest the circumstances of his incarceration and those of his escape, is an extraordinarily vivid and interesting piece of acting, and a striking example of Salvini's power to lift great weights — the length of the recital constituting a direct presumption against its success, and violating every prejudice of the English spectator, who often seems to carry to the theatre — and with reason, perhaps, when one thinks what he is sometimes exposed ·to — an insurmountable mistrust of human speech. The part of Corrado is also a capital example of the simple way in which Salvini conceives his characters. They present themselves to him — as they naturally do to the Italian imagination — as embodiments of feeling, without intellectual complications; the creature to be represented appears a creature of passion, of quick susceptibility, of senses lying close to the surface, in whom expression is immediate and complete. The picture given in *La Morte Civile* is a picture of suffering pure and simple, or of suffering illumined at most by one or two fitful rays of reflection and resistance. Nothing could be more natural, almost more sensual (for it is the torment of the whole sentient being, sick with suffering), more Italian — at any rate more expressive and more alien to the English theory of how a man should meet trouble. I have heard a lady say she did not care to see *La Morte Civile* because Corrado is not manly; and I confess I have not recovered from the impression made upon me by this way of considering an artistic effort. I should as soon think of objecting to the Faun of Praxiteles because he is not a picture, or to the Sistine Madonna because she is not a statue. Poor

Corrado, as played by Salvini, has no such refinements; it is enough for him that he is intensely human and bewildered, that his pluck is tremendously gone, that he is in a situation from which he sees no issue, and that when the Sicilian temperament feels the pressure of fate it turns and turns in blind pain, and finally collapses. Corrado is completely demoralized, and I can imagine no picture of demoralization more poignant.

The actor represents Othello in the same general way; it is a study of pure feeling — of passion, with as little as possible of that intellectual iridescence which, in a piece of portraiture, is the sign of Shakespeare's hand, but which, less visible, or at any rate less essential, in the Moor of Venice than in the other great parts, puts the character much more within Salvini's grasp than the study of Hamlet, of Lear, of Macbeth. There are various things his version of the part does not contain, but I prefer to judge it by those it does, in such rich and overflowing measure. I have heard it called brutal and truculent; but I do not think the actor exaggerates the signs by which a man who is about to smother his wife, while insane from jealousy, may be supposed to have preluded to such a catastrophe. It is easy for us English auditors to imagine the character interfused with different tones, played by an Othello more saturated with the text, more charged with "the pity of it," more awe-stricken at what he feels himself impelled to do, hanging over Desdemona at the supreme moment with a tenderness more hushed to horror, and which should give to some of his broken sentences a meaning more exquisite. It is an important defect in Salvini's rendering that Othello at the last does not hang over Desdemona at all, and that the incomparable pathos of some of his final speeches is wasted. But with this restriction it is impossible to imagine anything more living, more tragic, more suggestive of a tortured soul and of generous, beneficent strength changed to a purpose of destruction. With its tremendous force, it is magnificently quiet, and from beginning to end has not a touch of rant or of crudity. His Macbeth, his Lear, are less deeply assimilated; they are, on Shakespeare's part, less simple creations. They are figures of many facets, complicated and thoughtful, throwing out the strangest imaginative rays. Salvini simplifies them, but he makes them deeply dramatic, and his splendid powers of execution give back to them in vividness and reality what they lose in the poetical line. I cannot speak of a representation of *King Lear* without protesting primarily against the play being acted at all; it is, in my opinion, impossible to imagine a drama that accommodates itself less to the stage. Salvini, however, makes a great figure in it; and when I say that both his passion and his tenderness rise to the level of the part, I say everything that is required. *Il Gladiatore* is a desperately bad play, but it appears, comparatively speaking, to have pleased the town. It is better to see Salvini in this forcible-feeble production than not to see him at all; but it is, in my opinion, the least interesting thing that he does; his opportunities are mainly of a coarse kind, and he paints his picture with a big brush. Fortunately his stroke is always superb. I see, as I close these remarks, that he is announced to play Hamlet in a single occasion—his farewell —next week. He will need his finest touches for that; it will take all the resources of his art to bridge over the difference between a sensuous Italian and a melancholy Dane. But Salvini is capable of wonders; his dramatic instinct has extraordinary flexibility, and in an artist of his great dimensions one always, in one way or another, finds one's account. However Signor Salvini may play Hamlet—he has done it in London of old but I had not the fortune to see him—he will play it, as he plays everything, in the grand style—that grand style which will have made the brevity of his visit such a regret, the memory of his genius such a lesson and such a standard.

In London "Tommaso Salvini" ap- peared, under the title ".A Study of Salvini" by a Casual Critic, in the Pall Mall Gazette, *March 27, 1884.*   *Credit for the discovery of this article is due to Miss Edna Kenton, who was able to trace the reprinting of it in the* Pall Mall Budget *(a weekly* compendium which reproduced the more important articles from the week's issues of the Gazette *itself*) of March 28, 1884. Comparing this with the signed article of the previous year, and observing their identical judgments, Miss Kenton was able to establish, beyond doubt, that the 'Casual Critic' was none other than Henry James.

A POOR PLAY WELL ACTED

1883

IT WOULD seem that (in addition to products still more necessary to existence) we are destined to import from America not only actors but pieces. American performers have more than once appeared in London with plays of transatlantic construction as part of their outfit; but we just now remember no instance previous to the production on Saturday evening of the new piece at the St. James's of an American dramatic work interpreted wholly by English actors. It remains to be seen whether the London stage will receive encouragement to draw from this mine, if mine it should prove to be. The experiment just made by Messrs. Hare and Kendal is at any rate an incident to be noted in the exchange of international courtesies, which appear for the moment to be so brisk. *Young Folks' Ways* (the title is not an inspiration) is the production of Mrs. Burnett, the Anglo-American novelist, and has been extracted from one of her tales (*Esmeralda* by name), with the assistance of a collaborateur. Brought out two years ago in New York, the piece had, we believe, considerable success, and ran for some months in that city and others. It treats of matters that take place in the first act in North Carolina, and in the three others in Paris; so that, from the American point of view, it may be said to be genuinely national. These matters, we fear, are not of a nature to hold very powerfully the attention of an English audience, though the acting the play receives at the St. James's Theatre is for the most part effective and zealous. Considering, indeed, that *Young Folks' Ways* was not written for the company of Messrs. Hare and Kendal, it fits them better than might have been expected. The national illusion they do not particularly produce. The Rogers family, under their treatment, hardly realize the type of the "poor white" of the Southern States, and Mr. Alexander represents the love-stricken young man at large, rather than the Carolinian contending with adversity. But every one acts with a will and a manifest conviction that the piece cannot safely be left to take care of itself. It is not, we may say at once, a drama with a very sensible life of its own, and that it should be exactly what it is, and yet be, as we may say, where it is, suggests a good many reflections as to the sources at which the English stage, so robustly constituted in so many ways, and yet so sadly athirst, is at present compelled to drink. It is composed of elements of a touching simplicity, put together with an ingenuousness which would be commendable in a moral tale for the young. Old Rogers, a "Britisher," who has emigrated to North Carolina (a very hopeless field for this sort of enterprise) long enough ago to have acquired several of the locutions prevailing there, but not to have divested himself of the habitual tones of Mr. Hare, has a shrewish wife, a daughter of much sensibility, and a tract of land which is coveted by an unscrupulous speculator, who suspects in it the existence of "ore." The seductive mineral, if we mistake not, is not further defined; but young Dave Hardy, a son of the soil, the accepted lover of Mr. Rogers's daughter, accidentally confirms the speculator in his belief, and then just manages to foil him in an attempt to purchase the land for a mere nominal sum from the vixenish Mrs. Rogers, whose soul is above her station, and who, regretting the lost opportunities of Elizabethville, the county town where she was "raised," and hating the narrowness of her lot, is ready to part with her acres on the easiest terms. Her daughter's lover, interfering, brings about a much better bargain, in consequence of which the ambitious woman, rich with the proceeds of a brilliant operation, is able to transport her family to Paris, leaving young Hardy, the author of her good fortune, to languish in North Carolina, separated from his sweetheart, whom Mrs. Rogers now wishes, much to the young lady's distress, to marry to a marquis. The adventures of the Rogerses in Paris occupy the rest of the play, or rather they occupy very little of it, for the foreground is pervaded, during the greater part of three out of the four acts, by a family of Desmonds, who have not very much to do with the piece except that they are friends of the Rogerses, and that they have the good fortune to count Mrs. Kendal among their members. The ancient Mr. Rogers, wrapped up in pastoral things, is not happy in the American paradise, thanks, doubtless, to his being, as a "Britisher," not sufficiently Americanized. The part is played by Mr. Hare as elaborately as the absence of a ground to work upon allows; but the spectator has some difficulty in grasping the mixture of Paris, North Carolina, and Mr. Rogers's remoter origin. We lose sight of Esmeralda (the daughter who has been torn from her betrothed) almost completely; for it is revealed to us only in two or three fitful gleams that she grieves for the young man and the "little house" at home, and that she is secretly preparing to turn and rend her worldy mother—that "finished feminine fiend," as one of the characters calls her. She is abetted in this scheme by Miss Desmond, who is not only the cause of matrimony in others—she takes a gushing interest in young Hardy, who has come out from North Carolina, penniless and foodless, to irritate himself at a distance, from a bench in the Champs Elysées, with the sight of the Marquis who is to succeed him in the privilege of being Mrs. Rogers's son-in-law—but an eligible subject herself, in the opinion of a certain Mr. Estabrook. This gentleman, as an artist sketching in North Carolina, has known the Rogerses at home (we have seen him in their cottage in the first act) and makes them known to Miss Desmond, who is determined that Esmeralda shall be reunited to her early love—a course which has everything to recommend it, inasmuch as she has a letter in her pocket proving that the mysterious mineral is all on young Hardy's farm after all,

and not on that of the Rogerses, so that the wicked speculator
has been taken in and Hardy has the prospect of millions. Esmeralda emerges for a moment from that position in the wings to
which, in spite of her position as heroine of the piece, she has been
constantly relegated, to rant, in a manner for which we have not
been prepared, and which nothing leads up to, at her mother, and
faint away; then throws herself into the arms of young Hardy,
whom she rescues from the extremity of woe. Miss Desmond, who
has flirted inordinately with Estabrook for the greater part of
three acts — the artlessness with which the play suspends itself for
this long interlude is one of its most curious features — bestows
her hand upon him, together with certain pairs of gloves, on
which, on two or three occasions, the interest of the piece has
been surprised to find itself centred, and then the Rogerses, relieved of their Marquis and their illusions, return to North
Carolina.

Such a production as *Young Folks' Ways* strikes us as a considerable challenge to the spectator's ingenuity, so difficult is it
to find a point of view from which the phenomenon may be profitably considered. It would be unfair to criticise it seriously, it is
so very primitive an attempt at dramatic writing; and yet the
fact that it has achieved success in the United States, and has been
thought by competent judges to be capable of achieving success
in England, would appear to demand some sort of explanation.
The play would be infantine if infants ever expressed themselves
in falsetto. The story is mawkish and unreal, and after the first act
there is scarcely any attempt to tell it. The beautiful scenery
which the management of the theatre have given the second and
third acts throws into almost cruel relief the attenuation of the
action. It would be interesting to attempt to ascertain what level of
taste, what range of ideas as to what constitutes a play and what
a play is supposed to represent, the prosperity of such a piece
would give us the right to imagine. It is probable that Messrs.
Hare and Kendal have simply seen in the matter a problem which

might be solved by good acting. The acting is for the most part as good as acting can be which has to struggle constantly with the absence of opportunity. After the first act, which is much the best, there is nothing like a situation, and the performers may be said to be working against time. Mr. Hare attempts a portrait of a mild old rustic, whose spirit has been broken by a violent wife, and whose mind is bewildered by foreign travel and luxuries acquired too late to displace from his mind the image of "Old Bald," the mountain in whose shadow he has tilled the soil. Like everything that Mr. Hare does, the sketch is full of delicate intention, and the sweetness and quaintness of the incongruous Mr. Rogers are very happily rendered. But the part suffers from there being nothing for the actor to do but to wander in and out, and (towards the end) mispronounce a few French words. Mrs. Kendal contrives to be brilliant with very little material, and her Norah Desmond is a good example of what may be done by an actress who is determined to be vivacious at any price. Mr. Kendal assists her, though there is nothing in the piece to assist *him*, and between them the two manage to extract a good deal of rather prolonged and inexpensive comedy from the idea that a gentleman is trying to make love to a lady by innuendo and the lady is trying by innuendo to reciprocate. The whole thing is a *hors d'oeuvre*, absurdly out of perspective, and it is a pity to see Mrs. Kendal, with her lightness of touch, her real "authority," expend herself upon a task so fruitless. It is time we should see her again in a part involving some of those strong feelings which she renders so well. Mr. Kendal has really nothing to do but to put his glass to his eye and look jocose and gentlemanly, and of this he easily acquits himself. Mr. Alexander, as the forsaken young lover, stranded in Paris, and taking his situation as hard as possible, acts with abundant zeal and care; but we think he rather neglects the realities of the part, scantily as they are indicated in the drama. He has not had enough in his eye the particular young man whom Miss Rogers would have been likely to be engaged to, but is a trifle too romantic and rhapsodical, as well as too undermined and relaxed by his troubles. The part, in truth, however, strikes us as vague and false. Mrs. Vezin does her best with the too unamiable Mrs. Rogers, a termagant unrelieved by humour or by any niceties of characterization. A monotone of scolding is difficult to make not only sympathetic but acceptable, and the strenuous Mrs. Rogers varies her note not at all. As the ill-used but rebellious Esmeralda, Miss Webster, who made her first appearance, showed plenty of intention and aplomb, and it is not her fault if she has only to make herself disagreeable. The girl's violent outbreak and defiance of her mother in the third act, which, with the exception of her fit of weeping in the first, is the only glimpse we have of the heroine, is almost grotesquely abrupt, and is wanting, even under provocation, in maidenly gentleness. There is no occasion whatever for heroics; for Esmeralda has only to say that she will not marry the Marquis and the difficulty disappears of itself. Miss Webster shows signs of a familiarity with the stage and a dramatic temperament verging on the robust. If there is little for the principal characters to do, there is still less for the subsidiary ones, which are filled with discretion. The piece is worth seeing as an example of how an inanimate production may be, within limits, vivified.

"A Poor Play Well Acted" appeared under this title and as *"By a Casual Critic"* in the Pall Mall Gazette, *October 24, 1883.*

Miss Edna Kenton traced the reprint of this in the Pall Mall Budget, *October 26, 1883. She was set on the track of this discovery by a reference in the* Athenaeum, *October 27, 1883, which definitely stated that the criticism was from the pen of Henry James.*

Confirmation was found later by Leon Edel in an unpublished letter, dated October 25, the day after the article's appearance. In this James wrote: "[I] . . . have written an article (anonymously—don't mention it) for the Pall Mall Gazette, which wishes me to become its dramatic critic (declined) —don't mention this . . ."

He had returned to England in August of this year, and was now again leading his settled life in London, devoting himself more and more to his fiction and writing criticisms only very occasionally.

COQUELIN

—————— 1 8 8 7 — 1 9 1 5 ——————

Reprinted from Constant Coquelin, Art and the Actor, *translated by Abby Landgon Alger. Copyright 1915 by Dramatic Museum of Columbia University.*

IT WAS nearly seventeen years ago and the first time that the
writer of these remarks had taken his seat in that temple of
the drama in which he was destined afterwards to spend so many
delightful evenings, feel the solicitation of so many interesting
questions and welcome so many fine impressions, these last
crowned by the conviction that the Théâtre Français was such a
school of taste as was not elsewhere to be found in the world.
The spectator of whom I speak felt the education of his theatric
sense fairly begin on the evening M. Coquelin was revealed to
him in *Lions et Renards* — and revealed in spite of a part of rather
limited opportunity. Many parts since have continued the revelation, these more important, more marked for success (Émile
Augier's comedy to which I allude was, not undeservedly, a
failure); but I have retained in its vividness my image of the hour,
and of all that this actor in especial contributed, because it was the
first step of an initiation. It opened a door through which I was in
future to pass as often as possible into a world of delightful, fruitful
art. M. Coquelin has quitted the Comédie, his long connection
with that august institution has come to an end, and he is to
present himself in America not as a representative of the richest
theatrical tradition in the world, but as an independent and enterprising genius who has felt the need of the margin and elbow-
room, the lighter, fresher air of a stage of his own. He will find
this stage in the United States as long as he looks for it, and an
old admirer may hope that he will look for it often and make it the

scene of new experiments and new triumphs. His visit is in fact itself a new experiment, the result of which can scarce fail of interest for those who watch with attention the evolution of taste in our great and lively land. If it should be largely and strikingly successful that sacred cause will quite of necessity, I think, have scored heavily.

It is nevertheless to be noted that foreign performers, lyric and dramatic, descending upon our shores by the thousand, have encountered a various, by no means always an assured, fortune. Many have failed, and of those who have succeeded it is safe to say that they have done so for reasons lying pretty well on the surface. They have addressed us in tongues that were alien and to most of us incomprehensible, but there was usually something in them that operated as a bribe to favour. The peculiarity of M. Coquelin's position and the cause of the curiosity with which we shall have regarded the public's attitude toward him are in the fact that he offers no bribe whatever, none of the lures of youth or beauty or sex or of an insinuating aspect, and none of those that reside in a familiar domestic repertory. The question is simply of appreciating or not appreciating his admirable talent and his not less admirable method. Great singers speak, or rather sing, for themselves; music hath charms, and the savage breast is soothed even when the "words" require a handy translation. Distinguished foreign actresses have the resource of a womanhood which a chivalrous people is much more willing than not to take for lovely. Madame Sarah Bernhardt was helped to relieve the burden of the French tongue to the promiscuous public by being able to add to her extraordinary cleverness her singular beauty, and then to add ever so many wonderful dresses and draperies to that. M. Coquelin will have had to please with nothing like the same assistance; he is not beautiful, he is not pictorial, and his clothes scarcely matter. The great Salvini has successfully beguiled us in Italian, but has had the advantage of the bravest address to the eye of which a man can be well capable, and of representing with his romantic type characters that have on our stage a consecration, a presumption, in their favour. M. Coquelin's type is not romantic, and whatever in him is most immediately visible would seem to have been formed for the broadest comedy. By a miracle of talent and industry he has forced his physical means to serve him also, and with equal felicity, in comedy that is not broad, but surpassingly delicate, and even in the finest pathetic and tragic effects. To enjoy the refinement of his acting, however, the ear must be as open as the eye, must even be beforehand with it; and if that of the American spectator in general learns, or even shows an aptitude for learning, the lesson conveyed in his finest creations, the lesson that acting is an art, and that the application of an art is style, and that style is expression and that expression is the salt of life, the gain will have been something more than the sensation of the moment — it will be a new wisdom.

In M. Augier's comedy which I have mentioned and which was speedily withdrawn, there was frequent reference to the "robe of innocence" of the young Vicomte Adhémar, an interesting pupil of the Jesuits, or at least of the clerical party, who, remarkable for his infant piety and the care taken to fence him in from the corruptions of the town, goes sadly astray on coming up to Paris and inflicts grievous rents and stains on that precious garment. I well remember the tone of humbugging juvenile contrition in which Coquelin, representing the misguided youth, confessed that it was no longer in a state to be worn. He had a little curly flaxen wig, parted in the middle, a round and rosy face and a costume resembling the supposed uniform in New York to-day, of that illusive animal the dude; yet he was not a figure of farce, but a social product, so lightly touched in as he was definitely specified. I thought his companions as delightful as himself, and my friendliness extended even to the horrible stalls in which at that time one was condemned to sit, and to the thick hot atmosphere of the house. I suspect the atmosphere has never been cleared since then — that the place has never had a thorough airing; but certain

mitigations have been wrought, new chairs and wider passages
supplied, with frescoes on the ceilings and fresh upholstery in box
and balcony. It is still however of the dingy and stuffy old theatre
I think, haunted as it then more sensibly was by the ghosts of the
great players of the past, the mighty presences of Talma and
Mars and Rachel. It has seemed to me ever since that the "improvements" have frightened these sacred shades away; the ancient lack of ease was a part of the tradition—a word which
represents the very soul of the Comédie and which, under the great
dim roof that has echoed to so many matchless sounds, one pro-
nounces with bated breath. The tradition was at that time in the
keeping of MM. Regnier, Bressant, Delaunay and Got, of Mesdames Plessy, Nathalie and Favart, to say nothing of the subject of
this sketch, the latest comer in the great generation of which these
were some of the principal figures. Much has been changed with
the lapse of the years, and M. Coquelin, though still in the happy
prime, was the other day almost a senior. Regnier, Bressant,
Delaunay had disappeared, and from the boards of the Français
the most robust depositary of the tradition in the younger line—
for to this title our visitor has certainly a right—has also vanished.
Gone is the brilliant, artificial, incomparable Plessy; gone is that
rich and wise *comédienne*, the admirable, elderly, discreet, the
amusing and touching Nathalie; gone is poor Madame Favart,
whose utterance I remember I couldn't understand the first time
I saw her (she was still playing quite young persons and represented, in a very tight dress, the aristocratic heroine of *Lions et
Renards*,) but whom I afterwards grew to admire as an actress of
high courage and a great tragic range.

It took a certain time for a new spectator to discriminate and
compare, to see things, or rather to see persons, in the right proportion and perspective. I remember that the first evenings I
spent in the Rue de Richelieu I thought everyone equally good, I
was dazzled by the general finish, by the harmony unbroken, a
regulated tone and observed propriety which at that time affected

me as an almost celestial order. Everyone *was* good — I don't say it of everyone to-day; even if afterwards the new spectator perceived differences. He was to discover indeed that, such is the grossness intermixed with the noblest human institutions, there could be sometimes a failure of taste behind that stately *rampe*. And now he has heard common voices, has had the shock of the imperfect illusion there, has seen the dead letter of the famous tradition uninformed by a free spirit. He has seen gentlemen put down their hats with great accuracy on the first chair on the right of the door as they come in, but, even when the further convincing grace might be much required of them, achieve very little more than that. He has seen actresses for whom all the arts of the toilet, all the facility of the Frenchwoman and all the interest they had in producing the right impression could not conduce to the representation of a lady. These little roughnesses, however, inherent, as I say, in every mundane enterprise, were not frequent enough for the general glamour to suffer from them. I nevertheless rejoice to-day in a certain confidence of having even at the very first dimly discerned the essence of the matter, the purest portions of the actor's art, to abide in young Coquelin — he was then young — with unsurpassable intensity. It concerns his history that he was born at Boulogne-sur-Mer in 1841, and was christened Benoît-Constant; that his vocation defined itself at the earliest age, and that he became a pupil of the Conservatory in 1859. From this nursery of histrionic hopes he entered the Théâtre Français, where he at once drew attention to his presence. At the age of twenty-three he was a *sociétaire* of the great house. His features, his cast of countenance, the remarkable play and penetration of his voice, which combines the highest metallic ring with every conceivable human note, marked him out for parts of extreme comic freedom as well as for the finer shades of what is called character. Much before I had seen him I was to retain the impression of the liveliest, received from a friend's account of him in Théodore de Banville's touching little poetic piece *Gringoire*,

where, in the part of a medieval Bohemian of letters condemned
to hanging by Louis XI. and reprieved when the halter is already
round his neck—I have not seen the piece for a long time and
rather forget the argument—he showed a mastery of that mixture
of the appeal to the pity of things with the appeal to their absurdity
which always so succeeds with the French. *Gringoire* is an excellent
example of that range, and has taken its place in M. Coquelin's
regular repertory, where he has matched it, in comparatively
recent times, with M. Coppée's *Luthier de Crémone;* a like sensitive
and slightly morbid personage this last, represented by the actor
with wondrous discretion, delicacy and fancy, and dear to the
French public from the fact that he may be introduced to families
and young ladies. The pathetic, the "interesting"—including,
where need be, the romantic and even the heroic, these and the
extravagantly droll mark the opposite terms of our performer's
large gamut. He turns from end to end of this scale, he ranges
between his extremes, with incomparable freedom and ease. Into
the *emploi* of the impudent extravagant serving-men of the old
comedies, the Mascarilles, the Scapins, the Frontins, the Crispins,
he stepped from the first with the assurance of a conqueror; from
hand to foot, in face, in manner, in accent, in genius, he was cut
out for them, and it is with his most shining successes under that
star that his name has become synonymous for the public at large.
If his portrait is painted for the *foyer* of the Comédie—which was
doubtless long since the case—it should perhaps be in particular
as the Mascarille of Molière's *Étourdi.*

This must have been, I think, the second part in which I gaped
at him, when Delaunay, with but little less nature and art and
effect of his own delightful kind, was the incorrigibly scatter-
brained hero. I see Mascarille, I hear him, the incarnation of
humorous effrontery and agility, launch again his prodigious voice
over the footlights, fairly trumpet his "points" to the dome and
give an unparalleled impression of life and joy. I have acclaimed
him in the character many times since then, and found it, save for

his astonishing image of the false marquis in the *Précieuses Ridi- cules*, the most exuberant in his repertory. Of this fantastic exuberance, the special chartered license of the whole family, he is a master whom one watches very much as one watches some supreme dancer or trickster on the vertiginous tense wire, feeling him as certain to pile danger high as not to risk his neck by excess. This safe playing with the danger of excess—which is a defiance of the loss of balance under exhilaration—connects itself with the actor's command of the effects that lie entirely in self-possession, effects of low tone, indications of inward things. The representative of Don Annibal in the *Aventurière*, of Don César de Bazan in *Ruy Blas*, under both of which names this master is superb, is also the representative of various prose-talking and concentrated gentlemen of to-day (the Duc de Septmonts in the *Étrangère* of the younger Dumas, the argumentative, didactic Thouvenin in the same author's *Denise*) caught in various tight places, or suspicious of them, as gentlemen must be in a play, but with no accessories *à la* Goya to help them out. The interpreter of the tragic passion which is the subject of *Jean Dacier*, a piece I have not seen for many years, lurks in the stupendously droll and dreadful evocation of M. Loyal, the canting little pettifogger or *clerc d'huissier*, who appears in a single brief scene of the last act of *Tartuffe* and into whom M. Coquelin, taking up the part for the first time in the autumn of 1885, injected an individuality of grotesqueness and baseness which gave him, all in the space of five minutes, one of his greatest triumphs.

The art of composition is in the various cases I have mentioned the same, but the subjects to which it is applied have nothing in common. I have heard members of the public say with complacency: "Coquelin has great talent, he does ever so many different things, but somehow he is always the same Coquelin." He is indeed always the same Coquelin, which truth to himself crowns our comfort, considering the damage that in so gallant a genius any breach of his identity might have wrought. It is exactly by being fixed so firm at his centre that he is able to reach out, reach ever so far, to the perfect Jean Dacier one night and to the perfect Don Annibal another. If it be meant by the remark that he makes Don Annibal resemble Jean Dacier, or gives the two personages something in common that they could not really have possessed, no criticism could well be less just. What it really points to, I suppose, is the infallibility and punctuality of the great artist's method, the fact of its *always* reporting his observation and his experience, just as the postman always delivers the letters he starts out on his round with. The letters are various, but the postman remains the postman. It is, however, above all by his voice that M. Coquelin is (in the degree denounced, I suppose) exposed and betrayed, that voice which no art of composing a particular character or adopting a particular tone can well render a less astounding organ at one moment than at another. Don César is Coquelin and M. Thouvenin is Coquelin, because on the lips alike of Don César and of M. Thouvenin sit a range and a use of tone, a directed application of it, which are peculiar to the artist who commands them and are surely the most wondrous in their kind that the stage has ever known. It may be said that his voice does fairly give him away, that he cannot escape from it, and that whatever he does with it he still pays the penalty of reminding us that only he can command such service.

This idiosyncrasy it is in short that, by so intimately connecting him with his characters, connects them inevitably with each other and shuts them up together as prisoners of war, so to speak, are shut up in their ring fence. Its life and force are such that we seem at times to hear it run away with him, take a "day off" and engage in antics and exercises on its own account. The only reproach it would occur to me to make to a *diseur* so endowed is that he may perhaps at moments show as the victim rather more than as the master of his gift, may occasionally lose the idea while he listens to the form. That beguilement is doubtless not to be grudged, however, as a reward to so much toilsome forging and polishing of the vocal arm; the result gives us something unsurpassably addressed to the stage, where the prime necessity of the least thing done, as well as of the greatest, is that it shall "tell" for every creature in the house. When this master speaks the sound is not sweet and caressing, though it adapts itself beautifully, as I have hinted, to the most human effects; it has no analogy with the famous romantic murmur of Delaunay, a thing of ineffable quavers and enchanting cadences, dying falls and semitones calculated to a hair's breadth. It is not primarily the voice of a lover, or rather—for I hold that any actor, given the indulgence of the public to this particular easy appeal, may be a lover with any voice—it is not primarily, like that of M. Delaunay, the voice of love. There was no urgent reason why it should be, for the passion of love is not what M. Coquelin was cut out to represent or has usually been concerned with.

He has usually had to represent the passion of impudence, and it is, I think, not too much to say that in this portrayal he has won his greatest victories. His inimitable force of accent enables him to place supremely before us the social quality which, beyond question, leads straightest to social success. The valets of Molière and Regnard are nothing if not impudent; impudent are Don César and Don Annibal; impudent, as I remember him, M. Adolphe de Beaubourg in *Paul Forestier;* impudent the Duc de Septmonts; impudent even—or at least decidedly impertinent— the copious moralist M. Thouvenin. I select thus but a handful of instances from our actor's immense repertory; there are doubtless others at least as much to the point in parts in which I have not seen him. He is believed moreover—and nothing could be more natural—to have aspirations of the liveliest character in respect to Tartuffe, and it may be predicted that on the day he embraces that fine opportunity he will give a supreme sign of his power to depict the unblushing. It need hardly be remarked that the Mephistopheles which he is at the moment I write rumoured to have his eye on in an arrangement of Goethe's drama will abound in the same sense. If M. Coquelin's art of tone meanwhile is not the art of sweetness it is in an extraordinary degree that of firmness and distinctness, that of penetration, of the power to "carry" sound and sense. I hear it as I write ascend again like a rocket to the great hushed dome of the old theatre, under which, vibrating and lashing the air, it seems to have sprung from some mechanism of still greater science even than the human throat. In the great cumulative *tirades* of the old comedy, which grow and grow as they proceed, but the difficulties of which are pure sport for our artist's virtuosity, it flings down the words and the verses as a gamester precipitated by a run of luck flings *louis d'or* upon the table. I am not sure that the most perfect piece of acting I have seen him achieve, in the sense of the exhibition of things intensely felt and reacted upon, is not a prose character, but to appreciate to the full his mastery of form, his authority, as they say, we must listen to and enjoy his delivery of verse; since it represents all the breadth of the difference, of the abyss, one may indeed say, between the French dramatic manner and any claim to a manner open to ourselves in the same connection, that verse has remained among M. Coquelin's countrymen, till within recent years, the supposedly most congruous language of comedy—a distinction from any familiarity with which our theatre was long ago to fall away, save in so far as parts of the Shakespearean comedy saved it. That armour-plated assurance, that perfection of confidence which is but the product of the most determined study, shines forth in the example before us, at any rate, in proportion as the problem is complicated. The problem does not indeed as a general thing become so in the old rhymed parts psychologically speaking; but in these parts the question of elocution, of delivery, of *diction*, or even simply the question of breath, bristles both with opportunities and with dangers. It is true as a rule that wherever M. Coquelin has a very long and composite speech to utter, be it in verse or prose, there one gets the cream of his talent, or at least of his virtuosity. There one perhaps even sees why it is sometimes critically declared of him that he is not an actor in anything like the same sense in which he is a *diseur;* the criticism with which the genius of his country so restlessly invites the artist ever to reckon dealing thus in a discrimination not familiar from any act of frequency among ourselves.

Our distinctions in that order are between smaller things, things too, I think, in every way less apprehended; so that we never have for instance such a matter to consider as the wondrous length of some of the speeches in French plays, and of the detailed responsibility laid thereby on exponents. The longest continuous aggregation of lines that has had to face French footlights, not excepting the famous soliloquy of Figaro in the second comedy of Beaumarchais, and that of Charles the Fifth in *Hernani*, is, I should suppose, the discourse placed in the mouth of our above-mentioned M. Thouvenin in the last act of *Denise*. It occupies nearly four close pages in the octavo edition of the play — oh those delightful octavo editions, with their projection into litera-ture of the dignity of the theatre, unless indeed one says their projection upon the theatre of the dignity of literature! — and if it is not in strictness a soliloquy, being the product of an age posterior to that innocence and enjoying an audience on the stage as well as in the house, it is a delivered address, an uttered homily, a series of insistent remarks on many things. English or American spectators would have sunk into settled gloom by the time the long rhythm of the thing had declared itself, and even at the Théâtre Français the presumption was against the actor's ability to take safely into port a vessel drawing such a prodigious depth of water. M. Coquelin gave the affair life, light, colour, natural movement and that variety any absence of which would have wrecked it — gave it in short an interest that made it a triumph. We held our breath not altogether perhaps to hear what Thou-venin would say — it didn't quite come to that, but certainly to hear how Coquelin would bring Thouvenin through. Such a suc-cess as this case represents the actor's art at its highest and serenest, because built up straight from the humanity and all the moral facts that underlie it.

"Saying" things is on our own stage quite out of fashion — if for no other reason than that we must first have them to say. To *do* them, with a great reinforcement of chairs and tables and articles of clothing, of traps and panoramas and other massive carpentry, is the most that ever occurs to our Anglo-Saxon star of either sex. The ear of the public, that field of the auditive intelligence which is two-thirds of the comedian's battle-field, has simply ceased to respond for want of use; for where in very fact is the unfortunate comedian to learn to speak? Is it the unfortunate public, sitting all on this side in deepest darkness, that is to teach him? From what sources shall the light of usage, of taste, of tact, the breath of harmony and the tone of civilization, the perception in a word of anything approaching to a standard, have descended upon the society itself out of which the actor springs? Gone at any rate are the days — if they ever really were with us — when any situation not grossly obvious, any interest *latent* in anything and thereby involving for its issue our finer attention and our nobler curiosity, could look for help from the play of tone, *the* great vehicle of communication. What this comes to is that histrionic lips have ceased — so far as they ever began! — to be able to tell a story worth telling or to gratify a taste worth gratifying. The brilliant stage-carpenter, that master of supreme illusion the scene-painter, that mistress of inordinate variety, or of the only variety we may look to, the dressmaker, have taken over the whole question.

One September night ten years ago, a frequent haunter of Paris, though returning to it but after a considerable absence, was drawn to the Comédie by M. Lomon's *Jean Dacier*, four acts in verse and of a highly tragic cast. When this spectator came out he was too excited to go home, to go to bed, to do anything but live the piece over and walk off his agitation. He made several times the circuit of the Place de la Concorde, he patrolled the streets till night was far gone and his emotion had somewhat subsided. It had been produced by Coquelin's representation of the hero of the piece, and no tribute to the actor's power could have been more hearty and unrestricted. Many years have passed since then; the play, for reasons social and political, I think, rather than artistic, has not been repeated, and the visitor of whom I relate this harmless anecdote has consequently had no chance of renewing his impression of it. He has often wondered whether his recollection is to be trusted, whether some shade of a mistake, of extraneous fortuitous felicity doesn't hang about it. That evening abides with him none the less as well-nigh the most memorable ever spent by him in a theatre. Was there something in his inward condition that happened exceptionally to help the case, or was the whole thing really as fine, and was Coquelin's acting in particular as splendid, as his subsequent ecstatic perambulation would have proved? Why on the one hand should Coquelin's acting not have been splendid, and why on the other, if it was as splendid as I have ever since ventured to suppose, has it not been more celebrated, more commemorated, more of a household word? I fail to have noted any general awareness of this eminent triumph, and in fact to remember anywhere catching so much as a reference to it. Inexcusably, I admit, I have retained no memory of the action on its fate of the overwhelming attention of M. Sarcey, who must have had at such a crisis in our artist's career innumerable remarks to make. Why, at any rate, social and political reasons to the contrary notwithstanding, has the play never again been brought forward, allowing its effect to have been even but half as great as I thus fondly suppose it? Whatever the answer to this question my own impression must warrant me—Jean Dacier is a part which, now that he is his own master and may claim his property where he finds it, M. Coquelin will consult the interests of his highest reputation by taking up again at an early day.

As the beauty of this creation comes back to me I am almost ashamed to have described his strong point just now as the rep-

resentation of impudence. There is not a touch of that excess in the
portrait of the young republican captain who has sprung from the
ranks and who finds himself, by one of the strange complications
of circumstances that occur in great revolutions, married before
he can turn round to the daughter of his former seigneur, the lord
of the manor, now ruined and proscribed, under whom he grew up
in his Breton village. The young man, naturally, of old, before
being swept into the ranks, has adored in secret, and in secret
only, the daughter of the noble house, divided as he is from her by
the impassible gulf which in the novel and the drama, still more
than real life, separates the countess and the serf. The young
woman has been reprieved from the scaffold on condition of her
marrying a republican soldier—cases are on record in which this
clemency was extended to royalist victims—and the husband
whom chance reserves for her is a person who was in the days of
her grandeur and his own obscurity as dust beneath her feet. I
speak of chance, but as I recover the situation it was not purely
fortuitous, inasmuch as Jean had already recognized the object of
his passion—he naturally escapes recognition himself—as she
passes the windows of the guard-house at Nantes in the horrible
cart of the condemned. A "republican marriage," with the drum-
head for the registrar's table, has just been celebrated before the
spectator's eyes and those of the appalled young man; a stout
Breton damsel (not in this case a royalist martyr) has cheerfully
allowed herself to be conjoined by a rite not even civil, and of
scarce more military grace than if performed by a court-martial,
with one of her country's defenders. This strikes the note of
Jean's being able to save his former mistress—the idea flashing
upon him as he sees her—if she will accept a release at such a
price. But how can she herself know whether or not she accepts
it?—she is too dazed, too bewildered and overwhelmed. The
revulsion is too great and the situation too shocking to leave her
for the moment her reason; and an extraordinarily striking passage, as well as one of the most consummately performed things

I remember to have seen, was the entrance of Madame Favart as
the heroine at this stage of the piece. She has at a moment's
notice been pulled down from the tumbril, and with her hands
just untied, her hair disordered, her senses confounded, and the
bloody vision of the guillotine still in her eyes, she is precipitated
into the roomful of soldiers with the announcement of the inconceivable terms of her pardon in her ears. The night I saw the
play the manner in which Madame Favart, in this part, rendered
in face and step all the amazement of the situation, drew forth a
long burst of applause even while she was still dumb.

The ceremony is concluded before this party to it regains her
senses, and it is not till afterwards that she discovers the identity
of her accomplice. I recall as a scene to which the actress's talent
gave almost as much effect as Coquelin's own the third act of
Jean Dacier, the episode of the poor room that sees the young
republican captain introduce her as his bride—where the waiting
éclaircissement takes place of course between the couple so portentously brought together. As I thus refer to it a certain analogy
with the celebrated cottage-scene in the *Lady of Lyons* occurs to
me; but I was not struck with this in watching the play. The step
the young man has taken has, it appears, been only to save the
life of his unwitting mistress; this service rendered, he wished but
to efface himself, worship her though he does, without insisting
on the rights of a husband. The situation is of course foredoomed
to still richer romance and still sharper tragedy; by the time
Marie, whose noble surname I forget, apprehends in her companion the moral beauty of this effort of sacrifice, by the time a
new passion on her side begins to supplant her first impression
of his plan to take a base advantage of her, by this time it is
inevitably too late and we are close up against the catastrophe.
I forget how the climax occurs; I roughly recover it as determined
by Jean's taking or appearing to take part in a secret movement
for putting the life of the girl's father, his old feudal superior, so
to speak, in safety as against his own colleagues, the republican

chiefs. The attempt, the virtual treachery to *them*, comes to light
after it has succeeded, and the young man's life, either by his own
hand or by military justice, is the terrible forfeit. What I am most
distinct about is that while the curtain falls the once proud Marie,
who has fathomed the depths of his heroism, flings herself upon
his inanimate form. All this is of the finest high pitch — the interest of M. Lomon's play, you see, must have been intense; and
my theory would be that M. Coquelin's rendering of his part was
a marvel. Not formed by nature for depicting romantic love, he
triumphed over every obstacle superficially presented to his zeal,
and gave signal support to the interesting truth that if a player
have in him the active imagination of his opportunity, which is
the root of the matter, with a superiority in two or three of the
arts of suggestion, his mere outward facts needn't at all interfere
with the consistency of the figure he desires to impose.

Without the root of the matter, as in every other art, nothing
else, however it may disconnectedly pretend, has any contributive
virtue — whereas that inward force may occasionally cause the
physical desert itself to flower, or to seem to for the hour, which
comes to the same thing. The impression of the ear, it can scarce
be too often repeated, may always at the worst charm away the
objections raised by the eye; though I have never known the impression of the eye to charm away a protest strongly made by the
ear. In proof of the former of which propositions, one may ask,
who does not recall from experience some case of the happy
process so exhibited? The immediate alarm, after the rise of the
curtain or on the entrance of the apparently ill-starred figure, has
been dispelled, genius taking its time to intervene; the omens
have been boldly reinterpreted and the claim to interest and con-
vince us made good. Vivid for me to this day my disconcertment,
long years ago, by the prime aspect of that sincerest of artists and
most attaching of heroines Aimée Desclée, who "came on" in
Froufrou, the part she was to launch on its prodigious career, only
to surround herself at once with the cloud of doubts that she was

within the next ten minutes so triumphantly to sweep away that no one of them lifted its head again during the whole of the piece. I cherish that memory for its supremely exquisite support of the truth most precious in all this connection, the truth that expression and persuasion so depend on the actor's intelligence, on its being of the finest possible order for the particular application, and so take effect in proportion as it *is* of such an order, that other measurements and tests cease in comparison to be urgent. I see some of these indeed claiming an importance on behalf of the pantomimist, the *mime* pure and simple; but even then what are his motions, what is his play of face, but so many tones and syllables, so many signified mute words, all making sentences and with the sole difference of their being addressed to the mental instead of the physical ear. Language is not the less in question for its but *appearing* to be uttered; when the art is consummate we fail to distinguish between appearance and sound. All of which brings me round again without inconsequence to my point, on behalf of Coquelin's Jean Dacier, that youth, passion, patriotism, tenderness, renunciation, everything gallant and touching and that causes the sense to thrill and melt, are embodied for me, without attenuation by the years, in the little republican officer with the meagre material presence, the weather-worn uniform, the *retroussé* nose and that far-ringing, nerve-stirring voice which in certain of the patriotic couplets of the first act played through the place like a clarion. I note moreover that the part is tragic without a moment's look-in, as the phrase goes, of that apology for truth when truth becomes difficult which is known in the theatre as the "relief" of an altered pitch. The strings of the lyre are individual, and when the tune and the harmony are all in the graver ones I hate to find the others irrevelantly twanged.

It comes over me further, to revert, that if that admirable old Alsatian country schoolmaster in the *Ami Fritz*, of whom our intending visitor makes so inimitable a figure is not tragic, neither is he in any degree impudent. I recall this character as a finished image of quaint old-world geniality and morality, of patriarchal and peaceful *bonhommie*. Wondrously elaborated, yet never exaggerated, it reproduces the individual in his minutest particularities, and yet keeps him closely related to the medium, the sheltered social scene, in which he moves — keeps him perfect in tone, perfect above all in taste. The taste in which MM. Erckmann-Chatrian's schoolmaster is embalmed I judge it would be impossible to M. Coquelin under any betrayal of opportunity whatever to depart from. It bears him company as a classic temperance — not less in the grotesque unctuousness of M. Loyal above-mentioned than in the extravagance of the grimacing, chanting, capering footman of the *Précieuses*. Which comes back, as I have already hinted, to his letting go of the treasure of style as little in his lowest comedy as in his highest. His presentment of the Duc de Septmonts in the *Étrangère*, to which I have already alluded, is an instance of his highest and of the conditions in which he draws upon the treasure most considerately and quietly. I have left myself no space to devote to this consummate creation, which I had in mind in speaking just now of his Jean Dacier as surpassed for "importance" but by one other case in his repertory. (I can only answer of course for those I have seen, and there are several I have unluckily missed. Among these are three or four characters of the last few years, such as the chief in the *Député de Bombignac*, and the chief in Octave Feuillet's *Chamillac*, figures, I believe, with nothing whatever in common save an intimate actability, of which he appears to have taken with equal ease an extraordinary advantage. Such light studies of the infinitely modern as the former of the things just named, and as the hero of *Un Parisien*, happily within my ken, are a new extension of his range, and help to represent in him that liveliest of the self-respecting actor's ideals, and the greatest honour of the craft, I think, the placing at the two ends of his scale the most different images conceivable.) It is not on our artist's lighter efforts, however, that I should waste words — his marvellous virtuosity just *finds* ease in material

out of which his weaker brethren have to extract it by the sweat
of their brow; and it is more to the purpose that if Jean Dacier
is his highest flight in the line of rhymed parts the Duc de
Septmonts is his finest stroke in the field of a closer realism. Fine
indeed the aesthetic sense and the applied means that can invite,
that can insidiously encourage, a conception to so mature and
materialize, and that can yet so keep it in the tone of life as we
commonly know life, keep it above all "in the picture" in which
it is concerned and in relation to the other forms of truth that
surround it, forms it may not barbarously sacrifice. M. Coquelin's
progress through this long and elaborate part, all of fine shades
and pointed particulars, all resting on the keenest observation as
well as appealing to it, resembles the method of the "psychological" novelist who (when he is in as complete possession of his
form as M. Coquelin of *his*) builds up a character, in his supposedly
uncanny process, by touch added to touch, line to line, illustration
to illustration, and with a vision of his personage breathing
steadily before him. It wouldn't take much more than my remembrance of the Duc de Septmonts at the Français to make me pronounce his exponent really the Balzac of actors. The effect that
his farewell to the great theatre (taken in conjunction with some
other recent commotions, some other rifts within the lute, now
indeed a goodly number,) will have upon the classic scene itself
belongs to a range of considerations which, though seductive, are
not open to us here. But it is impossible not to follow with interest, in fact with a lively suspense, the future of the distinguished
seceder; his endowment, his capacity, his fortune up to this time,
with the remaining possibilities of such an ambition, have so the
weight of assurance, the exploring, conquering air. He is an image
of success as well as of resolution, and with so much of the booty
of his general quest appropriated, we look to see where the rest
of it may be stored. If he draws it forth, as well he may, in forms
as yet unsuspected and undiscovered, his career must still have a
scope, and our attention a thrill, at least proportionate to what

COQUELIN

the past has done for us. The defect of his activity, if I may "drag in" again that note—no very assured one at the best—is a certain technical hardness, an almost inhuman perfection of surface; but the compensation of this on the other hand is that it suggests durability and resistance, resistance I mean to the great corrupting contact with the public. May that virtue in him not break down under such a test as our American conditions have it in their dread power to apply!

"Coquelin" originally appeared, with a portrait of its subject, in the Century Magazine, *January, 1887. At the end of his essay on the visit of the Comédie Française to London in 1879 Henry James wrote: "I said just now that Mlle. Sarah Bernhardt was supposed to be going to America. That is all very well; but what I really wish is that M. Coquelin would go." Seven years later Coquelin resigned from the Comédie and prepared to undertake an extensive tour which was to include America. James's wish was about to be fulfilled, and it is hardly presumptuous to suppose that in writing and publishing his essay he had the intention of giving a friendly recommendation of the great actor to the American theatre-going public.*

As a small boy James had been educated for a short time at the Collège Communal of Boulogne, where he had for a fellow pupil a boy two years older than himself, Benoît-Constant Coquelin, son of a local pastry cook. In his Notebooks, *under date December 26, (1881), James makes a long entry recalling his emotion at Coquelin's performance in* Jean Dacier, *in September, 1877: "He threw me into a great state of excitement: I thought seriously of writing to Coquelin, telling him I had been his schoolmate, &c." He then goes on to recount his meeting with the actor at breakfast at Andrew Lang's, when the Comédie*

Française came to London, and the tremendous effect Coquelin made on him—"his personality, his talk, the way the artist overflowed in him"—although the occasion was unpropitious, James having to devote himself largely to translating the remarks of the other guests. But he concludes: "I may say that these two little moments are landmarks."

Early in 1915 Brander Matthews asked James to allow him to reprint the Coquelin essay in one of a small series of books then being issued by the Dramatic Museum of Columbia University which was to contain Coquelin's lecture on Art and the Actor. In the letter of February 2, 1915, already quoted, James writes, from 21, Carlyle Mansions, Cheyne Walk, S.W.:

". . . the 'four little books' of the Dramatic Columbia connection have not yet turned up. They will doubtless do so in due course, and I shall not less presumably appreciate and enjoy them. As for the Coquelin article, let me ask you if I mayn't have a sight of it again, after long years before I definitely let you know about reprinting it? I have no copy, and have had none, since the hour of its appearance, and only seem to remember that it came out in the Century, and that there was never any question for me of republishing it. I'm afraid you impute to me a more continued interest

217

THE SCENIC ART

in the theatre than I am conscious of, or have been for long; I am only now, and in a deeply obscured and discouraged way, interested in the drama—which is in our conditions so very different a thing. However, I shan't at all oppose your use of the Coquelin paper if I find I can myself read it again. I scarce know how to put my hand on it here, but doubtless you can help me."

By March 24, 1915, he had read and revised his essay, and wrote to Matthews:

"I am sending you back for your public use the article on Coquelin, but sending it back as much 'done over' as was absolutely inevitable. I have, as you will see, so very much re-expressed the sense of it as to have had recourse to a new text, that is a new pen and new paper, altogether; and I must ask you to be so good as to take it in this way or not to take it at all. It has been really dreadful to me to be reminded of how filthily (yes, je maintiens le mot,) I could at one time write, how imperfectly I could leave my intention expressed. This paper, as the Century printed it (without so much as a proof sent me in common decency) simply bristles with those intentions baffled and abandoned; and nothing could have induced me, from the moment of owning any relation to them again, not pityingly to re-father them, not decently to feed and clothe them, not, in short, to pop them into the hideous gaps that have so long and so disgracefully awaited them. The article has now, accordingly, some shadow of a right to exist—and I shall therefore welcome its existence in your volume. I beg you to be intelligent about this, as you so easily can, and to like it very much as it now, for the first time, stands. It didn't in the least stand before—it but waggled on one leg! Kindly refer it to its former identity by some such footnote (say on the first page or somewhere) as: "The substance of this paper appeared in the Century Magazine for"—such and such a date, which I have no note of and the excision received from you gives me no clue to. (1)

(1) A thousand pardons—it is of course, from your hand, January, 1887.

In the original text of the essay James refers to the author of Jean Dacier *as* Thomond. *This may be due to a printer's error, as he says he saw no proof. In the revised version he gives the name as* Lomond, *but actually there is no final 'd.'*

218

THE ACTING
IN MR. IRVING'S "FAUST"

—————— 1 8 8 7 ——————

AS AN assistance to making clear to ourselves some of the
questions suggested by the wonderful modern art of "staging" a piece, and in particular the effect that traps and panoramas,
processions and coloured lights, may have in their exuberance,
their obtrusiveness upon the personal interpretation, the manner
in which, at the Lyceum, Mr. Henry Irving has produced a version
of Goethe's *Faust* (for which he has been indebted to the fruitful
pen of Mr. Wills) is greatly to be welcomed. Nothing lights up a
subject like a good example, and Mr. Irving's examples are always
excellent. His production of *Faust* has been largely acclaimed and
still more largely witnessed; it has had one of the longest of long
runs, which, at the moment these words are written, shows no
signs of abating. To the richness and ingenuity of the spectacle
innumerable pens will have testified. The critic gives his impression, and that impression has been abundantly uttered. There is
another one which also naturally has its turn. The *mise-en-scène*
in the light of the acting, and the acting in the light of the *mise-en-
scène*, are the respective halves of the interesting question. It is
with the second half only that we ourselves are concerned.

In this connection the first thing that strikes us is a certain
perversity in the manner in which Mr. Irving has approached and
regarded his task, a perversity most singular on the part of a
manager to whom the interests of the dramatic art have long
appeared to be so dear. Saying to himself that he would give great

attention to the machinery of the piece, he omitted to indulge at
the same time in this indispensable reflection,—that to prevent
the impression of triviality which might easily arise from an abuse
of pantomimic effects, he should take care to put at the service of
the great story a consummate interpretation; to see that Faust
and Margaret and Martha, as well as Mephistopheles, were embodied in such a manner as to enable them to hold up their heads
and strike their respective notes in the midst of the wilderness of
canvas and paint. To the canvas and paint—since he feels Goethe's
poem, or indeed simply the wondrous legend, in that way; or
even, as we may say, since he feels in that way the manner in
which Mr. Wills feels Goethe and the legend—he was perfectly
welcome; but surely he ought to have perceived that, given the
grandly poetic, ironic, but at the same time very scantily dramatic
nature of his drama; given the delicacy and subtlety of a work of
genius of the complexion of *Faust*, special precautions should be
taken against the accessories seeming a more important part of
the business than the action. Evidently, however, Mr. Irving
argued in directly the opposite way. It is as if he had said that he
would pile the accessories so high that the rest of the affair
wouldn't matter, it would be regarded so little.

It wouldn't matter, in the first place, that Mr. Wills should
have turned him out an arrangement of Goethe so meagre, so
common, so trivial (one really must multiply epithets to express
its inadequacy), that the responsibility of the impresario to the
poet increased tenfold, rather than diminished, with his accepting
it, there being so much more, as it were, to make up for. It
wouldn't matter that from the beginning to the end of the play,
thanks to Mr. Wills's ingenious dissimulation of the fact, it might
never occur to the auditor that he was listening to one of the
greatest productions of the human mind. It wouldn't matter that
Mr. Irving should have conceived and should execute his own
part in the spirit of somewhat refined extravaganza; a manner
which should differ only in degree from that of the star of a

Christmas burlesque,—without breadth, without depth, with
little tittering effects of low comedy. It wouldn't matter that
Faust should be represented by a young actor, whose general
weakness should prevent him, in spite of zealous effort, from
giving stature and relief to his conception of the character, and
whose unformed delivery should interfere in the same degree
with his imparting variety of accent to his different speeches. It
wouldn't matter that, with Mr. Wills's version and such an interpretation, the exquisite episode of the wooing of Margaret
should hold no place in the play—should literally pass unperceived.
It wouldn't matter that Miss Ellen Terry, as picturesque and
pleasing a figure as usual, should give perhaps a stranger exhibition than she has ever given before of her want of art and style,
and should play the divine, still, concentrated part of Margaret
without apparently a suspicion of what it consists. If it wouldn't
matter that Mr. Irving himself should be thin, that Mr. Alexander
should be insignificant, that Miss Terry should be rough, and
that Mr. Wills should be all three, of course it would matter
still less that the two extremely mature actresses who were successively to attempt Martha should give the English public (so
far at least as represented at the Lyceum) a really rare opportunity
to respond to bad taste with bad taste, to greet with artless and
irrepressible glee the strange gruntings and snortings with which
the performers in question have seen fit to enrich the character.
All these things, to our sense, *should* have mattered; it was far
better that the overtopping scenery should have been sacrificed
than that a concession should have been made in regard to the
personal rendering of the piece. It was far better that the "points"
should remain the points that Goethe made, even if the background had to be bare for it; that the immortal group of the
scholar with his passions rekindled, the girl who trusts and suffers,
and the mocking, spell-weaving fiend should hold itself well together, detach itself, and stamp itself strongly, even if the imagination had to do the work of putting in the gardens and spires of

the German city, the mist and goblins of the Brocken, and the blue fire that plays about Mephistopheles. Of course if Mr. Irving could both have mounted the play and caused the acting of it to be an equal feature, that would have been best of all; but since the personal representation of a work at once so pregnant poetically and so faulty as a dramatic composition was the problem to challenge by its very difficulties an artist of his high reputation, — an artist universally acclaimed as leading the public taste, not as waiting behind its chair, — he would have consulted best the interests of that reputation by "going in" for a dramatic as distinguished from a spectacular success.

We may as well confess frankly that we attach the most limited importance to the little mechanical artifices with which Mr. Irving has sought to enliven *Faust*. We care nothing for the spurting flames which play so large a part, nor for the importunate limelight which is perpetually projected upon somebody or something. It is not for these things that we go to see the great Goethe, or even (for we must, after all, allow for inevitable dilutions) the less celebrated Mr. Wills. We even protest against the abuse of the said lime-light effect: it is always descending on some one or other, apropos of everything and of nothing; it is disturbing and vulgarizing, and has nothing to do with the author's meaning. That blue vapours should attend on the steps of Mephistopheles is a very poor substitute for his giving us a moral shudder. That deep note is entirely absent from Mr. Irving's rendering of him, though the actor, of course, at moments presents to the eye a remarkably sinister figure. He strikes us, however, as superficial — a terrible fault for an archfiend — and his grotesqueness strikes us as cheap. We attach also but the slenderest importance to the scene of the Witches' Sabbath, which has been reduced to a mere bald hubbub of capering, screeching, and banging, irradiated by the irrepressible blue fire, and without the smallest articulation of Goethe's text. The scenic effect is the ugliest we have ever contemplated, and its ugliness is not paid for by its having a

meaning for our ears. It is a horror cheaply conceived, and executed with more zeal than discretion.

It seems almost ungracious to say of an actress usually so
pleasing as Miss Terry that she falls below her occasion, but it
is impossible for us to consider her Margaret as a finished creation. Besides having a strange amateurishness of form (for the
work of an actress who has had Miss Terry's years of practice),
it is, to our sense, wanting in fineness of conception, wanting in
sweetness and quietness, wanting in taste. It is much too rough-
and-ready. We prefer Miss Terry's pathos, however, to her
comedy, and cannot but feel that the whole scene with the jewels
in her room is a mistake. It is obstreperous, and not in the least in
the poetic tone. If the passages in the garden fail of their effect,
the responsibility for this is not, however, more than very partially
with the Margaret. It is explained in the first place by the fact
that the actor who represents Faust is, as we have hinted, not
"in it" at all, and in the second by the fact that the conversation
between Mephistopheles and Margaret is terribly overaccented —
pushed quite out of the frame. Martha's flirtation, especially as
Mrs. Stirling plays it, becomes the whole story, and Faust and
Margaret are superseded. What can have beguiled Mr. Irving
into the extraordinary error of intrusting the part of Martha first
to one and then to another actress of (on this occasion at least)
signally little temperance and taste? The fault has been aggravated
by being repeated; the opportunity of retrieving it might have
been seized when Mrs. Stirling laid down her task. But Mrs.
Chippendale has even a heavier hand. We should be sorry to fail
of respect to the former actress, who, to-day full of years and
honours, has always shown an eminent acquaintance with her art
and has been remarkable for a certain old-fashioned richness of
humour. As such matters go, on the English stage, she is supposed
to have the "tradition." It is to be hoped, however, for the tradition's sake, that she violates it to-day by her tendency to spread,
to "drag," as the phrase is, to take too much elbow-room. This

defect was sufficiently marked when a year or two ago she played the Nurse of Juliet; whom she put sadly out of focus. It is manifested in an even greater degree by her Martha, and it must be said that if she renders the part in the spirit of the tradition, the tradition will on this occasion have been strangely coarse. Yet Mrs. Stirling is distinction itself compared with the displeasing loudness to which her successor treats us; and of this latter lady's acting, it is enough to say that it compelled us to indulge in a melancholy "return" on an audience moved by such means to such mirth. The scene between Mephistopheles and Martha is the most successful of the play, judged by the visible appreciation of the public—a fact which should surely minister to deep reflection on the part of those who, as artists, work for the public. All the same, Mr. Irving would have been well advised, from the artistic point of view, in causing Martha, by contact and example, to be represented in a higher style of comedy. We shall not attempt to point out still other instances in which, as it seems to us, he would have been well advised; we have said enough to substantiate our contention that it is not for the interest of the actor's art that it should be too precipitately, or too superficially, assumed that the great elaboration of a play as a spectacle is a complete expression of it—a complete solution of the problem.

"*The Acting in Mr. Irving's Faust*" *appeared, signed* * * *, in the* Century Magazine, *December, 1887.*

The discovery and identification of this article were made by Miss Edna Kenton, who traced it through the mention made of it in Joseph Pennell's The Adventures of an Illustrator, *1925, and in E. R. Pennell's* Life and Letters of Joseph Pennell, *1929. The idea of an article on Irving's* Faust *production originated with Joseph Pennell, his wife says; she was to describe the scenery and he to illustrate it. To this plan the* Century *agreed. But Joseph Pennell, writing earlier,* says: "*It was arranged that I should draw the scenery of* Faust . . . *and that James should write of the production.*" *The question of how Henry James was drawn into the project is thus left still rather obscure; possibly the suggestion may have come from Edmund Gosse who was the* Century's *European representative and with whom Henry James was at this time already on friendly terms. Both books describe at some length the way in which the Pennells were made free of the Lyceum Theatre, in the auditorium and behind the scenes. Eventually Pennell decided not to do his draw-*

ings; and the Century *published two articles in the same issue, "Pictorial Successes of Mr. Irving's Faust," signed by both Pennells, followed by James's essay. "I never did the drawings," Pennell says, "and James did not write exactly the article Irving looked for, and the situation became somewhat strained." It seems unlikely that James would have shared in the hospitality extended to the Pennells;* he valued his critical integrity too highly to have accepted favours on the understanding that he would produce a panegyric in return. Although the essay did not actually bear his name, "nobody could doubt," says Mrs. Pennell, "that its author was Henry James. I doubt if Ellen Terry and Irving ever forgave us." Less than a decade afterwards Ellen Terry was inviting James to write a play for her.

AFTER THE PLAY

————————— 1 8 8 9 —————————

THE PLAY was not over when the curtain fell, four months ago; it was continued in a supplementary act or epilogue which took place immediately afterwards. "Come home to tea," Florentia said to certain friends who had stopped to speak to her in the lobby of the little theatre in Soho—they had been present at a day performance by the company of the Théâtre Libre, transferred for a week from Paris; and three of these—Auberon and Dorriforth, accompanying Amicia—turned up so expeditiously that the change of scene had the effect of being neatly executed. The short afterpiece—it was in truth very slight—began with Amicia's entrance and her declaration that she would never again go to an afternoon performance: it was such a horrid relapse into the real to find it staring at you through the ugly daylight on coming out of the blessed fictive world.

DORRIFORTH: Ah, you touch there on one of the minor sorrows of life. That's an illustration of the general change that comes to pass in us as we grow older, if we have ever loved the stage: the fading of the glamour and the mystery that surround it.

AUBERON: Do you call it a minor sorrow? It's one of the greatest. And nothing can mitigate it.

AMICIA: Wouldn't it be mitigated a little if the stage were a trifle better? You must remember how that has changed.

AUBERON: Never, never: it's the same old stage. The change is in ourselves.

FLORENTIA: Well, I never would have given an evening to what we have just seen. If one could have put it in between luncheon and tea, well enough. But one's evenings are too precious.

DORRIFORTH: Note that—it's very important.

FLORENTIA: I mean too precious for that sort of thing.

AUBERON: Then you didn't sit spell-bound by the little history of the Duc d'Enghien?

FLORENTIA: I sat yawning. Heavens, what a piece!

AMICIA: Upon my word I liked it. The last act made me cry.

DORRIFORTH: Wasn't it a curious, interesting specimen of some of the things that are worth trying: an attempt to sail closer to the real?

AUBERON: How much closer? The fiftieth part of a point—it isn't calculable.

FLORENTIA: It was just like any other play—I saw no difference. It had neither a plot, nor a subject, nor dialogue, nor situations, nor scenery, nor costumes, nor acting.

AMICIA: Then it was hardly, as you say, just like any other play.

AUBERON: Florentia should have said like any other *bad* one. The only way it differed seemed to be that it was bad in theory as well as in fact.

AMICIA: It's a *morceau de vie,* as the French say.

AUBERON: Oh, don't begin on the French!

AMICIA: It's a French experiment—*que voulez-vous?*

AUBERON: English experiments will do.

DORRIFORTH: No doubt they would—if there *were* any. But I don't see them.

AMICIA: Fortunately: think what some of them might be! Though Florentia saw nothing I saw many things in this poor little shabby *Duc d'Enghien,* coming over to our roaring London, where the dots have to be so big on the "i's," with its barely audible note of originality. It appealed to me, touched me, offered me a poignant suggestion of the way things happen in life.

AUBERON: In life they happen clumsily, stupidly, meanly. One goes to the theatre just for the refreshment of seeing them happen in another way — in symmetrical, satisfactory form, with unmistakable effect and just at the right moment.

DORRIFORTH: It shows how the same cause may produce the most diverse consequences. In this truth lies the only hope of art.

AUBERON: Oh, art, art — don't talk about art!

AMICIA: Mercy, we must talk about something!

DORRIFORTH: Auberon hates generalizations. Nevertheless I make bold to say that we go to the theatre in the same spirit in which we read a novel, some of us to find one thing and some to find another; and according as we look for the particular thing we find it.

AUBERON: That's a profound remark.

FLORENTIA: We go to find amusement: that, surely, is what we all go for.

AMICIA: There's such a diversity in our idea of amusement.

AUBERON: Don't you impute to people more ideas than they have?

DORRIFORTH: Ah, one must do that or one couldn't talk about them. We go to be interested; to be absorbed, beguiled and to lose ourselves, to give ourselves up, in short, to a charm.

FLORENTIA: And the charm is the strange, the extraordinary.

AMICIA: Ah, speak for yourself! The charm is the recognition of what we know, what we feel.

DORRIFORTH: See already how you differ. What we surrender ourselves to is the touch of nature, the sense of life.

AMICIA: The first thing is to believe.

FLORENTIA: The first thing, on the contrary, is to *dis*believe.

AUBERON: Lord, listen to them!

DORRIFORTH: The first thing is to follow — to care.

FLORENTIA: I read a novel, I go to the theatre, to forget.

AMICIA: To forget what?

FLORENTIA: To forget life; to throw myself into something more beautiful, more exciting: into fable and romance.

DORRIFORTH: The attraction of fable and romance is that it's about *us*, about you and me—or people whose power to suffer and to enjoy is the same as ours. In other words, we *live* their experience, for the time, and that's hardly escaping from life.

FLORENTIA: I'm not at all particular as to what you call it. Call it an escape from the common, the prosaic, the immediate.

DORRIFORTH: You couldn't put it better. That's the life that art, with Auberon's permission, gives us; that's the distinction it confers. That is why the greatest commonness is when our guide turns out a vulgar fellow—the angel, as we had supposed him, who has taken us by the hand. Then what becomes of our escape?

FLORENTIA: It's precisely then that I complain of him. He leads us into foul and dreary places—into flat and foolish deserts.

DORRIFORTH: He leads us into his own mind, his own vision of things: that's the only place into which the poet *can* lead us. It's there that he finds *As You Like It*, it is there that he finds *Comus*, or *The Way of the World*, or the Christmas pantomime. It is when he betrays us, after he has got us in and locked the door, when he can't keep from us that we are in a bare little hole and that there are no pictures on the walls, it is then that the immediate and the foolish overwhelm us.

AMICIA: That's what I liked in the piece we have been looking at. There was an artistic intention, and the little room wasn't bare: there was sociable company in it. The actors were very humble aspirants, they were common—

AUBERON: Ah, when the French give their mind to that—!

AMICIA: Nevertheless they struck me as recruits to an interesting cause, which as yet (the house was so empty) could confer neither money nor glory. They had the air, poor things, of working for love.

AUBERON: For love of what?

AMICIA: Of the whole little enterprise—the idea of the Théâtre Libre.

FLORENTIA: Gracious, what you see in things! Don't you suppose they were paid?

AMICIA: I know nothing about it. I liked their shabbiness — they had only what was indispensable in the way of dress and scenery. That often pleases me: the imagination, in certain cases, is more finely persuaded by the little than by the much.

DORRIFORTH: I see what Amicia means.

FLORENTIA: I'll warrant you do, and a great deal more besides.

DORRIFORTH: When the appointments are meagre and sketchy the responsibility that rests upon the actors becomes a still more serious thing, and the spectator's observation of the way they rise to it a pleasure more intense. The face and the voice are more to the purpose than acres of painted canvas, and a touching intonation, a vivid gesture or two, than an army of supernumeraries.

AUBERON: Why not have everything — the face, the voice, the touching intonations, the vivid gestures, the acres of painted canvas, *and* the army of supernumeraries? Why not use bravely and intelligently every resource of which the stage disposes? What else was Richard Wagner's great theory, in producing his operas at Bayreuth?

DORRIFORTH: Why not, indeed? That would be the ideal. To have the picture complete at the same time the figures do their part in producing the particular illusion required — what a perfection and what a joy! I know no answer to that save the aggressive, objectionable fact. Simply look at the stage of to-day and observe that these two branches of the matter never do happen to go together. There is evidently a corrosive principle in the large command of machinery and decorations — a germ of perversion and corruption. It gets the upper hand — it becomes the master. It is so much less easy to get good actors than good scenery and to represent a situation by the delicacy of personal art than by "building it in" and having everything real. Surely there is no reality worth a farthing, on the stage, but what the actor gives, and only when he has learned his business up to the hilt need he concern himself with his material accessories. He hasn't a decent respect for his art unless he be ready to render his part as if the whole illusion depended on that alone and the accessories didn't exist. The acting is everything or it's nothing. It ceases to be everything as soon as something else becomes very important. This is the case, to-day, on the London stage: something else *is* very important. The public have been taught to consider it so: the clever machinery has ended by operating as a bribe and a blind. Their sense of the rest of the matter has gone to the dogs, as you may perceive when you hear a couple of occupants of the stalls talking, in a tone that excites your curiosity, about a performance that's "splendid."

AMICIA: Do you ever hear the occupants of the stalls talking? Never, in the *entr'actes*, have I detected, on their lips, a criticism or a comment.

DORRIFORTH: Oh, they say "splendid"—distinctly! But a question or two reveals that their reference is vague: they don't themselves know whether they mean the art of the actor or that of the stage-carpenter.

AUBERON: Isn't that confusion a high result of taste? Isn't it what's called a feeling for the *ensemble?* The artistic effect, as a whole, is so welded together that you can't pick out the parts.

DORRIFORTH: Precisely; that's what it is in the best cases, and some examples are wonderfully clever.

FLORENTIA: Then what fault do you find?

DORRIFORTH: Simply this—that the whole is a pictorial whole, not a dramatic one. There is something indeed that you can't pick out, for the very good reason that—in any serious sense of the word—it isn't there.

FLORENTIA: The public has taste, then, if it recognizes and delights in a fine picture.

DORRIFORTH: I never said it hadn't, so far as that goes. The public likes to be amused, and small blame to it. It isn't very partic-

ular about the means, but it has rather a preference for amuse-
ments that it believes to be "improving," other things being
equal. I don't think it's either very intelligent or at all opin-
ionated, the dear old public; it takes humbly enough what is
given it and it doesn't cry for the moon. It has an idea that fine
scenery is an appeal to its nobler part, and that it shows a nice
critical sense in preferring it to poor. That's a real intellectual
flight, for the public.

AUBERON: Very well, its preference is right, and why isn't that
a perfectly legitimate state of things?

DORRIFORTH: Why isn't it? It distinctly *is!* Good scenery and poor
acting are better than poor scenery with the same sauce. Only
it becomes then another matter: we are no longer talking about
the drama.

AUBERON: Very likely that's the future of the drama, in London —
an immense elaboration of the picture.

DORRIFORTH: My dear fellow, you take the words out of my mouth.
An immense elaboration of the picture and an immense sacrifice
of everything else: it would take very little more to persuade
me that that will be the only formula for our children. It's all
right, when once we have buried our dead. I have no doubt that
the scenic part of the art, remarkable as some of its achievements already appear to us, is only in its infancy, and that we
are destined to see wonders done that we now but faintly conceive. The probable extension of the mechanical arts is infinite.
"Built in," forsooth! We shall see castles and cities and mountains and rivers built in. Everything points that way; especially
the constitution of the contemporary multitude. It is huge and
good-natured and common. It likes big, unmistakable, knock-
down effects; it likes to get its money back in palpable, com-
putable change. It's in a tremendous hurry, squeezed together,
with a sort of generalized gape, and the last thing it expects of
you is that you will spin things fine. You can't portray a character, alas, or even, vividly, any sort of human figure, unless, in

some degree, you do that. Therefore the theatre, inevitably accommodating itself, will be at last a landscape without figures. I mean, of course, without figures that count. There will be little illustrations of costume stuck about — dressed manikins; but they'll have nothing to say: they won't even go through the form of speech.

AMICIA: What a hideous prospect!

DORRIFORTH: Not necessarily, for we shall have grown used to it: we shall, as I say, have buried our dead. To-day it's cruel, because our old ideals are only dying, they are *in extremis*, they are virtually defunct, but they are above-ground — we trip and stumble on them. We shall eventually lay them tidily away. This is a bad moment, because it's a moment of transition, and we still *miss* the old superstition, the bravery of execution, the eloquence of the lips, the interpretation of character. We miss these things, of course, in proportion as the ostensible occasion for them is great; we miss them particularly, for instance, when the curtain rises on Shakespeare. Then we are conscious of a certain divine dissatisfaction, of a yearning for that which isn't. But we shall have got over this discomfort on the day when we have accepted the ostensible occasion as merely and frankly ostensible, and the real one as having nothing to do with it.

FLORENTIA: I don't follow you. As I'm one of the squeezed, gaping public, I must be dense and vulgar. You do, by-the-way, immense injustice to that body. They do care for character — care much for it. Aren't they perpetually talking about the actor's conception of it?

DORRIFORTH: Dear lady, what better proof can there be of their ineptitude, and that painted canvas and real water are the only things they understand? The vanity of wasting time over that!

AUBERON: Over what?

DORRIFORTH: The actor's conception of a part. It's the refuge of observers who are no observers and critics who are no critics. With what on earth have we to do save his execution?

FLORENTIA: I don't in the least agree with you.

AMICIA: Are you very sure, my poor Dorriforth?

AUBERON: Give him rope and he'll hang himself.

DORRIFORTH: It doesn't need any great license to ask who in the world holds in his bosom the sacred secret of the right conception. All the actor can do is to give us *his*. We must take that one for granted, we make him a present of it. He must impose his conception upon us—

AUBERON (*interrupting*): I thought you said we accepted it.

DORRIFORTH: Impose it upon our *attention*, clever Auberon. It is because we accept his idea that he must repay us by making it vivid, by showing us how valuable it is. We give him a watch: he must show us what time it keeps. He winds it up, that is he executes the conception, and his execution is what we criticise, if we be so moved. Can anything be more absurd than to hear people discussing the conception of a part of which the execution doesn't exist—the idea of a character which never arrives at form? Think what it is, that form, as an accomplished actor may give it to us, and admit that we have enough to do to hold him to this particular honour.

AUBERON: Do you mean to say you don't think some conceptions are better than some others?

DORRIFORTH: Most assuredly, some are better: the proof of the pudding is in the eating. The best are those which yield the most points, which have the largest face; those, in other words, that are the most demonstrable, or, in other words still, the most actable. The most intelligent performer is he who recognizes most surely this "actable" and distinguishes in it the more from the less. But we are so far from being in possession of a subjective pattern to which we have a right to hold him that he is entitled directly to contradict any such absolute by presenting us with different versions of the same text, each completely coloured, completely consistent with itself. Every actor in whom the artistic life is strong must often feel the challenge to do that. I should never think, for instance, of contesting an actress's right to represent Lady Macbeth as a charming, insinuating woman, if she really sees the figure that way. I may be surprised at such a vision; but so far from being scandalized, I am positively thankful for the extension of knowledge, of pleasure, that she is able to open to me.

AUBERON: A reading, as they say, either commends itself to one's sense of truth, or it doesn't. In the one case—

DORRIFORTH: In the one case I recognize, even—or especially—when the presumption may have been against the particular attempt, a consummate illustration of what art can do. In the other I moralize indulgently upon human rashness.

FLORENTIA: You have an assurance *à toute épreuve;* but you are deplorably superficial. There is a whole group of plays and a whole category of acting to which your generalizations quite fail to apply. Help me, Auberon.

AUBERON: You're easily exhausted. I suppose she means that it's far from true everywhere that the scenery is everything. It may be true—I don't say it is!—of two or three good-natured playhouses in London. It isn't true—how can it be?—of the provincial theatres or of the others in the capital. Put it even that they would be all scenery if they could; they can't, poor things—so they have to provide acting.

DORRIFORTH: They have to, fortunately; but what do we hear of it?

FLORENTIA: How do you mean, what do we hear of it?

DORRIFORTH: In what trumpet of fame does it reach us? They do what they can, the performers Auberon alludes to, and they are brave souls. But I am speaking of the conspicuous cases, of the exhibitions that draw.

FLORENTIA: There is good acting that draws; one could give you names and places.

DORRIFORTH: I have already guessed those you mean. But when it isn't too much a matter of the paraphernalia it is too little a matter of the play. A play nowadays is a rare bird. I should like to see one.

FLORENTIA: There are lots of them, all the while — the newspapers talk about them. People talk about them at dinners.

DORRIFORTH: What do they say about them?

FLORENTIA: The newspapers?

DORRIFORTH: No, I don't care for *them*. The people at dinners.

FLORENTIA: Oh, they don't say anything in particular.

DORRIFORTH: Doesn't that seem to show the effort isn't very suggestive?

AMICIA: The conversation at dinners certainly isn't.

DORRIFORTH: I mean our contemporary drama. To begin with, you can't find it — there's no text.

FLORENTIA: No text?

AUBERON: So much the better!

DORRIFORTH: So much the better if there is to be no criticism. There is only a dirty prompter's book. One can't put one's hand upon it; one doesn't know what one is discussing. There is no "authority" — nothing is ever published.

AMICIA: The pieces wouldn't bear that.

DORRIFORTH: It would be a small ordeal to resist — if there were anything in them. Look at the novels!

AMICIA: The text is the French *brochure*. The "adaptation" is unprintable.

DORRIFORTH: That's where it's so wrong. It ought at least to be as good as the original.

AUBERON: Aren't there some "rights" to protect — some risk of the play being stolen if it's published?

DORRIFORTH: There may be — I don't know. Doesn't that only prove how little important we regard the drama as being, and how little seriously we take it, if we won't even trouble ourselves to bring about decent civil conditions for its existence? What have we to do with the French *brochure?* how does that help us to represent our own life, our manners, our customs, our ideas, our English types, our English world? Such a field for comedy, for tragedy, for portraiture, for satire, as they all make — such subjects as they would yield! Think of London alone — what a matchless hunting-ground for the satirist — the most magnificent that ever was. If the occasion always produced the man London would have produced an Aristophanes. But somehow it doesn't.

FLORENTIA: Oh, types and ideas, Aristophanes and satire —!

DORRIFORTH: I'm too ambitious, you mean? I shall presently show you that I'm not ambitious at all. Everything makes against that — I am only reading the signs.

AUBERON: The plays are arranged to be as English as possible: they are altered, they are fitted.

DORRIFORTH: Fitted? Indeed they are, and to the capacity of infants. They are in too many cases made vulgar, puerile, barbarous. They are neither fish nor flesh, and with all the point that's left out and all the naïveté that's put in, they cease to place before us any coherent appeal or any recognizable society.

AUBERON: They often make good plays to act, all the same.

DORRIFORTH: They may; but they don't make good plays to see or to hear. The theatre consists of two things, *que diable* — of the stage and the drama, and I don't see how you can have it unless you have both, or how you can have either unless you have the other. They are the two blades of a pair of scissors.

AUBERON: You are very unfair to native talent. There are lots of *strictly original* plays —

AMICIA: Yes, they put that expression on the posters.

AUBERON: I don't know what they put on the posters; but the plays are written and acted — produced with great success.

DORRIFORTH: Produced — partly. A play isn't fully produced until it is in a form in which you can refer to it. We have to talk in the air. I can refer to my Congreve, but I can't to my Pinero.*

FLORENTIA: The authors are not bound to publish them if they don't wish.

* *Since the above was written several of Mr. Pinero's plays have been published.* [1893].

DORRIFORTH: Certainly not, nor are they in that case bound to insist on one's not being a little vague about them. They are perfectly free to withhold them; they may have very good reasons for it, and I can imagine some that would be excellent and worthy of all respect. But their withholding them is one of the signs.

AUBERON: What signs?

DORRIFORTH: Those I just spoke of—those we are trying to read together. The signs that ambition and desire are folly, that the sun of the drama has set, that the matter isn't worth talking about, that it has ceased to be an interest for serious folk, and that everything—everything, I mean, that's anything—is over. The sooner we recognize it the sooner to sleep, the sooner we get clear of misleading illusions and are purged of the bad blood that disappointment makes. It's a pity, because the theatre—after every allowance is made—*might* have been a fine thing. At all events it was a pleasant—it was really almost a noble—dream. *Requiescat!*

FLORENTIA: I see nothing to confirm your absurd theory. I delight in the play; more people than ever delight in it with me; more people than ever go to it, and there are ten theatres in London where there were two of old.

DORRIFORTH: Which is what was to be demonstrated. Whence do they derive their nutriment?

AUBERON: Why, from the enormous public.

DORRIFORTH: My dear fellow, I'm not talking of the box-office. What wealth of dramatic, of histrionic production have we, to meet that enormous demand? There will be twenty theatres ten years hence where there are ten to-day, and there will be, no doubt, ten times as many people "delighting in them," like Florentia. But it won't alter the fact that our dream will have been dreamed. Florentia said a word when we came in which alone speaks volumes.

FLORENTIA: What was my word?

AUBERON: You are sovereignly unjust to native talent among the actors—I leave the dramatists alone. There are many who do excellent, independent work; strive for perfection, completeness —in short, the things we want.

DORRIFORTH: I am not in the least unjust to them—I only pity them: they have so little to put *sous la dent*. It must seem to them at times that no one will work for them, that they are likely to starve for parts—forsaken of gods and men.

FLORENTIA: If they work, then, in solitude and sadness, they have the more honour, and one should recognize more explicitly their great merit.

DORRIFORTH: Admirably said. Their laudable effort is precisely the one little loop-hole that I see of escape from the general doom. Certainly we must try to enlarge it—that small aperture into the blue. We must fix our eyes on it and make much of it, exaggerate it, do anything with it that may contribute to re-store a working faith. Precious that must be to the sincere spirits on the stage who are conscious of all the other things— formidable things—that rise against them.

AMICIA: What other things do you mean?

DORRIFORTH: Why, for one thing, the grossness and brutality of London, with its scramble, its pressure, its hustle of engage-ments, of preoccupations, its long distances, its late hours, its nightly dinners, its innumerable demands on the attention, its general congregation of influences fatal to the isolation, to the punctuality, to the security, of the dear old playhouse spell. When Florentia said in her charming way—

FLORENTIA: Here's my dreadful speech at last.

DORRIFORTH: When you said that you went to the Théâtre Libre in the afternoon because you couldn't spare an evening, I recognized the death-knell of the drama. *Time*, the very breath of its nostrils, is lacking. Wagner was clever to go to leisurely Bayreuth among the hills—the Bayreuth of spacious days, a paradise of "development." Talk to a London audience of "development"! The long runs would, if necessary, put the whole question into a nutshell. Figure to yourself, for then the question is answered, how an intelligent actor must loathe them, and what a cruel negation he must find in them of the artistic life, the life of which the very essence is variety of practice, freshness of experiment, and to feel that one must do many things in turn to do any one of them completely.

AUBERON: I don't in the least understand your *acharnement*, in view of the vagueness of your contention.

DORRIFORTH: My *acharnement* is your little joke, and my contention is a little lesson in philosophy.

FLORENTIA: I prefer a lesson in taste. I had one the other night at the *Merry Wives*.

DORRIFORTH: If you come to that, so did I!

AMICIA: So she does spare an evening sometimes.

FLORENTIA: It was all extremely quiet and comfortable, and I don't in the least recognize Dorriforth's lurid picture of the dreadful conditions. There was no scenery — at least not too much; there was just enough, and it was very pretty, and it was in its place.

DORRIFORTH: And what else was there?

FLORENTIA: There was very good acting.

AMICIA: I also went, and I thought it all, for a sportive, wanton thing, quite painfully ugly.

AUBERON: Uglier than that ridiculous black room, with the invisible people groping about in it, of your precious *Duc d'Enghien?*

DORRIFORTH: The black room is doubtless not the last word of art, but it struck me as a successful application of a happy idea. The contrivance was perfectly simple — a closer night effect than is usually attempted, with a few guttering candles, which threw high shadows over the bare walls, on the table of the court-martial. Out of the gloom came the voices and tones of the distinguishable figures, and it is perhaps a fancy of mine that it made them — given the situation, of course — more impressive and dramatic.

AUBERON: You rail against scenery, but what could belong more to the order of things extraneous to what you perhaps a little priggishly call the delicacy of personal art than the arrangement you are speaking of?

DORRIFORTH: I was talking of the abuse of scenery. I never said anything so idiotic as that the effect isn't helped by an appeal to the eye and an adumbration of the whereabouts.

AUBERON: But where do you draw the line and fix the limit? What is the exact dose?

DORRIFORTH: It's a question of taste and tact.

FLORENTIA: And did you find taste and tact in that coal-hole of the Théâtre Libre?

DORRIFORTH: Coal-hole is again your joke. I found a strong impression in it — an impression of the hurried, extemporized cross-examination, by night, of an impatient and mystified prisoner, whose dreadful fate had been determined in advance, who was to be shot, high-handedly, in the dismal dawn. The arrangement didn't worry and distract me: it was simplifying, intensifying. It gave, what a judicious *mise-en-scène* should always do, the essence of the matter, and left the embroidery to the actors.

FLORENTIA: At the *Merry Wives*, where you could see your hand before your face, I could make out the embroidery.

DORRIFORTH: Could you, under Falstaff's pasteboard cheeks and the sad disfigurement of his mates? There was no excess of scenery, Auberon says. Why, Falstaff's very person was nothing *but* scenery. A false face, a false figure, false hands, false legs — scarcely a square inch on which the irrepressible humour of the rogue could break into illustrative touches. And he is so human, so expressive, of so rich a physiognomy. One would rather Mr. Beerbohm Tree should have played the part in his own clever, elegant slimness—that would at least have represented life. A Falstaff all "make-up" is an opaque substance. This seems to me an example of what the rest still more suggested, that in dealing with a production like the *Merry Wives* really the main quality to put forward is discretion. You must resolve such a production, as a thing represented, into a tone that the imagination can take an aesthetic pleasure in. Its grossness must be transposed, as it were, to a fictive scale, a scale of fainter tints and generalized signs. A filthy, eruptive, realistic Bardolph and Pistol overlay the romantic with the literal. Relegate them and blur them, to the eye; let their blotches be constructive and their raggedness relative.

AMICIA: Ah, it was *so* ugly!

DORRIFORTH: What a pity then, after all, there wasn't more painted canvas to divert you! Ah, decidedly, the theatre of the future must be that.

FLORENTIA: Please remember your theory that our life's a scramble, and suffer me to go and dress for dinner.

"After the Play" appeared in the first number of the New Review, *June, 1889, and was reprinted in* Picture and Text, *1893.*

In the earlier part of this year Henry James was in London, hard at work on his novel The Tragic Muse *and writing little else. His thoughts were now centered on the theatre for he was intending to devote himself to writing plays, and it is evident that he used the occasion of the visit of the Théâtre Libre to London to arrange and clarify his ideas of what the contem-porary theatre was doing and what it might do; was he not envisaging his own future plans when he wrote of representing "our own life, our manners, our customs, our ideas, our Eng-lish types, our English world. Such a field for comedy, for tragedy, for portraiture, for satire, as they all make— . . ." It is significant, too, that of the four critical papers which he published in 1889 two of them— "After the Play" and "An Animated Conversation" in* Scribner's Maga-*zine of March—were cast "in scenic form."*

———————— 1891, 1893 ————————

I. *On the occasion of Hedda Gabler (1891)*

WHETHER or no Henrik Ibsen be a master of his art, he has had a fortune that, in the English-speaking world, falls not always even to the masters — the fortune not only of finding himself the theme of many pens and tongues, but the rarer privilege and honour of acting as a sort of register of the critical atmosphere, a barometer of the intellectual weather. Interesting or not in himself (the word on this point varies from the fullest affirmation to the richest denial), he has sounded in our literary life a singularly interesting hour. At any rate he himself constitutes an episode, an event, if the sign of such action be to have left appearances other than you found them. He has cleared up the air we breathe and set a copy to our renouncement; has made many things wonderfully plain and quite mapped out the prospect. Whenever such service is rendered, the attentive spirit is the gainer; these are its moments of amplest exercise. Illusions are sweet to the dreamer, but not so to the observer, who has a horror of a fool's paradise. Henrik Ibsen will have led him inexorably into the rougher road. Such recording and illuminating agents are precious; they tell us where we are in the thickening fog of life, and we feel for them much of the grateful respect excited in us at sea, in dim weather, by the exhibition of the mysterious instrument with which the captain takes an observation. We have held

Ghosts, or *Rosmersholm,* or *Hedda Gabler* in our hand, and *they* have been our little instrument — they have enabled us to emulate the wary mariner; the consequence of which is that we know at least on what shores we may ground or in what ports we may anchor. The author of these strange works has in short performed a function which was doubtless no part of his purpose. This was to tell us about his own people; yet what has primarily happened is that he has brought about an exhibition of ours.

It is a truly remarkable show, for as to where *nous en sommes,* as the phrase goes, in the art of criticism and the movement of curiosity, as to our accumulations of experience and our pliancy of intelligence, our maturity of judgement and our distinction of tone, our quick perception of quality and (peculiar glory of our race) our fine feeling for shades, he has been the means of our acquiring the most copious information. Whether or no we may say that as a sequel to this we know Dr. Ibsen better, we may at least say that we know more about ourselves. We glow with the sense of how we may definitely look to each other to take things, and that is an immense boon, representing in advance a wonderful economy of time, a saving of useless effort and vain appeal. The great clarifying fact has been that, with *Hedda Gabler* and *Ghosts* and all the rest, we have stood in an exceptionally agitated way in the presence of the work of art, and have gained thereby a peculiarly acute consciousness of how we tend to consider it. It has been interesting to perceive that we consider the work of art with passion, with something approaching to fury. Under its influence we sweep the whole keyboard of emotion, from frantic enjoyment to ineffable disgust. Resentment and reprobation happen to have been indeed in the case before us the notes most frequently sounded; but this is obviously an accident, not impairing the value of the illustration, the essence of which is that our critical temper remains exactly the *naïf* critical temper, the temper of the spectators in the gallery of the theatre who howl at the villain of the play.

It has been the degree in general, of the agitation that has been remarkable in the case before us, as may conveniently be gathered from a glance at the invaluable catalogue of denouncements drawn up by Mr. William Archer after perusal of the articles lately dedicated by the principal London journals to a couple of representations of Ibsen; that, if I mistake not, of *Ghosts* and that of *Rosmersholm*. This catalogue is a precious document, one of those things that the attentive spirit would not willingly let die. It is a thing, at any rate, to be kept long under one's hand, as a mine of suggestion and reference; for it illuminates, in this matter of the study of Ibsen, the second characteristic of our emotion (the first as I have mentioned, being its peculiar intensity): the fact that that emotion is conspicuously and exclusively moral, one of those cries of outraged purity which have so often and so pathetically resounded through the Anglo-Saxon world.

We have studied our author, it must be admitted, under difficulties, for it is impossible to read him without perceiving that merely book in hand we but half know him—he addresses himself so substantially to representation. This quickens immensely our consideration for him, since in proportion as we become conscious that he has mastered an exceedingly difficult form are we naturally reluctant, in honour, to judge him unaccompanied by its advantages, by the benefit of his full intention. Considering how much Ibsen has been talked about in England and America, he has been lamentably little seen and heard. Until *Hedda Gabler* was produced in London six weeks ago, there had been but one attempt to represent its predecessors that had consisted of more than a single performance. This circumstance has given a real importance to the undertaking of the two courageous young actresses who have brought the most recent of the author's productions to the light and who have promptly found themselves justified in their talent as well as in their energy. It was a proof of Ibsen's force that he had made us chatter about him so profusely without the aid of the theatre; but it was even more a blessing to have the aid at last. The stage is to the prose drama (and Ibsen's later manner is the very prose of prose) what the tune is to the song or the concrete case to the general law. It immediately becomes apparent that he needs the test to show his strength and the frame to show his picture. An extraordinary process of vivification takes place; the conditions seem essentially enlarged. Those of the stage in general strike us for the most part as small enough, so that the game played in them is often not more inspiring than a successful sack-race. But Ibsen reminds us that if they do not in themselves confer life they can at least receive it when the infusion is artfully attempted. Yet how much of it they were doomed to receive from *Hedda Gabler* was not to be divined till we had seen *Hedda Gabler* in the frame. The play, on perusal, left one comparatively muddled and mystified, fascinated, but — in one's intellectual sympathy — snubbed. Acted, it leads that sympathy over the straightest of roads with all the exhilaration of a superior pace. Much more, I confess, one doesn't get from it; but an hour of refreshing exercise is a reward in itself. The sense of being moved by a scientific hand as one sits in one's stall has not been spoiled for us by satiety.

Hedda Gabler then, in the frame, is exceedingly vivid and curious, and a part of its interest is in the way it lights up in general the talent of the author. It is doubtless not the most complete of Ibsen's plays, for it owes less to its subject than to its form; but it makes good his title to the possession of a real method, and in thus putting him before us as a master it exhibits at the same time his irritating, his bewildering incongruities. He is nothing, as a literary personality, if not positive; yet there are moments when his great gift seems made up of negatives, or at any rate when the total seems a contradiction of each of the parts. I premise of course that we hear him through a medium not his own, and I remember that translation is a shameless falsification of colour. Translation, however, is probably not wholly responsible for three appearances inherent in all his prose work, as we possess it, though in slightly differing degrees, and yet quite unavailing to destroy in it the expression of life; I mean of course the absence of humour, the absence of free imagination, and the absence of style. The absence of style, both in the usual and in the larger sense of the word, is extraordinary, and all the more mystifying that its place is not usurped, as it frequently is in such cases, by vulgarity. Ibsen is massively common and "middle-class," but neither his spirit nor his manner is small. He is never trivial and never cheap, but he is in nothing more curious than in owing to a single source such distinction as he retains. His people are of inexpressive race; they give us essentially the *bourgeois* impression; even when they are furiously nervous and, like Hedda, more than sufficiently fastidious, we recognise that they live, with their remarkable creator, in a world in which selection has no great range. This is perhaps one reason why they none of them, neither the creator nor the creatures, appear to feel much impulse to *play* with the things of life. This impulse, when it breaks out, is humour, and in the scenic genius it usually breaks out in one place or another. We get the feeling, in Ibsen's plays, that such whims are too ultimate, too much a matter of luxury and leisure for the stage of feeling at which his characters have arrived. They are all too busy learning to live—humour will come in later, when they know how. A certain angular irony they frequently manifest, and some of his portraits are strongly satirical, like that, to give only two instances, of Tesman, in *Hedda Gabler* (a play indeed suffused with irrepressible irony), or that of Hialmar Ekdal, in *The Wild Duck*. But it is the ridicule without the smile, the dance without the music, a sort of sarcasm that is nearer to tears than to laughter. There is nothing very droll in the world, I think, to Dr. Ibsen; and nothing is more interesting than to see how he makes up his world without a joke. Innumerable are the victories of talent, and art is a legerdemain.

It is always difficult to give an example of an absent quality, and, if the romantic is even less present in Ibsen than the comic, this is best proved by the fact that everything seems to us inveterately observed. Nothing is more puzzling to the readers of his later work than the reminder that he is the great dramatic poet of his country, or that the author of *The Pillars of Society* is also the author of *Brand* and *Peer Gynt*, compositions which, we are assured, testify to an audacious imagination and abound in complicated fantasy. In his satiric studies of contemporary life, the impression that is strongest with us is that the picture is infinitely *noted*, that all the patience of the constructive pessimist is in his love of the detail of character and of conduct, in his way of accumulating the touches that illustrate them. His recurrent ugliness of surface, as it were, is a sort of proof of his fidelity to the real, in a spare, strenuous, democratic community; just as the same peculiarity is one of the sources of his charmless fascination — a touching vision of strong forces struggling with a poverty, a bare provinciality, of life. I call the fascination of Ibsen charmless (for those who feel it at all), because he holds us without bribing us; he squeezes the attention till he almost hurts it, yet with never a conciliatory stroke. He has as little as possible to say to our taste; even his large, strong form takes no account of that, gratifying it without concessions. It is the oddity of the mixture that makes him so individual — his perfect practice of a difficult and delicate art, combined with such aesthetic density. Even in such a piece as *The Lady from the Sea* (much the weakest, to my sense, of the whole series), in which he comes nearer than in others — unless indeed it be in *Hedda Gabler* — to playing with an idea from the simple instinct of sport, nothing could be less picturesque than the general effect, with every inherent incentive to have made it picturesque. The idea might have sprung from the fancy of Hawthorne, but the atmosphere is the hard light of Ibsen. One feels that the subject should have been tinted and distanced; but, in fact, one has to make an atmosphere as one reads, and one winces considerably under "Doctor Wangel" and the pert daughters.

For readers without curiosity as to their author's point of

view (and it is doubtless not a crime not to have it, though I think it is a misfortune, an open window the less), there is too much of "Doctor Wangel" in Ibsen altogether—using the good gentleman's name for what it generally represents or connotes. It represents the ugly interior on which his curtain inexorably rises and which, to be honest, I like for the queer associations it has taught us to respect: the hideous carpet and wall-paper and curtains (one may answer for them), the conspicuous stove, the lonely centre-table, the "lamps with green shades," as in the sumptuous first act of *The Wild Duck*, the pervasive air of small interests and standards, the sign of limited local life. It represents the very clothes, the inferior fashions, of the figures that move before us, and the shape of their hats and the tone of their conversation and the nature of their diet. But the oddest thing happens in connection with this effect—the oddest extension of sympathy or relaxation of prejudice. What happens is that we feel that whereas, if Ibsen were weak or stupid or vulgar, this parochial or suburban stamp would only be a stick to beat him with, it acts, as the case stands, and in the light of his singular masculinity, as a sort of substitute—a little clumsy, if you like—for charm. In a word, it becomes touching, so that practically the *blasé* critical mind enjoys it as a refinement. What occurs is very analogous to what occurs in our appreciation of the dramatist's remarkable art, his admirable talent for producing an intensity of interest by means incorruptibly quiet, by that almost demure preservation of the appearance of the usual in which we see him juggle with difficulty and danger and which constitutes, as it were, his only coquetry. There are people who are indifferent to these mild prodigies; there are others for whom they will always remain the most charming privilege of art.

Hedda Gabler is doubtless as suburban as any of its companions; which is indeed a fortunate circumstance, inasmuch as if it were less so we should be deprived of a singularly complete instance of a phenomenon difficult to express, but which may perhaps be

described as the operation of talent without glamour. There is
notoriously no glamour over the suburbs, and yet nothing could
be more vivid than Dr. Ibsen's account of the incalculable young
woman into whom Miss Robins so artistically projects herself.
To "like" the play, as we phrase it, is doubtless therefore to give
one of the fullest examples of our constitutional inability to control our affections. Several of the spectators who have liked it most
will probably admit even that, with themselves, this sentiment has
preceded a complete comprehension. They would perhaps have
liked it better if they had understood it better — as to this they are
not sure; but they at any rate liked it well enough. Well enough
for what? the question may of course always be in such a case. To
be absorbed, assuredly, which is the highest tribute we can pay to
any picture of life, and a higher one than most pictures attempted
succeed in making us pay. Ibsen is various, and *Hedda Gabler* is
probably an ironical pleasantry, the artistic exercise of a mind
saturated with the vision of human infirmities; saturated, above
all, with a sense of the infinitude, for all its mortal savour, of
character, finding that an endless romance and a perpetual challenge. Can there have been at the source of such a production a
mere refinement of conscious power, an enjoyment of difficulty
and a preconceived victory over it? We are free to imagine that in
this case Dr. Ibsen chose one of the last subjects that an expert
might have been expected to choose, for the harmless pleasure of
feeling and of showing that he was in possession of a method that
could make up for its deficiencies.

The demonstration is complete and triumphant, but it does not
conceal from us — on the contrary — that his drama is essentially
that supposedly undramatic thing, the picture not of an action but
of a condition. It is the portrait of a nature, the story of what
Paul Bourget would call an *état d'âme*, and of a state of nerves as
well as of soul, a state of temper, of health, of chagrin, of despair.
Hedda Gabler is, in short, the study of an exasperated woman; and
it may certainly be declared that the subject was not in advance,

as a theme for scenic treatment, to be pronounced promising. There could in fact, however, be no more suggestive illustration of the folly of quarrelling with an artist over his subject. Ibsen has had only to take hold of this one in earnest to make it, against every presumption, live with an intensity of life. One can doubtless imagine other ways, but it is enough to say of this one that, put to the test, it imposes its particular spectacle. Something might have been gained, entailing perhaps a loss in another direction, by tracing the preliminary stages, showing the steps in Mrs. Tesman's history which led to the spasm, as it were, on which the curtain rises and of which the breathless duration—ending in death—is the period of the piece. But a play is above everything a work of selection, and Ibsen, with his curious and beautiful passion for the unity of time (carried in him to a point which almost always implies also that of place), condemns himself to admirable rigours. We receive Hedda ripe for her catastrophe, and if we ask for antecedents and explanations we must simply find them in her character. Her motives are just her passions. What the four acts show us is these motives and that character—complicated, strange, irreconcilable, infernal—playing themselves out. We know too little why she married Tesman, we see too little why she ruins Lövborg; but we recognise that she is infinitely perverse, and Heaven knows that, as the drama mostly goes, the crevices we are called upon to stop are singularly few. That Mrs. Tesman is a perfectly ill-regulated person is a matter of course, and there are doubtless spectators who would fain ask whether it would not have been better to represent in her stead a person totally different. The answer to this sagacious question seems to me to be simply that no one can possibly tell. There are many things in the world that are past finding out, and one of them is whether the subject of a work had not better have been another subject. We shall always do well to leave that matter to the author (*he* may have some secret for solving the riddle); so terrible would his revenge easily become if we were to accept a responsibility for his theme.

The distinguished thing is the firm hand that weaves the web, the deep and ingenious use made of the material. What material, indeed, the dissentient spirit may exclaim, and what "use," worthy of the sacred name, is to be made of a wicked, diseased, disagreeable woman? That is just what Ibsen attempts to gauge, and from the moment such an attempt is resolute the case ceases to be so simple. The "use" of Hedda Gabler is that she acts on others and that even her most disagreeable qualities have the privilege, thoroughly undeserved doubtless, but equally irresistible, of becoming a part of the history of others. And then one isn't so sure she is wicked, and by no means sure (especially when she is represented by an actress who makes the point ambiguous) that she is disagreeable. She is various and sinuous and graceful, complicated and natural; she suffers, she struggles, she is human, and by that fact exposed to a dozen interpretations, to the importunity of our suspense. Wrought with admirable closeness is the whole tissue of relations between the five people whom the author sets in motion and on whose behalf he asks of us so few concessions. That is for the most part the accomplished thing in Ibsen, the thing that converts his provincialism into artistic urbanity. He puts *us* to no expense worth speaking of—he takes all the expense himself. I mean that he thinks out our entertainment for us and shapes it of thinkable things, the passions, the idiosyncrasies, the cupidities and jealousies, the strivings and struggles, the joys and sufferings of men. The spectator's situation is different enough when what is given him is the mere dead rattle of the surface of life, into which *he* has to inject the element of thought, the "human interest." Ibsen kneads the soul of man like a paste, and often with a rude and indelicate hand to which the soul of man objects. Such a production as *The Pillars of Society*, with its large, dense complexity of moral cross-references and its admirable definiteness as a picture of motive and temperament (the whole canvas charged, as it were, with moral colour), such a production asks the average moral man to see too many things at once. It will never help Ibsen with the multitude that the multitude shall feel that the more they look the more intentions they shall see, for of such seeing of many intentions the multitude is but scantily desirous. It keeps indeed a positively alarmed and jealous watch in that direction; it smugly insists that intentions shall be rigidly limited.

This sufficiently answers the artless question of whether it may be hoped for the author of *The Pillars of Society* that he shall acquire popularity in this country. In what country under heaven might it have been hoped for him, or for the particular community, that he *should* acquire popularity? Is he in point of fact so established and cherished in the Norwegian theatre? Do his countrymen understand him and clamour for him and love him, or do they content themselves—a very different affair—with being proud of him when aliens abuse him? The rumour reaches us that *Hedda Gabler* has found no favour at Copenhagen, where we are compelled to infer that the play had not the happy interpretation it enjoys in London. It would doubtless have been in danger here if tact and sympathy had not interposed. We hear that it has had reverses in Germany, where of late years Ibsen has been the fashion; but, indeed, all these are matters of an order as to which we should have been grateful for more information from those who have lately had the care of introducing the formidable dramatist to the English and American public. He excites, for example, in each case, all sorts of curiosity and conjecture as to the quality and capacity of the theatre to which, originally, such a large order was addressed: we are full of unanswered questions about the audience and the school.

What, however, has most of all come out in our timid and desultory experiments is that the author of *The Pillars of Society*, and of *The Doll's House*, of *Ghosts*, of *The Wild Duck*, of *Hedda Gabler*, is destined to be adored by the "profession." Even in his comfortless borrowed habit he will remain intensely dear to the actor and the actress. He cuts them out work to which the artistic nature in them joyously responds—work difficult and interesting, full of stuff and opportunity. The opportunity that he gives them is almost always to do the deep and delicate thing—the sort of chance that, in proportion as they are intelligent, they are most on the look out for. He asks them to paint with a fine brush; for the subject that he gives them is ever our plastic humanity. This will surely preserve him (leaving out the question of serious competition) after our little flurry is over. It was what made the recent representation of *Hedda Gabler* so singularly interesting and refreshing. It is what gives importance to the inquiry as to how his call for "subtlety" in his interpreters has been met in his own country. It was impossible the other day not to be conscious of a certain envy (as of a case of artistic happiness) of the representatives of the mismated Tesmans and their companions—so completely, as the phrase is, were they "in" it and under the charm of what they had to do. In fact the series of Ibsen's "social dramas" is a dazzling array of parts. Nora Helmer will be undertaken again and again—of a morning, no doubt, as supposedly, though oddly, the more "earnest" hour—by young artists justly infatuated. The temptation is still greater to women than to men, as we feel in thinking, further, of the Rebecca of *Rosmersholm*, of Lona Hessel and Martha Bernick in the shapely *Pillars*, of the passionate mother and the insolent maid in the extraordinarily compact and vivid *Ghosts*—absurd and fascinating work; of Mrs. Linden, so quietly tragic, so tremulously real, in *The Doll's House*, and of that irresistibly touching image, so untainted with cheap pathos, Hedvig Ekdal, the little girl with failing eyes, in *The Wild Duck*, who pores over her story-book in the paltry photographic studio of her intensely humbugging father. Such a figure as this very Hialmar Ekdal, however, the seedy, selfish—subtly selfish and self-deceptive—photographer, in whom nothing is active but the tongue, testifies for the strong masculine side of the list. If *The League of Youth* is more nearly a complete comedy than any other of Ibsen's

prose works, the comedian who should attempt to render Stens-
gard in that play would have a real portrait to reproduce. But the
examples are numerous: Bernick and Rosmer, Oswald and Mand-
ers (Ibsen's compunctious "pastors" are admirable), Gregers
Werle, the transcendent meddler in *The Wild Duck*, Rörlund, the
prudish rector in the *Pillars*, Stockmann and the Burgomaster in
The Enemy of the People, all stand, humanly and pictorially, on
their feet.

This it is that brings us back to the author's great quality, the
quality that makes him so interesting in spite of his limitations,
so rich in spite of his lapses—his habit of dealing essentially with
the individual caught in the fact. Sometimes, no doubt, he leans
too far on that side, loses sight too much of the type-quality and
gives his spectators free play to say that even caught in the fact
his individuals are mad. We are not at all sure, for instance, of the
type-quality in Hedda. Sometimes he makes so queer a mistake
as to treat a pretty motive, like that of *The Lady from the Sea*, in
a poor and prosaic way. He exposes himself with complacent, with
irritating indifference to the objector as well as to the scoffer, he
makes his "heredity" too short and his consequences too long, he
deals with a homely and unaesthetic society, he harps on the
string of conduct, and he actually talks of stockings and legs, in
addition to other improprieties. He is not pleasant enough nor
light enough nor casual enough; he is too far from Piccadilly and
our glorious standards. Therefore his cause may be said to be
lost; we shall never take him to our hearts. It was never to have
been expected, indeed, that we should, for in literature religions
usually grow their own gods, and *our* heaven—as every one can
see—is already crowded. But for those who care in general for
the form that he has practised he will always remain one of the
talents that have understood it best and extracted most from it,
have effected most neatly the ticklish transfusion of life. If we
possessed the unattainable, an eclectic, artistic, disinterested

theatre, to which we might look for alternation and variety, it
would simply be a point of honour in such a temple to sacrifice
sometimes to Henrik Ibsen.

"Henrik Ibsen: On the Occasion of
Hedda Gabler" appeared in the New
Review, *June, 1891, and was re-
printed as the first part of the essay
"Henrik Ibsen" in* Essays in London
and Elsewhere, *1893.*

The date at which Henry James
made the discovery of Ibsen may be
gathered from an unpublished letter to
Edmund Gosse of January 29, 1889,
in which he says: "I have perused your
very interesting account of Ibsen, as I
always peruse you when I find you.
You must tell me more about I. That
is not in this case female-American
for me." A little later in the year
came the first impact of Ibsen on the
London stage (for two earlier attempts at adaptation had made no
mark) with the appearance of Janet
Achurch as Nora in A Doll's House
at the Novelty Theatre on June 7. If
Henry James was in London during
that month it seems certain that his
interest in Ibsen would have taken him
to see the performance, which indeed
made a considerable stir. Possibly he
may also have attended a morning
performance, ten days later, of The
Pillars of Society at the Opera
Comique in which Elizabeth Robins
played the part of Martha. It is, at
any rate, certain that he accompanied
Geneviève Ward to see a revival of the
Doll's House at Terry's Theatre on
January 27, 1891, in which Elizabeth Robins was playing Mrs. Linden.
The next month, on February 28,
Rosmersholm was played at the
Vaudeville, with Florence Farr as
Rebecca, and on March 13 the Independent Theatre, to which James
was a subscriber, gave its celebrated
performance of Ghosts in defiance of
the Lord Chamberlain's veto. Finally,
on April 20, came the production of
Hedda Gabler by Elizabeth Robins
and Marion Lea which formed the
"occasion" of Henry James's essay.
He wrote it, he says, six weeks after
the production, so that it would have
been finished by the end of May, and
it was promptly published in the New
Review, at that time still edited by
Archibald Grove.

II. *On the occasion of The Master Builder (1893)*

IN SPITE of its having been announced in many quarters that
Ibsen would never do, we are still to have another chance, which
may very well not be the last, of judging the question for ourselves. Not only has the battered Norseman had, in the evening
of his career, the energy to fling yet again into the arena one of
those bones of contention of which he has in an unequalled degree
the secret of possessing himself, but practised London hands have
been able to catch the mystic missile in its passage and are flour-

ishing it, as they have flourished others, before our eyes.[1] In addition to an opportunity of reading the play I have had the pleasure of seeing a rehearsal of the performance—so that I already feel something of responsibility of that inward strife which is an inevitable heritage of all inquiring contact with the master. It is perhaps a consequence of this irremediable fever that one should recklessly court the further responsibility attached to uttering an impression into which the premature may partly enter. But it is impossible, in any encounter with Ibsen, to resist the influence of at least the one kind of interest that he exerts at the very outset, and to which at the present hour it may well be a point of honour promptly to confess one's subjection. This immediate kind is the general interest we owe to the refreshing circumstances that he at any rate gives us the sense of life, and the practical effect of which is ever to work a more or less irritating spell. The other kind is the interest of the particular production, a varying quantity and an agreeable source of suspense—a happy occasion in short for that play of intelligence, that acuteness of response, whether in assent or in protest, which it is the privilege of the clinging theatre-goer to look forward to as a result of the ingenious dramatist's appeal, but his sad predicament for the most part to miss yet another and another chance to achieve. With Ibsen (and that is the exceptional joy, the bribe to rapid submission) we can always count upon the chance. Our languid pulses quicken as we begin to note the particular direction taken by the attack on a curiosity inhabiting, by way of a change, the neglected region of the brain.

In *The Master Builder* this emotion is not only kindled very

[1] *In the* Pall Mall Gazette *the article continued at this point:* "The English version of Bygmester Solness *lately prepared by* Mr. Edmund Gosse *and* Mr. William Archer *and now, under the title of* The Master-Builder, *about to appear as a volume, is, on Monday afternoon next and on* the following afternoons, to be presented at the Trafalgar Square Theatre by a company of which Mr. Herbert Waring, Miss Elizabeth Robins, and Miss Louise Moodie are the principal members."

This paragraph was omitted when the article was reprinted in Essays in London.

early in the piece—it avails itself to the full of the right that Ibsen always so liberally concedes it of being still lively after the piece is over. His independence, his perversity, his intensity, his vividness, the hard compulsion of his strangely inscrutable art, are present in full measure, together with that quality which comes almost uppermost when it is a question of seeing him on the stage, his peculiar blessedness to actors. *Their* reasons for liking him it would not be easy to overstate; and surely, if the public should ever completely renounce him, players enamoured of their art will still be found ready to interpret him for that art's sake to empty benches. No dramatist of our time has had more the secret, and has kept it better, of making their work interesting to them. The subtlety with which he puts them into relation to it eludes analysis, but operates none the less strongly as an incitement. Does it reside mainly in the way he takes hold of their imagination, or in some special affinity with their technical sense; in what he gives them or in what he leaves it to them to give; in the touches by which the moral nature of the character opens out a vista for them; or in the simple fact of connection with such a vivified whole? These are questions at any rate that Mr. Herbert Waring, Miss Robins, Miss Moodie, enviable with their several problems, doubtless freely ask themselves, or even each other, while the interest and the mystery of *The Master Builder* fold them more and more closely in. What is incontestable is the excitement, the amusement, the inspiration of dealing with material so solid and so fresh. The very difficulty of it makes a common cause, as the growing ripeness of preparation makes a common enthusiasm.

I shall not attempt to express the subject of the play more largely than to say that its three acts deal again, as Ibsen is so apt to deal, with the supremely critical hour in the life of an individual, in the history of a soul. The individual is in this case not a Hedda, nor a Nora, nor a Mrs. Alving, nor a Lady from the Sea, but a prosperous architect of Christiania, who, on reaching a robust maturity, encounters his fate all in the opening of a door.

This fate—infinitely strange and terrible, as we know before the curtain falls—is foreshadowed in Miss Elizabeth Robins, who, however, in passing the threshold, lets in a great deal more than herself, represents a heroine conceived, as to her effect on the action, with that shameless originality which Ibsen's contemners call wanton and his admirers call fascinating. Hilda Wangel, a young woman whom the author may well be trusted to have made more mystifying than her curiously charmless name would suggest, is only the indirect form, the animated clock-face, as it were, of Halvard Solness's destiny; but the action, in spite of obscurities and ironies, takes its course by steps none the less irresistible. The mingled reality and symbolism of it all give us an Ibsen within an Ibsen. His subject is always, like the subjects of all first-rate men, primarily an idea; but in this case the idea is as difficult to catch as its presence is impossible to overlook. The whole thing throbs and flushes with it, and yet smiles and mocks at us through it as if in conscious supersubtlety. The action at any rate is superficially simple, more single and confined than that of most of Ibsen's other plays; practically, as it defines itself and rises to a height, it leaves the strange, doomed Solness, and the even stranger apparition of the joyous and importunate girl (the one all memories and hauntings and bondages, the other all health and curiosity and youthful insolence), face to face on unprecedented terms—terms, however, I hasten to add, that by no means prevent the play from being one to which a young lady, as they say in Paris, may properly take her mother. Of all Ibsen's heroines Hilda is indeed perhaps at once the most characteristic of the author and the most void of offence to the "general." If she has notes that recall Hedda, she is a Hedda dangerous precisely because she is *not* yet *blasée*—a Hedda stimulating, fully beneficent in intention; in short "reversed," as I believe the author defined her to his interpreters. From her encounter with Halvard Solness many remarkable things arise, but most of all perhaps the spectator's sense of the opportunity offered by the two rare parts; and

in particular of the fruitful occasion (for Solness from beginning
to end holds the stage), seized by Mr. Herbert Waring, who has
evidently recognised one of those hours that actors sometimes
wait long years for—the hour that reveals a talent to itself as
well as to its friends and that makes a reputation take a bound.
Whatever, besides refreshing them, *The Master Builder* does for
Ibsen with London playgoers, it will render the service that the
curious little Norwegian repertory has almost always rendered
the performers, even to the subsidiary figures, even to the touching Kaia, the touching Ragnar, the inevitable Dr. Herdal, and the
wasted wife of Solness, so carefully composed by Miss Moodie.

"Henrik Ibsen: On the Occasion of The Master Builder" appeared, under the title "Ibsen's New Play," in the Pall Mall Gazette, *February 17, 1893, and was reprinted as the second part of the essay "Henrik Ibsen" in* Essays in London and Elsewhere, *1893.*

The whole story of Miss Robins's heroic adventure in Ibsen production and of the devoted interest in it mani-fested by Henry James may be read in her volume Theatre and Friendship, *1932. It was, no doubt, with the in-tention of stimulating public interest that James wrote his article, which appeared three days before the first performance of the play. Miss Robins has reprinted it in her book in its original form, which included a short paragraph afterwards omitted.*

DUMAS THE YOUNGER

———————————— 1 8 9 5 ————————————

Reprinted from Notes on Novelists with Some Other Notes *by Henry James; copyright 1914 by Charles Scribner's Sons, 1942 by Henry James; used by permission of the publishers.*

ONE OF the things that most bring home his time of life to a man of fifty is the increase of the rate at which he loses his friends. Some one dies every week, some one dies every day, and if the rate be high among his coevals it is higher still in the generation that, on awaking to spectatorship, he found in possession of the stage. He begins to feel his own world, the world of his most vivid impressions, gradually become historical. He is present, and closely present, at the process by which legend grows up. He sees the friends in question pictured as only death can picture them—a master superior to the Rembrandts and Titians. They have been of many sorts and many degrees, they have been private and public, but they have had in common that they were the furniture of this first fresh world, the world in which associations are formed. That one by one they go is what makes the main difference in it. The landscape of life, in foreground and distance, becomes, as the painters say, another composition, another subject; and quite as much as the objects directly under our eyes we miss the features that have educated for us our sense of proportion.

Among such features for the author of these lines the younger Dumas, who has just passed away, was in the public order long one of the most conspicuous. Suffused as he is already with the quick historic haze, fixed, for whatever term, in his ultimate value, he appeals to me, I must begin by declaring, as a party to one of these associations that have the savour of the prime. I knew him only in his work, but he is the object of an old-time sentiment for the beginning of which I have to go back absurdly far. He arrived early—he was so loudly introduced by his name. I am tempted to say that I knew him when he was young, but what I suppose I mean is that I knew him when I myself was. I knew him indeed when we both were, for I recall that in Paris, in distant days and undeveloped conditions, I was aware with perhaps undue and uncanny precocity of his first successes. There emerges in my memory from the night of time the image of a small boy walking in the Palais Royal with innocent American girls who were his cousins and wistfully hearing them relate how many times (they lived in Paris) they had seen Madame Doche in *La Dame aux Camélias* and what floods of tears she had made them weep. It was the first time I had heard of pocket-handkerchiefs as a provision for the play. I had no remotest idea of the social position of the lady of the expensive flowers, and the artless objects of my envy had, in spite of their repeated privilege, even less of one; but her title had a strange beauty and her story a strange meaning— things that ever after were to accompany the name of the author with a faint yet rich echo. The younger Dumas, after all, was then not only relatively but absolutely young; the American infants, privileged and unprivileged, were only somewhat younger; the former going with their *bonne*, who must have enjoyed the adventure, to the "upper boxes" of the old Vaudeville of the Place de la Bourse, where later on I remember thinking Madame Fargueil divine. He was quite as fortunate moreover in his own designation as in that of his heroine; for it emphasized that bloom of youth (I don't say bloom of innocence—a very different matter) which was the signal-note of the work destined, in the world at large, to bring him nine-tenths of his celebrity.

Written at twenty-five *La Dame aux Camélias* remains in its combination of freshness and form, of the feeling of the springtime of life and the sense of the conditions of the theatre, a singular, an astonishing production. The author has had no time to part with his illusions, but has had full opportunity to master the most difficult of the arts. Consecrated as he was to this mastery he never afterwards showed greater adroitness than he had then done in keeping his knowledge and his *naïveté* from spoiling each other. The play has been blown about the world at a fearful rate, but it has never lost its happy juvenility, a charm that nothing can vulgarize. It is all champagne and tears—fresh perversity, fresh credulity, fresh passion, fresh pain. We have seen it both well done and ill done, and perhaps more particularly the latter—in strange places, in barbarous tongues, with Marguerite Gautier fat and Armand Duval old. I remember ages ago in Boston a version in which this young lady and this young gentleman were represented as "engaged": that indeed for all I know may still be the form in which the piece most enjoys favour with the Anglo-Saxon public. Nothing makes any difference—it carries with it an April air: some tender young man and some coughing young woman have only to speak the lines to give it a great place among the love-stories of the world. I recollect coming out of the Gymnase one night when Madame Pierson had been the Marguerite—this was very long since—and giving myself up on the boulevard to a fine critical sense of what in such a composition was flimsy and what was false. Somehow, none the less, my fine critical sense never prevented my embracing the next opportunity to expose it to the same irritation; for I have been, I am happy to think to-day, a playgoer who, whatever else he may have had on his conscience, has never had the neglect of any chance to see this dramatist acted. Least of all, within a much shorter period, has it undermined one's kindness to have had occasion to admire in connection with the piece such an artist for instance as Eleanora Duse. We have seen Madame Duse this year or two in her tattered translation, with few advantages, with meagre accessories and with one side of the character of the heroine scarcely touched at all—so little indeed that the Italian version joins hands with the American and the relation of Marguerite and Armand seems to present itself as a question of the consecrated even if not approved

"union." For this interesting actress, however, the most beautiful
thing is always the great thing, and her performance—if seen on
a fortunate evening—lives in the mind as a fine vindication of the
play. I am not sure indeed that it is the very performance Dumas
intended; but he lived long enough to have forgotten perhaps
what that performance was. He might on some sides, I think,
have accepted Madame Duse's as a reminder.

If I have stopped to be myself so much reminded, it is because
after and outside of *La Dame aux Camélias* Dumas really never
figured among us all again—a circumstance full of illustration of
one of the most striking of our peculiarities, the capacity for
granting a prodigious ear to some one manifestation of an author's
talent and caring nothing whatever for the others. It is solely the
manifestation and never the talent that interests us, and nothing
is stranger than the fact that no critic has ever explained on our
behalf the system by which we hurl ourselves on a writer to-day
and stare at him tomorrow as if we had never heard of him. It
gives us the air of perpetually awaking from mistakes, but it
renders obscure all our canons of judgement. A great force makes a
great success, but a great force is furthermore no less a great
force on Friday than on Monday. Was the reader a sorry dupe on
the first day, or is the writer a wanton sacrifice on the second?
That the public is intelligent on both occasions is a claim it can
scarcely make: it can only choose between having its acuteness
impugned or its manners condemned. At any rate if we have in
England and the United States only the two alternatives of the
roar of the market and the silence of the tomb the situation is apt
to be different in France, where the quality that goes into a man's
work and gives it an identity is the source of the attention excited. It happens that the interest in the play of the genius is
greater there than the "boom" of the particular hit, the concern
primarily for the author rather than the subject, instead of, as
among ourselves, primarily for the subject rather than the author.
Is this because the French have been acute enough to reflect that

authors comprehend subjects, but that subjects can unfortunately not be said to comprehend authors? Literature would be a merry game if the business were arranged in the latter fashion. However such a question may be answered, Dumas was in his own country, to the end, the force that, save in connection with his first play, he failed to become elsewhere; and if he was there much the most original worker in his field one of the incidental signs of his originality was that, despite our inveterate practice, in theatrical matters, of helping ourselves from our neighbour's plate, he was inveterately not a convenience to us. We picked our morsels from the plates of smaller people — we never found on that of the author of *Le Fils Naturel* any we could swallow. He was not to our poor purpose, and I cannot help thinking that this helps a little to give his artistic measure. It would be a bad note for him now if we had found him amenable to that graceless game of which we show signs to-day of having grown ashamed, but which flourished for years in two imperturbable communities as the art of theatrical adaptation. A Dumas adaptable is a Dumas inconceivable; and in point of fact he was touched by the purveyors of the English-speaking stage only to prove fatal to them. If the history of so mean a traffic as the one here glanced at were worth writing it would throw light on some odd conceptions of the delicacy in the abused name of which it was carried on. It is all to the honour of our author's seriousness that he was, in such conditions, so unmanageable; though one must of course hasten to add that this seriousness was not the only reason of it. There were several others, not undiscoverable, and the effect of the whole combination was, in view of the brilliant fortune of his productions at home and the eager foraging of English and American speculators, to place him on a footing all his own. He was of active interest among us only to individual observers — simply as one of the most devoted of whom I trace these few pages of commemoration.

It takes some analysis, yet is not impossible, to explain why among the men of his time to whom the creative gift had been granted his image, for sundry such admirers, always presented him as somehow the happiest consciousness. They were perhaps not always aware of it, but now that he is gone they have a revelation of the place he occupied in the envious mind. This envy flowed doubtless, to begin with, from the sense of his extraordinarily firm grasp of his hard refractory art; the grasp that had put him into possession of it without fumblings or gropings made him canter away on the back of it the moment he had touched the stirrup. He had the air through all his career of a man riding a dangerous horse without ever being thrown. Every one else had a fall — he alone never really quitted the saddle, never produced a play that was not to stay to be revived and in the case of his comparative failures enjoy some sort of revenge, even to that of travelling in the repertory of great actresses round the globe. Such travels, moreover, much as they may please his shade, are far from having been the only felicities of his long career. The others strike me as so numerous that I scarcely indeed know where to begin to reckon them. Greatly even if oddly auspicious for instance was just his stark sonship to his prodigious father, his having been launched with that momentum into the particular world in which he was to live. It was a privilege to make up for the legal irregularity attaching to his birth; we think of it really almost to wonder that it didn't lift him on a still higher wave. His limitations, which one encounters with a sort of violence, were not to be overlooked; it expresses them in some degree to say that he was bricked up in his hard Parisianism, but it is also incontestable that some of them were much concerned in producing his firm and easy equilibrium. We understand, however, the trap they set for him when we reflect that a certain omniscience, a great breadth of horizon, may well have seemed to him to be transmitted, in his blood, from such a boundless fountain of life. What mattered to him the fact of a reach of reference that stopped at the *banlieue,* when experience had sat at his cradle in the shape not at all of a fairy godmother but of an immediate progenitor who was at once fabulous and familiar? He had been encompassed by all history in being held in such arms—it was an entrance into possession of more matters than he could even guess what to do with. The profit was all the greater as the son had the luxury of differing actively from the father, as well as that of actively admiring and, in a splendid sense, on all the becoming sides, those of stature, strength and health, vividly reproducing him. He had in relation to his special gift, his mastery of the dramatic form, a faculty of imagination as contracted as that of the author of *Monte Cristo* was boundless, but his moral sense on the other hand, as distinguished from that of his parent, was of the liveliest, was indeed of the most special and curious kind. The moral sense of the parent was to be found only in his good humour and his good health—the moral sense of a musketeer in love. This lack of adventurous vision, of the long flight and the joy of motion, was in the younger genius quite one of the conditions of his strength and luck, of his fine assurance, his sharp edge, his high emphasis, his state untroubled above all by things not within his too irregularly conditioned ken. The things close about him were the things he saw—there were alternatives, differences, opposites, of which he lacked so much as the suspicion. Nothing contributes more to the prompt fortune of an artist than some such positive and exclusive temper, the courage of his convictions, as we usually call it, the power to neglect something thoroughly, to abound aggressively in his own sense and express without reserve his own saturation. The saturation of the author of *Le Demi-Monde* was never far to seek. He was as native to Paris as a nectarine to a south wall. He would have fared ill if he had not had a great gift and Paris had not been a great city.

It was another element of the happy mixture that he came into the world at the moment in all our time that was for a man of letters the most amusing and beguiling—the moment exactly when he could see the end of one era and the beginning of another and join hands luxuriously with each. This was an advantage to which it would have taken a genius more elastic to do full justice, but which must have made him feel himself both greatly related and inspiringly free. He sprang straight from the lap of full-grown romanticism; he was a boy, a privileged and initiated youth, when his father, when Victor Hugo, when Lamartine and Musset and Scribe and Michelet and Balzac and George Sand were at the high tide of production. He saw them all, knew them all, lived with them and made of them his profit, tasting just enough of the old concoction to understand the proportions in which the new should be mixed. He had above all in his father, for the purpose that was in him, a magnificent springboard—a background to throw into relief, as a ruddy sunset seems to make a young tree doubly bristle, a profile of another type. If it was not indispensable it was at any rate quite poetic justice that the successor to the name should be, in his conditions, the great casuist of the theatre. He had seen the end of an age of imagination, he had seen all that could be done and shown in the way of mere illustration of the passions. That the passions are always with us is a fact he had not the smallest pretension to shut his eyes to—they were to constitute the almost exclusive subject of his study. But he was to study them not for the pleasure, the picture, the poetry they offer; he was to study them in the interest of something quite outside of them, about which the author of *Antony* and *Kean*, about which Victor Hugo and Musset, Scribe and Balzac and even George Sand had had almost nothing to say. He was to study them from the point of view of the idea of the right and the wrong, of duty and conduct, and he was to this end to spend his artistic life with them and give a new turn to the theatre. He was in short to become, on the basis of a determined observation of the manners of his time and country, a professional moralist.

There can scarcely be a better illustration of differences of national habit and attitude than the fact that while among his own people this is the character, as an operative force, borne by the author of *Le Demi-Monde* and *Les Idées de Madame Aubray*, so among a couple of others, in the proportion in which his reputation there has emerged from the vague, his most definite identity is that of a mere painter of indecent people and indecent doings. There are, as I have hinted, several reasons for the circumstance already noted, the failure of the attempt to domesticate him on the English-speaking stage; but one states the case fairly, I think, in saying that what accounts for half of it is our passion, in the presence of a work of art, for confounding the object, as the philosophers have it, with the subject, for losing sight of the idea in the vehicle, of the intention in the fable. Dumas is a dramatist as to whom nine playgoers out of ten would precipitately exclaim: "Ah, but you know, isn't he dreadfully immoral?" Such are the lions in the path of reputation, such the fate, in an alien air, of a master whose main reproach in his native clime is the importunity and the rigour of his lesson. The real difference, I take it, is that whereas we like to be good the French like to be better. We like to be moral, they like to moralise. This helps us to understand the number of our innocent writers — writers innocent even of reflection, a practice of course essentially indelicate, inasmuch as it speedily brings us face to face with scandal and even with evil. It accounts doubtless also for the number of writers on the further side of the Channel who have made the journey once for all and to whom, in the dangerous quarter they have reached, it appears of the very nature of scandal and evil to be inquired about. The whole undertaking of such a writer as Dumas is, according to his light, to carry a particular, an aesthetic form of investigation as far as it will stretch — to study, and study thoroughly, the bad cases. These bad cases were precisely what our managers and adapters, our spectators and critics would have nothing to do with. It defines indeed the separation that they should have been, in the light in which he presented them, precisely what made them for his own public exceptionally edifying. One of his great contentions is, for instance, that seduced girls should under all circumstances be married — by somebody or other, failing the seducer. This is a contention that, as we feel, barely concerns us, shut up as we are in the antecedent conviction that they should under no circumstances be seduced. He meets all the cases that, as we see him, we feel to have been spread out before him; meets them successively, systematically, at once with a great earnestness and a great wit. He is exuberantly sincere: his good faith sometimes obscures his humour, but nothing obscures his good faith. So he gives us in their order the unworthy brides who must be denounced, the prenuptial children who must be adopted, the natural sons who must be avenged, the wavering ladies who must be saved, the credulous fiancés who must be enlightened, the profligate wives who must be shot, the merely blemished ones who must be forgiven, the too vindictive ones who must be humoured, the venal young men who must be exposed, the unfaithful husbands who must be frightened, the frivolous fathers who must be pulled up and the earnest sons who must pull them. To enjoy his manner of dealing with such material we must grant him in every connection his full premise: that of the importunity of the phenomenon, the ubiquity of the general plight, the plight in which people are left by an insufficient control of their passions. We must grant him in fact for his didactic and dramatic purpose a great many things. These things, taken together and added to some others, constitute the luxurious terms on which I have spoken of him as appearing to the alien admirer to have practised his complicated art.

When we speak of the passions in general we really mean, for the most part, the first of the number, the most imperious in its action and the most interesting in its consequences, the passion that unites and divides the sexes. It is the passion, at any rate, to which Dumas as dramatist and pamphleteer mainly devoted himself: his plays, his prefaces, his manifestos, his few tales roll exclusively on the special relation of the man to the woman and the woman to the man, and on the dangers of various sorts, even that of ridicule, with which this relation surrounds each party.

This element of danger is what I have called the general plight, for when our author considers the sexes as united and divided it is with the predominance of the division that he is principally struck. It is not an unfair account of him to say that life presented itself to him almost wholly as a fierce battle between the woman and the man. He sides now with one and now with the other; the former combatant, in her own country, however, was far from pronouncing him sympathetic. His subject at all events is what we of English race call the sexes and what they in France call the sex. To talk of love is to talk, as we have it, of men and women; to talk of love is, as the French have it, to *parler femmes*. From every play of our author's we receive the impression that to *parler femmes* is its essential and innermost purpose. It is not assuredly singular that a novelist, a dramatist *should* talk of love, or even should talk of nothing else: what, in addition to his adroitness and his penetration, makes the position special for Dumas is that he talks of it—and in the form of address most associated with pure diversion—altogether from the anxious point of view of the legislator and the citizen.

Diane de Lys, which immediately followed *La Dame aux Camélias*, is, so far as I can recall it, a picture pure and simple, a pretty story, as we say, sufficiently romantic and rather long-winded; but with *Le Demi-Monde* began his rich argumentative series, concluding only the other day with *Denise* and *Francillon*, the series in which every theme is a proposition to be established and every proposition a form of duty to be faced. The only variation that I can recollect in the list is the disinterested portraiture of *Le Père Prodigue*, with its remarkable presentation, in the figure of Albertine de la Borde, of vice domesticated and thrifty, keeping early hours and books in double-entry, and its remarkable illustration, I may further add, of all that was the reverse of infallible in the author's power to distinguish between amiable infirmities and ugly ones. The idea on which *Le Père Prodigue* rests belongs more distinctively to the world of comedy than

almost any other situation exhibited in the series; but what are
we to say of the selection, for comic effect, of a fable of which the
principal feature is a son's not unfounded suspicion of the attitude
of his own father to his own wife? The father is the image of a
nature profusely frivolous, but we scent something more frivolous
still in the way his frivolity is disposed of. At the time the play
was produced the spectator thought himself warranted in recognising in this picture the personal character (certainly not the
personal genius) of the elder Dumas. If the spectator *was* so
warranted, that only helps, I think, to make *Le Père Prodigue* a
stumbling-block for the critic—make it, I mean, an exhibition of
the author off his guard and a fact to be taken into account in an
estimate of his moral reach; a moral reach, for the rest, at all
events, never impugned by any obliquity in facing that conception
of the duty imposed which it is the main source of the writer's
interest in the figured circumstances that they may be held to
impose it, and which he was apt to set forth more dogmatically, or
at least more excitedly, in an occasional and polemical pamphlet.
These pamphlets, I may parenthetically say, strike me as definitely compromising to his character as artist. What shines in
them most is the appetite for a discussion, or rather the appetite
for a conclusion, and the passion for a simplified and vindictive
justice. But I have never found it easy to forgive a writer who,
in possession of a form capable of all sorts of splendid application,
puts on this resource the slight of using substitutes for it at will,
as if it is good for but parts of the cause. If it is good for anything
it is good for the whole demonstration, and if it is not good for
the whole demonstration it is good for nothing—nothing that *he*
is concerned with. If the picture of life doesn't cover the ground
what in the world *can* cover it? The fault can only be the painter's.
Woe, in the aesthetic line, to any example that requires the escort
of precept. It is like a guest arriving to dine accompanied by
constables. Our author's prefaces and treatises show a mistrust
of disinterested art. He would have declared probably that his

art was not disinterested; to which our reply would be that it had then no right to put us off the scent and prepare deceptions for us by coming within an ace of being as good as if it were.

The merits of the play — that is of the picture, in these hands — are sometimes singularly independent of the lesson conveyed. The merits of the lesson conveyed are in other cases much more incontestable than those of the picture, than the production of the air of life or the happiest observance of the conditions of the drama. The conclusion, the prescription, of *Denise* strikes me (to give an instance) as singularly fine, but the subject belongs none the less to the hapless order of those that fail to profit by the dramatic form though they have sacrificed the highest advantages of the literary. A play — even the best — pays so tremendously by what it essentially can not do for the comparatively little it practically can, that a mistake in the arithmetic of this positive side speedily produces a wide deviation. In other words the spectator, and still more the reader, sees such a theme as that of *Denise*, which may be described as the evolution of a view, presented most in accordance with its nature when the attempt is not made to present it in accordance with the nature of the theatre. It is the nature of the theatre to give its victims, in exchange for melancholy concessions, a vision of the immediate not to be enjoyed in any other way; and consequently when the material offered it to deal with is not the immediate, but the contingent, the derived, the hypothetic, our melancholy concessions have been made in vain and the inadequacy of the form comes out. In *Francillon*, partly because the thing has nothing to do with anybody's duty — least of all with the heroine's, which would be surely to keep off the streets — the form happens to be remarkably adequate. The question is of the liberty of the protagonist, the right of a wronged and indignant wife to work out her husband's chastisement in the same material as his sin, work it out moreover on the spot, as a blow is repaid by a blow, exacting an eye for an eye and a tooth for a tooth. The play has all the kinds of life that the theatre can achieve, because in the first place Dumas, though acting as the wife's advocate, has had the intelligence to give us a solution which is only a scenic sequence and not a real, still less a "philosophic" one; and because in the second it deals with emotions and impulses, which can be shown by the short measure, and not with reflections and aspirations, which can be shown but by the long.

I am not pretending to take things in turn, but a critic with a generous memory of the spell of Dumas should not, however pressed, neglect to strain a point for *Le Demi-Monde*. I doubt my competence, however, to consider that admirable work scientifically—I find myself too condemned to consider it sentimentally. A critic is lost, as a critic, from the moment his feeling about the worse parts of the matter he investigates fails to differ materially from his feeling about the better. That is an attitude even less enlightened than being unconscious of the blemishes; all the same it must serve me for the present case. I am perfectly aware that Olivier de Jalin is a man of no true delicacy; in spite of which I take when I see them represented the liveliest interest in his proceedings. I am perfectly aware that Madame d'Ange, with her *calme infernal*, as George Sand calls it, is tainted and tortuous; in spite of which my imagination quite warms to Madame d'Ange. Perhaps I should indeed rather say that this interest and this sympathy have for their object the great total of the play. It is the member of the series in which Dumas first took up the scales in one hand and the sword in the other, and it is a wonderful piece of work, wonderful in kind of maturity, for a man of thirty. It has all the easy amplitude we call authority. I won't pretend to say what I think, here, of the author's justice, and if I happen to think ill of it I won't pretend to care. I see the thing through too many old memories, old echoes, old charms. In the light of the admirable acting of ancient days, of the faded image of the exquisite Desclée, of a dim recollection of the prehistoric Rose Chéri and of Mademoiselle Delaporte, it represents too many of the reasons why I saw him always ideally triumphant. To practise an art which for its full, its rich effect depended on interpretation, and to be able to do one's work with an eye on interpretation of that quality — this had in common with supreme bliss the element at any rate of being attainable only by the elect. It partook of a peace the world cannot give. To be a moralist with the aid of Croizette, a philosopher with the aid of Delaunay, an Academician, even, with the aid of Bartet — such things suggested an almost equivocal union of virtue and success. One had never seen virtue so agreeable to one's self, nor success so useful to others. One had never seen a play that was a model so alive in spite of it. Models in the theatre were apt to be dead and vivacities vulgar. One had never above all seen on the stage a picture so comfortable to deep pictorial art, a drama so liberally, gradually, scientifically flushed with its action. Beautiful in *Le Demi-Monde* is the way the subject quietly, steadily, strongly expands from within.

It was always the coercive force that his tone gave one the strongest sense of life, and it remains the interesting thing that this element in Dumas abounds in spite of not being fed from the source that we usually assume to be the richest. It was not fed from the imagination, for his imagination, by no means of the great plastic sort, has left us a comparatively small heritage of typical figures. His characters are all pointed by observation, they are clear notes in the concert, but not one of them has known the little invisible push that, even when shyly and awkwardly administered, makes the puppet, in spite of the string, walk off by himself and quite "cut," if the mood take him, that distant relation his creator. They are always formal with this personage and thoroughly conscious and proud of him; there is a charm of mystery and poetry and oddity, a glory of unexpectedness, that they consistently lack. Their life, and that, in each case, of the whole story (quite the most wonderful part of this) is simply the author's own life, his high vitality, his very presence and temperament and voice. They do more for him even than they do for the subject, and he himself is at last accordingly the most vivid thing in every situation. He keeps it at arm's length because he has the instinct of the dramatist and the conscience of the artist, but we feel all the while that his face is bigger than his mask. Nothing about his work is more extraordinary than this manner in which his personality pervades without spoiling it the most detached and most impersonal of literary forms. The reasons for such an impunity are first that his precautions, the result of a great intelligence, were so effective, and second that his personality, the result of a great affiliation, was so robust. It may be said that the precautions were not effective if the man himself was what one most enjoyed in the play. The only answer to that can be that I speak merely for myself and for the fresher sensibility of the happy time. Other admirers found certainly other things; what I found most was a tall figure in muscular motion and the sense of a character that had made admirably free with life. If it was mainly as an unabashed observer that he had made free, and if the life supplied was much of it uncommonly queer, that never diminished the action of his hard masculinity and his fine intellectual brutality. There was an easy competence in it all, and a masterful experience, and a kind of vicarious courage. In particular there was a real genius for putting all persons—especially all bad ones—very much in their place. Then it was all, for another bribe, so copious and so close, so sustained and so quiet, with such fascinating unities and complex simplicities and natural solutions. It was the breath of the world and the development of an art.

All the good, however, that I recollect thinking of Dumas only reminds me how little I desired that my remarks in general should lead me into vain discriminations. There are some indeed that are not vain—at least they help us to understand. He has a noble strain of force, a fulness of blood that has permitted him to be tapped without shrinking. We must speak of him in the present tense, as we always speak of the masters. The theatre of his time, wherever it has been serious, has on the ground of general method lived on him; wherever it has not done so it has not lived at all. To pretend to be too shocked to profit by him was a way of covering up its levity, but there was no escaping its fate. He was the kind of artistic influence that is as inevitable as a medical specific; you may decline it from a black bottle to-day—you will take it from a green bottle to-morrow. The energy that went forth blooming as Dumas has come back grizzled as Ibsen, and would under the latter form, I am sure, very freely acknowledge its debt. A critic whose words meet my eyes as I write very justly says that: "Just as we have the novel before Balzac and the novel after Balzac, the poetry that preceded Victor Hugo and the poetry that followed him, so we have the drama before Alexandre Dumas and the drama after him." He has left his strong hand upon it; he remodelled it as a vehicle, he refreshed it as an art. His passion for it was obviously great, but there would be a high injustice to him in not immediately adding that his interest in the material it dealt with, in his subject, his question, his problem, was greater still than this joy of the craftsman. That might well be, but there are celebrated cases in which it has not been. The largest quality in Dumas was his immense concern about life—his sense of human character and human fate as commanding and controllable things. To do something on their behalf was paramount for him, and *what* to do in his own case clear: what else but act upon the conscience as violently as he could, and with the remarkable weapons that Providence had placed within his grasp and for which he was to show his gratitude by a perfectly intrepid application? These weapons were three: a hard rare wit, not lambent like a flame, but stiff and straight like an arrow from a crossbow; a perception not less rare of some of the realities of the particular human tendency about which most falsities have clustered; and lastly that native instinct for the conditions of dramatic presentation without which any attempt to meet them is a helpless groping.

It must always be remembered of him that he was the observer of a special order of things, the moralist of a particular relation as the umpire of a yacht-race is the legislator of a particular sport. His vision and his talent, as I have said, were all for the immediate, for the manners and the practices he himself was drenched with: he had none of the faculty that scents from afar, that wings away and dips beyond the horizon. There are moments when a reader not of his own race feels that he simplifies almost absurdly. There are too many things he didn't after all guess, too many cases he didn't after all provide for. He has a certain odour of bad company that almost imperils his distinction. This was doubtless the deepest of the reasons why among ourselves he flourished so scantly: we felt ourselves to be of a world in which the elements were differently mixed, the proportions differently marked, so that the tables of our law would have to be differently graven. His very earnestness was only a hindrance—he might have had more to say to us if he had consented to have less application. This produced the curious dryness, the obtrusive economy of his drama—the hammered sharpness of every outline, the metallic ring of every sound. His terrible knowledge suggested a kind of uniform—gilt buttons, a feathered hat and a little official book; it was almost like an irruption of the police. The most general masters are the poets, with all the things they blessedly don't hold for so very certain and all the things they blessedly and preferably invent. It is true that Dumas was splendid, in his way, exactly because he was not vague: his concentration, all confidence and doctrine and epigram, is the explanation of his extraordinary force. That force is his abiding quality: one feels that he was magnificently a man—that he stands up high and sees straight and speaks loud. It is his great temperament, undiminished by what it lacks, that endears him to his admirers. It made him still of the greater race and played well its part in its time—so well that one thinks of him finally as perhaps not, when all is said, of the very happiest group, the group of those for whom in the general affection there is yet more to come. He had an immense reverberation—he practised the art that makes up for being the most difficult by being the most acclaimed. There is no postponed poetic justice for those who have had everything. He was seconded in a manner that must have made success a double delight. There are indications that the dramatist of the future will be less and less elated. He may well become so if he is to see himself less and less interpreted.

"Dumas the Younger" appeared, under the title "On the Death of Dumas the Younger," in the New Review *(under W. E. Henley's editorship) March, 1896, and was reprinted in* Notes on Novelists, *1914.*

Leon Edel discovered that this essay was first published in America in the New York Herald, *February 23, 1896, and in the* Boston Herald *of the same date, under the title "Henry James on Dumas the Younger"; it was plentifully bedecked with sub-headings of the kind which Henry James so much disliked. A note of James's, dated February 13, 1896, tells us that his article had been rejected by R. U. Johnson as "shocking." It had presumably been offered to the* Century Magazine *of which Johnson was Associate Editor.*

The work of Dumas fils had exercised a fascination on Henry James from very early days. In addition to what appears in the text of this volume he had written, at the end of his article "Occasional Paris" of 1877, printed in Portraits of Places:

"The Demi-Monde of M. Dumas fils is not a novelty either; but I quite agree with M. Francisque Sarcey that it is on the whole, in form, the first comedy of our day. I have seen it several times, but I never see it without being forcibly struck with its merits. For the drama of our time it must always remain the model. The interest of the story, the quiet art with which it is unfolded, the naturalness and soberness of the means that are used, and

by which great effects are produced, the brilliancy and richness of the dialogue—all these things make it a singularly perfect and interesting work. Of course it is admirably well played at the Théâtre Français. Madame d'Ange was originally a part of too great amplitude for Mademoiselle Croizette; but she is gradually filling it out and taking possession of it; she begins to give a sense of the 'calme infernal,' which George Sand somewhere mentions as the leading attribute of the character. As for Delaunay, he does nothing better, more vividly and gallantly, than Olivier de Jalin. When I say gallantly I say it with qualification; for what a very queer fellow is this same M. de Jalin! In seeing the *Demi-Monde* again I was more than ever struck with the oddity of its morality and with the way that the ideal of fine conduct differs in different nations. The *Demi-Monde* is the history of the eager, the almost heroic, effort of a clever and superior woman, who has been guilty of what the French call 'faults,' to pass from the irregular and equivocal circle to which these faults have consigned her into what is distinctively termed 'good society.' The only way in which the passage can be effected is by her marrying an honourable man; and to induce an honourable man to marry her, she must suppress the more discreditable facts of her career. Taking her for an honest woman, Raymond de Nanjac falls in love* with her, and honestly proposes to make her his wife. But Raymond de Nanjac has contracted an intimate friendship with Olivier de Jalin, and the action of the play is more especially De Jalin's attempt—a successful one—to rescue his friend from the ignominy of a union with Suzanne d'Ange. Jalin knows a great deal about her, for the simple reason that he has been her lover. Their relations have been most harmonious, but from the moment that Suzanne sets her cap at Nanjac, Olivier declares war. Suzanne struggles hard to keep possession of her suitor, who is very much in love with her, and Olivier spares no pains to detach him. It is the means that Olivier uses that excite the wonderment of the Anglo-Saxon spectator. He takes the ground that in such a cause all means are fair, and when, at the climax of the play, he tells a thumping lie in order to make Madame d'Ange compromise herself, expose herself, he is pronounced by the author 'le plus honnête homme que je connaisse.' Madame d'Ange, as I have said, is a superior woman; the interest of the play is in her being a superior woman. Olivier has been her lover; he himself is one of the reasons why she may not marry Nanjac; he has given her a push along the downward path. But it is curious how little this is held by the author to disqualify him from fighting the battle in which she is so much the weaker combatant. An English-speaking audience is more 'moral' than a French, more easily scandalised; and yet it is a singular fact that if the *Demi-Monde* were represented before an English-speaking audience, its sympathies would certainly not go with M. de Jalin. It would pronounce him rather a coward. Is

it because such an audience, although it has not nearly such a pretty collection of pedestals to place under the feet of the charming sex, has, after all, in default of this degree of gallantry, a tenderness more fundamental? Madame d'Ange has stained herself, and it is doubtless not at all proper that such ladies should be led to the altar by honourable young men. The point is not that the English-speaking audience would be disposed to condone Madame d'Ange's irregularities, but that it would remain perfectly cold before the spectacle of her ex-lover's masterly campaign against her, and quite fail to think it positively admirable, or to regard the fib by which he finally clenches his victory as a proof of exceptional honesty. The ideal of our own audience would be expressed in some such words as, 'I say, that's not fair game. Can't you let the poor woman alone?' "

More than thirty years later, when Henry James was writing the eleventh of his Prefaces to the New York Edition and endeavoring to trace the origin of his story The Siege of London, *his memory of this evening is as vivid as ever, and he returns to the charge. He writes:*

"I get no nearer to the birth of the idea than by recalling a certain agitation of the spirit, a lively irritation of the temper, under which, one evening in the autumn of 1877, that is more than thirty years ago, I walked away from the close of a performance at the Théâtre Français. The play had been *Le Demi-Monde* of the younger Dumas, a masterpiece which I had not heard for the first time, but a particular feature of which on this occasion more than ever yet filled up the measure of my impatience. I could less than ever swallow it, Olivier de Jalin's denunciation of Madame d'Ange; the play, from the beginning, marches toward it—it is the main hinge of the action; but the very perfection with which the part was rendered in those years by Delaunay (just as Croizette was pure perfection as Suzanne) seemed to have made me present at something inhuman and odious. It was the old story—that from the positive, the prodigious *morality* of such a painter of the sophisticated life as Dumas, not from anything else or less edifying, one must pray to be delivered."

And he adds—it is like a sigh of farewell!—:

"Far away and unspeakably regretted the days, alas, or, more exactly, the nights, on which one could walk away from the Français under the spell of such fond convictions and such deep and agitating problems."

MR. HENRY IRVING'S PRODUCTION
OF "CYMBELINE"

1896

THOSE lovers of the theatre with whom it is a complaint that they are not more often treated to Shakespeare encounter in *Cymbeline* one of those stumbling-blocks with which the path of this particular regret is not unplentifully strewn: it brings them face to face with so many of the questions that flutter up in the presence of all attempts to put the plays to the proof of the contemporary stage. None of them practically takes so little account as *Cymbeline* of the general effort of the theatre of our day to hug closer and closer the scenic illusion. The thing is a florid fairy-tale, of a construction so loose and unpropped that it can scarce be said to stand upright at all, and of a psychological sketchiness that never touches firm ground, but plays, at its better times, with an indifferent shake of golden locks, in the high, sunny air of delightful poetry. Here it disports itself beyond the reach of all challenge. Meanwhile the mere action swings, like a painted cloth in the wind, between England and Italy, flapping merrily back and forth and in and out, alternately crumpling up the picture and waving it in the blue. It is these latter charming moments, of so happy a fairy-tale quality, that tempt the producer. This is so much the case with all the moments allotted to Imogen, that it was inevitable the play should sooner or later be attempted by a manager so fortunate as to command the services of Miss Ellen Terry. As Mr. Irving gives it, he gives it frankly for Miss Terry's sake, contenting himself with a very moderate personal chance.

So far as she is concerned he gives it with great success; no part that she has played of late years is so much of the exact fit of her particular gifts. Her performance is naturally poetic, has delightful breadth and tenderness, delightful grace and youth. Youth above all — Miss Terry has never, without effort, been so young and so fresh. Short-skirted and free, crowned with roses by Mr. Alma-Tadema's hand, and dressed in the unmistakable "note" of one of that painter's learned visions, she is exactly the heroine demanded by an old-time story for a circle — not too critical — round the fire. That is the formula of *Cymbeline*, and Mr. Irving has accepted it without making difficulties. The spirit in which he has accommodated himself to the question of mounting shows the happy tact of not taking any part of the business too seriously. He has had the co-operation of Mr. Alma-Tadema, and Mr. Tadema, it is true, is nothing if not archaeological; but by avoiding an aggressive solidity the documentary stamp, the "reconstruction" as it were, has been kept in the right key — the key of the amusing. The Britons are figures on a tapestry, the Romans are figures on a mock triumphal arch, and as the play never leaves us for many minutes in one place, the place is indulgently impressionistic. When Romans and Britons meet, at the end, in the shock of battle, the carnage is as merry a game as all the rest. When Iachimo, at dead of night, emerges from the trunk in Imogen's room, hovers about her bed, takes off her bracelet, and catalogues at his leisure the items of proof by which he shall win his wager, we are in an order of things as delightfully idle as the verse in which he subsequently retails his observations:

> *"The chimney*
> *Is south the chamber; and the chimney-piece*
> *Chaste Dian, bathing."*

Imogen, in a soft lamp-light that seems to confound itself with the radiance of her purity, sleeps under the protection of this goddess, and that of a cloud canopy, which, like the curtain in an old-fashioned portrait, is vaguely caught up to where

> *"The roof o' the chamber*
> *With golden cherubim is fretted;"*

and when her gentlewoman has retired, and the lid of the big gruesome box has begun slowly to rise, we feel the thrill of early years, a shudder almost pantomimic. There is not much to be done with Iachimo but to make him picturesque, and Mr. Irving wisely lets him abound in the sense of his villany, qualified as it is by the quaintness of a masquerade, of which the "happy ending" is "pardon's the word for all." He gives the character the benefit of his great art of visible composition—a duskiness of romance, an eccentricity of distinction—and is content to let it, so far as it *is* a character, profit by the half-reluctant good humour into which we settle when the story, at once so disagreeable and so pretty, brings us at last to Milford Haven and the delightful cave in Wales. Why should the reprobate Roman be more "natural" than the lamentable Briton? The Kembles and Keans and Macreadys used, I believe, to amuse themselves in their lighter hours with Posthumus, but he can scarcely be said to be first-rate sport— there is still less to be done with him than with Iachimo. The wicked queen is a fine scarlet patch, which Miss Geneviève Ward keeps full in the light; she is like some vivified portrait-bust of the Vatican or the Capitol, some hard, high-frizzled Agrippina or Faustina. But there is no great sport for any one save Imogen till we reach the fourth act, which fairly hums, like a bee among flowers, with the spirit of poetry. Belarius in his cave, the hidden young princes—with the Briton's love of sport—in their goat-skins, the frightened Fidele, the decapitated Cloten, the clothes of Posthumus, the invading Romans, the enchanting verse, make a sweet jumble, from which even the footlights can scarcely brush the bloom. Italy crops up in a sense still different from that of "the legions garrisoned in Gallia"—even those who come under the conduct of "bold Iachimo, Sienna's brother." The whole scene becomes a carnival procession, a fantasy of the Renaissance. Miss Terry, as Fidele, grows younger and younger, and in her beautiful melancholy boy's dress shows admirably that the more chance she has for freedom of motion the more easily she surmounts its dangers. Her immense naturalness throughout the character is of the highest value, through its enabling her to throw all her weight, without any of the arts usually employed to that end, into the positive innocence of it—that of the young wife youthfully in love with her absent husband. The impulsiveness of this innocence, breaking out in confident high spirits, draws, by its vivid opposition to the evil that is believed of her, the one happy effect that *can* be drawn from the foolish story of the husband's instantaneous surrender. But everything in *Cymbeline* is instantaneous—doubt and faith, love and hate, recognition and despair, damnation and forgiveness, victory and defeat—everything, down to the lively congruity of the figures with old, vague, but remembered, pictorial types—a sort of success that is stamped with the *coup de pouce* of Mr. Tadema and the great scenic art of Mr. Irving.

"Mr. Henry Irving's Production of Cymbeline*" appeared in* Harper's Weekly, *November 21, 1896.*

IRVING'S "RICHARD III.;
LITTLE EYOLF"

——————————— 1 8 9 7 ———————————

IT IS more difficult, on this dusky threshold of the new year, to say exactly what London, at the dim aperture, is looking for than to say what—so far as, in the air we live in, mere eyes may avail—she is looking *at*. It is only the nearest objects that can, in such a medium, be descried, and I fall with instant relief to the easier task—comfortably conscious indeed of the blessed support of the Christmas void, the big brown desert of a town laid waste by the fond fancy (sweetest, for the London-lover at least, of all English superstitions,) that this is the time of year for the breast of nature. "Every one" is in the country—every one but the superlatively wise for whom the sense of such a shrinkage is an old and charming story, a story rich in impressions of the way things loom larger in the comparative solitude, the way "productions" of almost any kind, become striking and the pink and gold of the shop-fronts irradiate the fog. If the spirit of pantomime pervades in this manner the very streets, I hasten to add that theirs is the truest felicity who have schoolboys at large to take to the play. The pantomime, it is true, is not the play to the extent it used to be; but that difference is made up by the fact that the play is more and more the pantomime. I mean it is more and more one of the "productions aforesaid"—a great show and a great picture, an exhibition of which the pecuniary cost (the only cost ever mentioned, or of which a work of art, the interpretation of an author, appears to be deemed susceptible,) is promptly commemorated in the newspapers. And the vividness of this truth is not, I think, dimmed by the accident that if what the theatres are just now offering us is Shakespeare, one of them has but just ceased to offer us Ibsen.

Sir Henry Irving's Richard III. is not his first playing of the part, but it is his first presentation of the piece. Upwards of twenty years ago it was produced at the Lyceum by the management immediately preceding his own, and was then one of the successes which presumably determined him to take over the theatre from failing hands. His Richard of those days, as I remember it, strikingly showed his gifts, but he has had the artistic patience, all these years, to leave the character alone. His gifts have not changed, though they have visibly developed, and his power to use them has matured. His present creation has the benefit of this maturity, though I seem to remember that even the earlier one, when so much of his reputation was still to come, had that element of "authority" which is a note by itself in an actor's effect, independent of the particular case, and almost as distinguishable in what he does worst as in what he does best. What Sir Henry Irving does best, as happens in this instance, is exactly what he does with Richard—makes, for the setting, a big, brave general picture, and then, for the figure, plays on the chord of the sinister-sardonic, flowered over as vividly as may be with the elegant-grotesque. No figure could have more of this livid complexion and Gothic angularity than, singly and simply seen, the monster drawn by Shakespeare. Singly and simply—in this light—Sir Henry Irving sees him, and makes him, very obvious yet very distinguished, hold the Lyceum stage with any of his predecessors. But I confess that, in regard to the whole matter, the question of the better and the worse, of whether such a Richard as this is or isn't, in his frank enjoyment of the joke, a "comic character," leaves me cold compared with the opportunity of testifying afresh to an impression now quite wearily mature—an acute sense that, after all that has come and gone, the repre-

sented Shakespeare is simply no longer to be borne. The reason
of this impatience is of the clearest — there is absolutely no representing him. The attempt to make real or even plausible a loose,
violent, straddling romance like *Richard III.* — a chronicle for the
market-place, a portrait for the house wall — only emphasizes
what is coarse in such a hurly-burly and does nothing for what is
fine. It gives no further lift to the poetry and adds a mortal
heaviness to the prose. The thing suffers (till it positively howls)
from everything to which, in fiction — the fiction of the theatre or
any other — the present general cultivation of a closer illusion
exposes it. The more it is painted and dressed, the more it is
lighted and furnished and solidified, the less it corresponds or
coincides, the less it squares with our imaginative habits. By what
extension of the term can such a scene as Richard's wooing of
Lady Anne be said to be represented? We can only use the word
to mean that Sir Henry Irving shows his experience and his art.
It leaves us doggedly defying any actress whatever to give a
touch of truth, either for woe or for weal, to the other figure of
the situation — leaves us weltering, at this and at the great majority of the other moments, in a sea of weak allowances from
which we at last scramble ashore with (for all spoil of the wreck,)
a sore sense that the more Shakespeare is "built in" the more we
are built out.

If after this I say that I took, earlier in the month, a lively
interest in the production, at the Avenue Theatre, by Miss Elizabeth Robins, of *Little Eyolf*, I shall be quite prepared to hear it
asked if I think Ibsen, then, so superior to the Bard of Avon. I
am afraid it won't take me long enough even for decency to reply
that for the purpose to which he has just been so successfully
applied I prefer him a hundred times. I like Shakespeare better —
let me hurry to declare — "for reading;" but I like Ibsen better
for — Northumberland Avenue; and Northumberland Avenue is
after all but a moment's walk from that stronghold of art, the
Strand. Ibsen has the merit, not vain for an author of plays, of

being at his best in the theatre. He is in our chords, on our scale; he profits, up on the hilt, by the inevitable effort of our time to make the reflection of life, in the different arts, have the look and motion and sound of life. *Little Eyolf* had had to wait two years to come to the London stage; during which I dare say he has had his nine days' run in America, as these are matters in which other countries—countries other than England, I mean—are apt to be quicker on the trigger. It is true that we have at present the promise of all proper quickness in the case of *John Gabriel Borkman*, the four-act piece which embodies the very last biennial revolution—a series unfailing in its regularity and as punctual to a day as the mill of fate—of the wonderful old man of Christiania. Mr. William Archer has just translated it, Mr. Heinemann is about to publish it, and it is shortly to be produced by Miss Robins, who, in England, has rendered Ibsen all the pious service of a priestess of the altar. I have read the play with the sense of a great warming of the critical heart, and I emphasize the prospect because I profess no vagueness as to the fact that it belongs to that very small group of impressions theatrical which—as things appear mainly to be going—denote a calculable comfort. The comfort supplied by Ibsen—I use the term in the sense of the "higher amusement"—springs indeed from more sources than I can now attempt to enumerate, freshly opened as some of them were by the handful of performances of *Little Eyolf*. They began to operate, they always begin, within five or ten minutes of the rise of the curtain—a moment at which this special spectator becomes aware of an adjustment of his aesthetic sense as definite as a material "click." It is simply the acceptance of the small Ibsen *spell*, the surrender of the imagination to his microcosm, his confined but completely constituted world, in which, in every case, the tissue of relations between the parts and the whole is of a closeness so fascinating. The odd thing—I speak of course from the point of view of my particular stall—is that the fascination appears quite independent either of the merit of the interpretation or of the place held by the play in the Ibsen list. The place of *Little Eyolf* is not of the highest, and even in London, on other occasions, the author has had, on the whole, I think, more acting. Yet prompt to the moment the charm descended—as sharp as ever rang the little silver bell. Let me hope that I shall be able, on the production of *John Gabriel*, to express more arithmetically the mysterious force applied to it. Meanwhile there are other things to do.

"Irving's Richard III.; Little Eyolf" appeared, under the heading "London" and the date of January 1, in Harper's Weekly, *January 23, 1897; only that part of the letter which deals with the theatre is here reproduced.*

After nearly twenty years' avoidance of any continuous journalism, Henry James contributed a series of fourteen letters, at irregular intervals, to Harper's Weekly *between January and September, 1897. Except for the last, which was devoted to Old Suffolk, the letters are all headed "Lon-don"; they deal with art exhibitions and theatre productions, review a number of recent publications, and occasionally discuss current events.*

The letter on Richard III *is the first of the series. In a letter to W. E. Norris of December 23, 1896, four days after the revival, Henry James wrote: "I have yet had nothing worse to suffer than a first night at the Lyceum—the too great Irvingism of which—mainly in Ellen Terry's box —had been, the same day, pleasantly mitigated in advance, by Tessa Gosse in Sheridan's* Critic.*"*

JOHN GABRIEL BORKMAN

——————— 1 8 9 7 ———————

Reprinted from Notes on Novelists with Some Other Notes *by Henry James;*
copyright 1914 by Charles Scribner's Sons, 1942 by Henry James; used by per-
mission of the publishers.

I AM afraid the interest of the world of native letters is not
at this moment so great as to make us despise mere translation
as an aid to curiosity. There is indeed no reason why we should
forbear to say in advance what we are certain, every time, to say
after (after the heat has cooled, I mean): namely, that nothing is
easier to concede than that Ibsen—contentious name!—would be
much less remarked if he were one of a dozen. It is impossible,
in London at least, to shut one's eyes to the fact that if to so
many ingenious minds he is a kind of pictorial monster, a grotesque on the sign of a side-show, this is at least partly because his
form has a monstrous rarity. It is one of the odd things of our
actual aesthetics that the more theatres multiply the less any one
reads a play—the less any one cares, in a word, for the text of
the adventure. That no one ever *does* read a play has long been a
commonplace of the wisdom of booksellers. Ibsen, however, is a
text, and Ibsen is read, and Ibsen contradicts the custom and
confounds the prejudice; with the effect thereby, in an odd way,
of being doubly an exotic. His violent substance imposes, as it
were, his insidious form; it is not (as would have seemed more
likely) the form that imposes the substance. Mr. William Archer
has just published his version of *John Gabriel Borkman*, of which,
moreover, French and German versions reach us at the same
moment. There are therefore all the elements of a fresh breeze in
the wind—one has already a sense as of a cracking of whips and a
girding of loins. You may by this time be terribly tired of it all in

America; but, as I mentioned a fortnight ago, we have had very recent evidence that languor here, in this connection, is by no means as yet the dominant note. It is not the dispute itself, however, that most interests me: let me pay it, for what it has been and what it still may be, the mere superficial tribute of saying that it constitutes one of the very few cases of contagious discussion of a matter not political, a question not of mere practice, of which I remember to have felt, in a heavy air, the engaging titillation. In London, generally, I think, the wandering breath of criticism is the stray guest at the big party—the shy young man whom nobody knows. In this remarkable instance the shy young man has ventured to pause and hover, has lighted on a topic, introduced himself and, after a gasp of consternation in the company, seen a little circle gather round him. I can only speak as one of the little circle, testifying to my individual glee.

The author who at the age of seventy, a provincial of provincials, turns out *John Gabriel* is frankly for me so much one of the peculiar pleasures of the day, one of the current strong sensations, that, erect as he seems still to stand, I deplore his extreme maturity and, thinking of what shall happen, look round in vain for any other possible source of the same kind of emotion. For Ibsen strikes me as an extraordinary curiosity, and every time he sounds his note the miracle, to my perception, is renewed. I call it a miracle because it is a result of so dry a view of life, so indifferent a vision of the comedy of things. His idea of the thing represented is never the comic idea, though this is evidently what it often only can be for many of his English readers and spectators. Comedy moreover is a product mainly of observation, and I scarcely know what to say of his figures except that they haven't the *signs*. The answer to that is doubtless partly that they haven't the English, but have the Norwegian. In such a case one of the Norwegian must be in truth this very lack of signs.

They have no tone but their moral tone. They are highly animated abstractions, with the extraordinary, the brilliant property of becoming when represented at once more abstract and more living. If the spirit is a lamp within us, glowing through what the world and the flesh make of us as through a ground-glass shade, then such pictures as *Little Eyolf* and *John Gabriel* are each a *chassez-croisez* of lamps burning, as in tasteless parlours, with the flame practically exposed. There are no shades in the house, or the Norwegian ground-glass is singularly clear. There is a positive odour of spiritual paraffin. The author nevertheless arrives at the dramatist's great goal—he arrives for all his meagreness at intensity. The meagreness, which is after all but an unconscious, an admirable economy, never interferes with that: it plays straight into the hands of his rare mastery of form. The contrast between this form—so difficult to have reached, so civilized, so "evolved," —and the bareness and bleakness of his little northern democracy is the source of half the hard frugal charm that he puts forth. In the cold fixed light of it the notes that we speak of as deficiencies take a sharp value in the picture. There is no small-talk, there are scarcely any manners. On the other hand there is so little vulgarity that this of itself has almost the effect of a deeper, a more lonely provincialism. The background at any rate is the sunset over the ice. Well in the very front of the scene lunges with extraordinary length of arm the Ego against the Ego, and rocks in a rigour of passion the soul against the soul—a spectacle, a movement, as definite as the relief of silhouettes in black paper or of a train of Eskimo dogs on the snow. Down from that desolation the sturdy old symbolist comes this time with a supreme example of his method. It is a high wonder and pleasure to welcome such splendid fruit from sap that might by now have shown something of the chill of age. Never has he juggled more gallantly with difficulty and danger than in this really prodigious *John Gabriel*, in which a great span of tragedy is taken between three or four persons—a trio of the grim and grizzled—in the two or three hours of a winter's evening; in which the whole thing throbs with an actability that fairly shakes us as we read; and in which, as the very flower of his artistic triumph, he has given us for the most beautiful and touching of his heroines a sad old maid of sixty. Such "parts," even from the vulgarest point of view, are Borkman and Ella Rentheim! But about all this there will inevitably be much more to say when the play is produced.[1]

"John Gabriel Borkman" appeared, under the heading "London" and the date of January 15, as the second letter in Harper's Weekly, February *6, 1897; only that part of the letter* which deals with the play is here reproduced. It was reprinted, under the heading "London Notes" and dated January, 1897, in* Notes on Novelists, 1914.*

[1] *This intention was not carried out; and the last sentence was omitted when the essay was reprinted in* Notes on Novelists.

THE BLIGHT OF THE DRAMA

———————— 1897 ————————

MR. WILLIAM ARCHER contributed a few months since to the *Fortnightly Review* an article on "The Blight of the Drama"; which, as it seemed to me at the time to offer a capital text, I regret to have missed the right occasion for speaking of. This leaves me crudely confronted with melancholy facts and yet unsupported in the still more charmless office of noting and expressing them. It leaves me in other words just nakedly committed to remark that everything appears more and more to point to a definite renunciation on the part of the English theatre of any attempt to make, in Europe, even ever so little of a figure. It is not indeed that Europe seems to heed or to care or to be ever so faintly interested: nothing could well express the absence of reverberation on the Continent of any performance or any production of any kind on any London stage. There are dozens and dozens of stages and thousands and thousands of shows; but the white cliffs of Dover continue to constitute, to the east, the rigid limit of their appeal to the civilized consciousness. The German theatre is generously devoted to Shakespeare; but the cases in which either one of those that we have so often laid under contribution—the French, the German, the Scandinavian, let alone the Spanish, the Italian, the Slav—has borrowed or translated or adapted, or in any degree appropriated, a contemporary English play are so rare as to belong practically to the rosy realm of fable. To the west, of course—fortunately for these communications— it is a very different matter: America has all the air of being as candidly agog as the rest of the world is candidly averse. Let me find in this circumstance such countenance as I may for saying, with never a hand held out nearer home, that if the drama round about us is, in Mr. Archer's phrase, at the present hour perhaps more than ever blighted, I have never seen more light thrown on the mystery than by two accidents, of recent occurrence, which, however, have, so far as I know, attracted no general attention. One of these indeed is of the sort that may come and go a thousand times and make no one the wiser unless it happen to have brushed an irritable critic with its wing. It was to be seen, then, a few weeks since, in a hundred newspapers and with the particular look of what is called, I believe, inspiration, that Mr. Forbes Robertson and Mrs. Patrick Campbell had, for the entertainment of the public, definitely made up their minds to incarnate respectively, as they had long desired to do, Lord Nelson and Lady Hamilton. That was all, and it may to the superficial mind seem so little as to cause the superficial mind to ask, like Oliver, for more. But I can scarce begin to tell you what the irritated critic may see in it. He sees simply something that would not have been conceivable in the newspaper press of any other country. (I speak always of course of the Chinese Orient.) The Lord Nelson of whom? the Lady Hamilton of what? Neither in Paris, in Berlin, in Vienna nor in Rome could the official intimation of an opportunity of inter-pretation for a couple of players, of an eminence however colossal, have taken a form so artlessly — so touchingly in its artlessness — exclusive of any mention of a link connecting their irrepressible genius with the perhaps even still greater names to be invoked. Lord Nelson and Lady Hamilton may well, together, in their historical intensity, form a subject for the capable poet; but the only thinkable one for the capable, or even incapable, actor is, to my sense, the one the playwright offers him. There is a certain little process which, however trifling it may seem, is simply the whole of the affair, and Lord Nelson and Lady Hamilton are a possibility and a play only in so far as such an intervention may be so good as to make them so. The "blight of the drama" is surely complete when it may appear a mere detail that in such a connection the core of the matter is not so much as mentioned. We have thereby — and the picture is droll enough — the actor and the actress communing straight across the ages with the irreducible elements of their make-up. The announcement would have been anywhere else an announcement of the dramatic opportunity and of the source — in the form of somebody distinct, even to somebody's loss, both from Mrs. Patrick Campbell and Mr. Forbes Robertson — to which a grateful public was to owe it.

There inevitably came, in the case I glance at, a day when the play had to be named, the connecting link, the dramatic span of the dizzy space, to be in some sort recognized as the practicable bridge. If these things had not been mentioned sooner this was doubtless perhaps, in some degree or other, because they were not inordinately mentionable; yet if *Nelson's Enchantress*, at the Avenue, justified, on production, almost any disposition to have treated it as a prize for silence, the incident itself, tiny as you may think it, showed with peculiar precision how the wind is blowing. I at all events cannot help seeing in it a massive moral, a prodigious lesson. The drama verily is blighted when the drama is dropped. Though dropped, I grant, from no great height, it may well die of the fall, so that our next business with it shall be merely to bury it. *Nelson's Enchantress* is, I believe, already buried, and I have no wish to hover unkindly, or indeed to hover at all, over its grave: I pause there but long enough to catch a faint, brief echo. I hate to let anything pass that may form a contribution, however small, to my favourite exercise and study, that pursuit for which I can devise no better name than the collation of authorities. These authorities are simply the voice of to-day and the voice of yesterday, and the amusement in question is the effort to bring them into some sort of — I won't say definite agreement, but traceable relation and neighbourhood. The diversion consists in sounding them again at each other, as it

were, and listening for what they may have to say. To each other
they have nothing indeed, but are as mum as members of a family
who cut each other dead. The explanatory speech is for the critic,
if the critic can puzzle it out. It is ten to one he cannot, and to
call it explanatory is in fact to flatter it grossly. The repudiation,
on either side, of all connection with the establishment over the
way is not accompanied with any attenuating grace. Lest my
image appear obscure I hasten to remark that what I speak of is
nothing but the old story of the two great publics—read at this
moment in the light projected upon them by the artistic career of
the actress named above. For the public of the other day, the
public of *The Second Mrs. Tanqueray*, the talent of Mrs. Patrick
Campbell, in that play triumphantly associated with the principal
part, revealed itself, if the general voice be ever the measure, as
supreme and unapproachable. Deafening were the acclamations
that surrounded it for the whole career of the piece. But *où sont
les neiges d'antan?* The public of *Mrs. Tanqueray* is what I have
called the establishment over the way; the establishment on the
hither side is of course the same public in a different mood, or
say even only confronted with different work—that is with *other*
work—from the same producers: the same public, at all events,
blank as to any connection with any opinion at any other time
expressed or any enthusiasm at any other time delirious. It com-
mits itself, the first of our authorities, up to its eyes; while the
second, on the same question, remains abysmally obscure. A
talent, an artistic temperament, is, in short, in one light infinitely
distinguished; in another its highest office is to produce, on
reference to it, the stony stare that asks what the deuce you
mean. What the deuce you mean is simply that a distinguished
talent and a great proficiency don't change at that rate from one
occasion to the other, and that the many-headed monster can
therefore not plead high intelligence or even common perception
on both occasions. On which does it decide that its intelligence
shall have been darkened? To come back to the pastime for which

I just expressed my relish, the game here is to wait for its answer.

While we wait—and we shall wait long!—I may go on to say that the second of the two straws I picked up at the beginning of these remarks, testifies, though much the larger, proportionately not much more to the direction of the breeze. There towers, at the moment I write, above the passer in the Haymarket, a structure massive and ornate, though still unfinished, which is labelled on a commensurate scale, and in commemoration of the historic site it partly occupies, as the house presently to be opened by Mr. Beerbohm Tree under the name of Her Majesty's Theatre. The striking thing in this connection is the impassable gulf that appears to yawn between the interest taken in Mr. Tree's building and the interest taken in Mr. Tree's repertory. The two curiosities would appear to have some common ground, but the latter, for the present, is completely obscured by the former. It is only in London, I think—unless it be also in New York—that an edifice of this character scales the skies without suggesting in any quarter an audible allusion to what is to be done in it. Mr. Beerbohm Tree may of course have up his sleeve a repertory of the first order, he may take his stand upon traditions piled up as high as his house; I confess it meanwhile an effect of a turn of mind perhaps too speculative that, from the street, the bricks and mortar, the uplifted cornices and pinnacles, show a complacency into which we must wait awhile to read a meaning.

There is occupation for the interval, fortunately, at the Criterion and at the St. James's, where Mr. Henry Arthur Jones and Mr. Pinero have just produced new plays. There are many ways of looking at a work of art, and the way we take, in a given case, is sometimes more imposed on us than chosen. It was therefore, I may say, not in my own discretion to resist the particular manner in which *The Physician*, Mr. Charles Wyndham's production, affected me, nor the degree in which it led me to wonder how far Mr. Jones's relation to *his* centre of resistance had been deliberate and how far beyond his control. It is rudimentary, of course, to grant your artist in the way of subject whatever he chooses to ask; just as you don't dispute, or discuss, when you dine with one of your friends, the motive of his hospitality. What you may dispute, what you may discuss, is the quality of his dinner, which is the particular form the hospitality takes. The subject of *The Physician* is the history of a great London doctor. He falls, at the height of success and from one day to another, so madly in love with a young lady who comes to consult him about her *fiancé*, that he throws up his practice on the spot and goes down into the country to devote himself to the object of his passion. She lives in a pretty parsonage with the parson her father, who represents, you will more than suspect, the element of comedy; and the young man to whom she is engaged is a leading light, a bright agitator and speech-maker, in the great cause of Temperance. This young man is afflicted with a malady at some of the symptoms of which we cease to wonder only when we have discovered, through the unerring *flair* of the doctor, that concomitantly with his public career he has long carried on the practice of secret and desperate drinking. The parson and his daughter have, like the rest of the world, never dreamed of his duplicity; but the enamoured *medico* is placed by the knowledge of it in the situation which forms the theme of the play and which, instinctively, the spectator looks to Mr. Henry Arthur Jones to treat. This situation is the doctor's predicament, his dilemma; call it, if we will, his temptation, his struggle and his resistance. He is so mad to possess the girl that an easy way stares him in the face: he has only to reveal to her the private turpitude of her lover and she will infallibly fall into his arms. She does so, of course, in the last act, but by ways remarkably devious.

The quarrel the spectator may have with these ways is not, I hasten to explain, that they *are* devious, for if the devious is not always the dramatic, the dramatic is on the other hand not inveterately the direct. It is not even that they are eccentric beyond what he may find acceptable: it is simply that they are not *pre-*

sented—which is what I mean by my reference to Mr. Jones's ambiguous relation to his subject. The subject had something, doubtless, at a pinch, to give; though it strikes me as dealing most with those things of gradual growth, of which the meagre theatric form, so brief and so bare, is usually but a rough expression; but this was only on condition of following it up and squeezing it. Mr. Jones may, I think, be said to have let it persistently alone; and the question we ask is whether he has done so by irreflection, or by a refinement of that aesthetic curiosity which sometimes leads an artist almost wantonly to multiply his difficulties. Has he wished to see, for technical amusement, if a play *can* be interesting with something else offered in the place of the idea on which it rests? The subject of *The Physician* is essentially a relation, the growth and development of one—that of the great doctor to the lovely girl for whose sake he has broken his life in twain. It is even more particularly his relation to *her* relation, that is to the tie that binds her, and above all to the object of that tie, her mendacious and hypocritical lover, who is on the verge of *delirium tremens* without her guessing it, and in the sight of her intercourse with whom he finds from day to day both fresh flame for passion and fresh opportunity for a departure from professional discretion. This was the relation that it seems to me the author's theme enjoined upon him to put before us, and yet he has done that so little that there is scarcely a moment in the piece—after a first meeting in the first act and a mere gleam in the second—at which we see the hero either in combination with his mistress or in combination with his rival. Least of all do we see him at any instant in combination with the two together— a situation from which I should have expected to see Mr. Jones draw the best of the few effects that his *donnée* may have been held to promise him. The line he has taken reduces him to the single one of Mr. Wyndham's merely describing, with a good deal of ubiquity, to other people, what we might have if we only could. Why and how the hero is so far gone there is much too little to show us; and the result of that is an imperfect entrance into sentiments of which we have not had the vision and of which we fail to embrace the cause. The case is infinitely interesting for the light it throws on the penalties paid—exacted sooner or later, to the last turn of the screw, by the outraged muse—for every deviation from the letter of the artistic law. The consequence of the construction of a part for Mr. Wyndham that shall place Mr. Wyndham in relation, practically, to nobody but Mr. Wyndham himself—the consequence of this curious *tour de force* is that Mr. Wyndham never seems, from beginning to end, to be anything *but* Mr. Wyndham. It may surely be regarded as the golden rule of real evocation that, if it takes two to make a bargain, it takes no less extravagant a number to sustain an action. Therefore it is that I speak of *The Physician* so much less as a work with a subject than as a subject without a work.

On these grim terms, indeed, how am I placed for speaking of *The Princess and the Butterfly?* Mr. Pinero's new drama, which is in five acts, and begins at 7.45, to end at 11.30, makes on the stage of the St. James's a series of beautiful pictures of the contemporary "interior," in the form, at least, in which unlimited pecuniary resources enable this feature of our manners to show. But what sort of a picture does it make of the idea from which it starts? That amounts to asking how the subject is treated. To tell you, however, I must first make up my mind what it is. Perhaps I shall have done so the next time I have occasion to speak of it.

"The Blight of the Drama" appeared, under the heading "London" and the date of April 3, as the fifth letter in Harper's Weekly, *April 24, 1897.*

EDMOND ROSTAND

THE PATH of the observer of human things who, on occasion, at the behest of the critical spirit, permits himself an excursion into the world of letters, is doubtless at no time particularly smooth; but such an adventurer finds himself arrested at the present hour by a perplexity that is of recent growth. We live in a day in which the term 'success' represents, for the composition that has carried off the crown, possibilities of recognition, of circulation, undreamt of by our fathers and unknown to simpler societies. The scale on which a work of imagination, so called, may, in especial, see itself multiplied, advertised, acclaimed, diffused, makes the mystery of popularity more than ever difficult to analyse, and in fact surrounds the phenomenon with a disquieting, anomalous element. The novel, and even the poem, that sells, sells half a million of copies; the play that draws, draws vast populations, and for months together; and this, accordingly, is the puzzle, the worry — though we hope, as we try to deal with it but the temporary one — that, do what we will, we are unable altogether to dissociate the idea of acclamation from the idea of distinction. We are in the presence of huge demonstrations, and we ask ourselves if there be really afloat in the world anything like a proportionate amount of art and inspiration. The demonstrations are insistent, the reverberation such as victory or peace, announced to distracted nations, would alone seem to justify, and we are consequently somewhat oppressed — which is the form taken by our embarrassment. Our old habit, as a first impression, our old prejudice, stick to us: what is universal recognition but glory, and what is behind glory, by the ancient rule, in these fields, but somebody's achievement of something supreme? The critic must appreciate, discriminate, hold his course, and he can, in a word, scarce help being put out by the colossal when the colossal breaks into his little garden, so neat on its traditional lines, in the manner of an escaped elephant from the nearest circus. He learns soon enough, probably, to allow for the elephant; but the question never quite wholly sinks to rest—the garden never feels altogether safe. The insidious part of the perplexity is that acclamation may swell to its maximum, and the production acclaimed, the novel, the poem, the play, none the less truly *be* the real thing and not the make-believe. It is so often the make-believe that we are all but driven comfortably to generalise—so great is the convenience of a simple law. The law, however, ceases to be simple from the moment even one book in five hundred does appeal, distinguishably, to a critical sense. The case, though of the rarest, occurs, and it thereby deprives the conscientious student we have postulated of the luxury of a hard-and-fast rule.

I have approached M. Rostand, under the immediate advantage of whose name I have ventured on the foregoing remarks, by a road that will perhaps not seem too devious if I succeed in marking him, for our puzzled spectator, as one of those accidents that figure as disturbing—disturbing precisely because they show, in their rare way, a fine and complex talent as enjoying the fortune of talents not usually so to be qualified, show it as carried, to the sound of drum and trumpet, round the globe. He is the author of plays that, in Europe and America, have broken the record, as we say, for 'runs,' and he accordingly constitutes, brilliant, consummate performer as he is, one of the most curious of contemporary cases—really a more important one for criticism, I think, than if, with more stuff in him still, he had had, as might very well have happened, a destiny obscure. The copy of *Cyrano de Bergerac* that I have before me is marked, at a date at which the

run of the play was yet young, as the sixty-first thousand —
numbers that, in respect to each publication, must have been
afterwards greatly exceeded. Such a show, then, is delightfully
confounding — testifying as it does to the residuum of sensibility
in publics capable of consuming 'quality' with such appetite. The
revealed affinity with quality is thus what cheeringly strikes us;
and we find ourselves immediately connecting it with the recent
brilliant anomaly in our English literary annals, the immense
'success' of Mr. Rudyard Kipling, achieved in spite of his wearing
so many of the signs that charm the ingenious and disconcert the
simple — those simple by whom, at present, the crown is mainly
conferred. It would be interesting, had we space, to carry our
parallel far, for it to a great extent imposes itself, and would
evidently throw up an abundance of fresh hints on the question of
differences, of contrasts, in neighbouring peoples. The case remains that the Anglo-American and the French public have each
had, almost at the same time, in their respective, their superlative
favourite, a subject in which criticism itself has delighted, so that
the favourites have to that extent much in common. They have
for their deepest note the patriotic note, the note of the militant
and triumphant race. This is the particular reason why comparison
would be suggestive. The races are different, but for each poet
each is the triumphant and the militant.

Taking the case indeed as we find it in M. Rostand, it throws up
more oddities and appeals than we can do justice to. For the
patriotic explanation becomes queer when the response to the
signal flows from quarters where the ideal, the allegiance, is of
quite another cloth. *Cyrano* has been enjoyed, if I am not mistaken,
through the length and breadth of the United States, and yet the
glamour of *Cyrano* is intensely, exquisitely, in passionate, almost
invidious national reference. The particular beauty of the play —
and the remark is practically as true of *L'Aiglon* — is in the fantastic, romantic, brilliantly whimsical expression of an ardent
French consciousness. The problem before the author was to

weave into a dense and glittering tissue every illustration, every
reminder that the poetry, history, legend of a particular period
would yield; and the measure of his 'success,' exactly, is in the
vividness of this tapestry. The tapestry is marvellously figured,
but it is scarcely too much to say that the light of the consciousness
aforesaid is required for following the design with intelligence.
How much of that intelligence do M. Rostand's spectators and
readers about the globe, those of his Anglo-Saxon public in
especial, bring to the task? To ask the question is to move again
in the world of wonder; for would not the upshot of pushing an
enquiry into the relation between the glamour, as I have called it,
of *Cyrano* and *L'Aiglon*, and the state of mind of the alien populations that have absorbed them—would not this consequence be to
make us ask ourselves what such exhibitions, in such conditions,
have been taken *for?* *Cyrano*, of the two pieces, has been, I believe, much the more acclaimed, and *Cyrano*, precisely, might
quite have passed for a wilful wager, an act of amused defiance
to any perception of its finer flavour not determined, on the part
of the public, by identities of origin. Nothing is easier than to
fancy the writer's saying to himself that he would construct such
a spectacle as would be balm to the imagination of every Frenchman—just in proportion too as the latter should be French not
only instinctively, but by reflection and culture as well—and that
would, by the same law, lead the apprehension of other communities such a dance as would mainly throw into relief the inaptitude
of the dancers. But, lo! to this ironic, this malicious fiddle the
barbarians have kicked their heels positively in time—as inscru-
tably, at any rate, as was to be required for decorum. An ingenious
American actor carries his nightly hundreds captive with a translated, an arranged—*how* arranged we inextinguishably wonder—
version of the five-act play; a dauntless *comédienne* works the
miracle of reducing the still larger Napoleonic panorama to the
same simplified idiom. If there be a quality of M. Rostand's own
idiom, the bristling bravery of his verse, the general frolic of his

vocabulary, especially under the happy crack of the whip of rhyme, it is that, surely, of resisting simplification to the death. What, therefore, has become of it beyond the seas? What is the equivalent offered for his merciless virtuosity of expression? The account of that matter is probably that as no impression of his virtuosity has been received, none of its influence has been missed. Only, this being so, we are thrown back—or all *but*—on the puzzle of his popularity. M. Rostand without his virtuosity—with that element either not rendered or not caught—what sort of a M. Rostand to excite enthusiasm is that? With what residuum does the magic work?

I hasten to confess that if I keep speaking as if such questions were worth while, it is because of my sense—perhaps excessive—of what I have just called their fascination: so disturbing, doubtless, is the habit, in the presence of a work of art with which the public appears to be in relation, of finding the public, as one of the parties to the encounter, the more infinite thing to consider. That scent is by no means, however, in these remarks, what I have proposed to follow; and I am relegated to my actual business by my having a moment ago struck the right one. The explanation, the solution of everything, and, with this, the supreme sign of our author, is just that he is inordinately romantic—so that the questions connected with his fortune in this character become, frankly, the real ones and supersede all others. I spoke a moment since of the reason that may, after all, be given for his being acclaimed even when he is not, on the literary side, tasted; which reason we immediately see present when we see his romantic—his extravagantly romantic—complexion recognised. The romantic in itself depends, I think, supremely little on virtuosity; therefore with virtuosity left out of the account there yet remains a great deal to taste. Virtuosity is a matter of expression, and M. Rostand would still be romantic without his expression. This circumstance has helped him prodigiously; it always helps where masses of men are involved; it is the charm, the spell, the golden key, operating *en gros* as nothing else does. The beauty of M. Rostand is that he is a sincere and consistent, and therefore a precious example of the character; and the refinements of extravagance that he adds to it give it a freshness where freshness might otherwise seem decidedly to fail. This is what virtuosity can do—as we have known it to do, moreover, nearer home, in a recent interesting case. Much of the work of Robert Louis Stevenson is an instance of the same combination; but Stevenson was less clear a case, being decidedly less simple a one. He cared signally for expression, and he admirably achieved it; but his romance was of a comparatively anxious, sceptical, preoccupied order, was but one of the features, though possibly the most marked, of a complex and restless mind. The whole mind will always be interesting in Stevenson; one seems to see it, round the edge of his special gift, as one sometimes sees the wider ring of light round the disc of the moon. The edge of M. Rostand's gift is sharp and hard, and breaks short off; its connections are, so to speak, all within it, only deepening the glitter. So far as he has given us his measure, he hangs, in other words, thoroughly together: he offers us our finest, freshest occasion for studying the possibilities, for watching the development, of the temperament at its best.

We have been living, so many of us, of recent years, in a continuous romantic wave that nothing is more natural than to grasp, in the welter—if but for the mere comfort of orientation—at any really palpable object, anything with the property of floating. It is something to hold on by while we try to make out where we are. Little enough of the wave, of course, has mattered, among us, for literature—it has mattered on the showing of R. L. Stevenson almost alone; so that, so far as any light from our own sources is concerned, we are quite in the dark as to what literature can, so to speak, do for it. We have too few plays to talk about, and there could be no better proof of our destitution than that, in discussing such fine exotics as the productions immediately before us, we find ourselves without terms of comparison drawn from our own literary scene. But the novel, of sorts, we at least can cite, and the novel, as it most besets us, as we most know it or most avoid it, the novel, in fine, multiplied and acclaimed, lives its hour mainly under favour of the romantic prejudice. The favour might have appeared, on occasion, likely to fail it, but no such catastrophe, so far as can be noted, has in fact taken place; though nothing, on the other hand, it must equally be said, has happened strikingly to regild its scutcheon. M. Rostand is a master in another form; but the stuff of romance lends itself, like the stuff of reality, to all forms, so that we are still on the ground of the question in seeking to read the lesson of *his* free use of that restorative gold-leaf of which our store seems to have run short. He lays it on thick, and gives it a splendid polish; the work he has hitherto done shines and twinkles with it in his clear morning of youth. We are infinitely amused, we are well-nigh dazzled, by the show; we are so drawn and beguiled that we ask ourselves, with appetite, with curiosity, how much more of the sovereign compound, so lavishly spent, he still has on hand — together with other wonderments as to how it will wear and 'wash,' how far it will go, what may be its further connections with life. I may seem, with all this, to be taking our author very hard; but, obviously, if such questions are interesting at all, they are interesting with intensity; and I can only, personally, confess to positive suspense as to what will absolutely *become* of the potent principle under the particular impetus he has given and will presumably again give it. As no one, anywhere, has recently expressed it with anything like his art, the case, one must repeat, is practically in his hands; they carry Caesar and his fortunes. But whither?

M. Rostand's sympathy was marked from the first; he struck in the three acts of *Les Romanesques*, in 1894, the note of the very question itself — the question, that is, of the influence of the principle. This slight, but delightful production — ingeniously and amusingly Englished, and not incongruously rhymed, by George Fleming — is in fact as charming an examination of the nature of

the romantic, as pleasant a contribution to any discussion, as can
be imagined. The small action takes place in that happy land of
nowhere — the land of poetry, comedy, drollery, delicacy, profuse
literary association — which the French theatre has so often and
so enviably — notably with Alfred de Musset, unsurpassed for the
right touch — made its hunting ground; and if the whole thing is
the frankest of fantasies, an excursion into the *pays bleu*, it is the
work of a man already conscious of all the values involved. Percinet and Sylvette love each other over the garden wall because they
believe in the ferocious mutual enmity of their respective fathers —
a situation that makes their snatched and stolen interviews dangerous and wonderful. Their resemblance to Romeo and Juliet
is complete, and their appetite for such developments as shall
recall the fortunes of the immortal pair constant and exalted. The
respective fathers, meanwhile, are really the best friends in the
world, and steal *their* interviews over the wall precisely because
they desire their children to marry. Knowing the young persons
to be romantically disposed, dreading the probable effect of in
any degree prescribing to them a mutual impression, and cal-
culating therefore the effect of ostensibly denouncing and for-
bidding it, they have invented the idea of danger, defiance,
adventure, in order to keep their offspring in tune. What happens,
of course, is that the offspring discover at a given moment that
they have been practised on, that their elders are in league, that
their danger is a fiction, that their safety is complete, that their
analogy with the *amants de Vérone* is in fact naught, that there is,
in fine, no more romance in their case than in that of any other
two approved and engaged young persons. The romance of having
pleased each other isn't enough — they desire the cup to be spiced;
and they fall apart just in proportion as the two parents, prematurely confident, fraternise over the prospect. The moral of
the anecdote is of course that they come together again on the
basis of reality, once reality itself has had time to be prettily and
picturesquely arranged. M. Rostand's lightness of hand shows in

his keeping the dose of this article too, for Sylvette and Percinet, in tone with their dose of the other. The thing is really too much made up of ribbons and flowers, of masks and mantles, to be rehandled, with whatever finger-tips; but we note as its especial charm the ease with which the author's fancy moves in his rococo world.

This it is that in each of his productions makes M. Rostand so enviable, because it makes him, apparently at least, so happy; his rococo world spreads about him in an extraordinarily furnished and appointed, painted and gilded way, and he shows it to us as the master of the house shows the state apartments, knowing their order and relation and name, guiding us among crowded objects and 'up' in their history and quality. It is in the rococo world that he has gone on living and flourishing, for he has positively placed in it the successive scenes of *L'Aiglon.* We shall come to that presently; the point is that his face was, from the first, turned so fortunately straight for the concentration of energy. There is plenty of that, all in the direction of mask-and-mantle imagery, in such a delightful flight as the flourish of Straforel advertising his business in *Les Romanesques*—his business being, for just those ends, present to the pair of plotting fathers, the furniture of elopements, the accessories of abduction. The plotting fathers contract for the *enlèvement* of the young lady, with consequent death-dealing rescue by the young man, and nothing can be more delicately droll than Straforel's spoken and rhymed 'circular,' his tariff and his styles—he undertakes abductions as in a prosaic age his descendants are reduced to undertaking funerals and movings. Yet these things are almost too much things of air to be quoted; besides which they are, in M. Rostand, too numerous. It is his sign that, in his kind, he is rich, and we scarce show a man as rich by showing one or two of his bank notes.

There are plenty of them, however, no doubt, between the leaves of *La Princesse Lointaine,* the four acts of which date from 1895; by which I mean plenty of short examples of the author's power, in the matter of beautiful and whimsical turns, to keep it up and up, to begin again and again. *La Princesse Lointaine*, at any rate, is characteristic for just another reason than the one cited for its predecessor — the reason that the romantic here, instead of being in any degree mocked at or 'given away,' is taken for granted in all its length and breadth. It is exactly the play in which Percinet and Sylvette themselves would have found their ideal. The poetic picture, as in *Les Romanesques*, as in *Cyrano*, is a thing all of consistent tone — tone ever so adroitly arrived at and artfully sustained. M. Rostand knows the special preparation in which his subject must steep itself as a musical ear knows shades of sound and proprieties of time, and he can take every sort of liberty of form, of rhyme, of reference, without fear of taking any with the essence. He embarks again, in short, for the *pays bleu*, the purple island, and sails and sails with never an accident. It is a port, no doubt, that the adventurer never absolutely reaches, so that the sail itself is what makes the success, and our author's skill is to keep, as he does, in the boat. The adventure of his pair of Provençal troubadours who go forth in quest of the far-away princess, the Princess of the East and Countess of Tripoli, because the fame of her beauty has made them languish at home for years, and because one of them, the Prince of Aquitaine (the other being his knight), knows that she knows, beyond the sea, of his love-sick state, and wishes to show her before he dies to what a man may be reduced for her — this is, clearly enough, the perfection of a starting-point for a deep romantic plunge.

The piece surpasses its predecessor in brilliancy by the same stride by which *Cyrano* was in turn to surpass it, and by which — as a mere literary, or, if it be preferred, scenic wager — *L'Aiglon* was to surpass *Cyrano;* and we begin to get a glimpse of the author's formula — which relieves the mind. We see how far the great mantle of Victor Hugo has, all these years, trailed, and how, out of a mere corner of it, the cleverest of his grandsons can cut a complete suit. The form of M. Rostand's style, is it not, broadly speaking, Victor Hugo's style brought down to date, attuned to the age of the interview, the automobile and the decennial exhibition, the age of the American campaign and Madame Sarah Bernhardt? I say it not in mockery, nor even in familiarity, for M. Rostand will always dazzle me; but is it not practically a fair account of his use of his magnificent master to assert that he has done with him what we do with everything nowadays—has reduced him to the terms of contemporary journalism? It is delightful to get hold of so interesting, so exquisite an instance of a process going on all round us and never so well to be observed, to be caught in the fact, as in a good concrete example. The terms of contemporary journalism more and more impose themselves, announce themselves as, increasingly, irresistibly, the universal, the only terms, and exactly by the same law as that by which so many other modern conveniences have become indispensable, by which new machinery supersedes old, the kodak displaces the camera. They represent the portable, and the portable now is everything; if we have Victor Hugo at all, we must have a Victor Hugo who will go round the globe and be back in Paris by a date. Dates are everything; they are the numbers on that great ubiquitous clock-face which—however outside the matter in the given case—has at present so much more to say to any production of the mind than any principle within it. We are struck, at all events, for our consolation, with the range of accomplishment with which our general fate is compatible, with all indeed that is gained in one quarter if lost in another. Victor Hugo adapted, adjusted, scheduled and expositionised, Victor Hugo, in short, newspaperised, may be less august and mysterious, but the medium that absorbs him, the great diffusive, assimilative idiom, is unmistakably enriched. Happy an age, certainly, in which the vulgarisers are of M. Rostand's pattern.

The finest thing in *La Princesse Lointaine*—as also the finest in *Cyrano*—is the author's gallantry under fire of the extrava-

gance involved in his subject; as to which, in each instance — and
not less, in fact, in *L'Aiglon* — we can easily see that it would have
been fatal to him to be timid. The pathos, the poetry, for the
successive situations, move arm-in-arm with their latent absurdity — the too-much that keeps rising to the brim and that
would easily overflow at a wrong touch; and I find a charm the
more, I confess, in the dramatist's affinity with such dangers.
They help to make up his medley — the tear on the cheek of his
comic mask, the glimmer of a wink in the eye of his tragic — and
they help to give us, above all, a sense of his naturally adventurous temperament. They keep up his spirit and excite him thus
to keeping up our own. If his spirit requires, for exhilaration, the
acrobatic tight-rope, we are willing enough to sit and watch, it
being the acrobatic tight-rope, exactly, that he stretches from one
end of each of his productions to the other. The tight-rope in
La Princesse is the high fantasy of the common upliftedness between the distant lady and the dying pilgrim, who *have never met*,
over their penetrating relation; all the more that their failure to
meet is prolonged, is represented, through a large part of the
play, and that the amount of communication that might have
served instead has been of the slightest. The tight-rope in *Cyrano*
is, visibly enough, the question of the hero's facial misfortune,
doubly great as opposed to his grand imagination, grand manners
and grand soul, the soul that leads his boisterous personality to
run riot, for love and for friendship, in self-suppression, in sentimental suicide. The tight-rope in *L'Aiglon* is — well, what is it?
One is tempted to say that it is simply everything. It is in particular, we surmise, just the challenged, the accepted peril of
dealing scenically with the subject at all, and especially of dealing
with it on the scale required; the subject being essentially that of
the *attitude*, imposed, fixed, of the hapless young man — a young
man whose main mark it is that mere attitude is his only life,
that anything like action is forbidden him. The rope is here
stretched higher and tighter than elsewhere; it becomes, in its

appeal to the author's agility, a veritable trapeze. For I mean, emphatically, that the extravagant—that extravagant in which, for M. Rostand, the romantic mainly resides—is all there.

The extravagant is reached when emotions, passions, manners have ceased to reckon with life at all, and yet have become the more absorbing; and it consists, on the part of the young Duke of Reichstadt, in the general immensity and intensity of his yearning. *Stat magni nominis umbra*—he lives in the shadow of his great father. He yearns somehow or other to reconstruct and revive him, to play a part, to escape from tutelage, to return to France, to drop like a thunderbolt on the monarchy, to be, in fine, heroically, the Napoleon II that he is kept from being. But above all he lives over the vast paternal legend, the glories, the victories, the successive battlefields, the anecdotes, the manners, the personal habits, the aspect and trick of the very clothes. The picture is by its nature condemned to be that, exclusively, of his perpetual tension, obsession, communion—of the hallucination that consumes him. The subject was thus beautiful—nothing could possibly be finer; and nothing could at the same time be more interesting than to see if it might be made successfully scenic. Invidious, potentially disastrous, is the light that the conditions of the theatre project upon subjects that hang at all in the balance; it is then that we measure the frequently ruinous rigour of those conditions. A subject may strike a dramatist as so fine that the theatre must have the benefit of it, and yet may, on experiment, no matter how ingeniously conducted, show itself only as of a fineness by which the theatre is unable to profit. To combine as much as possible of the theatric with as much of the universal as the theatric will take—that is the constant problem, and one in which the maximum and minimum of effect are separated from each other by a hair-line. The theatric is so apt to be the outward, and the universal to be the inward, that, in spite of their enjoying scarce more common ground than fish and fowl, they often manage to peck at each other with fatal results. The outward insists on

the inward's becoming of its own substance, and the inward resists, struggles, bites, kicks, tries at least to drag the outward
down. The disagreement may be a very pretty quarrel and an
interesting literary case; it is only not likely to be a successful
play.

There is a happy enough balance, however, in *La Princesse*, and
we have meanwhile left the Prince of Aquitaine and his attendant
knight in postures the most characteristic — the knight, Bertrand,[1]
going ashore from the pilgrim ship to announce his infatuated
friend, and himself becoming infatuated as soon as he sees the
lady. She, on her side, having taken him at first for the Prince,
finds him quite in the note of their sublime situation — the Prince's
and her own; and the couple, accordingly, before they can turn
round, have fallen very presently and personally, not at all ideally,
in love, while the Prince, on the ship, with his strength ebbing,
awaits the result of Bertrand's[1] mission. This result is, of course,
in the fourth act, all it should romantically be; the Princess and
the young knight, though much tempted to be faithless, nobly
overcome their inclination and go out to the ship just in time for
the dying man's blessing. He beholds, that is, before dying, the
beauty on the mere hearsay of which h e so long has lived, and
the passion of the others is sanctified by his surrender. These
things, however, are details — it is the central idea that the author
has made, as it were, amusing, has worked, as we say, for all it is
worth, and has offered us as a general light on the bias of his
imagination. He thus did promptly, in 1895, two things: he committed himself, up to the ears, to the sentimental-sublime, and he
started handsomely the question of whether or no he were a poet.
I may as well say at once that he has remained, to my sense,
exactly as much a poet as *La Princesse Lointaine* charmingly
showed him, but he has not, by the same token, become an inch
more of one. The reason of this is of the clearest: he could never

---

[1] *Henry James accidentally confused the names of the two men, and twice
printed 'Rudel' for 'Bertrand' in the* Cornhill Magazine.

become more of one and remain within the limits of his cosmic boom, remain what I have otherwise called portable, and above all *ex*portable. He is as much of one as is consistent with the boom, the latest, the next exhibition, the universal reporter, the special car, the orbit of Mme. Sarah Bernhardt, the state of exposed accessibility, in especial, to audiences ignorant of his language. Dazzling as his command of the fantastic, both in humour and in pathos, makes him, I confess I am struck with the amount of poetry that he has fairly succeeded in saving from the consequences of his adventure. His freely figurative, his boldly maccaronic style, his verbal gymnastics and pictorial somersaults, his general romp through the unexpected — which is largely his hunt for rhyme through not only the past and present but the future of the language — all represent the elements of toughness and good humour required for so much exposure and such a pitch of reverberation.

If I should quote certain passages in support of these remarks it would immediately be felt that such speeches, such parts altogether, must have been wholly conceived and elaborated for the actress I have named, so that largely in this manifestation M. Rostand was romantic because Mme. Sarah Bernhardt is so. Interesting enough thus, if we had time, to trace the influence of a particular set of personal idiosyncrasies, the voice, the look, the step, the very *physique* of a performer, with all its signs, upon literature, and curious thereby to see once more how closely in France literature is still connected with life. The theatre there is a part of life. A given actress may be a part, an immense part, of the theatre; and, as literature has also its share in the same, the performer passes more or less into the sphere of the eternal. When I say eternal I speak largely; yet I speak otherwise than I should speak, certainly, in referring to any such phenomenon among ourselves. Plays enough are patched up in London for the given actor without any similar consequence. The influence of the given actor, that is, fails to be sufficient to make any portion of them pass into the sphere of the eternal. They do not, in short, as literature, embalm audibly a voice, so that the player perishes altogether when he speaks his farewell. So long, on the other hand, as *La Princesse Lointaine* is read, the voice, face, motion, art of Mme. Sarah will be active and present. It is only a question, accordingly, of how long the play will be read. But for that, after all, the portents may be none of the worst. Happy Mme. Sarah! And happy M. Rostand too!

Was the case the same in respect of *Cyrano?* and was the author's original vision, the first flush of the idea, suggested to him across the footlights by a present personality? Did the happy thought of the character, in other words, glimmer into life as the happy consciousness of M. Coquelin's countenance and genius? The point, though far from the most pressing in connection with the piece, would be interesting to fix, for the simple reason that no theatrical work so begotten has ever had, I imagine, such a fortune. There have been lucky actors and lucky plays, but never such a fusion of the two forms of luck. Actors may be conveniently fitted in the highest degree without the least profit to the larger career of the play; and, *per contra*, the play may have the largest career and yet leave us neither caring nor knowing who on the stage was to or was not to be suited. Ibsen's *Doll's House*, a play of the theatre if ever there was one, is at the same time so much a play of the 'closet' that the representatives of the parts, for all we heed, may have been numbered counters on a table. Augier's *Gendre de M. Poirier*, by the same law, living alike on the stage and in the library, depends on no particular personality and embalms no particular memory. (And I have the heart, I have the consistency to say this, I may add, in spite of a vivid remembrance of the perfect Poirier of the late M. Got.) If, however, the individual player lives, and lives intensely, inexpugnably, in the magnificent movement of *Cyrano*, we simply say so much the better for the individual player. The peculiarity, the real felicity of the case for him is that, having floated on the straight tide of

the whole triumph into the 'closet,' he seems subject to no such
reflux, no such reaction, as will float him out again. Behold us,
consequently, with M. Coquelin permanently established in that
inner sanctuary, where he must share intimately the fate, whatever
it be, of his author. And it is precisely to the fate of his author
that we come back—to the question, that is, of the amount of life
the romantic wave that has so bravely carried M. Rostand so far
may have still to spend.

For it is charmingly evident, in the light of his admirable scenic
eloquence, and in spite of interposing scenic images, that he
naturally *sees*, as it were, romantic or fantastic, just as certain
persons before certain objects see blue or yellow or red. That is
how he gets at sensibility—by enlarging the scale; which is an
experiment that, for my part, I am delighted to see him make.
Let it be as dangerous as it will or merely as triumphant, every
experiment in aesthetics is interesting—I mean, of course, to the
critic—that is made in good faith (made, likewise, I need scarcely
add, with talent, inasmuch as it takes a certain amount of that
really to attest a faith as 'good'). Entrancing, in fact, to the critic
is just the faith, however different from the critic's own, that runs
away with a man, and never, for our own part, of a nature to
make us wish to stop him. We wouldn't stop him for the world;
we would rather lash him on. For so are exhibitions achieved, so
are temperaments affirmed, so are examples multiplied, and so
are little sermons preached. That is tantamount to saying, more
concretely, that I wouldn't, individually, part with an inch of
Cyrano's nose. Too much is involved, too much for premature
protest, in all the author has made depend on it—more for fame
and fortune than ever depended on a nose before. The value of it
in the plan, naturally, is that it is liberally symbolic—that it
stands for the evil star in the wider sense, the whole body and
office of natural affliction on the part of the afflicted. Cyrano is one
of the worst afflicted; his nose happens to be only the accident; he
might have been displeasing in some other way, for there are but

too many ways; and the poet happily caught at the drama that would reside in his being *most* formed to suffer. There we get immediately the romantic formula, the short cut of antithesis, the vital spark, for a conspicuous example, of the theatre of Victor Hugo. The antithesis is a short cut because it ignores shades and lives on high contrasts. Differences are simply successions of shades; but shades are thus transitions and links; and, transitions and links being comparatively quiet things, the deep joy of the close observer, the romantic effect will have none of them. This is what makes one extreme seek another — what made M. Rostand intensely see that his afflicted person should be in every other respect his most showily organised. Cyrano, for a romantic use, had not only to be sensitive, to be conscious, but to be magnificent and imperial; and the brilliancy of the creation is in the author's expression of this.

That is the romantic formula, which obviously deals in a different poetry from the poetry of the 'quiet,' and which is extremely dependent for success on a certain aggressiveness of style. M. Rostand's vehicle is half his victory: it performs such prodigies on its own account — by which I mean is so perpetually ingenious and amusing that we never quite focus, nor even want to, what he asks us to accept as his human truth. Cyrano, hopelessly in love with the incomparable Roxane, but finding that Roxane has fixed her affections on a gentleman who is also enamoured of her and whose fine military type and fine person (he is as handsome as the other is ugly) render him a conceivable aspirant, Cyrano undertakes the task of helping on his suit in every possible way, and especially by the expenditure of a dazzling genius. Roxane, a *précieuse* of the seventeenth century, needs, above all, first to be learnedly wooed; she dotes on genius, on poetry, on prosody, on metaphors and alembications, and, as her handsome lover, though properly gallant and deeply devoted, is as stupid as an owl, he has to borrow the wit, the sonnets to her eyebrow, and all the other fine turns, with which to bombard her. Cyrano not

only lends for the purpose his own armoury, but he himself so
directs the aim that the lady's heart is completely riddled. He
does, in short, all the work, stores up the honey of which he is
never to taste, giving others all the beauty of his passion and
keeping all the pain for himself. He ministers thus, through twenty
adventures, to Roxane's happiness, though indeed that happiness
is not crowned in the end — a platitude for which M. Rostand is
much too clever, as he is also too clever to give his hero an
eventual compensation. The end is properly as romantic as the
beginning and the middle, the perfect art of romance being that it
shall, at every point, surpass itself. The turns of the story, at any
rate, are details; what is suggestive in it is its exceptionally
distinguished congruity with the romantic idea, and the proof it
offers for our proposition about the medium. In prose, or in verse
the least bit pedestrian, the idea would have gone to pieces, and
one can well understand its having done so, from the point of
view of the glamour, in such English forms as have been put at
its service. It is not that M. Rostand's verse has, precisely, wings
— these are rather what, considering its quantity of movement, it
lacks; but it has legs of abnormal agility, legs that fly about in a
manner to forbid our calling it pedestrian. Eloquence can go on
legs as well as on wings — perhaps in fact better; and our author
is easily and admirably eloquent.

The fortune of the idea was made, at any rate, from the moment
M. Rostand put his hand on the particular morsel of history that
he had pressed into his service: so much of its own quality, and
all in the desired key, had it to give, and so little, in proportion,
was there to add to it. The Cyrano de Bergerac of literary anecdote
was, by the best luck, a Gascon; he flourished, by the best luck,
in an age of literary magniloquence, social rhodomontade and
free fencing, and the opportunity for the glamour of race, for the
recall of qualities only a little more fantastically French, was accordingly all there to seize. Cyrano doubtless never flourished in
fact as our author makes him flourish in fiction, but the inten-

sifications are of the right colour. With such things as these the medium, as I have called it, is already constituted, the form is imposed, the style springs up of itself, and author and actor have but to keep them going. M. Rostand has not missed an effect of high fantasy, of rich comedy, of costume, attitude, sound or sense that could be shaken out of them; and we scarce know better how to describe the whole result than as a fine florid literary *revanche* of wounded sympathies and of the old French spirit, or at least of the imagination of it — the French spirit before revolutions and victories and defeats had made it either shrill or sore. And such an account of the matter is none the less true even if it be not precisely easy to say *revanche* against what. Against everything, we surmise, that would have made the production of a *Cyrano* impossible anywhere but in France, where doubtless, moreover, such productions are, whether as revenges or as speculations, less and less to be counted on. It would be difficult, at all events, to say whether the *revanche* really gains or loses point from the eager absorption of the play by other communities. No one, however this may be, has 'gone in' so successfully for atmosphere, and the particular atmosphere in question, since Théophile Gautier's *Capitaine Fracasse*. And even that delightful work was not eloquent, though it was so many things else, and not being eloquent was not patriotic. On the other hand it was, I suspect, more frequently and more essentially exquisite, if only through being indebted to the medium of prose; which, strange to say, is what the romantic, on M. Rostand's lines, somehow forfeits. When shades of truth go, the exquisite goes — which indeed, fortunately, is by no means the same thing as the picturesque. The picturesque may abound, may triumph, without it, may cover the subject as with an embroidered mantle, and so bedrape and costume it that its anatomy doesn't in the least matter. This is the happy romantic principle, thanks to which, when extended from the voluminous mantle to other properties and features, we get the quantity of atmosphere aforesaid. And — the point is of a rare interest — the great thing with the latter is that the question of its truth, the suspicion of its falsity, becomes subordinate; the relevant question is the question of its density. It may with impunity — with present, immediate impunity — be as false as it will, if it be only rich and thick. Then it closes us in; we don't see, as may be said, *out* of it: we don't see half a yard out of *Cyrano* and *L'Aiglon* — which is all that was necessary.

The author of these things has thus such an imagination of vivifying detail that he makes us extremely wonder what such a faculty might not achieve without the romantic perversity. That is the concern at which I just hinted — the question of where continued deflection on such a scale is likely to land him. I have already expressed the interest and indulgence that accompany this wonder — which amounts to the hope that he will continue to deflect so long as a prize is really to be reached, and so long as so much entertainment comes to us by the way. That is in fact requisite to ensure us a good case to oppose to those other seekers of the prize — the prize of interest, beauty, truth — who may be described as going straight. I admit that it is not easy to say with exactitude what makes, on one side and the other, the straight line and the tangent, even though it be precisely because of M. Rostand's success that the critic becomes, yet again, acutely conscious of the difference. Why is it that, to choose an example from very near at hand, M. Paul Hervieu, in *La Course du Flambeau* strikes me, in comparison, and quite apart from the degree of talent, as starting and as keeping straight? Or indeed why, I should perhaps rather ask, does the author of *L'Aiglon*, in comparison and quite apart from the degree of talent, strike me as starting and as keeping crooked? Where does the comparison, in such an instance, reside? — with what standard of value, outside of each work, do we make it? By what sign in advance do we know the romantic? by what sign do we know the real? and by what instrument do we, as they diverge, measure their divergence? What proof is there, in short, that *L'Aiglon* has in fact diverged

and that *La Course du Flambeau* has not? Absorbing inquiries, for
the critic and for the artist alike, but which they will probably not
meet in the same way. The critic, at all events — certainly the critic
for whom I speak — will profess that he recognises the romantic
deflection by recognising on his own part an anxiety, general or
special, as to where it will come out if left only to itself. As that
apprehension sharpens — and there are several ways of dealing
with it — he himself grows more and more sure. He knows where
he is, and above all where he is not; he is not in the real — or in
the air of things that pass with him for belonging to it; inasmuch
as in the real he is without the particular anxiety I speak of —
however much suspense of another and much simpler sort the
real may easily create. This latter suspense is never, I think, as
to where the author and the system themselves will come out,
but as to where some person will, or the affairs of some person
in whom they have interested him. The author and the system,
he finds himself assuming, will come out wherever life itself does,
and he follows them with confidence so far. It is both the difficulty
and a part of the inspiration — as well as no small part of the glory
— of a writer like M. Rostand that he has himself to create the
confidence, and to keep it up in the face of difficulties; so that he
is perpetually drawing on his credit with us as he goes.

Well, why should he not, it may be asked, if he makes us continue to trust him, or at all events beguiles, bewilders, fascinates
us into going with him, causes us simple-mindedly to follow our
nose through his labyrinth, however little that may be his own
rule of progress? There is no answer to this question but to say,
let him follow who can. We ask but to follow as far as our simple-
mindedness permits. The critic's nose is a special nose, and who
can tell in what direction *it* may be turned? Even after it has led
him through M. Rostand from beginning to end, its possessor may
still be concerned with the possibility of anyone's going safely, in
the same direction, 'one better' — better than the idea of *La Princesse*, or than the idea of *Cyrano*, or than the idea of *L'Aiglon*.

Better than, in their way, the form and skill and spring of these things nothing could very well be—for the writer positively strikes us as having talent as thoroughly as you have small-pox; but where are fresh motives of the same family to come from, unless with the family features unduly, even monstrously, marked? M. Rostand may answer, naturally, that this is none of our business; that his future proceedings are his own affair, and that it will be time enough to take dark views of his possible mistakes when he has put them, with the inimitable last touches, before us. We can allow that he is right, and yet not feel snubbed; for anxiety is the tenderest of sentiments, and it is all from tenderness that we speak. Nothing is more probable than that if his power of illustration were even a trifle less, the inexorable logic of his fate would leave us indifferent. We should not in those conditions in the least mind that he cannot afford—and still have anything left—to be much more 'heroic.' The word is his own—he applies it to the type of comedy of *Cyrano*, which it excellently fits; so that we may take it as a convenient name for his danger. The heroic, if only as a mere subdivision, has, like the patriotic, a mystery, a shy pride, which we fain would ensure the respect of; nothing is more to be deprecated than that it should be too much named and numbered, too freely accosted. We know it *after*, for the most part, rather than before or at the time, and even, oddly enough, when it is present we often take it for something else. We must not, however, I admit, be too literal, and I gladly grant that the sources of romance are many and the sources of amusement more. I may go further still, go so far as to say that a student enamoured of the 'real' is doubtless in some degree moved, on behalf of this cause, by jealousy of our author's extraordinary variety of touch, his boundless animation. Let it be taken for natural, and let me, in accordance with it, confess that I should be grateful indeed for the fine sight of M. Rostand's animation fairly coming home to roost, or, otherwise expressed, to life.

Only, by all means, not prematurely, not compunctiously, not before we have seen the game played out. If there be as good fish in the sea as ever were caught—the sea, say, of the pilgrims of *La Princesse*—he will catch them as no one else can do. If he is likely to find anywhere the stuff of such another overflowing first act as that of the seventeenth-century playhouse, the Hôtel de Bourgogne in *Cyrano*, such another overtopping fourth as that of the siege of Arras, with its poetry and bravery of empty stomachs and delightfully theatric apparition of Roxane, let him go to the far end of his rope, for these are in truth full sources of amusement. I delight as well in the fifth act of *Cyrano*, that of the final peace in the convent garden, the quietude of the old literary swash-buckler, the old—or the older—beauty, the old extravagant, troubled time: as charming a fifth act, and as little perfunctory, as a romantic play often gives us. I delight not less in every step and stage of *L'Aiglon*, and forbear from citing and selecting only because the author's struggle with his hard task strikes sparks from the metal scarce more at one time than at another. The task, as I have already briefly described it, never relaxes the question of creating, intensifying, multiplying movement where movement is fundamentally not; so that the energy and ingenuity are always in the breach and always performing prodigies of valour. M. Rostand has in every act of the six his ladder stiffly against the wall; he is in every act all for getting over and getting in; the admirable scenic temperament returns again and again to the charge. *L'Aiglon* is on this ground quite as much a *comédie héroïque* as its predecessor; and I am well aware of causing it to be asked, in possible stupefaction, if I would then wish our author to write in the manner—since I have named that work—of *La Course du Flambeau*. Many things would come up in answer to such a challenge, but I can glance now at only one—the interesting fact that there is no degree of talent, no wealth of the dramatic temperament, that such an idea as that of *La Course du Flambeau* (in common with a great many other good ideas) necessarily excludes. It is a comparatively quiet matter, yet the dramatic temperament—which M. Paul Hervieu possesses, to my sense, but in a limited degree—might have discovered a world in its quietness. Three generations, in the persons of three women—the heroine, as it were, her mother and her daughter—are put in presence, and the thesis of the piece, I take it, is that, under a pressure involving sacrifice, the eldest generation is inevitably the one sacrificed most, the one by whose doom the others profit. As between her mother and her daughter, in other words, a woman's *passion*—for that is the point—is, uncontrollably, more maternal than filial: she conceivably arrives, in fine, like M. Hervieu's Sabine Revel, at dealing death to what is behind her in order to save what is in front. She kills her mother, practically—not, I hasten to add, wilfully or overtly—for her daughter's sake.

This perhaps sounds an odd subject to describe as 'quiet,' but I maintain the term; besides which everything is relative. The quietness, I hold, might have been greater even than the author has made it, for there is an element of the romantic, which is no help, in his heroine's particular case. She is romantic, that is, by irritability and egotism; she might have been a different character without the least injury to the expression of the idea. However, the idea is expressed, and almost vividly—the idea that the torch of life, in the passage from hand to hand, can *stay* in no grasp, and above all can never move backward, whatever the insistent clutch. If M. Hervieu's demonstration of the matter be spoken of as dry, dull, grey, as exactly wanting in the qualities in which M. Rostand abounds, let that exactly show why we wonder what it might not have become under the latter's care. The element of animation is, in the actual piece, so absent that the effect—though with science, with lucidity, measurably behind it—remains, in degree, as unlike as possible the effect of M. Rostand; we feel it present, but we feel it not salient; it scarcely at all *represents* itself. What does it do then, what does M. Hervieu do, to be not so very much the less interesting? He follows, so far as he sees it, he clings to, the line of life, and it is a wonder what that—when good faith assists—will do for almost any dramatist. The writer can follow it for itself, follow it with such profit that I must take some other occasion for reference to the experiments lately multiplied in France under this conviction—those of MM. Maurice Donnay, Brieux, Porto-Riche, de Curel, and others. Such an experiment as *La Course du Flambeau*—or at any rate such a complexion as it wears—reminds us afresh how a romantic idea would never have got off clear with an equal neglect of those precautions and diversions that I have described it as condemned by its nature to prepare for the bamboozlement of the reader. I am afraid, to conclude, that I simply want everything; I want the line of life, and I want the bamboozlement too. I am full of tenderness for M. Rostand—I detest the idea that anything should happen to him. Now, it may lucklessly happen that there be *not* as good fish in the romantic sea—as good, I mean, as those in respect to which his bamboozlement has hitherto so triumphed. There may be only such hauls as will render bamboozlement vain. It is dreadful to think of, but he will then not have, as the saying is, a loaf on the shelf. There is no question, for M. Paul Hervieu, of exactly bamboozling us; but even if there were it would practically make no difference. *His* loaf on the shelf is large and certain.

"Edmond Rostand" appeared in the Cornhill Magazine, *November, 1901, and in the* Critic *of the same date.*

From the letters, now preserved in the Bodleian Library, which Henry James addressed to Sir Sianey Lee, at that time editor of the Cornhill, *one may suppose that the suggestion of writing about Rostand originated with James and had been welcomed by Lee. On July 15, 1901, James writes:* "A word to mention that I have finished my weary novel, and that, assuming you would still care to have the paper on Rostand for the *Cornhill*, I will do it as soon as possible." *And on August 26 he says:*

"I send you today my paper on Rostand—separate from this: with much shame and compunction at having been so long about it. The truth is this month of August has been a very bad and complicated time for me—a slow producer at the best. However, beyond saying there have been reasons, I won't try to explain. I'm afraid my article will show you afresh how little *journalistic* talent I have—though perhaps some other; and I hope it isn't too long. And I've had to entitle it *E.R.* pure and simple—I found I couldn't talk of the rest in any coherent way in the space; and he is a distinct subject in himself.

APPENDIX

1. *Actors*

GEORGE ALEXANDER (1858–1918) whose real name was George Samson, was born at Reading, England. He first appeared on the stage as an amateur in 1875 at the Cabinet Theatre, King's Cross, London, and made his professional début at Nottingham. In 1881 he was engaged by Henry Irving, and in 1883 by John Hare and the Kendals at the St. James's. Later he rejoined Irving and accompanied him on his second American tour in 1884. He undertook management first at the Avenue Theatre in 1890, and next year at the St. James's, where he achieved great success. He was knighted in 1911. His last appearance, at his own theatre, was in 1917. On January 5, 1895 he produced Henry James's *Guy Domville* at the St. James's.

G. W. ANSON (1847–1920) made his first stage appearance at the Theatre Royal, Edinburgh, in 1865, and his first in London at the Olympic in 1873. He was at the Court Theatre in 1875. Between 1885 and 1892 he acted in Australia, and in 1897–1898 he toured the United States in *La Poupée*.

SQUIRE BANCROFT (1841–1926), born in London, first appeared at Birmingham in 1861. In 1865 he made his London début at the Prince of Wales's Theatre under the management of Marie Wilton, whom he married in 1867. The Bancrofts remained at the Prince of Wales's Theatre until 1879, after which they moved to the Haymarket. They retired in 1885 and Squire Bancroft was knighted in 1897. See *The Bancrofts: Recollections of Sixty Years* (London: Murray, 1909).

CHARLES HARRISON BARRON (1840–1918) was born at Roxbury, Massachusetts, and made his first appearance in 1861 at the Howard Athenaeum as Hueget to the Richelieu of Edwin Booth. In February, 1869, he became leading man at the Boston Museum, and played there for more than twenty years. In 1878 he toured with Lester Wallack, but returned to the Museum in 1885, and again in 1893–1894. In 1887 he toured with Booth, and in 1889 with Julia Marlowe as her leading man. He made a great success as Bill Sykes in *Oliver Twist* in 1895.

HARRY BECKETT (? – 1880) was born in England, the son of an actress, who educated him as a violinist. He made his début at Manchester, and was a great favourite with Charles Mathews. In 1868 he went to America, first appearing in New York in *To Oblige Benson*, and after experience in various parts of the States he became leading low comedian at Wallack's Theatre. His last appearance was in August, 1880, in Boucicault's *A Bridal Tour* at the Haymarket, London.

PIERRE FRANCISQUE SAMUEL BERTON (1843–1912) was born in Paris, the son of a celebrated actor Charles Berton of the Gymnase. He himself appeared at the same theatre in 1859, remaining there for many years, and in 1872 was engaged at the Comédie Française. He was the author of several plays, including *Zaza*.

JEAN BAPTISTE PROSPER BRESSANT (1815–1886) after being a lawyer's clerk made his first appearance in 1835 at the Théâtre de Montmartre. In 1839 he went to St. Petersburg and remained there for seven successful years. From 1846 to 1854 he played jeune premier rôles at the Gymnase, and on the conclusion of his engagement there he became sociétaire of the Théâtre Français in 1854. He retired in 1876.

CHARLES H. BROOKFIELD (1855?–1913) was the son of Prebendary W. H. Brookfield and his wife, the friend of Thackeray. He made his first appearance on the stage at the Alexandra Palace Theatre in 1879, and soon after joined the Bancroft company at the Haymarket, where he remained until 1885. Later he appeared with Mrs. Bernard Beere and with Beerbohm Tree. He left the stage in 1898 and devoted himself to the writing and adapting of plays, and in 1909 was appointed the Lord Chamberlain's Reader of Plays. He published a volume of short stories and also *Random Reminiscences* (London: Arnold, 1902). He was famous as a raconteur.

LIONEL BROUGH (1836–1909) was born at Pontypool, the son of Barnabas Brough, the dramatist. He first appeared at the Lyceum in 1854 under Vestris's management. He was an all-round actor, playing in every sort of play from Shakespeare and old Comedy to burlesque and musical farce. He visited America in 1886 with Violet Cameron, playing in opera bouffe. In 1894 he joined Beerbohm Tree's company where he remained till his death.

ARTHUR CECIL (1843–1896), whose real name was Arthur Cecil Blunt, after acting as an amateur, made his first professional appearance in 1869 at the Gallery of Illustration, London, with the German Reeds. He joined the Bancrofts at the Prince of Wales's Theatre in 1876, and went with them to the Haymarket in 1880. Later he appeared at the Court Theatre in the famous series of farces by A. W. Pinero, and that theatre was for a time under his management.

JOHN CLAYTON (1843–1888) whose real name was John Alfred Calthrop, was born in Lincolnshire, and made his first appearance at the St. James's Theatre in *She Stoops To Conquer* on February 27, 1866. He did much varied work in many London theatres, played Osip in *The Danicheffs* at the St. James's in 1877, and Henry Beauclerc in *Diplomacy* at the Prince of Wales's in 1879. He managed the Court Theatre with Arthur Cecil from 1881 till 1887. He married a daughter of Dion Boucicault, the dramatist.

CHARLES FRANCIS COGHLAN (c. 1844–1899), actor and dramatist, was born in Paris. He appeared at the Plymouth Theatre Royal in 1862, and made his début in London in Tom Taylor's *Sense and Sensation* at the Olympic on May 16, 1864. From 1870 to 1876 he was a member of the company at the Prince of Wales's Theatre. He first appeared in New York at the Fifth Avenue Theatre, in *Money*, September, 1876, and from 1887 to 1890 he was Mrs. Langtry's leading man in America. He died at Galveston, Texas.

H. B. CONWAY (1850–1909) whose real name was Coulson, first appeared at the Olympic in 1872. In 1873 he appeared at the Lyceum under the Bateman management. In 1875 he joined the Haymarket company, and in 1878 became a member of the Bancrofts' company at the Prince of Wales's, moving with them to the Haymarket in 1880. He played Faust at the Lyceum in 1885 but had to resign the part after a few performances and was an invalid for the rest of his life. He last appeared at the Vaudeville Theatre about 1891.

THOMAS POTTER COOKE (1786–1864) joined the navy in 1796 and left it to become an actor. His first appearance seems to have been made at the Royalty Theatre in 1804. He played a great deal in melodrama, and made an enormous success in 1829 at the Surrey Theatre as William in Douglas Jerrold's *Black-Ey'd Susan*. His last appearance was in March, 1860.

BENOÏT CONSTANT COQUELIN (1841–1909) was born at Boulogne. He was a pupil of Regnier's at the Conservatoire, and entered the Comédie Française in 1860. He became a sociétaire in 1864, but resigned his position in 1886 and toured in Europe and America, 1887–1889. He re-entered the Comédie Française as pensionnaire in 1890, but left it finally in 1892. His engagement at the Renaissance in 1895 led to an action against him by the Comédie. In 1897 he became director of the Porte Saint Martin Theatre where he created the part of Cyrano. In 1900 he toured in America with Sarah Bernhardt. He died suddenly during the rehearsals of Rostand's *Chantecler*.

LOUIS ARSÈNE DELAUNAY (1826–1903) after studying at the Conservatoire, made his first appearance at the Odéon in October, 1846. In 1848 he passed to the Théâtre Français, and became sociétaire in 1850. He retired in 1887. His *Souvenirs* were published in Paris (Calmann-Lévy, 1902).

ALEXANDRE FRÉDÉRIC FEBVRE (1834?–1916) was born in Paris and made his first appearance at Le Havre in 1850. He played in several Paris theatres, including the Odéon and Vaudeville, before appearing at the Comédie Française in 1866. He became sociétaire in 1867 and retired in 1894, after which he toured the principal European countries. He published several books including *Journal d'un Comédien* (Paris: 1896).

CHARLES FECHTER (1824–1879) was born in London (or Paris), his father being a Frenchman of German descent. He was educated in France and studied at the Conservatoire. He made his début at the Théâtre Français in 1844, and played in various theatres in Paris until 1860, making a particular success as Armand in *La Dame aux Camélias* in 1852. In 1860 he appeared at the Princess's Theatre, London, acting in English, in *Ruy Blas, Don Cézar de Bazan* and *Hamlet*. He managed and appeared at the Lyceum Theatre from 1863 to 1867. He first appeared in New York at Niblo's Gardens on January 10, 1870. In 1876, after breaking his leg, he retired to a farm near Philadelphia, where he died in 1879.

JOHNSTON FORBES-ROBERTSON (1853–1937) was born in London and was originally intended to be an artist. His first appearance on the stage was in 1874 at the Princess's Theatre. He played with the Bancrofts at the Prince of Wales's in 1878–1879 and went with them to the Haymarket. Later he was with John Hare at the Garrick. In 1895 he went into management at the Lyceum. He played much in America. He produced *The High Bid* by Henry James at Edinburgh in March, 1908. He was knighted in 1913.

EDWIN FORREST (1806–1872) was born in Philadelphia, and first appeared there at the Walnut Street Theatre in 1820. He made his first appearance in New York at the Park Theatre in 1826 as Othello. He produced *The Gladiator* by Robert M. Bird in 1831. He was extremely successful as an actor. His last appearance was in 1871.

FRANÇOIS JULES EDMOND GOT (1822–1901) entered the Conservatoire in 1841 and gained first prize for comedy in 1843. After a year in a cavalry regiment, he appeared at the Théâtre Français in 1844 and became a sociétaire in 1850. He retired in 1895. His *Journal* was published by his son, in two volumes (Paris: Plon-Nourrit, 1910).

JOHN HARE (1844–1921) whose real name was Fairs, first appeared on the stage at Liverpool in 1864, and a year later was engaged by the Bancrofts at the Prince of Wales's Theatre, remaining with them for nine years. He managed the Court Theatre from 1875 to 1879, and moved to the St. James's, in partnership with W. H. Kendal, on October 4, 1879. The partnership ended in 1888, after which Hare managed the New Court Theatre for some months and opened the Garrick Theatre in April, 1889, where he remained in management until 1895. He first appeared in New York at Abbey's Theatre on December 23, 1895, and again visited America in 1897. His later years were mainly devoted to touring in England and America. He was knighted in 1907. His last appearance on the stage was in 1917.

HENRY IRVING (1838–1905) really John Henry Brodribb, made his first appearance at Sunderland in 1856, and then played at Edinburgh for two years and a half. He first played in London in 1859 at the Princess's Theatre, but soon returned to the provinces for several hard-working years. Again in London at the St. James's in 1866, he made a success in *Hunted Down* by Dion Boucicault. He was engaged by H. L. Bateman who opened the Lyceum under his own management in 1871, and made a great sensation in *The Bells*. He took over the lease of the Lyceum from Mrs. Bateman in 1878, and continued to appear there, with tours from time to time in America and the English provinces, until 1902. He first appeared in America at the Star Theatre, New York, on October 29, 1883, and visited the United States eight times in all. He was knighted in 1895. See *The Life of Henry Irving* by Austin Brereton (London: Longmans, 1908).

JOSEPH JEFFERSON (1829–1905) the son and grandson of an actor, was born at Philadelphia, and is reported to have appeared on the stage at the age of four. In 1856, after much hard work in the South, he became a member of Laura Keene's company in New York. After four years in Australia, he appeared in London making a great success at the Adelphi on September 4, 1865, in a new version of *Rip Van Winkle*, a part he continued to play for the rest of his life.

His last appearance on the stage was made in 1904. See *The Auto-biography of Joseph Jefferson* (New York: Century Co. 1890).

CHARLES JOHN KEAN (1811?–1868) son of Edmund Kean, was born in Waterford. He first appeared on the stage in 1827. His Shakespearean productions at the Princess's Theatre are famous, his management of that theatre lasting from 1850 to 1859. Henry James, as a small boy, saw his production of *Henry VIII*. (May 16th, 1855). He began a world tour in 1863 and reached San Francisco in October, 1864. His performances in New York began on April 26, 1865.

WILLIAM HUNTER KENDAL (1843–1917) whose real name was Grimston, was born in London, and made his first appearance in 1861 as a member of the Soho (Royalty) Theatre stock company. After four years at Glasgow he reappeared in London at the Haymarket, in 1866, remaining there for some time. He married in 1869, and later appeared with John Hare at the Court, and with the Bancrofts at the Prince of Wales's Theatre. He joined John Hare in the management of the St. James's Theatre from 1879 to 1888. After this the Kendals spent much time in touring the English provinces and the United States, with occasional seasons in London. They appeared at the Fifth Avenue Theatre, New York, in October, 1889. In 1908 they left the stage, having amassed a fortune.

FRÉDÉRIC LEMAÎTRE (1800–1876) really named Antoine Louis Prosper Lemaître, was born at Le Havre, and studied at the Conservatoire; but made his first appearance on all fours in the rôle of a lion at the Variétés-Amusants on the Boulevard du Temple. He was engaged at the Odéon in 1826. In 1823 at the Folies Dramatiques he created the part of Robert Macaire in *L'Auberge des Adrets*, a part with which his name will always be associated, in a play of which he was part author. Soon after he was given parts specially written for him both by Victor Hugo and the elder Dumas. After a long theatrical career, during which he visited England five times, he died in poverty. A very full life of Lemaître was published by L. H. Lecompte (Paris: 1888).

WILLIAM J. LE MOYNE (1831–1905) made his first professional appearance on the stage at Portland, Maine, in 1852, and was actively at work on the American stage for almost fifty years. His engagement at the Boston Museum was from 1873 to 1876. He retired about 1900.

CHARLES JAMES MATHEWS (1803–1878) was born in Liverpool, the son of Charles Mathews, the actor. His early life was spent as an architect, but in 1835, after his father's failure, he went on the stage, first appearing at the Olympic Theatre. Many years in management followed and many tours in America and elsewhere. He married first Madame Vestris in 1838, and, after her death, Mrs. E. L. Davenport of Burton's Theatre, New York. He last appeared on the stage in 1878, the year of his death. He wrote or adapted many plays.

HENRY JAMES MONTAGUE (c. 1843–1878) whose real name was Mann, made his first appearance, under the name of Maxwell, at Astley's Theatre in Boucicault's *Trial of Effie Deans*. He played at several London theatres, notably the Olympic, 1865–1867, and the Prince of Wales's, 1867–1869. He was lessee and manager of the Globe Theatre, 1871–1874. He went to America in 1874 where he joined the Wallack organization, and quickly became a great favourite: the matinée idol of the seventies. He toured the States with a company playing *Diplomacy* in 1878 and died of consumption at San Francisco in August of that year.

JEAN MOUNET-SULLY (1841–1916) did not enter the Conservatoire until 1862 owing to his family's opposition to a stage career. In 1868 he won a first prize for tragedy and appeared at the Odéon without much success. An officer during the Franco-Prussian war, he had thoughts in 1871 of giving up the stage, but obtained an engagement at the Théâtre Français in 1872, and in eighteen months was elected a sociétaire.

HENRY NEVILLE (1837–1910) first appeared on the stage as an infant in arms. After experience in the provinces he appeared at the Lyceum, London, in 1860. One of his most famous parts was that of Bob Brierly in *The Ticket of Leave Man* (1863) which he played about two thousand times. From 1873 to 1879 he was manager of the Olympic Theatre, and after that acted at the Adelphi for two years. He visited America in 1890 with Augustus Harris's company. His last performance was in April, 1910, at His Majesty's Theatre.

FRANÇOIS JOSEPH RÉGNIER (1807–1885) born in Paris, was for a time an architect's pupil, but soon adopted a stage career, appearing at Montmartre and in the provinces. In 1831 he first played at the Théâtre Français in *Le Mariage de Figaro*. He became a sociétaire in 1834, and professor at the Conservatoire in 1854.

GEORGE RIGNOLD (1839–1912) was on the stage from boyhood and played for several years at the Bath and Bristol Theatres. He first appeared in London in 1870 at the Queen's Theatre, Long Acre. He played in the United States and also in Australia, where he finally settled in 1880, managing Her Majesty's Theatre, Sydney, for nine years from 1886, and making there many Shakespearean productions. His last appearance on the stage was made in Melbourne in 1907.

ERNESTO ROSSI (1827–1896) was born at Livorno and became an actor against his father's wish. He first acted about 1846. He was for a time member of Madame Ristori's company. He toured much abroad, and first visited the United States in 1883. In Italy he was particularly admired as a Shakespearean actor. He wrote his autobiography: *Quarant'anni di vita artistica* (Florence: 1887–1890).

TOMMASO SALVINI (1829–1915) born at Milan, first appeared on the stage at the age of 14. In 1847 he joined Ristori. For many years he was the leading Italian actor, and he toured much, visiting the United States five times. The visit to Boston of which Henry James writes began at the Globe Theatre on January 1, 1883, and lasted for two weeks; his performances in London at Covent Garden were in March and April, 1884. He retired in 1890. See *Leaves from the Autobiography of Tommaso Salvini* (London: Unwin, 1893).

TALBOT (1824–1904) whose real name was Denis Stanislas Montalant, was born in Paris. He was admitted to the Conservatoire in 1849, and next year appeared at the Odéon. In 1856 he passed to to the Théâtre Français and became a sociétaire in 1859. He retired in 1879 to devote himself to teaching.

EDWARD O'CONNOR TERRY (1844–1912) was born in London. He first appeared on the stage at Christchurch, Hants, in 1863, and made his London début at the Surrey Theatre in 1867. He played at the Strand Theatre, mainly in burlesque, from 1869 to 1875, and was at the Gaiety from 1876 to 1884. He opened Terry's Theatre in the Strand in 1887, his greatest success there being Pinero's *Sweet Lavender*.

JOHN LAWRENCE TOOLE (1830–1906) began life as a wine-merchant's clerk, and after some amateur performances appeared professionally at the Queen's Theatre, Dublin, in 1852. His first professional engagement in London was at the St. James's Theatre in 1854. He was at the Adelphi for nine years from 1858. In 1874 he was in management at the Globe, and in 1879 he leased the Folly Theatre (afterwards known as Toole's Theatre) for sixteen years. He visited America once only, and was not a great success there. He was seen at Wallack's Theatre on August 17, 1874, in various plays from his repertory, his season lasting until October 3, and again at the Lyceum in the following year from February 15 to 26. Toole retired from the stage in 1896, and was for the remainder of his life a helpless invalid. He died at Brighton.

HERBERT BEERBOHM TREE (1853–1917) was born in London. His first professional appearance on the London stage was made at the Olympic in 1878. In 1880 he played with Geneviève Ward in *Forget-Me-Not*. He became a manager at the Haymarket Theatre in 1887, and opened Her Majesty's Theatre, which was built for him, in 1897. He visited America in 1895 and 1896. He was knighted in 1909.

HERMANN VEZIN (1829–1910) was born in Philadelphia, went to England in 1850, and made his first appearance that year at the Theatre Royal, York. He appeared in London in 1852 at the Princess's Theatre under Charles Kean's management. For many years he was a leading London actor, and was the original Doctor Primrose in *Olivia*. In later life he devoted much time to teaching. His last appearance was at His Majesty's Theatre in 1909.

HERBERT WARING (1857–1939) whose real name was Rutty, was born in London and made his first appearance at the Adelphi in 1877 in *Formosa*. He was with Hare and the Kendals at the St. James's from 1883 to 1888, and in the latter year toured America with Mary Anderson. He played in *A Doll's House* in 1889, and in *The Master Builder* in 1893. In 1895 he appeared as Frank Humber in Henry James's *Guy Domville*.

CHARLES WARNER (1846–1909) whose real name was Lickfold, was born in London and made his first appearance on the stage in 1861 at Windsor Castle before Queen Victoria as a page in *Richelieu*. After much work in the provinces, he made his début in London at the Princess's in 1864. He did much varied work in London and made a sensational success with his performance of Coupeau in *Drink*, a part he played over a thousand times. He visited America in 1904, and eventually died there.

WILLIAM WARREN (1812–1888) son of theatrical parents, first appeared at the Arch Street Theatre, Philadelphia, in 1832, and for some years divided his time between that city and touring the West. He first appeared in New York in 1841 at the Park Theatre. In 1846 he was engaged for the opening of the Howard Athenaeum at Boston and played there until February, 1847. In August of the same year he began his connection with the Boston Museum, where he remained almost without a break until 1883 when he retired from the stage. For an interesting chapter on his work consult *Reminiscences of a Dramatic Critic* by Henry Austin Clapp (Boston and New York: Houghton, Mifflin & Co., 1902).

BENJAMIN WEBSTER (1798–1882) was born at Bath. He appeared in London in 1818, and in 1832 was with Madame Vestris at the Olympic. In 1837 he undertook the management of the Haymarket, which continued until 1853 when he took the Adelphi. He retired from the stage in 1874.

GUSTAVE HIPPOLYTE WORMS (1837–1910) was born in Paris, and was employed as a typographer before entering the Conservatoire. He was engaged by the Comédie Française and appeared there in 1858, remaining at that theatre for seven years. He then went to Russia for ten years, and on his return in 1875 was engaged at the Gymnase, where he made a great success. In 1877 he returned to the Comédie Française, became a sociétaire in 1878, and retired in 1901.

CHARLES WYNDHAM (1837–1919) whose original name was Culverwell, was born in Liverpool. He qualified as a doctor, but went on the stage in 1862. He went to America and served as an army surgeon in the Civil War, subsequently appearing on the stage in New York. He returned to England in 1865, but visited the States many more times. In 1876 he became manager of the Criterion Theatre and remained there until 1899. In that year he opened Wyndham's Theatre, and in 1903 the New Theatre. He was knighted in 1902.

II. *Actresses*

MARIE EFFIE BANCROFT (Marie Wilton) (1839–1921) was born at Doncaster and played children's parts in the provinces early in life. She first appeared in London on September 15, 1856, at the Lyceum, and for nearly ten years played at various theatres, notably the Strand, in farce, burlesque, and extravaganza. She undertook management of the Prince of Wales's Theatre with H. J. Byron in 1865, and on his retirement from the partnership built up a school of "modern" comedy. She married Squire Bancroft in 1867, and with him undertook management of the Haymarket Theatre in 1880. They retired in 1885.

JULIA BARTET (1854–1941) whose real name was Jeanne Julia Regnault, was born in Paris, and made a brilliant début at the Vaudeville in 1872. In 1879 she was engaged at the Comédie Française, and became sociétaire in 1881. For many years she played leading parts there with great success. She retired in 1919. See *Julia Bartet* by Albert Dubeux (Paris: Plon 1938.)

KATE JOSEPHINE BATEMAN (Mrs. Crowe) (1842–1917) was born at Baltimore and made her first appearance at Louisville in 1846. She appeared in New York in December, 1849. In 1851 she, with her sisters Isabel and Ellen, appeared at the St. James's Theatre, London, in acts and scenes from Shakespeare. In 1875 she played Lady Macbeth with Henry Irving at the Lyceum, following this with Emilia in *Othello* the next year, and Queen Margaret in *Richard III.* in 1878. After a long retirement from the stage she returned in September, 1891, to play the Marquise de Bellegarde in the London production of Henry James's *The American.*

SARAH BERNHARDT (1844–1923) was born in Paris. She was admitted to the Conservatoire in 1858, and made her début at the Théâtre Français in 1862 without much success. After playing at other Paris theatres, she was more successful at the Odéon during the sixties, and returned to the Comédie Française in 1873. She became Sociétaire in 1875, but for some years relations between her and the management of the theatre became increasingly strained. After her great success in England in 1879, she next year resigned her position and heavy damages were awarded against her. Under her own management she was brilliantly successful for many years, both in France, in England, and in America. Late in life she lost a leg, but continued to act even when her old power and charm had vanished.

MADELEINE BROHAN (1833–1900) daughter of the actress Suzanne Brohan, entered the Conservatoire at the age of fifteen, and in 1850, having been awarded first prize for comedy, was engaged by the Théâtre Français. In 1856 she was given a year's leave of absence (in consequence of an unhappy marriage) and went to St. Petersburg where she made a great success at the Théâtre Impérial, after which she returned to Paris and the Théâtre Français. She retired in 1885. See *Les Trois Brohan* by Paul Gaulot (Paris: Alcan, 1930).

MRS. PATRICK CAMPBELL (1865–1940) was born in London and made her first professional appearance at Liverpool in October, 1888. She first played in London at the Adelphi Theatre in 1890. In 1893 she made a great success in *The Second Mrs. Tanqueray* at the St. James's Theatre. She first appeared in New York at the Republic Theatre in January, 1902, as Magda. Her death took place at Pau in the South of France.

CÉLINE CELESTE (1814–1882) was born in Paris, first appeared there as a child, and in 1827 visited America with a troupe of French dancers. She made her début in London at Drury Lane in 1830, and for some years played only parts in dumb show as she could not speak English. In 1838 she is said to have played her first speaking part and soon became celebrated as the heroine of melodramas. In 1844 she undertook management at the Adelphi, and next year played her most famous part, Miami in *The Green Bushes*. She visited the States on several occasions, and made frequent "farewell appearances" in London. Her actual last performance took place in 1878. (See the article on her by W. J. Lawrence in *The Gentleman's Magazine* in 1888).

MARIE CÉLINE CHAUMONT (1848?–1926) was born at Le Mans and began her stage career at the age of eleven at the Théâtre Molière. She appeared first in comedies, and was given a child's part by Dumas *fils* in 1864 in *L'Ami des Femmes* at the Gymnase. In 1869 she gave up comedy for operetta and played at the Bouffes-Parisiens and in Brussels. In *La Cruche Cassée* she took the part of Colette. In 1881 she joined the Palais Royal company, and married, as her second husband, one of its two directors, her first husband having died in 1872.

ROSE MARIE CIZOS CHÉRI (1824–1861) the daughter of an actor, appeared on the stage at Bourges as early as 1830. In 1842 she first played in Paris at the Gymnase but without success, and was engaged as understudy to Mlle. Nathalie, but made her name on the first occasion she replaced her. In 1845 or 1847 she married Lemoine-Montiguy, the director of the Gymnase. She played many parts in the plays of Augier and Dumas *fils*. She died of an attack of croup, caught while nursing her children.

MARY JANE CHIPPENDALE (1832–1888) was born at Salisbury and began her professional career on tour in the North of England. She made her London début, under the name of Miss Snowdon, on October 14, 1863, at the Haymarket, where she remained for twelve years. In March, 1878, she began an engagement at the Lyceum, appearing in *Louis XI.* and *The Lady of Lyons.* She took up the part of Martha in Irving's production of *Faust* on the retirement of Mrs. Stirling.

ANNIE M. CLARKE (1845–1902) was born in Boston, and first acted with the Boston Museum company as a child in 1853. In 1856 she played at the Howard Athenaeum and toured the New England states. In 1861 she rejoined the Museum and after a few seasons became leading lady, remaining there until 1892. After that she toured, and while appearing with Julia Marlowe contracted pneumonia and died in Chicago. In her later years she was associated with John Mason, Olga Nethersole, and Richard Mansfield.

KATE CLAXTON (1848–1924) was born at Somerville, New Jersey and first appeared on the stage at the Dearborn Street Theatre, Chicago, in December, 1869. She joined Augustin Daly's company at the Fifth Avenue Theatre, New York, in 1870, appearing as Jo in *Man and Wife.* Her great success was made as the blind girl in *The Two Orphans* (1874), a part she played for many years. She married Charles Stevenson, an English actor, in 1878.

SOPHIE ALEXANDRINE CROIZETTE (1848–1901) was born in Russia. She entered the Conservatoire in 1867, studied under Bressant and won first prize for comedy in 1869. She appeared at the Théâtre Français in 1870, and was elected a sociétaire in 1873. She retired from the stage in 1882.

PAULINE VIRGINIE DÉJAZET (1797–1875) first appeared as a child of five at the Théâtre des Capucines, and played both in Paris and the provinces for many years. From 1831 to 1844 she was at the Palais Royal where she achieved great success, passing on to the Variétés in the latter year. In 1869 she was awarded a pension, and in 1874 a benefit performance for her realized more than 60,000 francs.

MARIE DELAPORTE (1838– ?) was born in Paris and entered the Conservatoire in 1852, studying under Samson and Regnier. She made her début at the Gymnase in 1855, remaining there for fourteen years. She had great success in ingenue roles and appeared in *Le Père Prodigue* (1859) and *Les Idées de Madame Aubray* (1867). In 1867 there was a question of her joining the Comédie Française, but she was nervous of appearing in classical plays, and in 1868 accepted an engagement at St. Petersburg. In 1875 she played again at the Gymnase with great success, and retired about 1878 to devote herself to the teaching of elocution.

AIMÉE OLYMPE DESCLÉE (1836–1874) made her first appearance at the Gymnase in 1856 with small success. After other appearances in Paris she went to Russia, to Turin, and to Brussels. In 1869 she was re-engaged at the Gymnase at the request of Dumas *fils*, and this time made a great success. She played in *Frou-frou, Diane de Lys*, and other plays.

DOCHE (Marie Charlotte Eugénie de Plunkett) (1821–1900) was born in Brussels, and made her first appearance at the Vaudeville, Paris, in 1838 under the name of Eugénie Fleury. She married Alexandre Doche, the composer, in 1839 and was separated from him soon after. In 1852 she made her great success in the creation of La Dame aux Camélias at the Vaudeville. She played also at the Ambigu, Gaité, Porte Saint Martin, and other theatres. She died in Paris.

ADELINE ÉLIE FRANÇOISE DUDLAY (1859–1934) whose real name was Dulait, was born in Brussels. In 1876 she obtained a first prize at the Brussels Conservatoire, and was then engaged for the Comédie Française, her first appearance being in *Rome Vaincue*. She was made a sociétaire in 1883, and retired in 1909.

ELEONORA DUSE (1859–1924) belonged to a theatrical family and was born while it was on a tour in Lombardy. She acted in a booth at the age of four. Her early life was one of hard struggle; she first achieved recognition at Naples in 1878 in Augier's *Les Fourcham-bault*. Thereafter she had great success in plays by Dumas *fils*, Augier, Sardou, etc., and later in Ibsen, D'Annunzio and Maeterlinck. She first visited Paris in 1884, and went to London and New York in 1893. In 1909 she retired from the stage for twelve years, but re-appeared after the first World War. She made a successful appearance in London in 1923 and then went to America, where she died, as the result of a chill, at Pittsburgh in 1924.

ADA DYAS (1844–1908) made her first appearance in London at Sadler's Wells in 1861 as Prince John in *Henry IV*. After various work in London she was engaged by Augustin Daly in 1872 for the Fifth Avenue Theatre, and thence went as leading lady to Wallack's for three seasons, 1874–1876. Later she toured the States.

ANAÏS FARGUEIL (1819–1896) was born at Toulouse, and entered the Conservatoire in 1831. She won the prize for singing in 1834 and appeared in February of that year at the Opéra Comique. In 1836 she was engaged at the Vaudeville, and after other appearances at the Palais Royal and the Gymnase she returned to the Vaudeville in 1852 where she remained for many years.

NELLIE FARREN (1848–1904) was born at Liverpool and is said to have made her first appearance on the stage at Exeter in 1853. She first appeared in London at Sadler's Wells in 1862 in a Christmas extravaganza. From 1864 to 1868 she was at the Olympic, at the end of which year she was engaged by John Hollingshead for the Gaiety where she remained, playing in burlesque and comedy, for the greater part of her career. In 1888–1889 she visited America and Australia with the Gaiety company. She retired in 1891 owing to ill health.

MARIE FAVART (1833–1908) whose real name was Pierette Ignace Pingaud, was born at Beaune. On leaving the Conservatoire in 1848 she was engaged at the Comédie Française, and in 1854 became a sociétaire. In 1880 she resigned her position, and toured

both in France and abroad; and in 1883 accompanied Coquelin to
Russia as his leading lady.

LYDIA FOOTE (1844?–1892) whose real name was Legge,
was a niece of the celebrated Mrs. Keeley, and made her first appearance as a child at the Lyceum Theatre, London, in 1852. She played
a great many parts at a great many theatres. She was Anna in *The
Danicheffs* at the St. James's in 1877, and Smike in *Nicholas Nickleby*
at the Adelphi in 1875 and again in 1879.

ANNA MARIE LOUISE JUDIC (1849–1911) born at
Sémur, was at first employed in a lingerie shop, but studied at the
Conservatoire under Regnier and took singing lessons. She made her
début in 1867 at the Gymnase. After obtaining much success in Belgium she was engaged at the Bouffes-Parisiens in 1872 and soon became a leading lady of opera bouffe. In 1876 she was at the Variétés.
She visited New York and toured America in 1885–1886.

MRS. KENDAL (Madge Robertson) (1849–1935) spent her
childhood on the stage, first appearing at the Marylebone Theatre
at the age of four. Her next appearance in London was at the Haymarket in 1865 as Ophelia. She married W. H. Kendal in that year.
Two of her greatest successes were made in *Peril* and *Diplomacy* with
the Bancrofts in 1876 and 1878. From 1879 to 1888 the Kendals were
in partnership with John Hare at the St. James's Theatre. In 1889
they toured the United States and Canada. They retired from management in 1908. See *The Kendals* by T. Edgar Pemberton. (London:
Pearson, 1900.)

GRACIOSA GLECH (c. 1860–1900) first appeared in children's parts, and was for some years a pupil of Adelaide Ristori. She
became leading lady in a succession of companies including that of
Ernesto Rossi. In 1891 she retired from the stage and married.

MARIE LITTON (1847–1884) made her first appearance in
1868 at the Princess's Theatre. She opened the Court Theatre,
Sloane Square, in 1871 and managed it for more than three years. In
1878 she took the theatre attached to the Royal Aquarium at West-

minster and renamed it the Imperial, reviving there old English comedies. She retired from the stage in 1883 owing to ill health.

SARAH JANE MELLON (1824–1909) was born at Gosport, Hampshire. She first appeared at Plymouth in 1836. Her London début was made at the Adelphi on October 9, 1843, in burlesque, and she remained at that theatre for many years. As an actress she was much admired by Dickens. She left the stage in 1883.

HELENA MODJESKA (1841–1909) was born at Cracow and first appeared on the stage in Poland in October, 1861. In 1876 she married and went to South California with the intention of giving up the stage, but decided to learn English and appeared in San Francisco as Adrienne Lecouvreur in August, 1877. A successful tour followed and she reached New York on December 22 at the Fifth Avenue Theatre. She appeared in London at the Court Theatre on May 1, 1880 (matinée) in *Heartsease*, an adaptation by James Mortimer of *La Dame aux Camélias*. On October 9 of that year she appeared in a version of Schiller's *Mary Stuart* made by the Hon. Lewis Wingfield. Most of her acting life was spent in America.

LOUISE MOODIE (1846–1934) made her début on the Continent and first appeared in London at the West London Theatre in 1870 as Camille. She played much in the provinces and in 1876 was a member of the Chippendale Comedy Company. In 1878 she appeared at the Haymarket in *The Crisis*, an English version by James Albery of Augier's *Les Fourchambault*, and in 1880 played Elizabeth to Modjeska's Mary Stuart at the Court. From 1881 to 1884 she was engaged in America. She is reported to have played in *East Lynne* in the English provinces over a thousand times. In 1891 she took the part of Mrs. Bread in the London production of Henry James's play *The American*.

CLARA MORRIS (1848–1925) was born in Toronto, Canada, and first appeared on the stage at the Cleveland Academy of Music as an "extra" at the age of fourteen. After work in various cities, she was engaged by Augustin Daly in 1870 and made a great success at the Fifth Avenue Theatre in *Man and Wife*. She remained with

Daly until 1873, and then went to A. M. Palmer at the Union Square Theatre. By 1876 she was recognized as the leading emotional actress of America, though her critics seem puzzled to account for this success. Her health was delicate, and she retired from the theatre in the nineties of the last century. In 1909 she lost her sight, but recovered it partially after five years of blindness.

ZARÏE MARTEL NATHALIE (1816–1885) first appeared at the Porte Saint-Antoine Theatre in 1835. After engagements at various theatres, notably at the Vaudeville from 1845 to 1848, she made her first appearance with the Comédie Française in 1849, and became a sociétaire in 1852. She retired in 1876.

ADELAIDE NEILSON (1848–1880) really named Elizabeth Ann Brown, was born at Leeds, and worked in a mill, as a nursemaid, and as a barmaid. In 1865 she made her début at Margate as Juliet, and repeated the performance in London the same year at the Royalty Theatre. She played much in the provinces, and visited America several times, her first appearance there being made at Booth's Theatre, New York, on November 18, 1872. She died in Paris.

BLANCHE ADELINE PIERSON (1842–1919) was born in the Ile de Réunion. She first appeared at the Ambigu in 1856. In 1858 she made a success at the Vaudeville, from which theatre she passed to the Gymnase where she remained until 1875, after which she returned to the Vaudeville. In 1884 she was engaged by the Théâtre Français, and became a sociétaire in 1885, remaining there until her death.

JEANNE ARNOULD-PLESSY (1819–1897) studied at the Conservatoire for one year, 1830. She first appeared at the Théâtre Français in 1834 and became a sociétaire at the end of that year. In July, 1845, she suddenly left Paris and married J. F. Arnould, a dramatist, in London. He died in 1854. Madame Plessy was condemned to pay a heavy fine to the Theatre and forfeited her rights as a sociétaire. She made a brilliant success at St. Petersburg for about ten years. In 1855 she reappeared at the Théâtre Français (but as a pensionnaire). She retired in 1876, her farewell performance taking place on May 8 of that year.

SUZANNE REICHEMBERG (1853–1924) received her early training from the Brohans and entered the Conservatoire in 1867. Next year, having taken a first prize for comedy, she made her appearance at the Théâtre Français. She became a sociétaire in 1872, and retired in 1898 on her marriage to Baron Pierre de Bourgoing.

ADELAIDE RISTORI (1822–1906) was born at Cividale, and acted from childhood, making her first success at the age of fourteen. In 1855 she created a sensation in Paris and was spoken of as a rival to Rachel. She toured much and visited the United States four times, her first appearance there being in 1866. She retired from the stage in 1885.

ELIZABETH ROBINS (1865–   ) born at Louisville, Kentucky, made her first stage appearance in 1885 at the Boston Museum. She came to England in 1889, and began a series of performances in Ibsen's plays which did much to establish his reputation in England, appearing in *The Pillars of Society* (1889), *A Doll's House* and *Hedda Gabler* (1891), *The Master Builder* (1893), and *Rosmersholm* (1893), *Little Eyolf* (1896), and *John Gabriel Borkman* (1897). She played Claire de Cintré in the London production of Henry James's *The American*. Her last appearance on the stage was in 1902. She is the author of many novels and also of *Theatre and Friendship* (London: Cape, 1932) containing many letters from Henry James.

CLARA MARION JESSIE ROUSBY (1852?–1879) was born at Parkhurst, Isle of Wight. She married a provincial theatre-manager and actor, and after appearing at Jersey made her first London appearance at the Queen's Theatre, Long Acre, on December 19, 1869, in *The Fool's Revenge*, an adaptation by Tom Taylor of *Le Roi s'amuse*. She was more famous for her beauty than for her acting ability. In New York she appeared in January and February, 1875, at the Lyceum in *'Twixt Axe and Crown* by Tom Taylor, and as Rosalind and Camille.

HORTENSE CATHERINE SCHNEIDER (1835?–1920) was born at Bordeaux and appeared on the stage there at the age of fifteen. After three years at Agen playing secondary parts, she went to Paris and was engaged at the Bouffe-Parisiens, appearing later at the Variétés and Palais Royal. Her greatest successes were made in the operas of Offenbach with which her name will always be associated, especially in *La Belle Hélène*, and *La Grande Duchesse*. In 1881 she married and left the stage. See *Hortense Schneider* by Marcel Rouff and Therese Casevitz. (Paris: Talendier, 1931.)

MARY ANNE STIRLING (1813–1895) was born in London and first appeared on the stage under the name of Fanny Clifton, probably in 1829 at the East London Theatre. She had a long and distinguished career, playing every sort of part, and was leading lady at a great many London theatres. Her last appearance was as Martha in *Faust* at the Lyceum, and she retired from the stage on July 31, 1886. When the run of *Faust* was resumed after the summer vacation, Mrs. Chippendale took over the part. *The Stage Life of Mrs. Stirling* by her grandson, Percy Allen, was published in 1922 (London: Fisher Unwin) and gives a long list of the parts she played.

ELLEN TERRY (1847–1928) was born at Coventry and first appeared on the stage on April 28, 1856, as Mamillius in *A Winter's Tale*. She was with Charles Kean at the Princess's Theatre from 1857 to 1859, and played at the Royalty in 1861. She was in the company that opened the Queen's Theatre, Long Acre, in October, 1867, and was with the Bancrofts at the Prince of Wales's in 1875, and with John Hare at the Court in 1876. She joined Henry Irving at the Lyceum in December, 1878, and remained with him as his leading lady for twenty-four years. Her first appearance in America was made at the Star Theatre, New York, in 1883. She toured the United States ten times. She was created G. B. E. in 1925. Her *Story of My Life* appeared in 1908 (London: Hutchinson). A revised and enlarged edition was published in 1933 (London: Gollancz).

MARION TERRY (1856–1930) made her first appearance on the stage at the Theatre Royal, Manchester, on July 21, 1873, and appeared in London at the Olympic the same year. She was at the Strand Theatre in 1874–1875 and at the Haymarket in 1876–1877. She was in the Bancrofts' company at the Prince of Wales's and Haymarket Theatres from 1879 to 1881. She played Mrs. Peverel in Henry James's *Guy Domville*. In 1908 she toured in America.

LYDIA THOMPSON (1836–1909) was born in London and first made a reputation as a dancer, appearing in ballet at Her Majesty's Theatre in 1852. Her greatest success was made as an actress in burlesque. She visited the United States several times. In 1899 she was given a complimentary benefit at the Lyceum. Her last appearance was in 1904 at the Imperial Theatre.

MRS. HERMANN VEZIN (1827–1902) was born in England but made her first appearance as a child actress in Australia. She first married Charles Young (1846), and appeared in London at Sadler's Wells under Phelps in 1857. In 1863 she married Hermann Vezin and next year began a long engagement at Drury Lane. She was with the Bancrofts at the Prince of Wales's in 1879. Her last engagement was with John Hare and the Kendals in *Young Folks' Ways* at the St. James's in 1883.

MARY ANN VINCENT (1818–1887) was born at Portsmouth, England, and first appeared in 1835 at a theatre in Cowes in the Isle of Wight. She made her first appearance in Boston at the National Theatre in 1846 with her husband. In 1852 she was engaged for the Boston Museum and remained there almost uninterruptedly for over thirty-five years, playing up to the day before her death.

GENEVIÈVE WARD (1838–1922) was born in New York. She began life as a singer and made her début in Paris in April, 1859. After losing her singing voice she studied for the stage and appeared at Manchester as Lady Macbeth in October, 1873. After studying at the Comédie Française, she played at Booth's Theatre, New York, on September 2, 1878. Her performance in *Forget-Me-Not* was repeated over two thousand times. She appeared in *John Gabriel Borkman* in London in 1897. Her last performance was in 1918.

ANNIE WEBSTER (1861–1940) a granddaughter of the celebrated Benjamin Webster, actor and Adelphi manager (1819–1882), she first appeared in 1883 at the St. James's Theatre under the Kendals' management. Later she played in Ben Greet's early productions, and toured South Africa with Miss Fortescue's company. She first married Mr. J. Bell and retired from the stage. After her second marriage in 1896 to A. E. George she appeared occasionally in special performances.

MRS. JOHN WOOD (1833–1915) was born in Liverpool and first appeared on the stage at Brighton in 1841. She went to the United States in 1854, first appearing in Boston. She was a success in America before she appeared in London in 1866 at the Princess's Theatre. In 1871 she again returned to the States for two years. In 1883 she was at the Court Theatre, London, where she remained as actress and later as manageress until 1891. Towards the end of her life she was seen in several of the big Drury Lane melodramas.

III. *Playwrights*

GUILLAUME VICTOR ÉMILE AUGIER (1820–1889) was born at Valence. He was grandson of the novelist Pigault-Lebrun. His first great success was made with *L'Aventurière* in 1848, a play of Renaissance Italy, but most of his later work was in the field of social comedy (*Théâtre Complet*; Paris: 7 volumes; 1890).

JEAN FRANÇOIS ALFRED BAYARD (1786–1853) was a prolific playwright, working in collaboration with many authors, particularly with Scribe whose niece he married. His collected plays fill twelve volumes (Paris: 1855–1858).

DION BOUCICAULT (1822–1890) actor and dramatist, was born in Dublin. He was the author of a very large number of plays and adaptations, among his great successes being *London Assurance* (1841), *The Colleen Bawn* (1859), and *The Shaugraun* (1875). He first appeared on the stage under the name of Lee Morton at Brighton and Cheltenham in 1838, and in London at the Haymarket in 1839.

He spent a great deal of time in America and produced many plays there.

EUGÈNE BRIEUX (1858–1932) was born in Paris of working-class origin. His first success was made at the Théâtre Libre, and his plays deal chiefly with "social problems." He was elected to the Académie in 1909.

FRANCIS COWLEY BURNAND (1836–1917) began to write plays when a boy. His first London play, *Dido*, was produced at the St. James's in 1860. He was the author of over 120 plays and burlesques. For 25 years he was editor of *Punch*, retiring in 1906. He was knighted in 1902.

HENRY JAMES BYRON (1834–1884) actor and dramatist, was born in Manchester. He was a prolific writer of plays and burlesques. His first appearance on the stage in London was made in 1869 at the Globe Theatre. He opened the Prince of Wales's Theatre in partnership with Marie Wilton (afterwards Lady Bancroft) in 1865, but resigned his connection there in 1867. His last appearance on the stage was in 1881 at the Court Theatre in W. S. Gilbert's *Engaged*.

FRANÇOIS DE CUREL (1854–1928) began his career with two novels but became an acted dramatist in 1892 at the Théâtre Libre. His *Théâtre Complet*, containing also the history of each play followed by the author's reminiscences, appeared in 6 volumes (Paris: Albin Michel, 1919–1924).

CHARLES MAURICE DONNAY (1859–1945) was born in Paris and began life as a civil engineer. His first successful play was *Lysistrata*, produced at the Grand Theatre, Paris, in 1892, with Réjane and Guitry. He became a member of the Académie in 1907. See *Maurice Donnay: Son Oeuvre* by Pierre Bathille. (Paris: Nouvelle Revue Critique, 1932.) Donnay's plays were published in 8 volumes (Paris: Fasquelle, 1907–1929).

PAUL HERVIEU (1857–1915) dramatist and novelist, was born at Neuilly-sur-Seine. He was called to the Bar, and qualified for the Diplomatic Service. He was elected to the Académie in 1900. His plays were published in four volumes (Paris: Lemerre, 1900–1909).

HENRY ARTHUR JONES (1851–1929) was born at Grandborough, Bucks, and began to write plays in 1878. His first great success was *The Silver King* (1882) written in collaboration. During the nineties and early nineteen-hundreds he was one of the leading English dramatists, among his successes being *The Dancing Girl*, *The Liars*, and *Mrs. Dane's Defence*.

LÉON LAYA (1810–1872) was for some years librarian at the Palace of Fontainebleu. As a dramatist he was very successful. He died by suicide.

EDWARD BULWER, first BARON LYTTON (1803–1873) is better known as a novelist than as a playwright. Some of his plays, however, were extremely successful in their day, particularly *The Lady of Lyons* (1838), *Richelieu* (1839), and *Money* (1840).

ARTHUR WING PINERO (1855–1934) born in London, first appeared as an actor in 1874 at Edinburgh, and in London, at the Globe Theatre, in April, 1876. He acted with Irving at the Lyceum and with the Bancrofts at the Haymarket, but left the stage in 1884. His first (one-act) play was produced in 1877. During the later years of the nineteenth and in the early twentieth Century he wrote many well-known and very successful plays. He was knighted in 1909.

GEORGES DE PORTO-RICHE (1849–1930) was born at Bordeaux. His first play, *Le Vertige*, was given at the Odéon in 1873, and *Amoureuse*, his best-known play, at the same theatre in 1891. He died in Paris. His *Theatre d'Amour* in four volumes was published in Paris (Albin Michel, 1926–1928). See also *Georges de Porto-Riche* by Hendrik Brugmans. (Paris: E. Droz, 1934.)

THOMAS WILLIAM ROBERTSON (1829–1871) actor and dramatist, was born at Newark-on-Trent. He first appeared on the stage in 1834, and for many years had a difficult life both in the provinces and London, acting and also writing and adapting plays. His first success was an adaptation, *David Garrick* (1864), and soon after he began, with *Society*, the series of comedies which made him and the Bancrofts famous at the Prince of Wales's Theatre. The best known of these, *Caste*, is still occasionally played. His *Principal Dramatic Works* were edited by his son, in two volumes (London: Sampson Low, 1889).

EDMOND ROSTAND (1869–1918) poet and dramatist, was born at Marseille, and died in Paris. A large illustrated edition of his works was published in Paris by Pierre Lafitte & Cie. (1910–1930).

VICTORIEN SARDOU (1831–1908) was born in Paris, and in his early youth had a hard struggle for existence. He began to be successful as a playwright about 1860, and wrote a succession of satirical comedies. Later he turned to the writing of historical melo-dramas, many of them for Sarah Bernhardt. He was elected to the Académie in 1878. His collected plays, now in course of publication, are designed to fill fifteen volumes (Paris: Albin Michel, 1934, etc.).

WILLIAM GORMAN WILLS (1828–1891) dramatist and painter, was born at Kilmurry, Ireland. After making some success with *The Man o'Airlie* at the Princess's in 1867 and doing adaptations and work in collaboration, he was engaged by Colonel Bateman as dramatist to the Lyceum, and wrote several plays in which Irving figured, culminating in his version of *Faust*. His later work is said to be of indifferent quality. Few of his plays were printed. See *W. G. Wills* by Freeman Wills. (London: Longmans, 1898.)

iv. *Plays*

L'AIGLON, a drama in verse in six acts by Edmond Rostand, was first produced at the Théâtre Sarah Bernhardt on March 15, 1900, with Sarah Bernhardt as the Duc de Reichstadt and Guitry as Flambeau.

ALL FOR HER, a drama in three acts by Herman Merivale and J. Palgrave Simpson, was first produced at the Mirror Theatre,

London, on October 18, 1875, with John Clayton and Horace Wigan in the cast.

L'AMI FRITZ, a comedy in three acts by Erckmann-Chatrian, was first produced at the Théâtre Français on December 4, 1876.

AS YOU LIKE IT was revived by Marie Litton at the Imperial Theatre, Westminster, on February 25, 1880. In addition to those members of the cast mentioned by Henry James it is worth noting that Orlando was played by Kyrle Bellew. The costumes for this revival were designed by Johnston Forbes-Robertson.

L'AVENTURIÈRE, a comedy in four acts in verse by Émile Augier, was first played at the Comédie Française on March 23, 1848. Regnier created the part of Don Annibal, Mme. Plessy that of Dona Clorinde, and Mme. Favart that of Célie.

LA BATAILLE DE DAMES, a comedy in three acts by Scribe and Légouvé, first played at the Théâtre Français on March 17, 1851. It was adapted into English by T. W. Robertson under the title *The Ladies' Battle*, and produced at the Court Theatre on March 17, 1879.

BELLE LAMAR by Dion Boucicault was produced on August 10, 1874, at Booth's Theatre, New York, where it ran until September 12. The play dealt with the Civil War and was written for the actor John McCullough; Katherine Rogers played the part of Isabel Lamar. The production at the Boston Theatre was presented by the stock company and ran for three weeks, beginning on October 12, 1874.

THE BELLS, a drama in three acts adapted by Leopold Lewis from *Le Juif Polonais* by Erckmann-Chatrian (produced at the Cluny Theatre, Paris, on June 15, 1869), was first played at the Lyceum Theatre on November 25, 1871, with Irving as Mathias. This was the performance which made his reputation in London; the play remained always one of the most popular and successful in his repertory.

BLACK EY'D SUSAN or "ALL IN THE DOWNS," a drama in three acts by Douglas Jerrold, was originally played at the

Surrey Theatre, London, on June 8, 1829. The production mentioned by Henry James took place at the Connaught Theatre, Holborn (now demolished) on December 26, 1879, with George Rignold as William.

CASTE, a comedy in three acts by T. W. Robertson, was originally produced at the Prince of Wales's Theatre on April 6, 1867, and was frequently reproduced there. The revival of which Henry James here writes took place on January 11, 1879, with the Bancrofts, Arthur Cecil, and John Clayton in the cast. The play is still occasionally performed.

UNE CHAINE, a comedy in five acts by M. E. Scribe, was first produced at the Théâtre Français on November 29, 1841, with Regnier and Mme. Plessy in the cast.

CHAMILLAC, a comedy in five acts by Octave Feuillet, was first performed at the Théâtre Français on April 9, 1886, with Coquelin in the title role.

CHARLES I, a drama in four acts in verse by William Gorman Wills, was first produced at the Lyceum Theatre, London, on September 28, 1872, with Henry Irving as Charles and Isabella Bateman as Henrietta Maria. It was revived at the Lyceum in June, 1879, and remained in Irving's repertory for many years.

LES CHEVALIERS DE LA PATRIE, a drama in five acts by Albert Depit, was produced at the Théâtre Historique on February 20, 1876. It was played 36 times to small audiences. Sad to relate, the play was never printed.

THE CORSICAN BROTHERS was an adaptation by Dion Boucicault of *Les Frères Corses*, a play by Grangé and Xavier de Montépin, founded on a story by Dumas *père*, which was produced at the Théâtre Historique, Paris, on August 10, 1850, with Fechter in the title parts. Boucicault's version was made for Charles Kean who produced it at the Princess's Theatre on February 24, 1852. Irving's revival of the play at the Lyceum took place on September 18, 1880.

LA COURSE DE FLAMBEAU, a play in four acts by Paul Hervieu, was first produced at the Vaudeville Theatre, Paris, on April 17, 1901, with Réjane as Sabine Revel.

LA CRÉOLE, an opera comique (book by Albert Millaud, music by Jacques Offenbach) was first performed at the Bouffes-Parisiens on November 3, 1875, with Mme. Judic in the part of Zoë.

LA CRUCHE CASSÉE, an opera comique (book by Jules Noirac and Jules Moineaux, music by Félix Augustin Léon Vasseur) was produced on October 27, 1875, at the Théâtre Taitbout, formerly a concert hall, which opened as a theatre on March 28, 1875, and closed in April, 1878, after a chequered career.

CYMBELINE was revived by Henry Irving at the Lyceum Theatre on September 22, 1896.

CYRANO DE BERGERAC, a heroic comedy in verse in five acts by Edmond Rostand, was first produced at the Porte Saint Martin Theatre on December 28, 1897, with Coquelin as Cyrano and Maria Legault as Roxane.

LA DAME AUX CAMÉLIAS, a drama in five acts by Alexandre Dumas *fils*, was first played at the Vaudeville Theatre, Paris, on February 2, 1852, with Charles Fechter as Armand Duval and Mme. Doche as Marguerite Gautier.

LES DANICHEFF, a comedy in four acts by Pierre Newsky (Petr Corvin de Krukovskoi) and Alexandre Dumas *fils*, was first produced at the Odéon Theatre on January 8, 1876. An English adaptation by Lord Newry was played at the St. James's Theatre on January 6, 1877.

THE DEAD HEART, a drama in a prologue and three acts by Watts Phillips, was first produced at the Adelphi Theatre on November 10, 1859. There was a revival there on February 8, 1869, which Henry James may have seen as he reached London on March 1 of that year. The play was subsequently revived by Henry Irving at the Lyceum on September 28, 1889.

LE DEMI-MONDE, a comedy in five acts by Alexandre Dumas *fils*, was first produced at the Gymnase on March 20, 1855, with Dupuis as Olivier de Jalin and Rose Chéri as Suzanne d'Ange. At the Comédie Française these parts were played by Delaunay and Sophie Croizette.

DENISE, a play in three acts by Alexandre Dumas *fils*, was first produced at the Théâtre Français on January 19, 1885, with Worms, Got, Coquelin, and Mlle. Reichemberg in the cast.

LE DÉPUTÉ DE BOMBIGNAC, a comedy in three acts by Alexandre Bisson, was first produced at the Théâtre Français on May 28, 1884, with Coquelin as de Chantelaur. An English adaptation by Justin Huntly McCarthy, *The Candidate*, was played at the Criterion Theatre, London, on November 22, 1884.

DIANE DE LYS, a drama in five acts by Alexandre Dumas *fils*, was first produced at the Gymnase on November 15, 1853, with Bressant and Rose Chéri in the cast.

DIPLOMACY, an adaptation of Sardou's *Dora*, by B. C. Stephenson and Clement Scott, was first produced at the Prince of Wales's Theatre on January 12, 1878. The original play, *Dora*, a comedy in five acts by Victorien Sardou, was first played at the Vaudeville Theatre, Paris, on January 22, 1877.

A DOLL'S HOUSE, a play in three acts by Henrik Ibsen translated by William Archer, was produced at the Novelty (now Kingsway) Theatre on June 7, 1889, with Janet Achurch as Nora. It was revived at Terry's Theatre on January 27, 1891, with Elizabeth Robins in the part of Mrs. Linden.

DRINK, a play in five acts adapted by Charles Reade from *L'Assommoir*, a dramatization of Zola's novel by W. Busnach and Gastineau (Ambigu Theatre, Paris, January 19, 1879), was first performed at the Princess's Theatre, London, on June 2, 1879, with Charles Warner as Coupeau and Amy Roselle as Gervaise.

LE DUC JOB, a comedy in four acts by Léon Laya, was first produced at the Théâtre Français on November 4, 1859, with Got, Worms, Monrose, Talbot, and Mme. Nathalie in the cast.

ELIZABETH, QUEEN OF ENGLAND, an historical drama in five acts by Paolo Giacometti, was translated into French by C. Ferrari in 1860, and into English by T. J. Williams in 1863.

L'ÉTRANGÈRE, a comedy in five acts by Alexandre Dumas *fils*, was first produced at the Théâtre Français on February 14, 1876, with Coquelin, Got, Mounet-Sully, Febvre, Sophie Croizette, Madeleine Brohan, and Sarah Bernhardt in the cast.

EUGENE ARAM, a drama in verse in three acts by William Gorman Wills, was first produced at the Lyceum Theatre, London, on April 19, 1873, with Henry Irving in the title part and Isabel Bateman as Ruth Meadows.

THE FALCON, a play in one act by Alfred, Lord Tennyson, was first performed at the St. James's Theatre on December 18, 1879.

FAUST, a tragedy in a prologue and five acts, adapted and arranged from the first part of Goethe's play by W. G. Wills, was first produced at the Lyceum Theatre on December 19, 1885. It was played by Irving in America at the Star Theatre, New York, on November 7, 1887. It is said to have been the most successful financially of all Irving's productions.

LA FEMME DE CLAUDE, a play in three acts by Alexandre Dumas *fils*, was produced for the first time at the Gymnase Theatre on January 16, 1873, with Aimée Desclée and Blanche Pierson in the cast.

FERRÉOL, a play in four acts by Victorien Sardou, was first played at the Gymnase Theatre on December 17, 1875.

UN FILS DE FAMILLE, a comedy in three acts by Jean François Alfred Bayard and de Biéville, first played at the Gymnase Theatre on November 25, 1852. It was adapted by G. W. Godfrey, under the title *The Queen's Shilling*, and produced at the Court Theatre on April 19, 1879.

LE FILS NATUREL, a comedy in five acts by Alexandre Dumas *fils*, was first produced at the Gymnase on January 16, 1858, with Dupuis and Rose Chéri in the leading parts.

A FOOL AND HIS MONEY, a comedy in three acts by H. J. Byron, was first played at the Globe Theatre, London, on January 17, 1878, with J. L. Toole in the cast. It was revived at the Folly Theatre on November 17, 1879.

FORGET-ME-NOT, a drama in three acts by Herman Merivale and Crawford Grove, was first played at the Lyceum Theatre on August 21, 1879, with Geneviève Ward as Stephanie and Forbes-Robertson as Sir Horace Welby. It was revived at the Prince of Wales's Theatre on February 21, 1880, with John Clayton as Sir Horace.

LES FOURCHAMBAULT, a comedy in five acts by Émile Augier was first played at the Comédie Française on April 8, 1878, with Coquelin, Got, Mlle. Reichemberg, and Mlle. Croizette in the cast.

FRANCILLON, a play in three acts by Alexandre Dumas *fils*, was produced at the Théâtre Français on January 17, 1887, with Thiron, Febvre, Worms, and Mme. Bartet in the cast.

FROUFROU, a comedy in five acts by Henry Meilhac and Ludovic Halévy, was first produced at the Gymnase Theatre on October 30, 1869, with Aimée Desclée as Gilberte. Sarah Bernhardt played Gilberte at the Porte Saint Martin in 1888, and the play was first given at the Théâtre Français on May 22, 1892.

LE GENDRE DE M. POIRIER, a comedy in four acts by Émile Augier and Jules Sandeau, was first played at the Gymnase on April 8, 1854, with Rose Chéri in the part of Antoinette. It was revived at the Comédie Française on May 3, 1864.

GHOSTS, a play in three acts by Henrik Ibsen, translated by William Archer, was produced at the Royalty Theatre on March 13, 1891, by the Independent Theatre.

LE GLADIATEUR, a tragedy in verse in five acts by Alexandre Soumet and Gabrielle Daltenheym, his daughter, was first produced at the Théâtre Français on April 24, 1841, with Ligier as the Gladiator.

THE GREEN BUSHES, a play in three acts by J. B. Buckstone was first performed at the Adelphi Theatre on January 27, 1845, with Madame Celeste as Miami. She took the play to America in 1851 when Henry James appears, according to *A Small Boy and Others*, to have seen her. He also mentions seeing her play the part at the Adelphi. There were revivals there in October, 1870; September, 1872; and October, 1874; he perhaps saw the second of these.

GRINGOIRE, a comedy in one act by Théodore de Banville, was first produced at the Théâtre Français on June 23, 1866, with Coquelin in the part of Pierre Gringoire.

LA GUEULE DU LOUP, a comedy in four acts by Léon Laya, was first played at the Gymnase Theatre on October 16, 1872, with Aimée Desclée in the part of Anna.

HAMLET. The revival by Henry Irving of which Henry James writes took place at the Lyceum Theatre on December 30, 1878. Irving had first played Hamlet under the Bateman management at the Lyceum on October 30, 1874, on which occasion the play ran for eight months.

HEDDA GABLER, a play in four acts by Henrik Ibsen, translated by William Archer and Edmund Gosse, was produced at the Vaudeville Theatre on April 20, 1891, with Elizabeth Robins as Hedda and Marion Lea as Thea.

HÉLÉNE, tragédie bourgeoise in three acts by Edouard Pailleron, was first produced at the Théâtre Français on November 14,

1872, with Delaunay, Febvre, Mesdames Favart, Nathalie, and Reichemberg in the cast.

HENRY V. The production in which George Rignold starred was brought to Booth's Theatre, New York, from the Theatre Royal, Manchester, and opened on February 8, 1875.

THE HUNCHBACK, a play in five acts by Sheridan Knowles, was first produced at Covent Garden on April 5, 1832. The revival at the Adelphi in which Adelaide Neilson appeared took place on March 22, 1879.

LES IDÉES DE MADAME AUBRAY, a comedy in four acts by Alexandre Dumas *fils*, was first produced at the Gymnase on March 16, 1867, with Pierre Berton and Mme. Delaporte in the cast.

JEAN DACIER, a drama in verse in five acts by Charles Lomon, was first produced at the Théâtre Français on April 28, 1877, with Coquelin and Madame Favart in the cast.

JOHN GABRIEL BORKMAN, a play in four acts by Henrik Ibsen, translated by William Archer, was produced at the (old) Strand Theatre on May 3, 1897, with Elizabeth Robins and Geneviève Ward in the cast.

JULIE, a drama in three acts by Octave Feuillet, was first produced at the Théâtre Français on May 4, 1869, with Febvre, Mme. Favart, and Mlle. Reichemberg in the cast.

KEAN, a comedy in five acts by Alexandre Dumas *père*, was first produced at the Variétés on August 31, 1836. The leading part was a favourite one of Frédéric Lemaître.

THE LADY OF LYONS, or "LOVE AND PRIDE," a play in five acts by Edward Bulwer Lytton, was first produced at Drury Lane on January 17, 1848. Henry Irving's revival of the play took place at the Lyceum on April 17, 1879.

LES LIONNES PAUVRES, a play in five acts by Émile Augier and Édouard Foussier, was first produced at the Vaudeville on May 22, 1858, and revived there on November 22, 1879.

LIONS ET RENARDS, a comedy in five acts by Émile Augier, was first produced at the Théâtre Français on December 6, 1869, with Got, Delaunay, Bressant, Coquelin, Mme. Favart, and Madeleine Brohan in the cast.

LITTLE DOCTOR FAUST, a burlesque by H. J. Byron, was produced at the Gaiety Theatre on October 13, 1877.

LITTLE EYOLF, a play in three acts by Henrik Ibsen, translated by William Archer, was produced at the Avenue Theatre (now the Playhouse) on November 23, 1896, with Janet Achurch, Mrs. Patrick Campbell, and Elizabeth Robins in the cast.

LONDON ASSURANCE by Dion Boucicault was first produced at Covent Garden on March 4, 1841. The play held the stage until nearly the end of the nineteenth century.

LOUIS XI., a play by Casimir Delavigne (Paris, Théâtre Français, February 11, 1832) was adapted by Dion Boucicault for production by Charles Kean at the Princess's Theatre on January 13, 1855. Henry Irving's revival of the play took place at the Lyceum on March 9, 1878. It remained in his repertory for many years.

LUCREZIA BORGIA, a drama by Victor Hugo, was first produced at the Porte Saint Martin Theatre on February 2, 1833.

LE LUTHIER DE CRÉMONE, a comedy in one act by François Coppée, was first produced at the Comédie Française on May 23, 1876.

MACBETH. Henry Irving's production of the play took place at the Lyceum on September 18, 1875, under the management of Mrs. S. F. Bateman. The production at Booth's Theatre, New York, with George Rignold and Clara Morris in the leading parts took place on May 17, 1875.

MADEMOISELLE DE BELLE ISLE, a drama in five acts by Alexandre Dumas *père*, was first produced at the Théâtre Français on April 2, 1839.

MAÎTRE GUÉRIN, a comedy in five acts by Émile Augier, was first produced at the Théâtre Français on October 29, 1864, with Got, Delaunay, Mesdames Nathalie, Plessy, and Favart in the cast.

LE MARIAGE D'OLYMPE, a play in three acts by Émile Augier, was first produced at the Vaudeville on July 17, 1855. Madame Fargueil played the part of Pauline.

LE MARQUIS DE VILLEMER, a comedy in four acts by George Sand, was first produced at the Odéon Theatre, Paris, on February 29, 1864.

MARY STUART, a tragedy in five acts by Schiller, was translated into Italian by Andrea Maffei and published in 1856.

THE MASTER BUILDER, a play in three acts by Henrik Ibsen, translated by William Archer and Edmund Gosse, was produced at the Trafalgar Square (now Duke of York's) Theatre on February 20, 1893, with Elizabeth Robins and Herbert Waring in the cast.

MEDEA, a tragedy in verse in three acts by Ernest Legouvé, was translated into Italian by Giusseppi Montanelli and played by Ristori in Paris at the Théâtre Italien on April 8, 1856.

THE MERCHANT OF VENICE. Henry Irving's revival of this play was given at the Lyceum Theatre on November 1, 1879.

THE MERRY WIVES OF WINDSOR. Beerbohm Tree's production of the play took place at the Haymarket Theatre on January 2, 1889.

MONEY, a comedy in five acts by Edward Bulwer Lytton, was first produced at the Haymarket Theatre on December 8, 1840. There was a revival at the Prince of Wales's Theatre under the Bancrofts' management in May, 1872, and another in 1875, which Henry James appears to have seen. The Bancrofts began their management of the Haymarket with another revival of the play on January 31, 1880.

LA MORT DU DUC D'ENGHIEN, a drama in three scenes by Léon Hennique, was first produced by the Théâtre Libre on December 10, 1888, at the Théâtre des Menus-Plaisirs, Boulevard de Strasbourg, Paris, with André Antoine as the Duc. The visit of the Théâtre Libre to London began on February 4, 1889, when *La Mort du Duc d'Enghien* and *Jacques Damour*, a one-act play by Léon Hennique, taken from Zola's short story, were performed for a week at the Royalty Theatre.

LA MORTE CIVILE, a drama in five acts by Paolo Giacometti, written in 1861, was first produced at the Teatro dei Fiorentini at Naples by Salvini in December, 1864.

NELSON'S ENCHANTRESS, a play in four acts by Risden Home, was produced at the Avenue Theatre, London, on February 11, 1897.

NEW MEN AND OLD ACRES, a comedy in three acts by Tom Taylor and A. W. Dubourg, was first produced at the Haymarket Theatre on October 25, 1869. The revival at the Court Theatre here mentioned took place on December 2, 1876.

NICHOLAS NICKLEBY, a drama in three acts by Andrew Halliday, taken from Dickens's novel, was first produced at the Adelphi Theatre on March 20, 1875, and revived there on December 30, 1879. It appears to have been the revival which Henry James saw.

ODETTE, a comedy in four acts by Victorien Sardou, was first performed at the Vaudeville Theatre, Paris, on November 17, 1881. The English adaptation, anonymous but actually by Clement Scott, was produced at the Haymarket Theatre on April 25, 1882.

THE OLD LOVE AND THE NEW, a play in five acts by Bronson Howard, was produced at the Court Theatre, London, on December 15, 1879. Originally played at Hooley's Theatre, Chicago, on September 4, 1877, as *Lilian's Last Love*, it was renamed *The Banker's Daughter* and produced with great success at the Union Square Theatre, New York, on September 30, 1878. The English adaptation was made with the help of James Albery. See *The Auto-biography of a Play*. (New York: Columbia College, 1914.)

OLIVIA, a play in four acts by W. G. Wills, founded on incidents in Goldsmith's *Vicar of Wakefield*, was produced at the Court Theatre on March 28, 1878, with Ellen Terry as Olivia and Hermann Vezin as Dr. Primrose. Henry Irving revived it at the Lyceum on April 22, 1891, playing the part of the Vicar himself.

LE PANACHE, a comedy in three acts by Edmond Gondinet, was first produced at the Palais Royal Theatre on October 12, 1875.

UN PARISIEN, a comedy in three acts by Edmond Gondinet, was first produced at the Théâtre Français on January 23, 1886, with Coquelin in the part of Brichanteau and Mlle. Reichemberg as Geneviève.

PAUL FORESTIER, a comedy in four acts in verse by Émile Augier, was first produced at the Comédie Française on January 25, 1868, with Got, Delaunay, Coquelin, and Mme. Favart in the cast.

UN PÈRE PRODIGUE, a comedy in five acts by Alexandre Dumas *fils*, was first produced at the Gymnase on November 30, 1859, with Lafont, Dupuis, and Rose Chéri in the cast.

PERIL, an adaptation by B. C. Stephenson and Clement Scott of Sardou's *Nos Intimes*, was produced at the Prince of Wales's Theatre on September 30, 1876. The original play, a comedy in four acts, was first produced at the Vaudeville Theatre, Paris, on November 16, 1861.

PETITE PLUIE, a comedy in one act by Edmond Pailleron, was first produced at the Théâtre Français on December 4, 1875.

PHILIBERTE, a comedy in three acts in verse by Émile Augier, was first produced at the Gymnase on March 19, 1853. Bressant took the part of Talmay and Rose Chéri that of Philiberte.

THE PHYSICIAN, a play in four acts by Henry Arthur Jones, was produced at the Criterion Theatre on March 25, 1897, with Charles Wyndham and Mary Moore in the cast.

LE POST-SCRIPTUM, a comedy in one act by Émile Augier, was first produced at the Théâtre Français on May 1, 1869, and played by Bressant and Madame Plessy.

THE PRINCESS AND THE BUTTERFLY, a comedy in four acts by Arthur Wing Pinero, was produced at the St. James's Theatre on March 29, 1897, with George Alexander and Fay Davis in the cast.

LA PRINCESSE LOINTAINE, a play in verse in four acts by Edmond Rostand, was first produced at the Renaissance Theatre, Paris, on April 5, 1895, with Sarah Bernhardt as the Princess, Guitry as Bertrand, and De Max as Rudel.

A QUIET RUBBER, a comedy in one act adapted by C. F. Coghlan from *Une Partie de Picquet* by Narcisse Fournier and Horace Meyer (Gymnase, Paris, February 5, 1854), was first produced at the Court Theatre on January 8, 1876. It remained for long a popular feature of John Hare's repertory.

RABAGAS, a comedy in four acts by Victorien Sardou, was first produced at the Vaudeville Theatre, Paris, on February 1, 1872.

RICHARD III. Henry Irving's first appearance in this part was made under Mrs. Bateman's management at the Lyceum Theatre on January 29, 1877, with Kate and Isabel Bateman in the cast. He revived the play at the Lyceum on December 19, 1896, and after the first night fell and injured his knee. The run of the play was not resumed until February 27, 1897; Henry James must therefore have been present on the first night of the revival.

RICHELIEU, a play in five acts in verse by Edward Bulwer Lytton, first produced at Covent Garden on March 7, 1839, was revived at the Lyceum on April 19, 1873, with Irving as Richelieu.

RIP VAN WINKLE. The first play based on Washington Irving's story was produced at Albany on May 26, 1828, and ten different versions are said to have been used. Jefferson first imitated a performance given by his half-brother, Charles Burke, but made alterations of his own and finally had a version made for him by Dion Boucicault which he produced at the Adelphi Theatre, London, on September 4, 1865.

ROBBING ROY or "SCOTCHED AND KILT" a burlesque by F. C. Burnand was produced at the Gaiety Theatre on November 11, 1879.

LES ROMANESQUES, a comedy in verse in three acts by Edmond Rostand, was first produced at the Comédie Française on May 21, 1894, with Mlle. Reichemberg as Sylvette and Le Bargy as Percinet. An English version by George Fleming (Constance Fletcher) entitled *The Fantastics* was produced at the Royalty Theatre on May 29, 1900, with Mrs. Patrick Campbell as Percinet.

ROME VAINCUE, a tragedy in five acts by Dominique Alexandre Parodi, was first produced at the Théâtre Français on September 27, 1876.

ROMEO AND JULIET. Henry Irving's revival of the play took place at the Lyceum on March 8, 1882.

ROSMERSHOLM, a drama in four acts by Henrik Ibsen, translated by Charles Archer, was produced at the Vaudeville Theatre, London, on February 23, 1891, with Florence Farr as Rebecca.

LES SCANDALES D'HIER, a comedy in three acts by Théodore Barrière, was first produced at the Vaudeville Theatre, Paris, on November 15, 1875, with Blanche Pierson and Pierre Berton in the cast. An English adaptation, *Scandal*, by A. Matthison was produced at the Royalty Theatre, London, on June 1, 1878.

THE SCHOOL FOR SCANDAL, by Richard Brinsley Sheridan, was first produced at Drury Lane on May 8, 1777. The revival of which Henry James here writes took place at the Boston

Museum on October 5, 1874, and ran for three weeks; the London revival to which he makes reference was probably that which had recently been made at the Prince of Wales's Theatre on April 4, 1874, with Mr. and Mrs. Bancroft, John Hare, and Charles Coghlan in the cast.

THE SECOND MRS. TANQUERAY, a play in four acts by Arthur Wing Pinero, was produced at the St. James's Theatre on May 27, 1893, with George Alexander and Mrs. Patrick Campbell in the cast.

THE SHAUGRAUN, by Dion Boucicault, was produced at Wallack's Theatre, New York, on November 14, 1874, and was an immense success, running for 143 performances. The cast included H. J. Montague, Ada Dyas, and the author. In London *The Shaugraun* was produced at Drury Lane on September 4, 1875.

THE SQUIRE, a play in three acts by Arthur Wing Pinero, was produced at the St. James's Theatre on December 29, 1881.

STILL WATERS RUN DEEP, a comedy in three acts by Tom Taylor, founded on Charles de Bernard's novel *Le Gendre*, was first produced at the Olympic Theatre, London, on May 14, 1855, with Alfred Wigan, George Vining, and Sam Emery in the cast. Henry James saw this production as a small boy. The revival by the Kendals at the St. James's Theatre took place on March 13, 1880.

LE SUPPLICE D'UNE FEMME, a drama in three acts by Émile de Girardin, was first played at the Théâtre Français on April 20, 1865, with Regnier and Mme. Favart in the cast.

TRUTH, a comedy in three acts by Bronson Howard was produced at the Criterion Theatre on February 8, 1879. Under its original title, *Hurricanes*, it had been played at Hooley's Theatre, Chicago, on May 27, 1878, and at the Park Theatre, New York, on August 31 of the same year. The adaptation for England was made by the author.

THE TWO ORPHANS, adapted by Hart Jackson from Cormon and d'Ennery's *Les Deux Orphelines* (Paris: Porte Saint Martin Theatre, January 29, 1874) was produced at the Union Square Theatre, New York, on December 21, 1874, and is described by Odell as "one of the greatest theatrical successes of all time in America." Kate Claxton made a great hit in the part of the blind girl, Henriette. The run ended on June 15, 1875, with 180 performances.

VANDERDECKEN, a drama by W. G. Wills and Percy Fitzgerald, was first produced at the Lyceum Theatre on June 8, 1878.

LE VILLAGE, a comedy in one act by Octave Feuillet, was first performed at the Théâtre Français on June 2, 1856, with Samson, Regnier, and Mme. Nathalie in the cast.

THE WILD DUCK, a play in five acts by Henrik Ibsen, translated by William Archer, was produced at the Royalty Theatre on May 5, 1894.

WILLIAM AND SUSAN, a drama in three acts by W. G. Wills, founded on Douglas Jerrold's *Black-Ey'd Susan*, was produced at the St. James's Theatre on October 9, 1880.

WOMEN OF THE DAY, by Charles Morton, was produced by Augustin Daly at the Fifth Avenue Theatre, New York, on January 20, 1875. It ran until February 17.

YOUNG FOLKS' WAYS, a comedy in four acts by Mrs. Hodgson Burnett and W. H. Gillette, was produced at the St. James's Theatre on October 20, 1883.

v. *Theatres*

BOOTH'S THEATRE was situated at the southeast corner of Sixth Avenue and 23rd Street. It was opened on February 3, 1869, with a production of *Romeo and Juliet* played by Edwin Booth and Mary F. McVicker. Eventually Booth went bankrupt owing to the magnificence of his productions here.

THE BOSTON MUSEUM was opened in 1846. It is said to have been at its zenith between 1873 and 1883 when it devoted itself mainly to the performance of Shakespeare and the English classic comedies, and possessed a fine stock company under the inspiration of William Warren.

THE BOSTON THEATRE was opened on September 11, 1854, under the management of Thomas Barry, with performances of Sheridan's *The Rivals* and J. R. Planché's *The Loan of a Lover*. *The History of the Boston Theatre, 1854–1901* by Eugene Tompkins was published by the Houghton Mifflin Co. in 1908.

COURT THEATRE. The first Royal Court Theatre which stood on the south side of Sloane Square was opened by Marie Litton in January, 1871. It was managed by John Hare from 1875 to 1879, and closed in 1887. A new theatre of the same name, also in Sloane Square, was opened in September, 1888, and was for a time under the management of Mrs. John Wood. It was later the scene of the famous Vedrenne-Barker performances (1904–1907) and eventually became a cinema. It was damaged during the air raids on London in the second World War.

CRITERION THEATRE in Piccadilly Circus was opened in 1874 and in 1876 came under the management of Charles Wyndham in whose hands it was for long associated with the production of farce and light comedy.

THE FIFTH AVENUE THEATRE on Broadway and 28th Street was opened by Augustin Daly on December 3, 1873.

THE FOLLY THEATRE in King William Street, Strand, originally a hall, was transformed into a small theatre and opened as the "Charing Cross" in 1869. For some years it was under the management of J. S. Clarke, the American comedian. J. L. Toole took the theatre in 1879, and rechristened it "Toole's" in 1882. Augustin Daly's company made their first appearance in England here in 1884. The theatre closed in 1895 and was absorbed into Charing Cross Hospital.

THE GAIETY THEATRE was built on the site of the old Strand Music Hall by Mr. Lionel Lawson, part proprietor of the *Daily Telegraph*, and opened on December 21, 1868, under the management of John Hollingshead. It was for many years the "home of burlesque"; later it produced musical comedy under George Edwardes's management. It closed and was demolished in 1903.

GLOBE THEATRE on Washington Street, Boston, was opened in 1867 by John H. Selwyn and at first bore his name.

LE GYMNASE, originally called Le Théâtre du Gymnase-Dramatique, this theatre opened at 38, Boulevard Bonne-Nouvelle on December 23, 1820; on September 8, 1824, it took the name of Théâtre de Madame, but in July, 1830, it again became the Gymnase.

HAYMARKET THEATRE. The present building was opened in 1821, having been built next door to "the Little Theatre in the Haymarket." It was managed from 1827 by Benjamin Webster, and by J. B. Buckstone from 1853 to 1877. The theatre was largely reconstructed for the Bancrofts who opened it on January 31, 1880, and managed it until 1885. From 1887 to 1897 it was managed by Beerbohm Tree.

HER MAJESTY'S THEATRE in the Haymarket, London, was opened by Herbert Beerbohm Tree on April 28, 1897, with *The Seats of the Mighty*, a play by Gilbert Parker.

LE THÉÂTRE HISTORIQUE, the third to bear this name, stood in the Place du Châtelet, having been rebuilt in 1874, the previous building having been burnt down in 1871. It opened on November 6, 1874, and closed on March 25, 1879. The site is now occupied by the Théâtre Sarah Bernhardt.

THE LYCEUM THEATRE (NEW YORK) was originally the Théâtre Français and was built in 1866 in 14th Street, near Sixth Avenue, on the site of the Cremorne Gardens. It was named the Lyceum by Fechter, September 11, 1873.

ODÉON. This theatre opened on May 20, 1797, where previously had been the Théâtre de la Nation. It frequently changed its name, being Théâtre de L'Impératrice from 1805 to 1815, Théâtre Royal under three kings, Impérial under Napoleon III., and today is the second Théâtre National, being subventioned by the State. The present building opened in 1819.

PALAIS-ROYAL. This, the second theatre to bear the name, opened on June 6, 1831. In 1848 it became the Théâtre de la Montansier until 1852 when it again became the Palais-Royal. It was almost entirely reconstructed in 1881.

PRINCE OF WALES'S THEATRE. This building was originally opened in Tottenham Street as the New Theatre in 1810. After bearing many other names it had sunk into obscurity and was usually known as the "dust-hole," when the Bancrofts reopened it in 1865 as the Prince of Wales's. Their management lasted until 1879. After they left it the theatre soon again sank into obscurity. The present Scala Theatre, opened in 1905, now occupies the site, the portico of the old Prince of Wales's still remaining outside the Scala stage entrance.

SADLER'S WELLS THEATRE in Islington is the oldest theatre in London, dating from 1765. In its earlier days it was managed by Charles Dibdin. From 1844 to 1862 it was under Samuel Phelps's direction; he made there many famous Shakespearean productions. It was rebuilt and opened by Mrs. H. L. Bateman on October 9, 1879, who produced there Shakespeare and other plays with her daughters in the cast and with Hermann Vezin and Charles Warner as leading actors, until her death in 1881. It was again rebuilt and reopened in 1931 and is now devoted to opera and ballet at "popular" prices.

ST. JAMES'S THEATRE in King Street, St. James's, was opened in December, 1835, by John Braham, the singer. For many years it had the reputation of being unlucky. In the sixties it was used as a French theatre. John Hare and the Kendals managed it from 1879 to 1888. Under George Alexander it had great prosperity from 1891 to 1918.

APPENDIX

THE UNION SQUARE THEATRE was opened as a variety house on September 11, 1871. It stood between Broadway and Fourth Avenue on 14th Street. For eleven years, from 1872 to 1883, it was under the successful management of Albert Marshall Palmer.

VARIÉTÉS. The present building bearing this name is situated at 7, Boulevard Montmartre, and was first opened in 1807.

VAUDEVILLE (PARIS). The theatre bearing this name was opened in 1869 on the Boulevard des Capucines at the corner of the Chausée d'Antin. In 1925 it became a cinema.

THE WESTMINSTER (AQUARIUM) THEATRE. This was first opened in 1876 as an adjunct to the Royal Aquarium. It was first managed by Henry Labouchère but changed hands many times. It was rebuilt and opened by Mrs. Langtry in 1902. Eventually it was sold and the building transferred to Canning Town where it was re-erected and used as a music hall.

VI. *Miscellaneous*

SIR LAWRENCE ALMA-TADEMA (1836–1912) was born in Holland. He came to London in 1870 and was very successful as a painter, especially of Roman subjects. He designed the scenery for Irving's productions of *Cymbeline* in 1896 and *Coriolanus* in 1901. He also worked for Beerbohm Tree's productions of *Hypatia* (1893) and *Julius Caesar* (1898).

WILLIAM ARCHER (1856–1924) was born in Perth, Scotland, and educated as a lawyer but never practised. He was dramatic critic for the *London Figaro*, 1879–1881, and, later, for *The World* and other papers. The devoted apostle of Ibsen in England, he translated most of his plays. Late in life he achieved great success with a melodrama, *The Green Goddess*, produced in America in 1921 and in England two years later. He died in London.

"The Blight of The Drama," an article by William Archer, was published in the *Fortnightly Review* for January, 1897.

SIDNEY FRANCES BATEMAN (1825–1881) was the wife of Col. H. L. Bateman. After his death in 1875 she continued the management of the Lyceum Theatre until August, 1878. She became lessee and manager of Sadler's Wells in 1879.

THE COMÉDIE FRANÇAISE IN LONDON. These performances took place at the Gaiety Theatre for six weeks, from June 2 to July 12, 1879. They were a great success with the London fashionable public. John Hollingshead, the lessee and manager of the theatre, states in his *Gaiety Chronicles* (London: Constable, 1898) that the director of the Théâtre Français, M. Perrin, fixed the terms at the average *maximum* of the Théâtre Français, £240 a night, and £160 for the matinée, making £1,600 a week, always payable in advance. Nevertheless the six weeks' season yielded Hollingshead a net profit of £7,000. Double prices were charged, and the receipts, especially on the nights when Sarah Bernhardt played, were very high. Hollingshead's book gives details of the company appearing.

COMÉDIENS ET COMÉDIENNES, by Francisque Sarcey was published by the Librarie des Bibliophiles in Paris. The first series, devoted to the Comédie Française, appeared in 1876. The second, which concerned Théâtres Divers appeared in 1884.

ÉMILE CÉSAR VICTOR PERRIN (1814–1885) was born at Rouen and began his career as a painter, showing several pictures at the Salon from 1840 to 1848. In the latter year he became director of the Opéra Comique, remaining there till 1857. In 1862 he was director of the Opéra but resigned in 1870. He was then nominated administrator general of the Comédie Française in which capacity he was extremely successful. He published an *Étude sur la Mise en Scène* (Paris: Quantin, 1883). He died in Paris.

FRANCISQUE SARCEY (1827–1899) dramatic critic, began his weekly article on the theatre in 1867 and continued it until his death. The best of his criticisms have been collected in *Quarante Ans de Théâtre* (Paris: 1900–1902; 8 volumes).

INDEX

(See also alphabetical lists of actors, actresses, plays, and playwrights in the Appendix, pp. 329-76)

DRAMABOOKS

HILL AND WANG aims to establish DRAMABOOKS as a permanent library of the great classics of the theatre of all countries, in an attractive, low-priced format.

Eric Bentley, Advisory Editor to Dramabooks, is Brander Matthews Professor of Dramatic Literature at Columbia University.

Published

In Preparation